ALKALI WASTELANDS ENVIRONMENT AND RECLAMATION

ALKALI WASTELANDS ENVIRONMENT AND RECLAMATION

By
Dr. I.C. Gupta
Dr. S.K. Gupta
Dr. D.P. Sharma

MD Publications Pvt Ltd
New Delhi

Published by
MD Publications Pvt Ltd
"MD House" 11, Darya Ganj
New Delhi-110002
Tel. : +91-11-41563325, 41562846
Fax : +91-11-29235450
E-mail : contact@mdppl.com
Website : www.mdppl.com

Revised and Enlarged Edition.

ISBN-978-81-7533-100-6

Price : Rs. 1295/-

Published and Printed by **MD Publications Pvt. Ltd.** at Times Press, 910, Jatwara Street, Darya Ganj, New Delhi.

CONTENTS

PREFACE

The arid and semi-arid zones are spread over an area of 31.7 and 95.7 million ha respectively. The two together cover more than a third of the landmass of India. The introduction of canal irrigation in these areas, in the absence of adequate drainage and scientific water management led to the development of water logging and soil salinity. These problems reported for the first time in 1858 in Western Yamuna canal command at Munak (Haryana), today occupy 12 M ha in different states of the country. This includes 4 M ha of alkali wastelands, also called as sodic soils, posing a serious threat to the environment. Although the exact cost to the exchequer is unknown, some estimates reveal that the twin problems are costing more than Rs. 15,000 million per annum. The problems of soil salinity/alkalinity are assuming a serious dimension because normal soils are being encroached upon by other sectors of economy such as housing and industries.

India's population has crossed 1000 million mark at the turn of the century and is likely to grow to 140 million by 2025 AD, the largest increase in the world, according to 'State of World Population Report 1994'. The latest World Watch Institute Report predicts massive grain deficits over the next 40 years on the Indian Subcontinent, if population continued to grow as projected. Our recent dilemma on wheat import is a pointer to the future state of affair. Our soils are becoming hungry and additional fertilizer use is no longer ending up in raising crop outputs. As such, for about the last one decade our food grain production is hovering at about 210 million tons. Since 1984, grain output per person has fallen roughly 1 per cent per year. India is committed to remove hunger and implement the night to food for all. In order to cope up with the increasing food requirement, agricultural production has to be stepped up substantially. The only feasible option is to increase the cultivable area by bringing under cultivation the approximate 100 M ha of so called wastelands, which include 8 M ha of saline and 4 M ha of alkali wastelands.

Reclamation of alkali wastelands is essential as not only do these soils occupy significant area, but also the lands are potentially fertile. Experience acquired through research and experimentation in laboratories and fields in the reclamation and management of alkali soils showed that a major part of the alkali lands can be utilized to grow several crops, if the soils are scientifically managed. Several institutions and more so the Central Soil Salinity Research Institute, its Regional Research Stations and Network Centers have generated a wealth of information on this subject. The latest available information on this subject has been collected, critically evaluated and synthesized before incorporating in the revised edition of this book. It is hoped that bringing information together in one volume will not only contribute to the advancement of knowledge but also help to solve the food problem of the nation. Since alkali soils are spread over the globe, the Indian experience would also be useful to the scientific communities working internationally. The authors take this opportunity to thank the scientists whose work has been quoted in this book, as without their efforts, achievements made in the gigantic task of land reclamation would have not been possible. At the current level, alkali land reclamation programme has added about 8 million tons of food grains to the national food grain stock.

We believe that this book will be immensely useful to researchers, teachers, extension specialists, progressive farmers, land use planners and postgraduate students.

Authors

1

HISTORICAL DEVELOPMENTS

The knowledge of fertile and infertile lands called as '*Urvar*' and '*Anurvar*' is as old as farming in India. However, the scientific knowledge of the factors causing infertility came into being only towards the beginning of the twentieth century. '*Anurvar*' soils were also called '*Usar*' soils. '*Usar*' word in a real sense is derived from '*Ushtra*' a Sanskrit word. In the past, all such lands, which used to be unfit for agriculture were called '*Ushtra*'. In addition, the lands affected with excess salts such as neutral NaCl or alkali ($NaHCO_3$, Na_2CO_3), were also called '*Reh*' by the geologists in mid-nineteenth century to characterize the appearance of salt efflorescence on the surface of lands, as a result of canal irrigation. The word 'Alkali' itself is of Arabic origin meaning ash-like. Since the surface soil looked like calcined wood ash to the Arabs, these soils were named as such. The alkali wastelands have developed under the influence of several factors but since their spread is timed with the birth of canal irrigation, the later has been held more often than not as one of the most potential factors responsible for the formation of alkali wastelands. As such, it would be desirable to trace out the development of canal irrigation in India.

Canal Irrigation

Western Jamuna Canal

Irrigation is an age-old practice in India. During the Vedic period (200-600 BC), the peasants dug wells and constructed canals to apply water to the croplands. Till this period, there is no record of salinity in irrigated tracts. The development of canal irrigation began in the second half of the 14th century at the initiative of Sultan Feroz Shah Tughlak (1351-1388), a pioneer in the history of canal irrigation. During his reign extensive irrigation works were planned and executed to stabilize the agricultural economy. Five big canals were dug to distribute the waters of Jhelum, Jamuna and Sutlej for irrigation. The most important was the Western Jamuna Canal, the oldest canal of north India, constructed in 1355. It carried the water of the Jamuna river to Hisar Firiza (Hisar), a newly constructed city, the hunting grounds of the King at Safidon and orchards of Hansi. In addition, it also provided irrigation to the limited cultivated areas in what are today known as Karnal, Rohtak, Hisar and Jind districts. In aligning the canal, advantage was taken of natural depression or drainage channels whose slope and direction were found suitable. The channel thus, took the form of a linked series of drainage channels and depressions rather than a canal as the word is understood today. Perceiving the scarcity of water, two streams were conducted into the city of Hisar from two rivers viz. Jamuna and Sutlej. Both these streams were conducted through the vicinity of Karnal, and after a length of about 80 kos (1 kos = 2.8km), discharged their waters by one channel into the city of Hisar. Sultan Feroz Shah was occupied for two years and a half in building the city. Later on he laid out many trees including all sorts of fruit trees. Prior to this time, spring harvest used to fail because wheat could not grow without water.

The canal that Sultan Feroz Shah had made could maintain only a scanty supply of water and thus, became ruinous after the death of the Sultan. The use of canal water for irrigation got an impetus during the time of Sher Shah Suri (1450-1545) and later during the reign of Akbar (1555-1605) in areas near Delhi. The proportion of the area that may have been irrigated by canals relative to that served by the wells can safely be regarded as minimal. He repaired the old canal and set it flowing again to fertilize the places in his *Jagir*, and hence it was called Nahr-I-Shabab; but for want of repairs, it again stopped flowing.

Shah Jahan (1628-1658) once again restored the canal and brought a channel from it to Shahjahanabad. At a time when the sublime attention was turned to the building of the Taj Mahal, the fort and the palace, it was commanded that the canal from Khizrabad to Safidon should be repaired, and a new channel excavated from the latter spot to the legal residence, a distance of 30 *kos*.

The salty patches in the soil that developed under irrigation disappeared when the canals went into disuse in the year 1750, after the fall of Mughal empire. In the primitive system of well irrigation there was no significant area affected with *reh* (salt efflorescence).

In 1813, the second Earl of Moira, later called Marquis of Hastings was appointed Governor-General of India. In January 1815, he saw the neglected bed of the Western Jamuna Canal and the surrounding countryside. He observed for a considerable distance the vestiges of the canal. It began where the Jamuna bursts through the hills into the plain and took direction nearly parallel to that of the river quite close to Delhi. Its objective was to fertilize the long tract of country from its source to its termination; the tract in which no tolerable water was available underground at shallow depth and sinking wells to an enormous depth was beyond the ambit of the ordinary farmer as it required extraordinary efforts and funds. All the water found in the higher strata was brackish and deleterious to vegetable crops as well as unsuitable for domestic purposes. During the wars, the banks of the canal were broken at many places and dykes were constructed in its course. The country had then in consequence, an air of desolation. Ruins of villages could be widely seen everywhere. The possibility of re-establishing the canal had struck Hastings. On a rough estimate, the engineers computed that an investment of Rs. three lakhs (0.3 million) would be needed to put the canal into perfect condition, but the estimates were seemingly on the higher side. In 1817, Blane was appointed by the Government of India to restore the Western Jamuna Canal. It took three years to do the job and due to paucity of funds, alignment of the old Mughal canal consisting of natural channels and depressions was adhered, which resulted in the formation of large swamps and extensive water logging. The canal took off from the River Jamuna near Hathnikund, flowed down an old creek of the river until it joined the Pathral and Somb torrents. There were no permanent head works built and the supplies fluctuated with the seasonal changes in the river level.

The famine of 1823-33 led to the enlargement and multiplication of branch and distributary channels. The financial aspect of the project proved satisfactory; for in 1947, it was yielding a net return of 13% on the capital invested.

Eastern Jamuna Canal

Little is known about early history but it seems the Eastern Jamuna canal taking off from the river Jamuna on its eastern bank near Naushehra in Uttar Pradesh, reported to have been originally designed by Ali Mardan Khan in the days of Shahjahan between 1628 and 1659. It was abandoned soon after construction due to declining power of the Mughals. Rohilla leader Zabitha Khan partly reconstructed the canal in 1764 to restore water supply into the canal but it proved futile. The alignment was faulty, and no great stream of water could have been carried down the channel for any prolonged period and the works were abandoned. From 1823, the canal was repaired under the British and reopened in January 1830. It irrigated tracts in Saharanpur, Muzaffarnagar and Meerut districts.

When first constructed, irrigation was practiced directly from the canal, water being supplied to the village watercourses through openings in the bank. This led to much waste, and the area commanded was small. An attempt to extend the system was made by utilizing the natural drainage lines, across which dams were constructed. The channels quickly silted up and it became necessary to excavate regular distributaries. The Eastern Jamuna Canal runs throughout its length almost parallel to, but a few kms distance from the river.

Ganga Canal

The history of the Ganga Canal belongs to the last years of the East India Company's rule. The work commenced during the period of Lord Auckland when he had to deal with the famine, which ravaged northern India in 1837-38. In this famine, about 8,000,000 people died. His successor, Lord Ellenborough, however suspended the work on the Ganga canal. In December 1839, Cautley, a military engineer, undertook a close examination of the country near Haridwar. He proposed to adopt a direct line from Haridwar to Roorkee. Lord Harding sanctioned the project in 1814. The canal was opened in April 1854 and thereafter irrigation in a grand manner began. With the opening of Agra canal and the Lower Ganges Canal in 1870s, large areas in Uttar Pradesh (Muzaffarnagar, Meerut, Bulandshahar, Aligarh, Mathura, Etah, Mainpuri, Farrukhabad, Partapgarh, Etawah, Kanpur, Fatehpur, Allahabad, Hardoi, Unnao, Lucknow, Rai Bareilly, Sultanpur, Partapgarh, Jaunpur etc.) and then Punjab (Rohtak, Gurgaon, Karnal) were covered under canal irrigation.

Without elaborating further on individual systems, it is heartening to note that between the beginning of the plan era (1951-56) and till the beginning of the VIII plan period, a total of 278 major, 894 medium and 146 extension/renovation/ modernization (ERM) schemes were taken up. About 120 major, 668 medium and 51 ERM projects had been completed. By the end of VIII plan, irrigation potential to irrigate 89.5 million ha was created (Table 1.1). While, this has lead to increase in production and stability against weather based

Table 1.1 Plan-wise position of irrigation created and utilized

Plan		*Potential created*				*Total*	*Potential utilised*				*Total*
		M & M	*S.W*[1].	*G.W*[2].	*Total*		*M & M*	*S.W*[1].	*G.W*[2].	*Total*	
Pre-Plan period	Up to 1951	9.70	-	-	12.90	22.60	9.70	-	-	12.90	22.60
At the end of											
-I Plan	(1951-56)	12.20	6.43	7.63	14.06	26.26	10.98	6.43	7.63	14.06	25.04
-II Plan	(1956-61)	14.33	6.45	8.30	14.75	29.08	13.05	6.45	8.30	14.75	27.80
-III Plan	(1961-66)	16.57	6.48	10.52	17.00	33.57	15.17	6.48	10.52	17.00	32.17
-Annual Plan	(1966-69)	18.10	6.50	12.50	19.00	37.10	16.75	6.50	12.50	19.00	35.75
-IV Plan	(1969-74)	20.70	7.00	16.50	23.50	44.20	18.69	7.00	16.50	23.50	42.19
-V Plan	(1974-78)	24.72	7.50	19.80	27.30	52.02	21.16	7.50	19.80	27.30	48.46
-Annual Plan	(1978-80)	26.61	8.00	22.00	30.00	56.61	22.64	8.00	22.00	30.00	52.64
-VI Plan	(1980-85)	27.70	9.70	27.82	3.52	65.22	23.57	9.01	26.24	35.25	58.82
-VII Plan	(1985-90)	29.92	10.99	35.62	46.61	76.53	25.47	9.97	33.15	43.12	68.59
-Annual Plan	(1990-92)	30.74	11.46	38.89	50.35	81.09	26.32	10.29	36.25	46.54	72.86
-VIII Plan	(1992-97)	32.96	N.A[3].	N.A[3].	53.31	86.27	28.37	N.A[3].	N.A[3].	48.77	77.24
-IX Plan (P)	(1997-2002)	37.06(P)	-	-	56.90	93.96	31.01	-	-	49.05	80.06

M & M = Major and medium projects [1] S.W.-Surface water; [2] G.W.-Ground water; [3] N.A.-Not available
Source: India (2005). P = Provisional

fluctuation, some serious environmental degradation problems have arisen both in the old and new projects. Drainage component in most projects continued to be ignored. It means we have not learnt appropriate lesson from our past mistakes while implementing irrigation projects.

Development of Alkali Wastelands and Early Investigations

The salt affected soils in India were known much before the British rule. The first ever account of such soils is available from the dairy of Mr. Sleeman who wrote that large areas of land are lying barren in the United Province near Agra and surrounding areas. He also mentioned some of the techniques used by the farmers to reclaim such lands near Raebreilly. It was in the year 1865, an executive engineer of the Punjab Irrigation Department noted that whole of the country in Punjab lying west of Jamuna is impregnated with *reh* (salts). The *Reh* in the form of efflorescence has spread in small and big patches from Lahore to Multan and Shahpur and onward to the Derajat in the west and foot of the Soolamani mountains in the north (Whitcomb, 1971).

Occurrence of Alkali Soils–First Report

Alarmed at the progressive deterioration of land in the command of the Western Jamuna Canal following the first-official notice through a complaint lodged in 1855 by a grower of village Munak (now in District Karnal) prompted the Government of Punjab for the first time in 1858 to draw the attention of then Governor-General to the seriousness of the problems of *reh* and *usar* tracts. The chief Commissioner of Punjab reported; "for some time past, it has been known that many villages in the Panipat, Delhi and Rohtak districts have been suffering from a destructive saline efflorescence. The accounts of poverty in some of these villages have been quite distressing. At present, about 60 villages or one-tenth of the total number of canal villages are affected. The mischief is increasing yearly. It would soon attain a very considerable proportion, and would entail fiscal loss to the Government and suffering to the people". On consultations, Colonel Baird Smith, Superintendent General of Irrigation in NWP, attributed appearance of this efflorescence to the percolation under pressure of the canal water through the soils in various directions. The controlling factors for seepage being the volume of water in the canal and the difference between the surface level of the water within the channel and the surface of the surrounding country (Whitcomb, 1971).

Early Investigations

Medlicott, the then Professor of Geology at Thomson College, Roorkee, was probably the first scientist who made scientific investigation of the problem of *reh* in 1863. His findings were the following:

(1) Because of the change in the rate of movement of sub-soil water through percolation, capillary movement and by the poor quality of irrigation water itself, progressive concentration of soluble and partially soluble salts, originally distributed more widely throughout the profile, takes place in the upper strata of the soil to a degree toxic to plant growth.

(2) Samples from the Ravi and Ganges rivers, which fed the West and East Jamuna Canals, contained high concentrations of sodium sulphate and sodium chloride, the predominant salt characterizing *reh* and *usar* lands.

(3) The canal water was an exacerbating agent but not a prime cause and the natural salt lands were made increasingly so by inefficient drainage and insufficient application of water.

(4) Soils in which salts accumulated through high rates of evaporation and through capillary action were parched, never thorough soaked; there was no natural sub-soil drainage and no 'free connection'

therefore, could be made with the ground water stratum.

(5) Canal water could well be used to provide the requisite soaking for the soil to wash down the salts and establish a ground water connection

A further set of independent chemical analysis of *usar* samples was made by T.E.B. Brown, Chemical Examiner of Punjab, in 1863. He corroborated that the local *usar*, known as '*kallar*' in Punjab, was of three kinds. The one, *Chikna Kallar*', consists of nitric acid and soluble lime neutralized *reh* affected soil due to excess of sodium chloride, sulphate and carbonate.

Meanwhile, samples of *reh* were also sent for analysis to Dr. Thomas Anderson, Professor of Chemistry at Glasgow. He corroborated in general the reports of his predecessors that *reh* may be described as mixture of common salt (sodium chloride), sulphates, soda, potash, lime and small quantity of alumina. The appearance of *reh* was ascribed to the presence in the soil of some alkaline mineral, the decomposition of which is promoted by the irrigation water. As a result, large quantities of these substances are converted into soluble form that gradually accumulates until they become so abundant as to become noxious to plants. Drainage was suggested as the cure of the problem.

By 1864, *usar* was well known in Faizabad, Behraich, Lucknow, Sitapur and Hardoi and reports were pouring in with the Government of India. *Usar* was in general a combination of *reh*, a mixture of highly soluble salts and *kankar*, a residual insoluble precipitation or hardpan. *Kankar* is impure calcium carbonate. Amongst soluble salts, carbonates rather than sulphates and chlorides predominated. Occurrence of *usar* was ascribed to the capillary action.

The correspondence on *reh* deterioration published in 1864 represents the first collected documentation on the problem and its scientific analysis. Copies were sent to the Secretary of State in England in 1865, with specimens of *reh* soil collected from village Munak and Asan-Kalan, both in the present district of Karnal, on the Western Jamuna Canal. Samples of canal and spring water were also sent. W.J. Ward in the metallurgical laboratory of the Royal School of Mines analyzed the samples. Ward observed that canal waters contained notably low amounts of chlorides and sulphates, a finding contrary to Medlicott. He also concluded that *reh* was a mixture of highly soluble salts, that water was the vehicle by which it was brought into prominence in the soil and that cure was the combination of sufficient irrigation with adequate drainage. Subsequent to the receipt of the reports and accompanying papers, the Lieutenant Governor, NWP, recommended by way of immediate action that experiments on leaching and drainage should be initiated, for which the central portion of the Eastern Jamuna Canal provided an opportunity. The progress of the modest experiments in reclamation was reported annually. They were shown to be of little practical value in that a return on investment was not immediately forthcoming. For example, canal silt enabled crops to be grown on *usar*, but the operation was not directly remunerative. By 1875, the most practical operation seemed to raise non-agriculture plantations. Meanwhile, coordination between the analysis and experiments on *reh* and in particular its connection with canal irrigation and the implementation of plans to extend the canal system was non-existent.

Occurrence of Alkali Soils-Second Report

In 1876, another alarm was raised about the disastrous spread of *reh* in parts of Aligarh, Meerut and throughout the Kali Nadi Valley of Uttar Pradesh. Through a petition, David Robarts, a substantial *Zamindar* of *pargana* Sikandra Rao, Aligarh district, to the Board of Revenue requested for relief on the ground that his land had deteriorated fast due to the appearance of saline efflorescence as a result of the introduction of canal irrigation. The condition had become far more obvious, sufficient to cause serious, if somewhat academic, concern on the part of Government Officers and this led to the formation of the historical Indian *Reh* Committee in 1877 (Agarwal and Gupta, 1968).

Center (1880) studied alkali soils and saline well water of Punjab. He ascribed occurrence of *reh* in soils to the decomposition of the elements of rocks and soils under the action of air and water. Nature of *reh* and its varieties, formation of *kankar,* causes of salt accumulation and methods of cure by sluicing and irrigation, manure and cultivation, arboricultural (Plantation of trees and grasses), chemical manure and nitrate of lime were discussed. Uses of *reh* for the recovery of Na_2SO_4 etc. were also mentioned.

Report of '*Reh*' Committee

The report of the *Reh* Committee was made available in 1886, which focussed attention on many important points related to canal irrigation, drainage and spread of alkali in the soil. The inquiry was far from adequate. No account, for instance, was given of the extent of *usar* tracts in the provinces. The report qualitatively stated that *usar* covered 'immense areas', without details as to acreage. No Agricultural Chemist was appointed to the committee nor even consulted during the investigations. The committee reported, "The canals were built for the purpose of affording abundance of irrigation water; and in order that it might be easily available, they were laid high so as to allow their waters when used to flow naturally over or through the agricultural lands. No provision for drainage was made". It was suggested that indiscriminate use of water through the flush system of irrigation (flood irrigation) should be stopped. Economizing the use of water could be achieved by raising the rates for flush irrigation charged by the Government. Since flush rates were already high, an increase would deter farmers altogether with disastrous results for the revenue accruing from canal charges. Alternatively, lift irrigation was suggested. Provision of deep drainage, straightening and opening of natural drainage ways and preparation of ground water maps were also suggested. It was also recommended that experiments in reclaiming *usar* tracts, which began in 1874 under the supervision of the newly created Department of Agriculture should be continued. The results had consistently shown that *usar* could be brought back into cultivation only by careful watering accompanied by intensive manuring. Nothing, however, was done on any scale to increase the local supply of manure near these tracts in order to keep pace with the increase in irrigation from the canal. Obviously the outcome of the modest series of reclamation experiments was as before. Whilst it was stated, for example, in 1888 that Government of India attached great importance to the experiments, Colonel J.G. Forbes, Irrigation Secretary to Govt., NWP and Oudh, admitted that so far all attempts at reclamation had proved unsuccessful.

Dr. J. A. Voelcker was first Agricultural Scientist appointed by Government to report on Indian agrarian conditions. He recorded that it is hardly surprising that enormous tracts especially in the plains of northern India are affected by *reh*. In the NWP alone, it was estimated to cover between 10,000 to 12,000 km^2 (Voelcker, 1897).

Scientific Investigations

Uttar Pradesh

Subsequently, with the implementation of Dr. Voelcker's recommendations, Dr. J.W. Leather was appointed as first Agricultural Chemist. Dr. Leather deserves to be called the first scientific worker on soil salinity in this country. He made a thorough systematic and scientific multi-pronged attack on *reh* (alkali) problem. Beginning his studies in 1893, Leather published his several research findings on the 'reclamation of *reh* or *usar* lands' in Agricultural Ledger during 1893 and 1897. The first and the foremost scientific treatise on the subject 'Investigations on *usar* Land in the United Provinces' by Leather, was published, in the form of a report, by Government Press, Allahabad in 1914. Some of the salient conclusions which emerged from his studies of *usar* (saline-alkali) patches at many locations in the districts of Etah and Mainpuri, in the vicinity of Lower Ganges canal in 1893 are as follows:

(1) *Usar* soils contained practically sodium carbonate and bicarbonate, which amounted to 0.06 to 0.90% respectively in the surface 60 cm depth. Total soluble

salt content seldom exceeded 2%. A good arable soil contained less than 0.1% soluble salts.

(2) Infertile (*usar*) patches were impervious, the water penetration being 1/10 to 1/1000 of normal soil and always less than 0.1cm per hour and associated with water logging at about 7 to 9 feet (2.8 to 3.6m) from the surface.

(3) Sub-soil water was considered to rise and fall freely below the impervious patches of *usar* soil which were 7 to 8 feet (2.8 to 3.2m) thick.

(4) In respect of frequency, infertility, nature and amount of salts or physical condition, there was substantially no difference between *usar* patch irrigated with canal water or unirrigated. The alkali in the soil was presumed to be a product of the soil itself. Canal water would possibly not create such patches, but there could be possible extension of *reh* due to water logging on the introduction of canal irrigation.

(5) Lowering of sub-soil water or opening of drains was though necessary to reclaim these soils but experiments showed that surface and subsurface drainage were ineffective.

(6) Gypsum and canal silt were found to reclaim *usar* land but prohibitive because of the high cost.

(7) Deep and good cultivation coupled with heavy manuring reclaimed only surface 1ft (30 cm) of the soil.

(8) Scrapping of salts was ineffective.

(9) Digging out the impervious soil, if not more than 4 ft (120 cm) thick was suggested as one of the measures to reclaim the soil.

(10) Allowing 2 ft (60 cm) of water to percolate through the soil for a prolonged period in well maintained dykes (*bunds*) coupled with small amounts of gypsum

of fine size was also supposed to remove salts to a lower stratum.

(11) Reclamation by tree (*babul* or *shisham*) planting or by growing of grasses after enclosing the land to avoid grazing for some period were found encouraging.

(12) Pot culture experiments revealed that sodium carbonate up to 0.4% and chloride and sulphate up to 1.0% were not generally fatal to maize, wheat, barley, cotton etc. but germination was severely affected at 0.7% sodium carbonate or sodium sulphate. The germination of leguminous plants, gram, peas and pigeon pea was interfered with 0.2-0.4% sodium carbonate or sodium chloride and 0.7 sodium sulphate.

(13) Investigation on the quality of waters of Mathura district showed that well waters were considerably saline as compared to canal waters, which were the purest form of irrigation water available. Some of the well waters contained 1,250-10,000 ppm salts. The upper limit of TSS of waters suitable for irrigation was fixed as 1000 ppm (EC 1.5 dS m^{-1}). This limit was considered safe only when the irrigation water was used in excess of what was required for maturing the crops.

(14) The origin of the salts was ascribed to four possible ways: (a) sub-soil bed of salts brought at least in part by the rivers when the alluvium of the plains was deposited; (b) those portions of the salt which have been rendered soluble by water, air and plants and rejected by the later, which are not drained away and (c) brought in part by the canal water used for irrigation. Imperfect drainage, surface washing, wind drift and canal were considered as causes for the accumulation of *reh*.

Duthie (1896) reported on the *usar* reserves in Chherat and Gursikran of Aligarh district in 1893-94 as compared to

1888. The grass called as *bat (Diplachne fusca)* was observed to be more useful than *usar* grass (*Sporobolus pallidus*) on the low lying regions, where water was liable to accumulate for any length of time. Planting of *Dhak* (*Butea frondosa*) tree was recommended. The *frash* tree (*Tamarix artculata*) also thrived on saline soil.

Although, Leather recognized as early as 1897 that calcium salts coagulated *usar* soil and made them permeable, he calculated gypsum requirement of the soil as simply the quantity which was equivalent to soluble carbonates present. The formation, characterization and reclamation of saline soils, in fact, remained obscure until the implication of the principles of Base Exchange were fully known.

Deccan

With the spread of irrigation farming, the awareness of the problem of soil salinity was extending throughout India since land was deteriorating due to canal irrigation. In the Deccan tract, the Nira valley irrigation canal was opened in 1884 to irrigate for the first time on a large scale the deep black cotton soil area and soon after, the land began to be affected by salt and water logging. Reports of water logging and soil salinity appeared in the year 1886 and by 1905 an area of 1600 ha was taken out of cultivation (out of an irrigated area of 14,800 ha). The problem areas increased to 5570 ha in 1947. In 1886, Dr. Ozanne, the then Director of Agriculture, was directed to make a survey of the problems. He reported that damage was due to seepage and percolation from canals. In 1893, Leather visited the tract and sampled some of the affected soils. The problem, in this tract, became so serious that in 1903, the Government of Bombay appointed a committee to consider the measure to be adopted to check the spread of the damage. The committee recommended that all *nalas* (natural drainage lines) should be opened without delay, salt affected lands should be surveyed and reclamation trails carried out. Mann and Tamhane (1910) estimated that 6-7 percent of the area was being damaged annually, and even those lands on which sugarcane was being raised had accumulated soluble salts, whose adverse effect was being suppressed by the amounts of manure and irrigation water being used. Drainage trails laid out remained unsuccessful. A symposium on the 'Alkali Soils of the Deccan' was held as early as in 1940 to take stock of the available information on this subject.

By 1947, for Deccan black cotton soil tract, where altogether different geomorphology existed, effective drainage and land improvement techniques were developed (Inglis and Gokhale, 1928), genetic soil survey were carried out and soil classification were made (Basu and Tagare, 1941). Talati (1947) successfully undertook the classification and reclamation of salt damaged lands in Baramati.

Talati (1941) reported that Deccan soils had four types of damaged soils excluding waterlogged areas: (i) mixed saline soils, (ii) saline soils, (iii) alkali soils and (iv) strongly alkali soils. These required different treatments for their improvement. The first type of soil improved merely by leaching while the saline soils became alkaline either under natural rainfall or artificial conditions of leaching and required fertilizer for their improvement. Gypsum and Sulphur in combination with FYM were found the best. Sugarcane variety CO 290 was observed to be alkali resistant and was tried after *dhaincha* (*Sesbania aculeata*) green manuring with a basal dose of gypsum and FYM. Talati (1947) also conducted field experiments on the reclamation of waterlogged salt affected lands in Baramati of the Bombay Deccan. The water table was lowered to a depth of more than 1.2 m by drainage followed by ploughing and levelling. Rainfall of 400 cm reduced salt content from 3 to less than 1% and reduced pH in top 1.5 m but increased in the lower horizon. For reclaimed soils under sugarcane, tilth was good up to pH 8.6 and yield decreased if the pH was beyond this value. Addition of $CaSO_4$ with FYM or sheep manure gave best results.

Punjab

Most of the canals in Punjab were constructed in the last quarter of nineteenth century. Bernee in 1908 conducted the survey of Lower Chenab canal area and field experiments on land reclamation began at Narwala in district Layallpur in 1914. By 1918 the problem of water logging and salinity was of so much concern that Government set up a Drainage Board. After the abnormal excessive rains in 1925, a Water Logging Inquiry Committee was constituted to carry out statistical investigations and experimental work pertaining to water logging and *thur* (saline soil). The Chakanwali Reclamation Farm in Gujranwala district (Now in Pakistan) was also opened with the simultaneous establishment of the Punjab Irrigation Research Laboratory at Lahore in 1924 to investigate all the problems connected with irrigation, drainage and salinity. This research laboratory rose to the status of a full-fledged Research Institute by 1931-32. Scientists like Mackenzie, Taylor, Puri, Ashghar and Mehta devoted themselves to research on the problems of soil salinity and water use. Standards of soil and water quality were established and the means of reclamation of deteriorated soils found. The implementation of these research findings in the field started in the late thirties. Since the problem continued to increase beyond all proportions, Water Logging Inquiry Committee was expanded and converted into Water Logging Board. In 1929 Punjab Government agreed to construct main and branch drains but the responsibility for the construction of field drains was left with the landowners. The position was reviewed annually in water logging conference presided over by the Governor.

Commencing from 1927 to 1941 was a period of fruitful research in India on the subject of saline-alkali soils. Puri and Associates (1933, 1937), Singh and Nijhawan (1932), Hoon and Associates (1937, 1949), Mehta (1940); Taylor and Associates (1933, 1934, 1941) in the undivided Punjab made valuable contributions to the subject of alkali soils, their characterization, diagnosis and reclamation. Singh and Nijhawan (1932) reported that calcium salts followed by farmyard manure could improve the alkali soils to the status of normal soil. Puri (1933) reported the relationship between exchangeable sodium and crop yield in Punjab soils. He observed that treatment of a Montgomery soil with $CaCl_2$ and leaching reduced base saturation from 67 to 20 percent and increased yields from 32 to 100 kg per ha. During the same period, some of the factors determining the hydrogen ion concentration in suspension of Punjab soils were also examined. Taylor *et al.* (1933) statistically analyzed the water table data for the last several decades and showed that a regular rise of water table has taken place in canal irrigated tracts. They attributed this to the combined effect of seepage from the eastern channels, heavy percolation from irrigated fields, pronounced effect of rainfall on the water table on account of percolation through ploughed cultivated fields, blockade of natural drains and above all lack of drainage.

Taylor *et al.* (1934) pointed out that the crop yields declined above pH 8.5. Application of gypsum was suggested to prevent base exchange reaction. Mehta (1940) observed that salt could be removed from *reh* soil by one or two crops of rice and the reclaimed land could produce excellent crops of cotton, wheat, sugarcane etc. for eight years without deterioration. The inclusion of rice in the crop rotation was recommended. Taylor and Mehta (1941) reported that taking a rice crop at the initial stage of irrigation could prevent land deterioration due to excess salts. Many leaching, drainage and reclamation trails were conducted at the Chakanwali Reclamation Farm and effective methods suited to Punjab soils were developed. Water rating, the problems of irrigation and rise of water table were also simultaneously studied at length to check the deterioration of land against indiscriminate use of water.

Land Reclamation Directorate

In 1940, Land Reclamation Board distinct from Water Logging Board was constituted and in 1945 a separate Land Reclamation Directorate was created. Valuable work on the movement of water and the salts in the soil was initiated before 1947. Unfortunately, the partition of the country in 1947 interrupted this work. Most of the reclamation and drainage work was confined to areas that now constitute a part of Pakistan.

U.P. *Usar* Land Reclamation Committee

Dhar and Mukherji (1936) and Dhar (1939) in Uttar Pradesh tried a number of reclaiming agents particularly molasses and press mud for the amelioration and reclamation of saline-alkali soils. But the gravity of the problem went on increasing as a consequence of which an *Usar* Land Reclamation Committee was constituted in 1938 by the State Government of U.P. to advise on all matters related to the characterization, reclamation and prevention of spread of *usar* land. The committee reviewed the work done on such soils, and examined the problem in great detail and reported that the alkaline conditions were mainly due to sodium carbonate. The profiles of these soils are generally associated with *kankar* or definitely a hard pan, which restricted the upward movement of water by capillary action and downward flow of water by percolation under force of gravity. The set-up of a Wasteland Reclamation Board to deal with all the problems of wastelands was suggested.

Punjab Action Committee

The problem created by the abnormal floods of 1947 and 1950 resulted in the formation of Water Logging Board for Punjab. The floods of 1954, 1955 and 1956 further aggravated the water logging and *thur* such that the problem of drainage became more serious.

The Punjab Government set up an Action Committee in 1957 in order to tackle this problem effectively on a top priority basis. The Action Committee recommended the following remedial measures:

(1) Flood from rivers, big streams and creeks should be minimized since total prevention is difficult.

(2) Improvement in surface drainage.

(3) Installation of an adequate number of tube wells and revival of percolation wells fallen into disuse to stabilize the sub-soil water at the proper level.

(4) Lining of watercourses, main canals and distributaries, if economically possible.

(5) Increase in the water allowance in *thur* affected areas so as to attain an intensity of 200 percent.

(6) Construction of seepage drains parallel to the existing channels.

Research and Developments

Post-Independence Period (1947-1962)

The 15 years of post-independence period (1947-1962) saw a great progress in research on saline-alkali soils of India. Agarwal and Associates (1956, 1957, 1961) studied several aspects of soil salinity problem in Uttar Pradesh. Likewise, Hoon and Associates (1950, 1953, 1955), Dhawan and Associates (1950, 1953, 1955, 1958), Asghar and Associates (1947, 1948), Kanwar and Associates (1960, 1961, 1962) contributed greatly in Punjab. Raychaudhary and Associates (1952, 1957) studied the salt affected soils at Delhi. Central Board of Irrigation and Power published three research monographs on Land Reclamation viz. Mehta (1951), Hoon (1955) and Dhawan (1964). In first monograph, formation of *thur* lands, movement of moisture and salts in the soil profile, rise of water table, water logging, reclamation in deep and high water table areas etc. had been discussed. Hoon (1955) pointed out that due to ability to withstand salt in the soil and a fair range of variation in irrigation intensity, sugarcane offered immense possibilities for soil amelioration, when the top of the soil profile is somewhat free from excessive salt content. Dhawan (1964) observed the main method of reclamation consisted of land levelling followed by planting of *dhaincha*. The water was allowed to stand 8 to 10 cm deep for about two and half months. *Dhaincha* was buried when its age was about 6 weeks. After these operations, the fields were dried, ploughed and rice seedlings were transplanted preferably in rows with two or more seedlings at each spot. After harvesting rice in October, gram or *berseem* was grown in the winter depending upon the degree of reclamation. Construction of drains was recommended. Some studies were also conducted in other states of India, e.g. in West Bengal (Banerjee, 1959); Gujarat (Shah and Associates 1954, 1958), Madras (Satyanarayana, 1953), Andhra Pradesh (Krishna *et al.*, 1960); Maharashtra (Basu, 1950); and U. P. (Khan, 1950).

Saline Alkali Soils Seminars

The Indian Council of Agricultural Research organized a well-planned Seminar on the Recent Advances in Agronomy and Soil Science at Shimla in 1959. The programme included a session on saline and alkali soils. While discussing many aspects of this subject, it was felt that the existing information on soils in the country is voluminous but the same has not been brought together and published. The Council desired that Dr. R.R. Agarwal and Dr. R.N. Gupta of Uttar Pradesh collect this information from the available sources and write a bulletin on the subject. In consequence, a bulletin entitled 'Saline-Alkali Soils in India' was prepared which covered research work on the subject since the time of inception to 1962. This was published by ICAR in 1968.

A seminar on 'Salinity and Alkali Soil Problems', held at Indian Agricultural Research Institute, New Delhi in 1962, recommended reclamation of saline and alkali soils on a war footing at the national level. It also recommended that establishment of a suitably manned and equipped Central Salinity and Alkali Laboratory, already approved in the Third Five Year Plan should be given the highest priority.

ICAR Schemes and Future Research Work

A number of schemes to conduct research on fundamental and applied aspects of the salinity problem were launched by the Indian Council of Agricultural Research. The scheme operated in Punjab from 1958 to 1961, Rajasthan from 1960 to 1963 and Andhra Pradesh from 1955 to 1960. A research scheme on possibilities of using charcoal for improvement and reclamation of soils was also sanctioned by ICAR (Puri, 1960). A scheme on treatment of saline waters was also sanctioned in Punjab during 1960-61. Another scheme was sanctioned for the study of composition of plants growing on *usar* lands under reclamation to Lucknow University during 1957-60.

During 1960-70 research work on the problem of soil salinity continued to be strengthened at Central Arid Zone Research Institute, Jodhpur; University of Udaipur, Udaipur and State Deptt. of Agriculture, Rajasthan; University School of Sciences, Gujarat Univesity, Ahmedabad; Irrigation Research Laboratory, Baroda; Govt. Agriculture College, Kanpur; B. R. College, Agra; B.H.U., Varanasi; Dept. of Chemistry, Allahabad University, Allahabad; Botany Deptt. Lucknow University, Lucknow; College of Agriculture, P.A.U., Ludhiana; Irrigation Research Institute, Amritsar in Punjab and Indian Agricultural Research Institute, New Delhi.

Planning Commission Report on Wastelands

While more or less systematic research work continued in some parts of the country, increasing need was being felt seriously for the intensification of the studies on the problem soils. Planning Commission Committee on Natural Resources (1963) prepared a study report on wastelands, including saline alkali and waterlogged lands and their reclamation measures. The report recommended setting up of three Regional Salinity Laboratories in the country. This recommendation was not accepted immediately and concerted efforts to solve the problem on national basis remained lacking, though the salinity continued to induce creeping death to the soil.

NEDCO Investigations in Gujarat

NEDCO (1968), a consultancy organization from the Netherlands, operated a Pilot Polder Project (1,500 ha) in Gujarat in order to suggest measure for the reclamation of the *Bhal* area, representing a former tidal flat abandoned by the sea. It comprised of Vertisols in the highest part and Halaquepts in the lower part, lying as wasteland or in use as poor pasture. The results obtained in the project had been poor due to various reasons including the presence of a layer of very low permeability in the upper meter of the soil profile. Swelling nature of the soil, low amount of fresh water carried by the rivers during the monsoon, irregular and short duration floods and absence of adequate sources of fresh ground water were mentioned as other causes. Discharge of water from the pilot polder could not be disposed off due to severe siltation of the outlet channel. Desalinization of the soil did not respond to improved drainage. A major recommendation emerged from the studies was not to proceed with the plans for reclaiming the entire area of saline soils in *Bhal* unless after extensive research more was known about desalinization. Other pre-requisites identified in the project were: whether or not in combination with flooding and drainage desalinization could occur, possibilities for storage of water (small dams) for irrigation in the area west of the Bhavnagar-Ahmedabad road, availability of fresh ground water in the area and possibilities of water storage in the Mithapur Depression. Measures to check erosion especially in the valley of the Khalkhalia and encroachment of the sea in the Sonrai creek area by low levels around the threatened arable lands were also suggested for investigations.

Recommendations of USAID-Indian Team

In 1967, Indian Council of Agriculture Research appointed a Consultant Team consisting of 3 American and 3 Indian scientists to suggest the need of the plan for research on water use and soil management towards meeting India's food shortages. The team made a thorough study of the problem. The team recommended that for increasing research effectiveness on immediate food production problems, research on applied or adaptive nature be considered immediately. Since it is of major concern, technical people for this activity should be identified immediately. For improving inter-departmental and inter-agency relations and coordination, the Ministry providing the leadership for the design and construction aspects of land and water development should also be responsible for the specialized research necessary to implement the programs. It is essential that these research activities be coordinated so that the efforts interlock but do not overlap. With the Ministry, ICAR should coordinate on water use and soil management research and training activities. In states, Agricultural Universities should carry out research pertaining to regional significance. To provide essential technological information for the water and soil management component of the 'Package of Practice', several research projects were recommended. Great emphasis was laid on pilot projects.

In addition, the team recommended for early initiation of the following measures:

(1) Establishment of a coordinated drainage-salinity pilot research project at one national center and regional centers (Black soils-Maharashtra or Madhya Pradesh; mixed Red and Black soils-Karnataka or Orissa; Coastal alluvial soils-Orissa or West Bengal) to evaluate the application of principles of drainage and the management of salinity and alkalinity in cultivated soils of India.

(2) In states other than those selected for the centers and where salt problems are acute, appointment of an Indian Scientist having in depth knowledge to aid cultivators.

(3) A research programme on basic properties in relation to soil and water management practices and production of crops should be initiated at four centers in India.

(4) Establishment of a Central Water Management Research Center at the Indian Agricultural Research

Institute to study water management problems of national significance.

(5) Research on problems of well design, construction and maintenance, including materials and equipment and evaluation of pumping costs.

(6) Research on tanks at catchment level and storage structures for water supplies.

(7) Studies on the problems of recharge of underground aquifers.

(8) Examination of existing approaches to research on rain fed lands and a substantial strengthening of programs at the Soil Conservation Research, Demonstration and Training Centers throughout India.

As a consequence of these recommendations, ICAR launched in 1968 an All India Coordinated Scheme for 'Studies on Soil Salinity and Water Management' at different locations and established Central Soil Salinity Research Institute (CSSRI) at Karnal and Water Technology Center at New Delhi (Indian Agricultural Research Institute) in 1969. It is just by coincident that CSSRI happens to be located on the banks of the Western Jamuna Canal (Fig. 1.1) and the village Munak where first reports of salinity appeared, is just 30 km away from its campus. Another Coordinated scheme on 'Use of Saline Water in Agriculture' came in operation in 1972 at 5 centers in the country in the states of Uttar Pradesh, Rajasthan, Karnataka, Andhra Pradesh and Maharashtra. Since then the scheme has been expanded under which number of states have increased as well as the mandate of the project has been widened. With the establishment of two Research Institute/Centers and two Coordinated Schemes, and with sufficient budget grants, the lacunae on the part of the Government had almost been removed. The outcome of the findings on the problem and its solution was expected to pave the path for sustainable irrigated farming in future.

Figure 1.1. Present day view of the Western Jamuna canal at Karnal

UNDP Investigations in Haryana

Introduction of canal irrigation in 1.2 million ha in Haryana proceeded with the rise of water table and consequential development of water logging and soil salinity. It has been estimated that State of Haryana is suffering annually a loss of 420 million due to twin problems of water logging and salinity. Out of the total geographical area of 4.4 million ha in Haryana, 3.5 million ha is under cultivation. About 2.8 million ha is underlain with saline ground water. The cost of reclamation of the entire area in Haryana for potential agricultural production through drainage and other measures has been estimated to be Rs. 7200 million (HSMITC, 1984). Recently a Master Plan for drainage of agricultural lands has been prepared. It is estimated to cost Rs. 2300 crores (Table 1.2). Clearly, in the absence of timely actions, the cost of land reclamation would increase tremendously.

Table 1.2 Salient recommendations on drainage in the drainage master plan of Haryana

Project	*Quantity*	*Cost (Rs. Crores)*
Surface drainage	($1,400\ km^2$) 14 lakh ha, 1,432 km length	1,231
Horizontal subsurface drainage	47,000 ha area	257
Vertical tube wells drainage	1,200 Nos. (24,000 ha)	43
Conjunctive use tube wells	1 lakh Nos. (2 lakh ha)	250
Bio-drainage	2 lakh ha area	385
Repair of canal water courses, water supply tanks	–	44
Road raising & cross drainage	–	58
Total cost		2,278

Source: Anonymous (2000)

Salinity Problems in Rajasthan

Rajasthan is located in the northwest part of India and is the second largest state in the country. With only 1 percent of India's total water supply in the state, the canal systems supplying much of the water used for irrigation purposes depend upon water sources located outside the state. Some of the identified problems include declining water table except in canal commands, increasing salinity of ground water and large pockets of waterlogged salt affected lands in the irrigation commands. As an example, one could site the Chambal Project, which is one of the integrated irrigation and power scheme with a culturable command area of 229,000 ha in Rajasthan. The area is characterized as arid to semi-arid with approximately 90% of the total annual precipitation occurring during the monsoon season. By 1972, approximately 10 years after irrigation development began, it was estimated that approximately 20,000 ha of land had a water table within 1.5 m of ground surface. It was also estimated that the affected area is increasing at the rate of 1%. Even after 40 years, it is believed that the problem is expanding as revealed through satellite imageries.

Another irrigation project that was initiated at about the same time is the Indira Gandhi Canal Project. It is one of the biggest irrigation projects of the world being implemented in the state and the work is now going on at a fast pace under stage II. The project would cover CCA of 19.64 lakh ha and irrigate 15.17 lakh ha in the districts of Sriganagnagar, Hanumangarh, Churu, Bikanar, Jaisalmer, Jodhpur and Barmer. A part of the area would be supplied water through lift irrigation. The project has transformed the destiny of this desert land and its inhabitants. In phase I, crops like wheat, rice, sugarcane, pulses, mustard, cotton and groundnut are being grown raising the economic standard of the people living in the area. Loonkaransar terrain comprising of a sub-soil hard pan, traditionally known as the no-man's-land (*Kalapani* of Bikaner) has been transformed into a prosperous land of plenty with the arrival of water by lift irrigation from Indira Gandhi canal. This one time forbidden land now produces groundnut worth Rs. 10 crore annually. While, these are issues of pride, environmental degradation resulting from lack of drainage has now become a matter of concern both for the project and for the nation, which has invested heavily in the project. In less than a decade now, the scarcity-prosperity-scarcity cycle seems to have run a full circle. Introduction of canal irrigation in the desert of western Rajasthan has completed journey from one wasteland (water starved) to another wasteland (water logging). In the year 1997-98, it is estimated that water logging has affected an area of 43,428 ha (area inundated with water and water table within 1.5 m of the ground surface) in stage I and 3,978 ha in stage II. The most serious aspect of this problem is that affected area is increasing over the years. Sub-soil conditions resulting in water logging, a rising water table (43 to 83 cm a year) and the inevitable salinity have already rendered major part of the land useless for agriculture (Fig. 1.2). Since the problem is still increasing (Fig. 1.3), it is anticipated that 20 to 60 percent of the canal-irrigated area may develop drainage and salinity problems within 30 to 100 years.

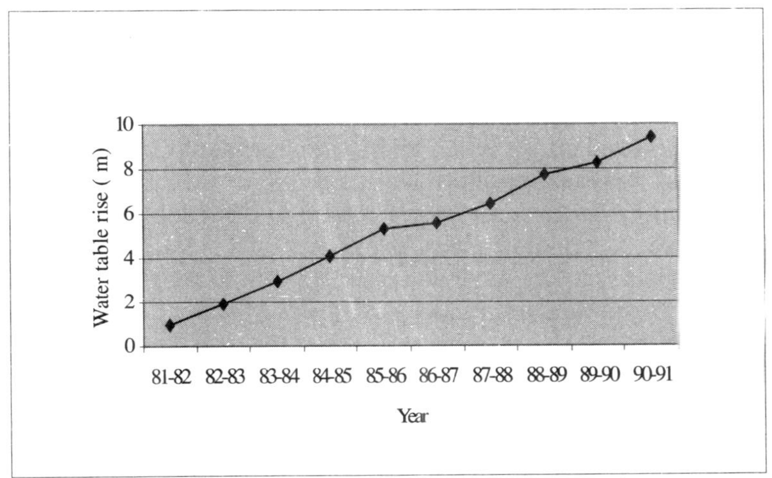

Figure 1.2 The rise in water table in Indira Gandhi *Nahar pariyojana*, Phase I (Anonymous, 2002)

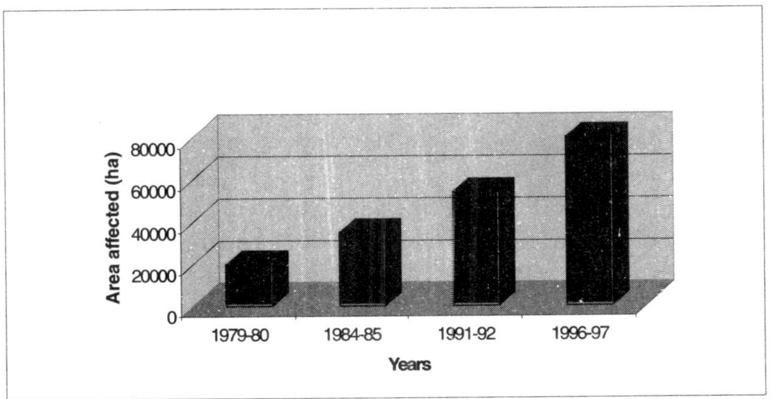

Figure 1.3 Bar chart showing increasing area under water logging and soil salinity in Tungabhadra command (Manjunatha *et al.*, 2004)

Irrigation Cost and Benefit-an Overview

History has witnessed rise and fall of the civilization associated with the development of irrigation and water logging respectively. The earliest recognition of salt lands dates back to 2400 BC from the Tigris-Euphrates alluvial plains in Iraq (Russel *et al.*,1965). In the ancient period, in Mesopotamia, people had taken recourse to wheat cultivation, which required more water than the area could digest in an ecologically non-destructive way. The result was that the area became infertile for millennia. It was here that salt lands were located and correlated with irrigation. In the Indian context, situation is not only grim in Haryana and Rajasthan but Punjab, Uttar Pradesh, Gujarat, Andhra Pradesh, Madhya Pradesh and Maharashtra states are equally affected with soil salinity problems accelerated through water logging after the introduction of canal irrigation. No doubt, during the first ten to twenty years of the inception of canal irrigation, spectacular results are obtained in terms of bumper production, but after this the adverse effects start appearing. The Sarda Sahayak canal for irrigation in U.P. has created such water logging problems that a drain had to be dug all along the canal and tube wells sunk along its banks to drain off the water. Tungabhadra, Nagarjunsagar and Sriramsagar projects in Andhra Pradesh have created grave water logging problems. In the Tungabhadra canal area alone, 83,000 ha of irrigated land have been affected and crop yields have been reduced by about 30 percent. The Tawa Command area in Madhya Pradesh, Purna Command area in Maharashtra and Chambal Command area in Madhya Pradesh and Rajasthan have become the farmer's ruin. "*Mitti Bachao Samities*' were formed as a result of environmental degradation upon introduction of water through the Tawa canal.

Although India has the world's largest irrigation system with the largest irrigated area of 89 million ha, it has not been able to benefit from it as the system has become highly inefficient. The gap between the potential created (89.5 million ha) and actual utilization (80.7 million ha) has been widening (Table 1.3). The cost of creating irrigation potential through major and medium schemes has increased from Rs. 1,520 per ha during first plan to Rs. 60,000 per ha in eighth plan.

Presently, its cost is assessed at Rs. 100,000 per ha or even more in few cases.

Table 1.3 Ultimate, created and utilized potential of irrigation in India

Source	*Ultimate (M ha)*	*Created (M ha)*	*Utilized (M ha)*
Major and Medium projects	58.5	32.8	28.4
Minor (Surface)	15.5	56.6	52.3
Minor (G. water)	64.1		
Total	138.1	89.4	80.7

The performance has not been commensurate with huge public investments due to poor crop productivity, uneven water distribution and rising problems of water logging and salinity (Table 1.4). Despite huge subsidy on surface irrigation system, the actual yield levels are far below the projected targets. The deprivation of tail enders is serious and an area of 6-10 million ha is losing productivity because of uneven water distribution (Joshi, 1990). While increasing water logging and salinity have led to wastage of resources, the time and cost overrun in the irrigation works have resulted in an expenditure of nearly Rs. 160 billion by Central and State Government between 1950 and 1984 to create an additional potential of 30 million hectares. As per the estimates of the World Watch Institute (1990), out of a total of 60.2 million ha damaged by water logging and salinity at the global level, 59.9 million ha occurred only in five countries namely India, China, USA, Pakistan and erstwhile USSR. According to another estimate, out of a total 76.6 million ha affected by soil salinity in the world, 45.4 million ha is in the irrigation commands (Ghassemi *et al.*, 1995). Nevertheless, 60 percent of total food production comes from 32 percent of irrigated land while farm produce from remaining 68 percent unirrigated land accounted for 40 percent of the total food grain production in the country. Thus, both food and nutritional security of the country hinge upon the sustainability of production from the irrigated lands.

Table 1.4. Extent of water logging and soil salinity in some irrigation projects

Irrigation project	*State*	*Extent (Thousand ha)*	
		Water logging	*Soil salinity*
Sriramsagar	Andhra Pradesh	60.00 (47.62)	1.00 (0.79)
Tungabhadra	Andhra Pradesh and Karnataka	4.65 (1.27)	24.84 (6.69)
Gandak	Bihar and Gujarat	211.01(21.11)	400.00 (40.03)
Ukai-Kakrapar	Gujarat	16.25 (4.32)	8.29 (2.20)
Mahi Kadana	Gujarat and Rajasthan	82.00* (16.81)	35.76 (7.33)
Malprabha	Karnataka	1.05* (0.99)	–
Chambal	Madhya Pradesh and Rajasthan	98.70 (20.31)	40.00 (8.23)
Tawa	Madhya Pradesh	–	6.64 (3.79)
Indira Gandhi	Rajasthan	43.10 (7.89)	29.11 (5.39)
Sarda Sahayak	Uttar Pradesh	303.00** (28.34)	50.00 (4.68)
Ramganga	Uttar Pradesh	195.00 (32.99)	352.42 (59.62)
Total		1,014.76	947.70

*Figures in parenthesis show the percentage of the irrigation created in command areas.
Source: Bowonder and Ravi (1984)

Interestingly, eighth plan period laid emphasis on the completion of the on-going works in the medium and major projects and on the improvement of quality of irrigation in the command areas of the existing projects. However, greater emphasis will be given to minor irrigation works both surface and ground water. Better utilization of completed projects, speedy completion of on-going projects, and efficient utilization of available water are expected to be substantially more in forthcoming plans.

The exact cost due to water logging and salinity to agricultural production in India is not known but has been conservatively estimated at Rs. 10,000 million per annum. The cost to society accounted for more than Rs. 6000 million alone in the eleven selected irrigation projects (Table 1.4 and 1.5). In view of the huge cost involved in the development of canal irrigation and being a source of social destabilization and environmental destruction, it is highly desirable that well irrigation is given proper emphasis and priority over canal irrigation. The development of well irrigation does not cause deforestation or seriously disturb the eco-system. It does not lead to over-irrigation, seepage and water logging in the nearby areas. However, it may be important not to over-exploit the ground water as then it would be as bad as canal irrigation as far as the environment degradation is concerned.

Table 1.5. Project-wise cost to the society due to water logging and salinity

Irrigation project	*Expenditure per ha (Thousand Rs.)*	*Production loss of rice* Quantity (million tons Rs.)	*Value (million*	*Total cost to society*
Sriramsagar	15.48	26.26	49.61	944.04
Tungabhadra	2.72	27.25	53.77	79.34
Gandak	2.95	296.75	582.61	1804.00
Ukai-Kakrapar	3.87	13.07	26.69	95.05
Mahi Kadana	4.02	60.97	149.77	473.80
Malprabha	9.84	0.75	1.50	10.29
Chambal	2.62	41.58	97.35	362.70
Tawa	4.70	3.75	6.27	31.20
Indira Gandhi	4.66	18.54	53.22	336.70
Sarda Sahayak	2.84	182.97	317.09	1002.00
Ramganga	2.20	297.77	516.04	1215.00
Total	-	969.66	1853.92	6354.12

Source: Joshi, P. K. (1990)

Need for Reclamation

The present population of the country as on 31st March, 2001 is 1027 million and the maximum annual food grain production has been to the tune of 200 million tonnes in 1999-2000, although it was of the order of only 50 million tonnes in 1950's. By the year 2020, the population would cross 1300 million mark. Thus, to keep the food grain availability at 512 g/person/day achieved in the year 1997, food grain production in year 2020 should exceed 240 million tonnes. With changing food habits and improved living standard, the mark of 512 g/person/day may be quite low. Thus, to cope up with the food requirement of the increasing population in the near future, the agricultural production has to be stepped up substantially. This can be done either by multi-cropping on the existing cultivated lands or by bringing the additional area under cultivation. In view of the projected increase in food grain requirement and remote possibility for the increase in the net cultivated area, it is obvious that our country must ensure higher yield per unit land area than ever before and limited resources of land and water must be used more efficiently. It is argued that the salt affected lands, which are estimated to be 8.5 million ha should be seen as an opportunity as it can alone contribute 45-55 million tonnes of food grains upon reclamation. It has been estimated that 1.3 million ha of alkali lands reclaimed in the states of Punjab, Haryana and Uttar Pradesh alone is contributing about 7.0 million tonnes of food grains (rice-wheat). If irrigation targets are kept and land and water are managed properly, India has the capacity to feed 2,621 million people by the turn of the century, 2.5 times the estimated population, according to a recent study by the Food and Agricultural Organization–Agricultural Towards 2000.

Environmental Issues

Adverse effects of water logging were experienced as early as in the beginning of the 20th century. It appeared in the form of large-scale migration of people from Amritsar due to increasing menace of malaria as a result of increasing population of mosquitoes due to water logging. It was decided to fight this menace through vertical drainage by installing tube wells. Since then, there have been increasing evidences linking water logging and salinization to health related problems in the irrigation commands. In a recent article 'Piecing together the water/malaria picture' published in Research Update of the International Water Management Institute (IWMI), Sri Lanka, IWMI proposes to study irrigation related malaria in the three main climatic and geographic areas where it affects the highest number of world's poor (IWMI, 2000). The hypothesis has been that the world of water and malaria are inextricably linked. One of the research goals is to prepare scientifically validated conclusions that describes the health, institutional and hydrological factors that must fit together for countries to create an effective malaria prevention strategy using water management. It may be interesting to look for the results of this study as one of the studies would be: 'semi-arid areas: will reduced salinity trigger new epidemic'.

The occurrence of alkali lands is generally linked with the canal system. This linkage tends to increase opportunities for human/water/vector contact in addition to the creation of habitats well suited to vector production. There is always a risk to health from vector-borne disease such as malaria, lymphatic filariasis, encephalitis, schistosmiasis etc. Adverse soil conditions in alkali lands characterized with low rates of infiltration result in longer periods of stagnant water during rainy season. Where the intensity of land use under irrigation is relatively low due to exposed water surface being greater than the irrigated area, the period of standing water is sufficient for a number of breeding cycles of vector and pest insects. The development of dense aquatic weeds and algal growth in canals is also responsible for the rise of some insect vectors, pest insect and snails. The use of domestic wastewater in irrigation, if any also serves the cause for increase in breeding of mosquitoes. The IWMI study in Mexico has concluded that the short-term benefits of wastewater irrigation could be offset by considerably high health and environmental costs of this activity. The association between alkali lands and vector borne disease is both complex and site specific.

Lining of canals, in addition to improving irrigation efficiencies and performance is an effective measure to reduce vector breeding and snail survival through minimizing water seepage and puddle formation, increasing water velocities in canals and reducing weed growth. However, problems associated with the quality of construction, sedimentation and maintenance of canals have to be considered.

Modification in water regimes at the farm level through intermittent irrigation and diversified cropping offers considerable scope for reducing vector breeding. When canals are closed either for repairs or due to water shortages, stagnant water in canal beds serves as breeding ground for vectors. In such situation, desilting and flushing wherever possible should be carried out to prevent vector breeding.

Methane is known to be one of the causes leading to global warning. Rice paddies have been found to contribute substantially to methane addition to the environment. As alkali lands upon reclamation are likely to be put under paddy, the question of methane emission need to be addressed. It is known that the methane emission is directly related to water regime. The contribution of methane emission from irrigated field is much less than the one assumed based on the world literature. According to Prashar *et al.,* (1994), the irrigated paddy may only contribute 0.112 Tg Yr^{-1} of methane which is less than 1/30th of the methane emission from rain fed areas and about 1/4th of deep water paddy. Thus environmental degradation on this account may not be as serious as one would think.

However, an adverse environmental effect of adopting rice-wheat rotation upon reclamation of alkali lands is due to declining water table. Besides impairing the water quality, excessive withdrawals from the ground water have lowered the water table. As the water table goes out of reach of an ordinary centrifugal pump, farmers go on deepening pits to install the centrifugal pumps to lower and lower levels. These pits accumulate toxic gases. Whenever, a farmer enter the pit, he upon inhalation of these gases gets entrapped in the pits and eventually looses his life and of others who try to save by entering the pits. These pits as a result have become death traps. But such a scenario may not be linked to reclamation alone. Rice-wheat rotation in general is expanding to non-conventional areas even under low rainfall conditions and light textures soils. Probably a check on such uncalled expansion is urgently required.

REFERENCES

Agarwal, R. R. 1957. Alkali soils can be reclaimed. Indian Farming. 7: 6-8.

Agarwal, R. R. 1961. Soil classification for the alluvium derived soils of the Indo-Gangetic plains in Uttar Pradesh. J. Ind. Soc. Soil Sci. 9: 219-232.

Agarwal, R. R., Mehrotra, C. L. and Gupta, C. P. 1957. Spread and intensity of soil alkalinity with canal irrigation in Gangetic alluvium of Uttar Pradesh. Indian J. gric. Sci. 27: 363-373.

Agarwal R. R. and Yadav, J. S. P. 1956. Diagnostic techniques for the saline and alkali soils of the Indian Gangetic alluvium in Uttar Pradesh. J Soil Sci. 7: 109-121.

Agarwal R.R. and Gupta, R.N. 1968. Saline Alkali Soils in India. Tech. Bull. (Agric. Series), ICAR, New Delhi. 221p.

Agarwal R.R. and Yadav, J.S.P., Gupta, R.N. 1979. Saline and Alkali Soils of India, ICAR, New Delhi. 286p.

Anonymous, 2000. Drainage Master Plan. A report Prepared by High Powered Committee of the Govt. of Haryana.

Anonymous, 2002. Indo-Dutch Network Project (IDNP). Recommendations on Waterlogging and Salinity Control Based on Pilot Area Drainage Research. CSSRI, Karnal and Alterra-ILRI, Wageningen, 100 p.

Ashgar, A. G. and Dhawan, C. L. 1947. Effect of irrigation and growing rice on saline soils. I. Manganese, nitrogen and phosphate status of soil. Indian J. agric. Sci. 17: 199-202.

Ashgar, A. G. and Dhawan, C. L. 1948. Quality of irrigation water. Effect on pH and exchangeable bases of soils. J. Indian Chem. Soc. 25: 179-184.

Banerjee, S. 1959. Some studies of salt-affected soils of Canning, West Bengal. Pl Soil. 10: 207-219.

Basu, J. K. 1950. Problems of saline soils in the Bombay state, India. Trans. 4th Int. Congr. Soil Sci. 3: 169-172.

Basu, J. K. and Tagare, V. D. 1943. Soils of the Deccan canals. IV. The alkali soils, their nature and management. Indian J. Agric. Sci. 13: 157-181.

Bowonder, B. and Ravi, C. 1984. Waterlogging from Irrigation Projects: an Environmental Management Problem. Centre for Energy, Environment and Technology. Administrative Staff College of India, Hyderabad. pp 49.

Center, W. 1880. Note on alkali or reh soils and saline water. Rec. geo. Survey. India 43:253-273.

Dhar, N. R. 1939. Molasses and pressmud in usar (alkali) land reclamation. J. Indian Chem. Soc. 2:105-111.

Dhar, N. R. and Mukherji, S. K. 1936.Reclamation of alkali soils by molasses and pressmud. Proc. Sug. Tech. Ass. India. 5: 15-24.

Dhawan, C. L. and Dhand, A. D. 1950. The occurrence and significance of trace elements in relation to soil deterioration. II boron. Indian J. agric. Sci. 20: 479-485.

Dhawan, C. L., Malhotra, M. M. L. and Singh, J. 1953. Reclamation of alkali soils-Jantar (Sesbania cannabina) root system in black alkali soils treated with different reclaimimg agents. Bull. Int. Comm. Irrig. Drain. 76-82.

Dhawan, C. L., Malhotra, M. M. L. and Singh, J. 1955.Reclamtion of alkali soils. Proc. Natn. Acad. Sci. India. 24A:625-630.

Dhawan, C. L. and Singh, J. 1958. Reclamation of alkali soils by different crop rotations. Proc. Natn. Acad. Sci. India. 27A:238-252.

Dhawan, C.L., 1964. Land Reclamation (Reclamation of Saline and Alkali Soils). Central Board of Irrigation and Power, New Delhi, 140p.

Duthi, J. F. 1896. Reclamation of reh or usar land. Agric. Ledger 3:1-8.

Ghassemi, F., Jakman, A.J. and Nix, H.A. 1995. Global salinization of land and water resources; Human and Environmental Studies. Australian National University, Canberrra.

Gupta, I.C. and Pahwa, K.N. 1978. A Century of Soil Salinity Research in India–A bibliography 1863-1976. Oxford & IBH Publishing Co., New Delhi. 400 p.

Manjunatha, M. V., Oosterbaan, R. J., Gupta, S. K., Rajkumar, H. and Jansen, H. 2004. Performance of subsurface drains for reclaiming waterlogged saline lands under rolling topography in Tungabhadra irrigation project in India. Agricultural Water Management. 69: 69-82.

Hoon , R. C. and Ahluwalia, G. S. 1953. The physico-chemical changes in deteriorated soils as a result of soil reclamation operation. II. J. Irrig. Pwr. 10: 38-42.

Hoon, R. C. 1955. Land Reclamation. Pub. Central Board of Irrigation and Power. 2: 160-178.

Hoon, R. C. , Jain, L. C. and Bhatnagar, B. B. 1950. The physico-chemical changes in deteriorated soils as a result of soil reclamation operation. IV. The occurrence of gypsum in soils. J. Cent Board Irrig. Simla Pwr. 7: 60=68.

Hoon , R. C. and Dewan, R. 1949. The physico-chemical changes in deteriorated soils as a result of soil reclamation operations. II. J. Central Board Irrig. Simla. 6:265-272.

Hoon , R. C. and Mehta, M. L. 1937. A study of the soil profile of the Punjab plains with reference to their natural flora. Res. Pub. Punjab Irrigation Res. Inst. 3:3.

HSMITC 1984. Studies for the Use of Saline Water in the Command Areas of Irrigation Projects in Haryana, India–Appraisal Document (Summary).115 p.

Inglis, C. C. and Gokhale, V. K. 1928. Report on drainage experiments at Baramati, Bombay. Tech. Report. Public Works Department Bombay. No. 14.

IWMI. 2000. Piecing together the water/malaria picture. Research Update. November 2000: 4.

Joshi, P.K. 1990. Influence of surface irrigation on crop productivity. Indian J. Agric. Sci. 60: 91-96.

Kanwar, J. S. and Bhumbla, D. R. 1960. Reclamation of alkaline and saline soils in the Punjab. Rep. ICAR, New Delhi.

Kanwar, J. S. 1961. Reclaiming deteriorated soils. Fertilizer News. 6: 19-21.

Kanwar, J. S. 1962. Reclamation of saline-alkali soils. Proc. Symp. Salinity and Alkalinity. IARI, New Delhi.

Khan, A. D. 1950. Usar soils: their identification and reclamation. Agric. Animal Husb. (U P). I:29-30.

Krishna, G. C.. Desai,. A. D. and Krishnamurthy, C. 1960. Deep black cotton soils of Raichur. Bull. Indian Council of Agric. Res. 83: pp 53.

Leather, J.W. 1914. Investigation on Usar Land in the United Provinces. Govt. Press, U.P. 87 p.

Mann, H.H., Tamhane, V.A. 1910. The salt land of Nira Valley. Bull. Deptt. Agric. Bombay, 35 p.

Mehrotra, V.L., Das, S.K. and Yadav, J.S.P. 1975. Nature of soils of Large Usar Blocks of Kanpur district. Tech. Bull. Deptt. Agric. U.P. Supdt. Printing and Stationery, Lucknow. 278p.

Mehta, K.M., Mathur, C.M., Shankarnarayana, H.S. and Moghe, V.B. 1969. Saline Alkali Soils in Rajasthan, their Nature, Extent and Management. Research Monograph No. J, Deptt. Agric. Rajasthan. 61 p.

Mehta, M.L. 1940. The Formation and the Reclamation of Thur Lands in Punjab. Punjab Irrigation Research Institute pub. 3. 64p.

Mehta, M.L. 1951. Land Reclamation. Central Board Irrigation Power, New Delhi. 117p.

NEDCO 1968. Bhal Reclamation Scheme (Govt. of The Netherlands and State of Gujarat, India). Delft Hydraulics Laboratory, Delft, The Netherlands. Vol. 1-6.

Planing Commission, India. 1963. Study of Wastelands including Saline Alkali and Waterlogged Lands and their Reclamation Measures. Res. Committee of Natural Resources, New Delhi. 237 p.

Prashar, D.C. et al. 1994. Methane budget from paddy fields in India. Current Sciences: 66: 938-941.

Puri, A. N. 1933. The relation between exchangeable sodium and crop yield in Punjab soils and a new method to characterise alkali soils. Res. Pub. Punjab Irrigation Res. Inst. 5:4.

Puri, A. N., Taylor, E. M., Mckenzie and Ashgar, A. G. 1937. Soil deterioration in the canal irrigated areas of Punjab. III. Formation and Characteristics of the soil profiles in the alkaline alluvium of the Punjab. Res. Pub. Punjab Irrigation Res. Inst. 4: 7.

Raychaudhury, S. P. and Shankaran, A. 1952. Studies on the saline soils of Delhi state. I. Some typical profiles of the Jamuna khadar area (north). Ind. J. agric. Sci. 22: 209-222.

Raychaudhury, S. P. and Sinha, N. S. 1957. Studies on the saline and alkaline soils of Delhi state villages. IV. Ind. J. agric. Sci. 27: 347-361.

Russel, J.C. Kadry, L. and Hanna, A.B. 1965. Sodic soils in Iraq. Agrokomia ES Talajtan. Tom 14(Suppl.): 91-97.

Satyanarayana, M. 1953. Crop and land improvement under the Krishna East Bank Canal (Madras state). Madras agric. J. 40:293-294.

Shah, R. K. and Trivedi, A. M. 1954. An investigation of the alkali soils in Gujaraf, preliminary report. J Soil Wat. Cons. 3: 28-31.

Shah, R. K. , Vora, J. C. and Trivedi, A. M. 1958. Possibilities of reclamation of alkali soils of the Little Rann of Kutch. Ind. J. App. Chem. 30: 96-99.

Singh, D. and Nijhawan, S. D. 1932. A study of the physico-chemical changes accompanying the process of reclamation in alkali soils. Indian J. agric. Sci. 2:1-18.

Talati, R. P. 1941. Damaged lands in the Daccan and their classification. Indian J. agric. Sci. 11: 959-977.

Talati, R. P. 1947. Field experiments on the reclamation of salt land in Baramati of Bombay Deccan. Indian J. agric. Sci. 17: 153-174.

Taylor, E. M. , Malhotra, J. K. and Mehta, M. L. 1933. An investigation of the rise of water table in the upper Chenab canal area, Punjab. Res. Pub. Punjab Irrigation Res. Inst. 1:39.

Taylor, E. M. and Mehta, M. L. 1941. Some irrigation problems in the Punjab. Ind. J. agric. Sci. 11: 137-169.

Taylor, E. M., Puri, A. N. and Asghar, A. G. 1934. Soil deterioration in the canal-irrigated area of the Punjab. I. Equilibrium between Ca and Na ions in base exchange reactions. Ind. J. agric. Sci. 4: 8.

U.P. Deptt. Agric. 1939. Usar Land Committee Report. Supdt. Printing and Stationery, Allahabad, 118 p.

Uppal, H.L. 1963. Reclamation of Land Rendered Barren by Salinity and Alkalinity. Food Production series No. 1, Land Reclamation, Irrigation and Power Research Institute, Amritsar. 17 p.

Voelcker, J. A. 1897. Report on the Improvement of Indian Agriculture.

World Watch Institute, 1990. State of the World. Norton and Co., New York.

Zende, G.K. 1968. Improvement of Saline and Alkali Soils in Maharashtra State. Res. Bull. 5, Deptt. Agric. Maharashtra, Poona. 65 p.

2

SAMPLING AND LABORATORY INVESTIGATIONS

To accurately characterize a soil or water to assess the nature of the salt stresses that would be encountered by the plants, soil/water sampling and laboratory investigations are essential pre-requisites. Aided by some field tests on soil physical properties of the soil, it should be possible to understand the nature and properties of the soils as well as to understand the kinds and degree of the problems. Guidelines on drawing soil and water samples and some essential field and laboratory investigations for alkali lands are included in this chapter. The information generated through these tests should help in understanding the nature and properties of the soil and to accurately diagnose the problems on the basis of guidelines provided in the next chapter.

Soil Sampling

The method for soil sampling depends on the purpose for which a sample is collected. For this reason, no common standard procedure can be suggested for all the situations. To meet the requirements of a good sample for laboratory investigations, the soil sampling procedure is outlined in the following sections.

Number of Samples

The size of the plot or the farm area that could be represented by one composite sample depends on the anticipated spatial variability in the fields. Field plots, which are more or less uniform, may make a single unit for the purpose of sampling. Normally 8 to 10 samples are required from a uniform field unit to make one composite sample representative of the area. However, salt-affected soils have large spatial variability. Therefore, for each acre field (0.4 ha), one composite sample may be sufficient. For this purpose an auger could be used. If a profile has been dug, a thin (1.25-2.0 cm) slice of soil from the required depth from all sides should be taken to prepare the sample. Take samples from 8–10 sites in 0.4 ha field, thoroughly mix them in a tray and draw a composite sample for laboratory analysis. The samples should normally be drawn after levelling and dyking (*bunding*) has been completed. When it is intended to improve a patchy field, model soil samples should be composited from a few representative samples taken from within the spot.

Soil samples should not be drawn immediately after rains, irrigation, fertilization or burning of crop residues. Similarly, do not sample the sites near to or along an irrigation canal, a collector or lateral drain, dyke (*bund)*, farmyard manure pits, shady trees, threshing floor and roads.

Depth of Sampling

The depth to which samples should be drawn depends on the land use. If the intention were to grow shallow to medium rooted crops like rice, wheat etc., it would suffice to draw samples to a depth of 30 cm. A major fraction of the roots of these crops is confined to this zone. If, on the other hand, it is proposed to grow deep-rooted crops like cotton, it would be advantageous to obtain samples up to a depth of about 60 cm. In case the intended land use is to grow trees (horticultural or forest tree species), it is essential to carry out a detailed study of the soil profile up to a depth of 150 to 180 cm. It is necessary because the performance of tree species on a long-term basis is strongly influenced by properties of the lower soil layers including the presence of a hard layer due to $CaCO_3$ concretions etc.

How to Obtain Samples

For samples up to 30 cm depth, a cut in the soil can be made with a spade and a thin slice of soil taken to a desired depth (0-15 and/or 15-30 cm) with the help of trowel (Mason's spatula, Fig. 2.1). If sample from deeper soil layers are needed, an auger should be used (Fig. 2.2). Alternatively, a soil profile can be exposed to a depth of 1.5 m, and sample can be drawn from appropriate depths. Once the profile is exposed, consult

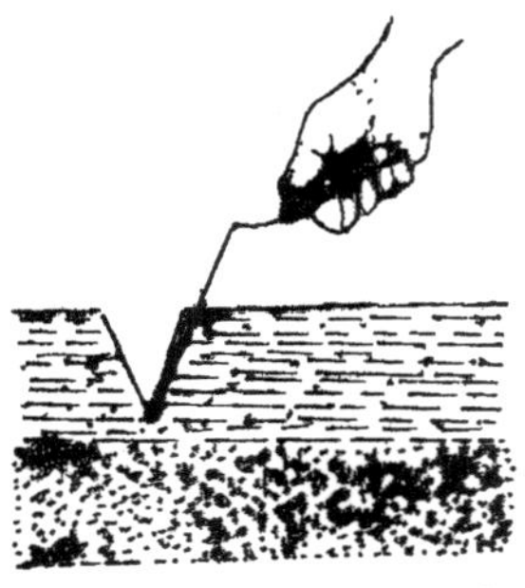

A. From each 1/2 ha, take 9-10 soil samples using mason's spatula

B. Thoroughly mix the soil samples on a dry cloth or in an iron pan

Mix | Divide in four parts | Take opposite 2 parts

C. Mix the samples as the quantity is more, divide in four parts and keep two opposite portions. Repeat the process if necessary.

D. Pack the sample in a cotton bag to send it for analysis

Fig. 2.1 A schematic diagram showing soil sampling technique

a specialist for examination and formulation of recommendations.

Size of the Sample

For conventional diagnostic analysis in a laboratory, it is sufficient to have about 500 to 750 g of soil sample.

Sampling Slick Spots

A slick spot can be best identified during the cropping season. It is better to sample when spots are visible. Samples representing slick spots should not be mixed with samples from good spots. Salt crust should not also be mixed with the soil samples. If salt crust is sampled, it should be kept and analyzed separately.

Packing of Soil Samples

Before packing the soil samples and their mailing to a soil testing laboratory, the following precautions should be taken:

- Remove stones/gravel from soil samples, air dry the samples in trays in shade.
- Air-dried soil should be packed in polyethylene / hard paper bags.

Fig. 2.2 Application of an auger to sample soils

- Insert the polyethylene bag in a cloth bag and put an appropriate tag for labeling.
- Cloth bags should be labeled with a coping pencil/ ink.
- Seal the bag properly and use wooden/hard paper board carton for mailing.

The packets of the samples should be dispatched to soil testing laboratories. In each state, the Department of Agriculture and the State Agricultural University have soil testing laboratories either at the district or at the *tehsil* level. These laboratories are generally responsible for undertaking soil and water testing and making appropriate recommendations for reclaiming salt-affected soils/waters, either free or on a nominal charge.

Table 2.1 Collector's observations on the soil sample

Specifications	
Name of the farmer	
Name of the collector	
Location of the site	
Any other character	
Proposed cropping pattern	
Observations (if already in use)	
On crops (give yield in kg/ha)	
Amount of water applied	
General observation	
Type of soil	
Soil fertility test required	Yes/No*
Whether water sample is being sent	Yes/No*
Sample Number and date	
Name of the laboratory where sample sent	
Signatures	

Encircle the appropriate word

Each sample should be accompanied by a detailed Performa to help make sound recommendations on the basis of soil analysis (Table 2.1). A sample sheet on which soil analysis results are provided to the user is given in Table 2.2 (Gupta *et al.*, 1995).

Sampling Procedure for Water Samples

Proper diagnosis of the nature and the amount of salts present in water is essential to assess the possible hazards, which it could pose to the soil or the crop. Collection of representative sample is, therefore, basic for correct diagnosis and for making sound recommendations for the management of poor quality waters. Following procedures may be adopted in collection and dispatch of the samples for analysis.

Selection of Containers

As far as possible plastic bottles should be used for collection of water samples. If plastic bottles are not available, glass bottles can be used. Bottles should be thoroughly cleaned and rinsed 2-3 times with water from the same source for which sample is to be taken. Avoid using metal containers for collection of water samples.

Time of Sampling

In case of gravity canal, take the sample of the water from the channel after irrigation has been in progress for about an hour. For ground water samples, take the sample after running the tube well for about 0.5 hr.

Quantity of Sample

Most routine salinity appraisal tests require about 100 ml of water. However, to be on the safer side and to allow specialized tests, if need be, as much as 500 ml of sample should be sufficient.

Table 2.2 Performa for soil test reports

Name of the laboratory ____________________

Name of the farmer ____________________

Sample No. ____________________

Date of Sample received ____________________

Sample analyzed on ____________________

Description	*Results*				
EC_e (dS m^{-1})					
pH					
Cations (meq l^{-1})	Ca^{++}	Mg^{++}	Na^-	K^+	Total
Anions (meq l^{-1})	CO_3^{--}	HCO_3^- SO_4^{--}	Cl^-	Total	
Special Analysis	ESP	GR	Nitrogen	Available Phosphorus	Potash
Analyzed by Checked by					
Recommendation (if any)					
					Signatures

Packing

Water containers should be properly screwed and if possible wax sealed. Containers should be properly labeled for identification. Each sample should be accompanied by a description conforming to the list (Table 2.3). A sample sheet on which water analysis results are provided to the user is given in Table 2.4 (Gupta *et al.,* 1995).

Table 2.3 Collector's observations on the irrigation water sample

Specifications	
Name of the farmer	
Name of the collector	
Location of the site	
Source of water Spring/canal/drain/well/lake*	
Additional details (if needed)	
Colour	
Odour	
Any other character	
Depth of water on sampling date	
Proposed application : Domestic/irrigation*	
Irrigation method employed : surface/sprinkler/drip*	
Proposed cropping pattern	
Observations (if already in use)	
On crops (give yield in kg/ha)	
On soil	
Amount of water applied	
General observation	
Type of soil	
Your opinion on water quality	
Any special test you require	
Whether soil sample is being sent	Yes/No*
Sample No. and date	
Name of the laboratory where sample sent	
Signatures	

* Encircle the appropriate word

Table 2.4. Performa for water test reports

Name of the laboratory ______________________

Name of the farmer ______________________

Sample No. ______________________

Date of Sample received ______________________

Sample analyzed on ______________________

Description	Results				
EC (dS m^{-1})					
pH					
Cations (meq l^{-1})	Ca^{++}	Mg^{++}	Na^{+}	K^{+}	Total
Anions (meq l^{-1})	CO_3^{--}	HCO_3^{-} SO_4^{--}	Cl^{-}	Total	
Special determinations	Boron (mg l^{-1})	Fluorine (mg l^{-1})	Silica (mg l^{-1})	NO_3 (me ql^{-1})	Any other

Analyzed by ______________ Checked by ______________

Recommendation (if any) ______________________

Signatures

Equipment and Procedures for Soil Investigations

Hand Augers

For soil or drainage investigations, most commonly used auger is the closed post-hole auger. These augers are usually provided with bits of 5, 10 or 15 cm diameter, which could be used interchangeably on the same pipe shaft or are permanently welded to it. The length of each auger is fixed or appropriate arrangements are made to add extension to the pipe shaft. With extensions, it is possible to explore up to about 2.0-2.5 m depth with such augers. Many variations of these augers are available and the one that suits to local soil conditions may be procured. These augers are used to take soil sample for various kinds of analysis, to make auger holes for conducting hydraulic conductivity tests or to make shallow temporary bore holes to measure depth to water table.

Power Augers

Power augers are usually required to explore sub-soil strata below 2.5 m, installation of observation wells and piezometers and for logging the soil profiles. This kind of equipment may not be required under the Indian conditions as most of the work could be completed with the help of local/ village mechanics who could be awarded contracts to undertake the job. The jetting equipment commonly used in installing a hand pump or a shallow tube well is quite sufficient for the kinds of works involved in drainage investigations.

Chemical Analysis of Soil and Water Samples

Often a question arises as to what kind of analysis be performed on soil and water samples. The decisions on this matter could be taken on the basis of information provided in Table 2.5. It could be seen that for scientific assessment more elaborate analysis would be needed compared to cropping on the land. It is usually recommended that a chemistry laboratory be an integral part of a reclamation/drainage project. It should have an EC meter, a pH meter, a flame photometer and chemical analysis facility for anions and cations. The laboratory facilities could be extended over the years depending upon the need for chemical determinations.

Preparation of Saturation Extract

Before most laboratory tests can be conducted, it is essential to draw saturation paste extract. For this purpose, following procedure is used :

Table 2.5 Kind of analysis and use of information

Analysis	*Use of information*
Total salts or Electrical Conductivity (EC) of soil/water	Leaching need for reclamation, crop selection and reuse and disposal of saline water including the drainage water
Exchangeable Sodium Percentage (ESP), pH (soil) and pH (water)	Need for amendment application, pH of the soil in many cases being an indicator of ESP, is used to have quick estimates of alkali problem. pH (water) is a general indicator of water quality
Sodium Adsorption Ratio (SAR) Soil /water	Need to assess leaching, envelope requirement in combination with clay % age. SAR of water helps to decide reuse of saline water including drainage effluent and need for amendment application.
Residual Sodium Carbonate (RSC)	Reuse of saline water including drainage effluent and need for amendment application
Iron, Manganese	Soil: Ochre formation; Water: Ochre formation and need to take corrective steps
Sulphates (Soil and water)	Reuse of saline water and fertilizer application, In drainage, it would dictate the kind of cement to be used in case of tile drains and in other structures
Nitrates (Drainage)	Nutritional requirement of saline water irrigated lands, to assess the leaching of nitrate so as to take corrective measure to minimize leaching
Specialized analysis	To assess the toxic nature of water, needed only when there are indications that Boron, Flouride or heavy metals in the water could occur.

Air dry the sample and pass through 2 mm sieve. Weigh 300 g of soil and place it into a plastic beaker. Add distilled water to sample of soil while stirring with a spatula. Add distilled water until the soil is nearly saturated. At saturation, the soil glistens as it reflects light, flows slightly when the container is tipped and the paste slides freely and cleanly off the spatula for all soils but for a soil with high clay content. Allow the paste to stand for few hours so that soil is fully wet.

Add more water, if necessary, to form a saturated paste. Cover the beaker and leave it this way overnight. Some more distilled water or weighed amount of dry soil should be added, if necessary. Mix the sample. Neither the free water should collect on the soil surface nor should the paste stiffen markedly. It should also not loose its glistening appearance on standing.

Place the paste in a Buchner funnel lined with a Whatman 50 filter paper. Apply the vacuum and collect the extract in a bottle or test tube as per requirement. The filtration is finished when air starts to pass through the paper. Add sodium hexametaphosphate solution to the filtrate (approximate one drop for each 25 ml of filtrate) to prevent calcium carbonate to precipitate.

The saturation per cent defined as mass of water in the saturated paste expressed as a percentage of oven dry weight of soil is measured as follows:

Transfer a portion of the saturated soil paste, prepared according to the above procedure to a tared soil can with lid. Weigh, dry to constant weight at 105 °C and weigh again. The saturation percentage (SP) is then given by

$$SP = \frac{\text{Loss in weight upon drying}}{\text{Weight of oven dry soil}} \times 100 \qquad (2.1)$$

Chemical Analysis

Electrical Conductivity (EC)

Electrical Conductivity is an indirect measurement of the soluble salts present in the soil solution or the water. It is defined as the reciprocal of the electrical resistivity (specific resistance). The resistivity is the resistance in ohms of a conductor whose length is 1 cm and cross-sectional area is 1 cm^2. Electrical conductivity which earlier used to be expressed in mmhos cm^{-1} is now commonly expressed in dS m^{-1} such that 1 dS m^{-1} = 1 mmhos cm^{-1}.

Equipment

- Conductivity bridge
- Conductivity cell
- Reagents: Standard potassium chloride solution (0.02 N KCl). It is prepared by dissolving 1.4912 g of KCl in water and making the volume 1liter. It has an electrical conductivity of 2.768 dS/m at 25°C.

Procedure

The first step is to determine the cell constant if already not available. The standard solution (Say EC =2.768) is filled into a 100 ml beaker and the conductivity cell previously rinsed with the standard solution is immersed into the beaker. Conductivity is noted. The cell constant is then determined from the following relation:

$$\text{Cell constant (k)} = \frac{\text{Known specific electrical conductance (2.768)}}{\text{Measured conductance of the standard solution (C)}} \quad (2.2)$$

Take out the conductivity cell and rinse the same with the distilled water. Use the test solution kept in the beaker and measure the conductance as before. The actual EC of the test solution is then given as

$$\text{Actual EC} = \text{Measured EC} * k \quad (2.3)$$

Temperature of the test solution is considered in evaluating the EC at 25°C. For this purpose, laboratory meters are provided with temperature correction. Tables are also available to convert EC measured at a given temperature to the EC at 25°C (Table 2.6). As a thumb rule, the electrical conductivity increases approximately by 2% per degree C rise in temperature. For example to convert values measured at 20°C to the values at 25°C , multiply by a factor of 1.112. However, use of table is recommended such that

$$\text{EC at } 25°\text{C} = \text{EC at } T°\text{C} \times f_t \quad (2.4)$$

Here, f_t = correction factor at temperature t (Table 2.6)

Soil Samples

For measuring the EC of the soil samples, use of saturation extract is recommended. The EC of the saturation extract is denoted as EC_e. However, in land reclamation works where numbers of sample are large and would need to be repeated over the years, EC is usually determined using 1:2 soil water paste. The EC of the 1:2 soil-water paste is denoted as EC_2. In heavy textured soil 1:2.5 or 1:5 soil-water pastes have also been used. To prepare 1:2 soil-water paste, weigh 100 gm of the soil sample and add 200 ml of water and shake well before testing. It is customary to denote EC as EC_e for soils. Following relation then determines the EC_e.

$$EC_e = \frac{\theta_2}{\theta_{sp}} * EC_2 \quad (2.5)$$

Here θ_2 and θ_{sp} are the soil moistures contents in soil-water paste and at saturation for a given soil.

It is prudent to prepare a standard curve by analyzing a good number of samples from the project area at the initial stage itself. For these samples, both EC_e and EC_2 are measured. The data are plotted as shown in Fig. 2.3. A best-fit line is drawn for the data set, which then can be used to report EC_e values for the soil samples (Fig. 2.3).

Table 2.6 Correction factors for correcting conductivity data at standard temperature of 25°C

°C	f_t	°C	f_t	°C	f_t
08.0	1.488	22.6	1.051	29.2	0.921
09.0	1.448	22.8	1.047	29.4	0.918
10.0	1.411	23.0	1.043	29.6	0.914
11.0	1.375	23.2	1.038	29.8	0.911
12.0	1.341	23.4	1.034	30.0	0.907
13.0	1.309	23.6	1.029	30.2	0.904
14.0	1.277	23.8	1.025	30.4	0.901
15.0	1.247	24.0	1.020	30.6	0.897
16.0	1.218	24.2	1.016	30.8	0.894
17.0	1.189	24.4	1.012	31.0	0.890
18.0	1.163	24.6	1.008	31.2	0.887
18.2	1.157	24.8	1.004	31.4	0.884
18.4	1.152	25.0	1.000	31.6	0.880
18.6	1.147	25.2	0.996	31.8	0.877
18.8	1.142	25.4	0.992	32.0	0.873
19.0	1.136	25.6	0.988	32.2	0.870
19.2	1.131	25.8	0.983	32.4	0.867
19.4	1.127	26.0	0.979	32.6	0.864
19.6	1.122	26.2	0.975	32.8	0.861
19.8	1.117	26.4	0.971	33.0	0.858
20.0	1.112	26.6	0.967	34.0	0.843
20.2	1.107	26.8	0.964	35.0	0.829
20.4	1.102	27.0	0.960	36.0	0.815
20.6	1.097	27.2	0.956	37.0	0.801
20.8	1.092	27.4	0.953	380	0.788
21.0	1.087	27.6	0.950	39.0	0.755
21.2	1.082	27.8	0.947	40.0	0.763
21.4	1.078	28.0	0.943	41.0	0.750
21.6	1.073	28.2	0.940	42.0	0.739
21.8	1.068	28.4	0.936	43.0	0.727
22.0	1.064	28.6	0.932	44.0	0.716
22.2	1.060	28.8	0.929	45.0	0.705
22.4	1.055	29.0	0.925	46.0	0.694

Source: Richards (1954)

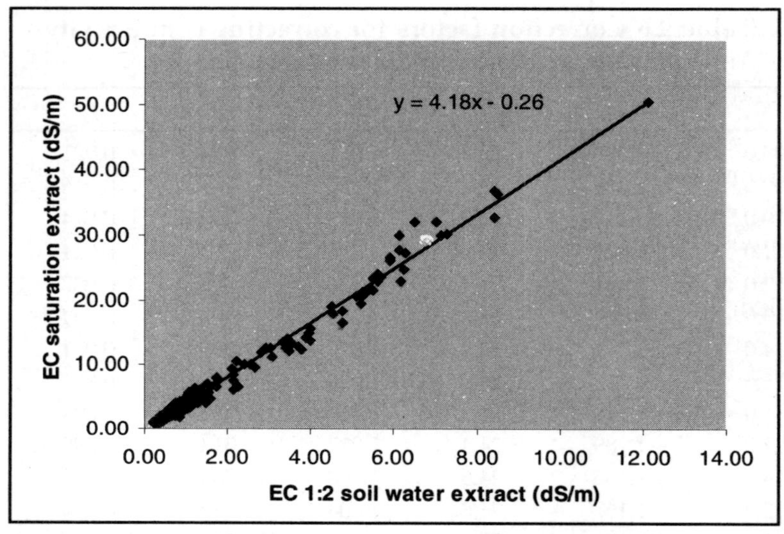

Fig. 2.3 Relationship between EC of the saturation extract and EC of the 1:2 soil water paste

pH

The pH of the soil solution or extract is an indicator of the nature of the soil whether it is acidic or alkali. A pH less than 7.0 indicates acidic nature while pH above 7.0 would indicate the alkali nature.

Apparatus

- pH meter with glass electrode
- Buffer tablets (4 & 7 or 7 & 9.2)

First wash the electrodes with water from a wash bottle. Dry the electrodes. Use buffer solution of pH 4 and adjust the pH meter to 4, the pH of the buffer solution. Repeat this determination with the other buffer solution of pH 7. Repeat these determination till the pH meter is set to both the buffer solutions correctly. The pH of the water or of the soil-water suspension is then read straight from the pH meter. It is advisable that buffer checks be repeated in between to ensure that the pH meter is calibrated appropriately during the determinations. For alkali soils, calibrate the pH meter at pH 7 and 9.2.

Although pH of the soil-water suspension (1:2) is recommended for use, the pH of the suspension should not be treated as pH_s (pH of the saturation paste). Usually pH_s values would be lower than pH_2 by 0.2 to 0.5 unit in normal and saline soils and by 0.5 to 1.0 units in alkali and saline alkali soils due to hydrolysis upon dilution.

Sodium and Potassium

- Flame photometer
- Sodium filter
- Potassium filter
- Sodium/Potassium standards

Preparation of sodium standard

First dry NaCl at 105°C for one hour and then cool it in a desiccator. Dissolve 0.254 g in water and make it up to 100 ml. Pipette 10 ml into a 100 ml volumetric flask and make it up to the mark. Then pipette 0, 2, 4, 7 and 10 ml of this diluted standard into 100 ml volumetric flasks and make up to the mark. These will contain 0, 2, 4, 7 and 10 mg Na respectively.

Place the sodium filter in the flame photometer and then set the milliammeter to zero on the zero standard and to full scale deflection with the 10 mg Na standard. Read all of the standards and prepare a standard curve from these measurements.

Once the standard curve is prepared, use the water and/or soil saturation extract for milliammeter readings. Find out the exact amount of sodium using the standard curve. If necessary, dilute the water/saturation extracts before use. In that case, the resulting figure is also multiplied by the dilution factor to arrive at the exact amount of sodium in the water/extract.

Same procedure is employed for potassium determinations. In this case KCl is used to prepare standard curve and potassium filter is used instead of sodium filter.

Calcium plus Magnesium

It is commonly recommended to use EDTA titration method for this analysis. Required reagents are as follows:

A. Ammonium chloride–Ammonium hydroxide buffer solution: It is prepared by dissolving 67.5 g of ammonium chloride in 570 ml of concentrated ammonium hydroxide and made to 1 liter.

B. Erichrome black T indicator: It is prepared by dissolving 0.5 g of Erichrome black T and 4.5 g of hydroxylamine hydrochloride in 100 ml of 95 % ethanol.

C. EDTA solution (0.01 N)

Take 5 ml of soil saturation extract or the water sample in a China dish. Add about 10 ml of distilled water to this solution. Add 0.5 ml of reagent A and 3 or 4 drops of reagent B. Titrate with reagent C. The colour change is from wine red to blue or green. Rotate the dish to ensure complete disappearance of the red colour at the end point.

(Ca+Mg) in meq l^{-1} = ml of EDTA used * (normality of EDTA * 1000)/ ml of aliquot taken

$$= 2\,V \qquad (2.6)$$

Where V is the volume of 0.01N EDTA used for 5 ml of the water/extract sample.

Carbonates and Bicarbonates

Carbonates and bicarbonates in water or soil saturation extract can be conveniently determined by titration of a known volume of water against standard (usually 0.01 N) H_2SO_4. Reagents required are:

A. Phenolphthalein indicator (1 per cent in 60% ethyl alcohol)

B. Methyle orange indicator, 0. 01 per cent in water

C. Sulphuric acid, H_2SO_4 (0.01N)

Take 5 ml of the sample in a glass flask. Add 1 of 2 drops of reagent A. If the solution turns pink, titrate against reagent C until the colour just disappears. Note volume of the acid consumed and designate it as N.

Add 2 drops of reagent B to the colorless content after the first titration. Again titrate it with reagent C to the first orange color and designate the reading as M.

Carbonates (meq l^{-1}) = 2 N * (normality of H_2SO_4 * 1000)/ ml of sample taken

$$= \frac{2\,N * 0.01 * 1000}{5} = 4\,N \qquad (2.7)$$

Bicarbonate (meq l^{-1})

$$= (M\text{-}2N)\ X - \frac{\text{Normality of } H_2SO_4 \ X\ 1000}{\text{ml of sample taken}} = 2\,(M-2\,N) \qquad (2.8)$$

Note : The titrated contents can be saved for determination of Chloride.

Chloride

The determination of chloride is made by titration against $AgNO_3$ solution. Reagents required are:

A. Potassium chromate : 5 per cent solution

B. Silver nitrate, 0.005 N.

To the sample preserved from the carbonate, bicarbonate determination, add 4 drops of reagent. A . While stirring, titrate with reagent B to the first reddish brown (brick red) colour.

Cl in meq l^{-1} = (ml of Ag NO_3 * 0.005 * 1000)/ ml of water sample

$$= x \qquad (2.9)$$

Where x is the ml of $AgNO_3$ used.

Same procedure is used for fresh soil saturation extract/ water sample. It is usually recommended to determine a blank correction by titrating a like volume of Cl-free distilled water. If this is done, then Cl in meqL^{-1} = (x-blank).

If a chloride meter is available, then the same can also be used to determine chloride as per the procedure.

Sulphate

By titration, sulphate is determined as follows.

Reagents

A: Magnesium chloride, 0.02 N

B: Barium chloride, 0.01 N

C: Versene solution, 0.01 N

D: Erichrome black T indicator

E: HCl, 0.1 N

F: A buffer solution of NH_4Cl and NH_4OH

Take 3 aliquotes of sample. In the first aliquote find out (Ca+Mg) in meq l^{-1} as described previously.

In the second aliquote determine carbonate and bicarbonate by reagent E.

In the third aliquote of 5 ml, add 0.01N HCl equivalent to total alkalinity plus slightly more to completely neutralize the alkalinity. Shake the solution to destroy carbonates. Add 2 ml of reagent B and boil for few seconds. Cool and add 10 ml of reagent F and 5 drops of reagent D. Titrate the solution against reagent C to the first end point (blue or green). Add 1 ml of reagent A and again titrate to obtain a second end point by titration with reagent C.

Sulphate, meq l^{-1} = (B+Ba+Mg-T) (2.10)

Here

B is the blank, meq of (Ca+Mg) in the original solution

Ba and Mg are the meq of Barium and Magnesium added

T is the meq of versene added in the total titration of sample with Ba and Mg.

Gypsum Requirement

Theoretically, the Gypsum Requirement (GR) can be calculated by the following relationship:

$$GR\ (me/100g) = \frac{CEC\ (initial\ ESP-final\ ESP)}{100} \qquad (2.11)$$

Since 1me of gypsum/100g of soil is equivalent to 860 mg of gypsum and since 1 ha of soil to a depth of 20 cm may be taken to weigh 3,100,000 kg, the amount of gypsum theoretically required to treat this depth of soil is calculated as follows:

$$GR/ha/20cm = GR\ (me/100g)\ 860 \times 10^{-6} \times 3.10^{6}$$

$$= GR\ (me/100g) \times 2580\ (kg) \qquad (2.12)$$

If the percentage purity of gypsum is less than 100, the quantity of gypsum has to be increased proportionately.

Usually 3 methods are used to work out the gypsum requirement in the laboratory.

A: Schoonover (1952) method

Prepare a saturated gypsum solution of known calcium concentration. It is prepared by adding 5 gm of chemically pure $CaSO_4$-$2H_2O$ to one liter of distilled water. Shake vigorously for about 10 min on a mechanical shaker or 1 hour by hand. Filter through Whatman filter paper no. 1.

Take 5 g of air dry soil in 250 ml conical flask. Add 100 ml of the saturated gypsum solution. Firmly put a stopper and shake for 5 minutes on a mechanical shaker or 50 min by hand. Filter the contents through Whatman filter paper no.1. Transfer 5 ml of aliquot into 100 ml porcelain dish. Determine the calcium and magnesium concentration as per the procedure outlined earlier in this chapter. Run a blank using 5 ml of the saturated gypsum solution prepared before.

GR (meq/100 gm soil) = 2 (Ca concentration in blank (meq L^{-1})-Ca concentration in the filtrate (meq L^{-1})

GR for 15 cm soil layer (t ha^{-1}) = GR (meq/100 gm soil) * 1.72 (2.13)

B: Modified Schoonover (1952) procedure (Abrol *et al.* 1975)

According to Abrol *et al.* (1975), the gypsum requirement as calculated with Schoonover method, also includes the gypsum required to neutralize the soluble sodium carbonate if present in alkali soils. It is therefore, prudent to leach the sample of the soil (5 gm) with 20 ml of 60% ethanol. It will leach down the soluble sodium carbonate and therefore, will not add to the gypsum requirement. Rest of the procedure is same as discussed before.

C: pH versus GR graph

The absolute quantity of exchangeable sodium percentage of the alkali soils will continue to be the basis for the accurate determination of the quantity of gypsum for reclamation. In practice, however, pH of the saturated soil paste (pH_s) or pH of 1:2 soil water suspension (pH_2) may also serve the useful purpose since for many alkali soils of the Indo-Gangetic plains, a fairly good co-relation exists between pH_2 and exchangeable sodium percentage. This technique would be specifically useful where skilled staff and laboratory facilities are not available to determine the exchangeable sodium and gypsum requirement. Abrol *et al.* (1973) prepared a graph between pH_2 and GR of the soils for different soil texture (Fig. 2.4) . The use of this graph is a quick and fairly good method to estimate GR of alkali soils of the Indo-Gangetic plains.

GR and Equivalent Amendment Values

GR is the equivalence of gypsum that must be added to reclaim the soil. However, depending upon the availability, other amendments are could be used in the field. Equivalence of amendments other than gypsum could be determined from the values reported in Table 2.7.

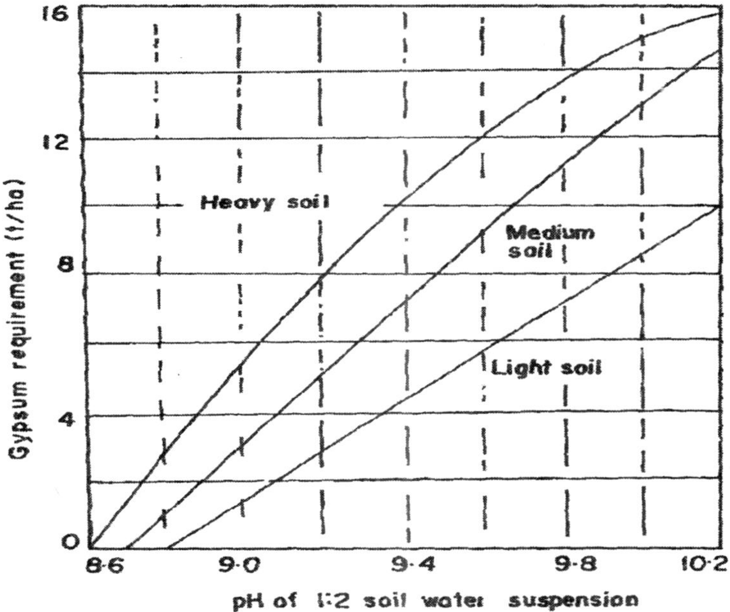

Fig. 2.4 pH and gypsum requirement of soils

Source: Abrol *et al.*, 1981

Assessment of Physical Properties

Soil Texture: Feel and Touch Method

In the field, soil texture is assessed by feel of the soil with the fingers. If necessary, this assessment can be verified later in the laboratory. The general definitions of soil textural classes in terms of field experience and feel that are included in the USDA Soil Survey Manual (1951) are as follow:

Sand: Sand is loose and single grained. The individual grains can be seen or felt readily. Squeezed in the hand when dry, sand falls apart when pressure is released. Squeezed when moist, it forms a cast but crumbles when touched.

Table 2.7: Commonly used amendments and their equivalent amendment values

Amendments (Chemical formula)	*Tons of amendment material equivalent to*	
	1 ton of pure gypsum	*1 ton of pure sulphur*
Gypsum ($CaSO_4 . 2 H_2O$)	1.00	5.38
Calcium chloride ($CaCl_2 . 2 H_2O$)	0.86	–
Calcium nitrate ($Ca (NO_3) . 2 H_2O$)	1.06	–
Press mud (lime-sulphur, 9% Ca + 24% S)	0.78	4.17
Sulphuric acid (H_2SO_4)	0.61	3.20
Iron sulphate ($FeSO_4 . 7 H_2O$)	1.62	
Ferric sulphate ($(Fe_2SO4)_3$.	1.09	5.85
Aluminium sulphate ($Al_2 (SO_4)_3 . 18 H_2O$)	1.29	6.34
Sulphur (S) **	0.19	1.00
Pyrites (FeS_2 . 30% S) **	0.63	

*The above quantities are based on 100% pure materials. If not 100%, then necessary corrections must be made. Thus, if gypsum is only 80% pure then the equivalent quantity to be applied would be 1.25 times to quantity mentioned in the Table.

** *For sulphur and pyrites 100 % oxidation is assumed.*

Sandy Loam: A sandy loam is a soil containing a high percentage of sand but having enough silt and clay to make it some what coherent. The individual sand grains can be readily seen and felt. Squeezed when dry, a sandy loam forms a cast that falls apart readily. If squeezed when moist, a cast can be formed that bears careful handling without breaking.

Loam: A loam is soil having a relatively even mixture of different grades of sand, silt and clay. It is mellow with a somewhat gritty feel but is fairly smooth and slightly plastic. Squeezed when dry, it forms a cast that bears careful handling, and the cast formed by squeezing the moist soil can be handled freely without breaking.

Silt Loam: A silt loam is having a moderate amount of fine sand and only a small amount of clay; over half of the particles are of the size called silt. When dry, a silt loam appears cloudy but the lumps can be broken readily; when pulverized, it feels soft and floury. When wet, the soil runs together readily and puddles. Either dry or moist, it forms a cast that can be handled freely without breaking; when moistened and squeezed between thumb and fingers, it does not ribbon but has a broken appearance.

Clay Loam: A clay loam is fine-textured soil that usually breaks into clods or lumps that are hard when dry. When the moist soil is pinched between the thumb and finger, it forms a thin ribbon that breaks readily, barely sustaining its own weight. The moist soil is plastic and forms a cast that bears much handling. When kneaded in the hand, it does not crumble readily but works into a heavy compact mass.

Clay: Clay is fine-textured soil that usually forms very hard lumps or clods when dry and is very plastic and usually sticky when wet. When the moist soil is pinched out between the thumb and finger, it forms a long, flexible ribbon. Some clays very high in colloids are friable and lack plasticity at all conditions of moisture.

Organic soils: These are soils in which organic-matter content ranges from 20 percent to as high as 95 percent. They generally are classified on the basis of degree of decomposition of the organic deposits. Those deposits that are only slightly decayed or non-decayed are called peat; in peat soils the kinds of plants that make up the deposits can be identified. Well-decomposed deposits in which the original plant parts cannot be identified are called muck. The word mucky is used also as an adjective in the textural class name for horizons of mineral soils that contain 15 percent or more partially decomposed organic matter. Examples are mucky loam and mucky silty loam.

Soil Texture (Laboratory Determination)

Soil texture is determined by mechanical analysis. The mechanical analysis consists of the determination of the percentage of particles of different sizes (coarse sand, fine sand, silt and clay) as they exist in the soil. The diameter of these particles is as under:

Kankar	More than 2 mm
Coarse sand	2-0.2 mm
Fine sand	**0.2-0.02 mm**
Silt	0.02-0.002 mm
Clay	below 0.002

For accurate determination, the international method called as pipette method is commonly employed (Piper, 1966; Chopra and Kanwar, 1991). This method is based on the Stokes' law. According to Stocks, law, a relationship exists between the radius of a spherical particle and the rate of its sedimentation in a liquid. Stocks stated that resistance offered by the liquid to the fall of the particle varied with the radius of the sphere and not with the surface. The equation to predict the velocity of fall is given as follows:

$$V = \frac{2\,g\,r^2\,(d_p - d)}{9\,\eta} \tag{2.14}$$

Where, V is the velocity of the falling particle in cm sec^{-1}, g is the acceleration due to gravity, d_p is the density of the particle, d is the density of the liquid, r is the radius if the particle in cm and η is the absolute viscosity of the liquid.

Procedure: pipette method

Amongst the (i) Sieve and hydrometer analysis and (ii) the sieve and pipette analysis, the second method is most commonly employed in the laboratories for mechanical analysis. The Tyler sieve set is generally used for the sieve analysis. The set is made up of the perforated brass sieves with round holes of opening sizes of 1 and 0.5 mm and standard numbers 60, 80, 140 and 300 mesh per inch with top lid and two bottom pans kept on appropriate shaking arrangements.

Procedure for destroying organic matter: Place about 20 g of oven dry soil that has been passed through a 2 mm Sieve in a 400 ml beaker, add 20 ml of 6% H_2O_2 solution (30 to 40 ml of H_2O_2 if the sample contains more than 3.5 % organic matter) and allow to stand overnight. Add another 10 ml of H_2O_2 solution and cover the beaker with a watch glass. Place the beaker on a steam plate or over boiling water bath for 15 minutes, then immerse it in boiling water for 5 minutes. Stir when necessary to control frothing. Repeat the heat treatment with another 10 ml of H_2O_2 solution if the colour of the soil has not become light enough to indicate that the organic matter has been destroyed. Boil the contents gently for 5 minutes.

After the above procedure, the sample is ready to begin with step 2 of the pipette analysis unless calcium carbonate is present.

If manganese compounds are present in the sample (manganese compounds are indicated if H_2O_2 fails to destroy the organic matter), begin by placing the soil in 40 ml of water and add 0.5 gram of $NaHSO_3$. Boil until water is half gone, and then continue as above.

Procedure for removal of carbonates: After the organic matter has been destroyed, cool the beaker and clean the sides of the beaker with a rubber pestle. Add 25 ml of 2N HCl and stir well (add more acid at the rate of 2.5 ml for each percent of $CaCO_3$ present above 2 percent). Stir occasionally while the reaction proceeds for about one hour. Test after one hour, to make sure that an excess of acid is present and filter the contents through a Buckner funnel using atman No. 50 filter paper.

Thereafter, the following step-wise procedure is adopted.

1. Wash the soil with hot distilled water till the excess acid is removed (Test with litmus paper or putting a drop of silver nitrate solution in the filtrate). Do

not attempt to wash the soil to the bottom of the filter as this decreases the rate of filtration and may cause some of the particles to pass through the filter.

2. After the soil has been washed nearly free from acid and drained, transfer it from the Buckner funnel to 1000 ml long neck beaker or in a dispersing cup. After removing the most of the soil, spread the filter paper on one of the clock glasses and clean the last traces of more soil from it by means of distilled water jet. When no more soil can be removed, roll the filter paper into a loose ball, wet it and thoroughly squeeze like a sponge. Repeat this process until no more turbid liquid can be obtained. Also wash the Buckner funnel rinsing it with jet of distilled water.

3. When the whole of the soil has been transferred to the 1000 ml beaker, add 10 ml of 1N sodium hydroxide.

4. Place the beaker beneath the dispersing unit, lower the propeller into position and set the later into motion, controlling the speed. Adjust the speed so that vigorous stirring is affected, avoiding loss from splashing. Continue for 10-15 min, then raise the motor propeller and rinze the propeller blades into the beaker.

5. Place a 70 mesh sieve, held over the month of a funnel which is placed over a 1000 ml cylinder, pour the suspension on to the sieve and, with a stream of distilled water from the wash bottle, wash as much material as possible through the sieve. Transfer the coarse material thus left on the sieve to a weighed dish. Dry it at 105°C in an oven and find its weight. Calculate the percentage of coarse sand as follows :

Weight of dish $= W_1$ g

Weight of dish + dry coarse sand $= W_2$ g

Weight of coarse sand $= W_2 - W_1$ g

$$\% \text{ coarse sand} = \frac{W_2 - W_1}{20} \times 100 \qquad (2.16)$$

6. Fill the cylinder to the 1000 ml mark with distilled water.
7. Check the temperature of the suspension. Stopper the top of the cylinder and thoroughly mix the contents by inverting it several times while shaking.
8. Set the cylinder on the table; record the time (hour, minute, second) immediately.
9. At the determined time against the suspension temperature (Table 2.8) insert a pipette into the suspension to a depth of 10 cm and withdraw a 25 ml sample. (Mark the depth on the pipette with a grease pencil)
10. Place the sample in a dish/beaker can that has been weighed accurately to 0.01 g. Evaporate the water by placing the dish in an oven set at 105°-110°C for at least 24 hours. Weigh the sample to 0.01 g. The % silt + clay in the sample is calculated as follows:

Weight of dish $= W_1$ g

Weigh of dish + silt + clay $= W_2$ g

Weight of silt +clay $= W_2 - W_1$ g

Weight of oven dry weight= 20 g

$$\% \text{ silt+clay} = \frac{(W_2 - W_1)\ 1000}{25 \times 20} \times 100 = Y \qquad (2.17)$$

11. Shake the contents of the cylinder again for 1 min and record the temperature and time. Sample in the same way at the depth of 10 cm after the setting

time for clay (Table 2.8). Dry it and weigh and calculate the clay percentage as follows :

Weight of dish = W_1 g

Weight of dish + clay = W_2 g

Weight of clay = W_2–W_1 g

$$\% \text{ of clay} = \frac{(W_2-W_1) \times 1000 \times 100}{25 \times 20} = X \quad (2.18)$$

$$\% \text{ silt} = Y-X \quad (2.19)$$

Fine sand :

Fine sand can be calculated either by difference or by sedimentation.

$$\% \text{ Fine sand} = 100-(\text{Silt} + \text{clay}) \quad (2.20)$$

or

Pour away the bulk of the supernatant liquid and transfer the sediment of cylinder to a 500 ml beaker, make up with water to a height of 10 cm above the base which should be marked with a pencil using foot rod. Stir well and allow to stand for the requisite period taken from the silt column in the table (Table 2.8) against the observed temperature. Then pour away the turbid suspension. Fill beaker again to the mark with distilled water and repeat this process till the liquid is no longer turbid at the end of the period. The residue is the fine sand which is dried at 105 $^{\circ}$C and weighed. Calculate the percentage of fine sand as follows :

Weight of dish = W_1 g

Weight of dish + fine sand = W_2 g

Weight of fine sand = W_2–W_1 g

$$\% \text{ of fine sand} = \frac{(W_2-W_1)}{20} \times 100 \quad (2.21)$$

Cautions

1. If air dry soil is taken for analysis, then moisture correction should be applied.
2. During the drying process, some loss due to ignition may occur, the correction should be applied.
3. Loss on solution in the case of soil means the loss due to the decomposition of $CaCO_3$ and oxidation of organic matter.

Expression of results

Tabulate the analysis showing the over dry percentage of each fraction in the original soil as follows :

1. Coarse sand, 2. Fine sand, 3. Silt (ignited), 4. Clay (ignited), 5. Loss on solution or loss on ignition + CaCO3, 6. Moisture (if air dry soil is taken) 7. Total.

Note : The summation should approximate to 100 and if the total is less than 98.5 or more than 102, the analysis should be repeated.

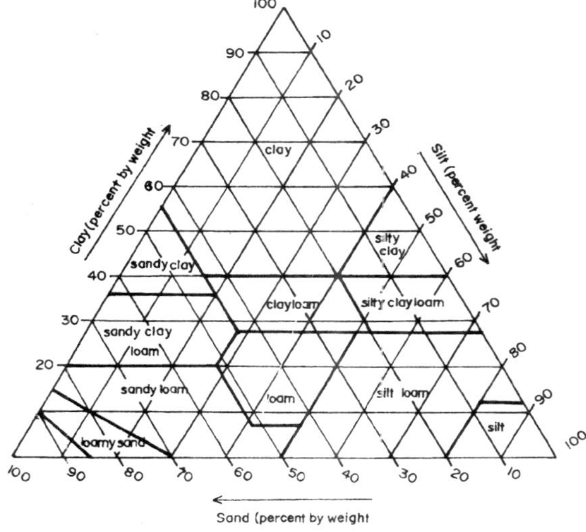

Fig. 2.5 The textural triangle for assigning the soil texture (after Hillel, 1980)

After the determination of sand (coarse + fine sand), silt and clay percentage, the soil texture is determined from the soil textural triangle (Fig. 2.5).

Table 2.8 The time of sedimentation for clay and silt fraction at different temperature

Temperature sampling °C	*Time for clay sampling*		*Time for silt + clay*	
	Hrs.	*Min.*	*Min.*	*Second*
8	11	-	6	40
9	10	40	6	30
10	10	25	6	20
11	10	10	6	10
12	9	54	6	10
13	9	35	5	50
14	9	20	5	40
15	9	05	5	30
16	8	50	5	20
17	8	35	5	10
18	8	25	5	05
19	8	10	5	00
20	8	00	4	48
21	7	50	4	40
22	7	40	4	30
23	7	25	4	30
24	7	15	4	20
25	7	05	4	15
26	6	55	4	10
27	6	45	4	05
28	6	40	4	00
29	6	30	3	55
30	6	20	3	50
31	6	15	3	45
32	6	05	3	40
33	5	55	3	35

Infiltration Rate

Infiltration rate of water through the soil surface is extremely important in soils because it determines the total water storage in the profile. From the standpoint of soil salinity, it determines how much and how fast the leaching of a given soil can be accomplished. In a saline environment, it will also determine whether salts will get leached (pushed downward), accumulate or flushed with runoff. From hydrological point of view, it is probably the most important hydrological process in a watershed and reveals the relative contribution to run off and ground water recharge.

Infiltration rate is a dynamic parameter and it changes with time. When excess water is applied continuously to the soil surface, not only infiltration rate decreases with time, the rate of the decrease also reduces with increasing time. The asymptotically decreasing curve has a tendency to approach a final minimum value, which is designated as the basic infiltration rate. Initial moisture content has a great bearing on the infiltration rate curve of a soil. The infiltration rate curve of a wet soil would always lie below that of an initially dry soil. The two curves may meet at a time when the infiltration rate approaches the basic infiltration rate. Whereas, total infiltration will determine the surface drainage requirement, basic infiltration rate is important in the design of a subsurface drainage system and to evaluate capability of the soil for leaching and the fastness with which a soil can be leached.

Infiltration is used to describe the process of water entry into the soil through the soil surface. A double ring infiltrometer is commonly used to measure infiltration. The double rings are two concentric cylinders open at both ends and about 250 to 300 mm in height. The inner cylinder is of about 225-300 mm diameter while the outer cylinder is of 600 mm diameter. The usual procedure is to insert the inner and outer cylinders about 75-100 mm deep in the ground as far as possible without disturbing the soil. For this purpose, a driving plate and a hammer is used to uniformly insert the cylinders into the ground. A hook gauge is placed in the inner cylinder to measure the depth of the water added in each step. 2-3 replicates at one site would be required to accurately assess the infiltration rate. The readings are recorded at 1-5 minute's interval initially and the time is gradually increased to cover at least 4-5 hours. Usually, the available water in the area is used to conduct the infiltration studies. Following procedure is used to calculate and fit Kostiakov (1932) type infiltration function to the data sets as follows :

Elapsed time (min)	*Volume of * water used (ml)*		*Accumulated intake (cm)***	*Intake during elapsed time (cm)*	*Infiltration rate (cm hr^{-1}) (col 5/ col 1) *60*
	Instant-aneous	*Cumulated*			
5	636	636	0.333	0.333	4.0
10	556.4	1192.4	0.625	0.29	3.5
15	381.6	1573.6	0.825	0.2	2.4
20	333.9	1907.5	1.000	0.175	2.1
25	238.5	2146.0	1.125	0.125	1.5
35	413	2559.0	1.342	0.216	1.3
45	381.6	2940.6	1.542	0.2	1.2
55	381.6	3322.2	1.742	0.2	1.2
85	1144.4	4466.6	2.342	0.6	1.2
115	1144.4	5611.0	2.942	0.6	1.2
145	1144.4	6755.2	3.542	0.6	1.2
205	2480.1	9235.5	4.842	1.3	1.3

* Observed, ** Column 3/area of the inner cylinder

The basic infiltration rate is calculated from the plotted data when the curve is nearly parallel to the x-axis.

According to Kostiakov, infiltration curve can be described by a power function of the following form:

$$Y = k\, t^{n} \qquad (2.22)$$

Where Y is the cumulative intake, t is the time in min and k and n are constants such that n is always less than 1. If we plot the data in column 1 and column 4 on a log-log paper, it results in a straight line. From the intercept on y axis, we get the value of k and from the slope, value of n. Upon differentiation, eq. (1) can be written as

$$I = kn\ t^{n-1} \text{ Or simply } \qquad I = k_1\ t^{-n1} \qquad (2.23)$$

Such that I is the infiltration rate, $k_1 = k * n$ and n_1 is (n-1). Instantaneous infiltration rate can be assessed using eq. (2.23). In practice, after sometime, the infiltration rate tends to be constant and infiltration rate at this time is taken as the basic infiltration rate (Fig. 2.6). The Kostiakov equation fails to realistically model this situation.

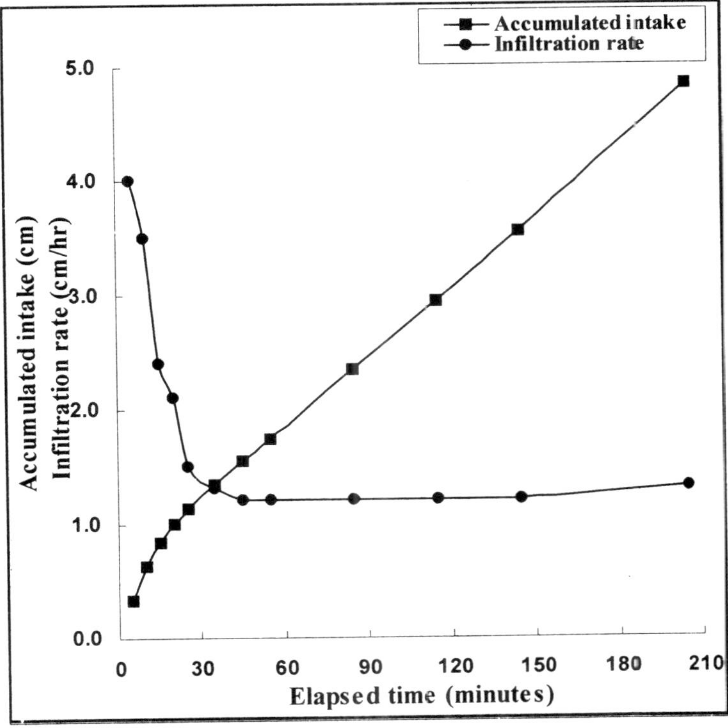

Fig. 2.6 Instantaneous and cumulative infiltration rate curves on a normal paper. Note the basic infiltration rate of around 1.2 cm hr^{-1}

In view of the above, many times equation given by Philip (1957) is used to describe the infiltration rate. According to this

$$I = 0.5\, s\, t^{-1/2} + A \tag{2.24}$$

Thus, the infiltration rate in (cm hr^{-1}) consists of a basic infiltration rate component given by A at very large times. On the arithmetic paper if data in column 1 and column 6 are plotted such that $t^{-1/2}$ is plotted on x-axis and infiltration rate in cm hr^{-1} on y-axis, it also results in a straight line. The intercept on y-axis would give A while slope of the line would provide the value of s. If we integrate eq. (2.24), the cumulative infiltration, Y is given by the relation:

$$Y = st^{1/2} + At \tag{2.25}$$

Visual Characters and Identification of Alkali/Saline Soils

The alkali soils can be visually and qualitatively identified and distinguished from saline and normal soil during reconnaissance surveys. Some visual characters that help to distinguish two kinds of soils are listed in Table 2.9.

A Quick Test for Assessing Sodicity

As per information available on the internet, on the basis of visual characters as reported in Table 2.9, a quick test to assess the sodicity problem has been developed in Australia. The step-wise procedure is as follows:

- Take soil samples from the surface 0-15 cm and the next layer of 15-30 cm. Air dry the soil and break the clods into pieces of 1cm diameter or less.
- From these samples, weigh 100 g sample each and transfer into clean 600 ml glass bottles/jars.
- Measure about 500 ml of rain/distilled water and pour down the side of the jar to give a 1:5 soil-water ratio. Ensure that soil at the bottom is not disturbed during this transfer.

Table 2.9. The visual observations for distinguishing alkali from saline soil

Observation	*Alkali soil*	*Saline soil*
Rain water stagnation	Stagnation for longer period	Relatively lesser period
Stagnated water type	Dark coloured, muddy, soapy	Clear
Surface salt crust	Dark brown or ash coloured clay crust	White salt efflorescence
Ground water	Usually good, occasionally with high Residual Sodium Carbonate (RSC)	Saline, some times with high Sodium Adsorption Ratio (SAR)
Presence of nodules	$CaCO_3$ nodules are present	Gypsum may be present at some depth
Natural vegetation (grasses)	*Sporobolus marginatus, Desmostachya bipinata, Suaeda maritma, Diplachne fusca, Dichanthium annulatum, Cynodon dactylon, Chloris barbata, Brachiaria mutica, Kochia indica, Panicum antidotale*	*Cressa cretica, Cyperus rotundus, Chloris pallida, Sporobolus pallidus, Haloxylon salicornicum, Aeluropus lagopoides, Zygophyllum simplex, Dichanthium annulatum, Suaeda fruticosa, Butea monosperma*

- Invert the jar slowly and gently once and then return to its original position. Avoid shaking during this process.
- Check the suspension above the soil at the bottom of the jar.
- The soil sodicity problem is estimated as follows:
  - Clear or almost clear — No sodicity
  - Partly cloudy — Medium sodicity
  - Very cloudy — Highly sodic

A white plastic spatula or spoon, that reflects light, could also be used. Visibility of the spatula (visible, partly visible,

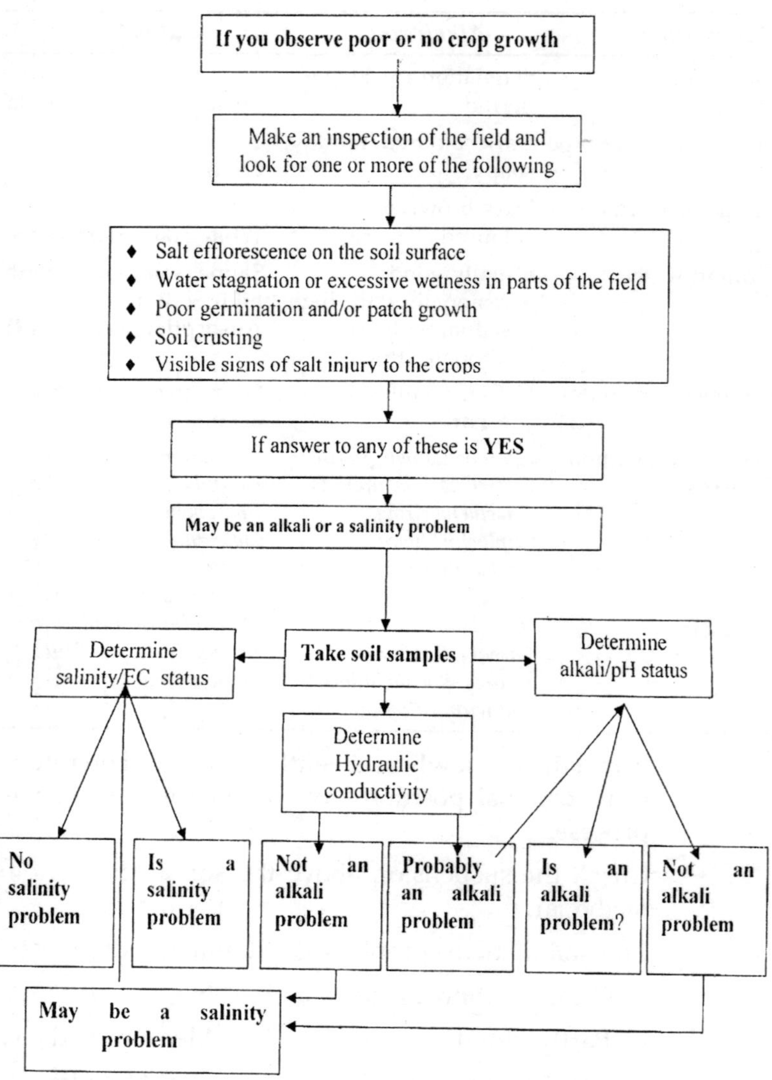

Fig. 2.7 Flow chart for the diagnosis of the problems

not visible) would determine the degree of sodicity as no, medium and high.

A flow chart that leads to differentiation between saline and alkali soils is shown in Fig. 2.7.

REFERENCES

Abrol, I. P., Chhabra, R. and Gupta, R. K. 1981. Diagnosing alkali soils. Indian Farming. 31:22-4, 37.

Abrol, I.P., Dargan, K.S. and Bhumbla, D.R. 1973. Reclaiming Alkali Soils. Bull. 2, CSSRI, Karnal.

Abrol; I.P., Dahiya, I.S. and Bhumbla, D.R. 1975. On the method of determining gypsum requirement of soils. Soil sci. 120: 30-36.

Chopra, S. L. and Kanwar, J. S. 1991. Analytical Agricultural Chemistry. Kalyani Publishers, New Delhi.

Gupta, S.K., Dinkar, V.S. and Tyagi, N.K. (Eds.) 1995. Reclamation and Management of Salt Affected Lands in Irrigation Commands. Published by CSSRI on Behalf of Ministry of Water Resources (GoI),New Delhi. pp 144.

Hillel, D. 1980. Fundamentals of Soil Physics. Academic Press, New York. 413 pp.

Kostiakov, A. N. 1932. On the dynamics of the coefficient of water percolation in soils and the necessity for studying it from a dynamic view for purpose of amelioration. Trans. 6th Cong. Int. Soc. Soil Sci. Russian Part A: 17-21.

Philip, J. R. 1957. The theory of infiltration 4. Sorptivity and algebraic infiltration equation. Soil Sci. 84: 257-264.

Piper, C. S. 1966. Soil and Plant Analysis. Hans Publishers, Bombay.

Richards L.A. (Ed.) 1954. Diagnosis and Improvement of Saline and Alkali Soils. USDA Hbk. 60, 160P.

Schoonover, W.R. (1952). Examination of soils for alkali. Univ. Of California. Extension Service, Berkley, California.

Soil Survey Staff. 1951. Soil Survey Manual. Agric. Handbook. 18, USDA, USA.

Van Alphen J.G. and Rice Romero F de Los. 1971. Gypsiferous Soils. Bull. 12, Int. Instt. Ld. Reclam. Improve., Wageningen

3

NATURE AND PROPERTIES

The accurate diagnosis of the problem, precise differentiation between saline and alkali soils and the diagnosis of the causes of low productivity of otherwise potentially productive land, are the primary pre-requisites to decide effective measures for economic exploitation of chemically degraded lands. It would ensure that the correct recommendations are made and implemented. Treatments decided on the basis of incorrect diagnosis would result in the loss of investments while the problems remain unresolved, the reclamation efforts are wasted and farmers get disenchanted with the technologies.

Nomenclature and Classification

No uniform nomenclature has been adopted in different parts of the world to classify salt affected lands because of the wide variations from one region to another. The USA, USSR, Hungary, Australia and other European countries evolved different criteria for the classification of salt affected soils. However, the most widely used criteria in many countries of the world and adopted in India was the one evolved by the United States Salinity Laboratory (Richards *et al.*, 1954). According to this criterion, salt affected soils are divided into three main classes, viz., (i) Saline (ii) Alkali and (ii) Saline-Alkali, primarily on the basis of pH, EC_e and ESP.

Saline Soil

The soils which have EC_e more than 4 dS m^{-1}, ESP less than 15 and ordinarily pH_s less than 8.5 were defined as saline soils. If adequate drainage is provided, leaching can reclaim these soils. Sodium seldom comprises more than half of the soluble cations and therefore, is not adsorbed to any significant extent. The chief anions are chloride and sulphate. Small amounts of bicarbonates may occur but soluble carbonate is almost invariably absent.

Alkali Soil

The soils having a variable EC_e (more or less than 4 dS m^{-1}), ESP greater than 15 and pH_s more than 8.5 usually between 8.5 and 10.0, are defined as alkali soils. Sodium is the most predominant cation and calcium occurs in unduly low concentration while the anions present consist mostly of chloride, sulphate and bicarbonate. Small amounts of carbonates often occur.

Saline-Alkali Soil

The soils which have EC_e more than 4 dS m^{-1}, ESP more than 15, pH_s generally less than 8.5 before leaching and greater than 8.2 after leaching of soluble salts are defined as saline-alkali soils.

The Soil Science Society of America (1974) has modified the definition and classification of salt affected soils. The critical limit of EC_e has been reduced from 4 dS m^{-1} to 2 dS m^{-1} and criterion of ESP has been replaced with SAR, critical limit of 15 remaining the same. Accordingly, a soil having EC_e greater than 2 dS m^{-1} is defined as saline. The soil may have any values of SAR and pH_s. A soil having SAR greater than 15 is defined as *alkali/sodic*. This soil may have any values of EC_e and pH_s. A soil having EC_e more than 2 dS m^{-1} and SAR more than 15 and

pH_s ordinarily less than 8.5 is defined as saline-alkali (saline-sodic soils).

In Hungary and other European countries, salt affected soils have been classified in two classes i.e. saline and alkali soils. The saline soils contain sufficient amount of neutral salts to adversely affect the growth of most crop plants. The salts are mainly chlorides and sulphates of sodium followed by those of magnesium and calcium (EC_e 4 dS m^{-1} occurring with in 125, 90 and 70 cm below the surface in case of coarse, medium and fine textured soils, respectively). Alkali soils also referred to as sodic soils containing sodium salts capable of alkaline hydrolysis, mainly Na_2CO_3 or $NaHCO_3$ or dominated by exchangeable sodium (ESP 15). The alkali soils have further been sub-divided into two groups, namely soils without structural B horizon, and soils with structural B horizon.

In India, saline soils are locally called as *Thur, Uppu, Shora, Soulu, Pekhali, Khar and Kari.* Alkali soils have been called as *Usar, Rakkar, Bara, Chopan and Karl.* The saline-alkali soils have been designated as *Usar, Kallar, Karl, Chopar, Bari, Reh, Choudu, Kshar and Jougu.* On the basis of management options that need to be applied, the salt affected soils have been grouped into two groups in India *i.e.* alkali and saline soils.

Alkali soils : These soils have ESP/SAR exceeding 15 which is reflected in the high pH_s of these soils (>8.2). The EC may or may not be high (Table 3.1). As a result, these soils have dispersed soil structure and after an irrigation or rainfall, water stagnates for long periods at low spots. Upon drying, alkali soils develop cracks 1-2 cm wide. Dissolved organic matter present in the soil solution of highly alkali soils may be deposited on the soil surface by evaporation causing dark black surface–the reason why these soils have been termed as black alkali. The cropped fields have spotty growth. When the alkali status is high, crops show scorching and leaf burn typical of sodium toxicity or the yellowing of leaves resulting from poor soil physical properties. In extreme cases, the soils remain bare with practically very little or no vegetation (Fig. 3.1).

Fig. 3.1 A view of barren alkali land being reclaimed. Note the barren land in the background

Saline soils: These soils have EC of the saturation paste extract (EC_e) exceeding 4 dS m^{-1} and have a variable ESP usually in the low range with pH <8.2 (Table 3.1). These soils supports patchy growth of crops and sometimes-visible signs of salt

Table 3.1 Characteristics of alkali and saline soils

Characteristics	*Alkali soils*	*Saline soils*
EC_e (dS m^{-1})	Variable	4.0 or more
ESP/SAR	15 or more	Variable
pH_s	8.2 or more	< 8.2
Chemistry of soil solution	Carbonates and bicarbonates always present	Dominated by chloride and sulphate
Main adverse effect on plants	Alkalinity of soil solution	High osmotic pressure of soil solution
Geographical distribution	Associated with semi-arid and sub-humid climates	Associated with arid and semi-arid climates
First step for reclamation	Lowering or neutralization of high pH by applying amendments	Removal of excess electrolytes through leaching

injury such as tip burn or chlorosis (pale yellow colour) of leaves can be seen. Soluble salts, which are invariably present in large quantities, form a white efflorescence on the soil surface (Fig. 3.2). For this reason, these soils are called white *kallar*.

Fig. 3.2 A view of barren saline land

Extent and Distribution

The salt affected soils are widely distributed in many parts of India, particularly in the arid and semi-arid regions and also in certain humid coastal areas. Till recently, several workers on the basis of limited information compiled the countrywide assessment on the extent and distributions of salt-affected soils. The extent varied from a low value of 2.05 million ha to 23.8 million ha. The salt affected soils occupy an area of about 12 million hectares (Sharma and Gupta, 1986). Elaborating further, authors reported that 4 million ha are spread over Indo-Gangetic alluvial plains (Uttar Pradesh, Delhi, Punjab, Bihar, Haryana and Parts of Rajasthan); 4 million ha in medium and deep black soil region (Madhya Pradesh, Rajasthan, Gujarat, Maharashtra, Karnataka, Andhra Pradesh and Tamil Nadu); 3 million ha in coastal region (West Bengal, Orissa, Kerala, Tamil Nadu, Andhra Pradesh, Maharashtra and Gujarat) and 1 million ha in arid and semi arid region (Rajasthan and Gujarat) (Gupta and Gupta, 1987).

It is estimated that in India about 4 million ha of agricultural lands are affected by the problem of alkali. Though, it occurs in small amounts here and there in many states of India, the major share of alkali land is confined to Indo-Gangetic plains of Punjab, Haryana and Uttar Pradesh (Fig. 3.3). The districts and states in which alkali soils have been reported to exist are listed in Table 3.2. It may not be out of place to mention here that in the last three decades more than 1.3 m ha of alkali land in these states has been reclaimed.

Table 3.2. Distribution of alkali soils in India

State	*Districts affected by alkali soils*
Andhra Pradesh	Nizamabad, Karim Nagar, Kurnool, Guntur, Anantapur, Cuddapah.
Bihar	Muzaffarpur, Shahabad
Delhi	Delhi
Gujarat	Navsari, Bharuch, Surat, Bhavnagar, Kaira
Haryana	Karnal, Kurukshetra, Jind and Parts of Rohtak, Sonepat and Gurgaon.
Karnataka	Bellary, Bijapur, Dharwar, Chital, Durg, Gulbarga.
Madhya Pradesh	Gwalior division, pockets in West and East Nimar districts and along Narmada in black soil area, Bhind, Morena.
Maharashtra	Sholapur, Nasik, Jalgaon, Parbhani, Ahmednagar, Satara.
Punjab	Amritsar, Kapurthala, Sangrur, Patiala, Gurdaspur and Ropar.
Rajasthan	Parts of Jaipur, Kota, Tonk, Bharatpur, Sawai Madhopur and Bhilwara.
Tamil Nadu	South Arcot, Salem, Thanjavur, North Arcot, Coimbatore, Madurai and Ramanathapuram.
West Bengal	24 Parganas, Midnapur
Uttar Pradesh	Aligarh, Etah, Etawah, Mainpuri, Hardoi, Kanpur, Unnao, Lucknow, Fatehpur, Rai Bareli, Sultanpur, Azamgarh, Ghazipur, Pratapgarh and Meerut.

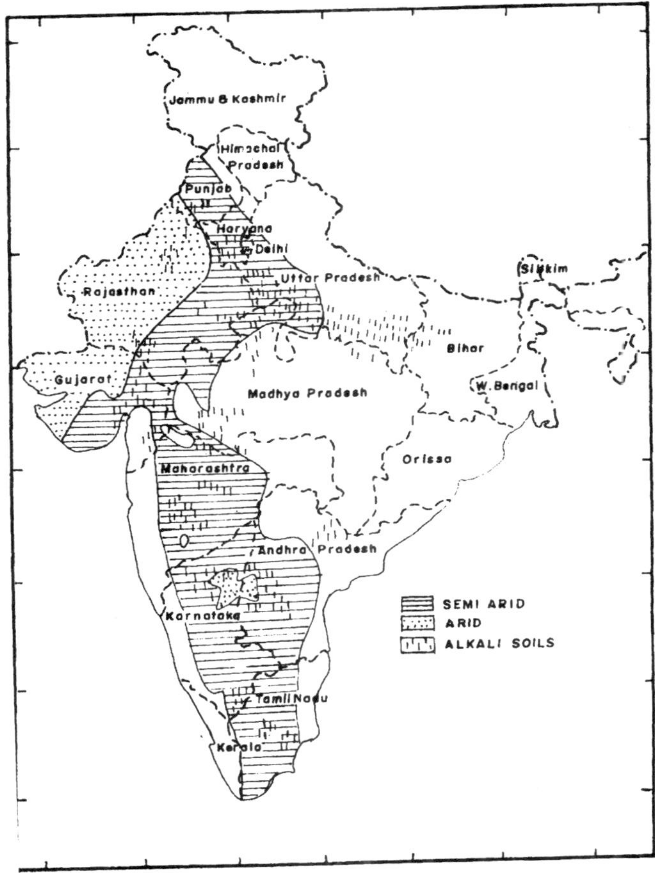

Fig. 3.3 Distribution of alkali soils in India

The current estimates of 6.73 million ha salt-affected soils measured by field verified remote sensing method showing the extent and spatial distribution on 1:250,000 scale map-sheets, appears realistic within the parameters set in this endeavour (Sharma *et al.*, 2004). For example, in the study by Sharma *et al.* (2004) some very small and isolated patches of salt-affected soils in the states of Delhi and Himachal Pradesh could not be detected due to the limitation of scale. The maps for Jammu and Kashmir and Goa were not available and thus, the information of salt-affected soils of these states could not be derived. In spite of these limitations, some interesting statistics have been arrived at. For example, out of 584 districts, 194 have salt affected soils. Four districts, three in Uttar Pradesh and one in West Bengal have more than 20 per cent of their geographical area under these soils. It is also estimated that 2.96 million ha are saline and the rest 3.77 million ha are sodic.

Given these limitations, it may not be out of place to mention that another estimate given by Gupta (2002) also seems to be in order (Table 3.3). According to this estimate, total salt-affected soils in the country have been assessed at 8.4 million ha. However, when both the estimates are compared, state to state variations as well as variations in the total extent of saline soils are clearly apparent. But the apparent decrease in the area by about 0.2 million ha since the estimate of Singh (1992) seems illusive. If the area under reclamation in the three states of Punjab, Haryana and U. P. of around 1.3 million ha is taken into account, there seems to be an increase in the affected area by about a million ha in about a decade. It is apparent that concerted efforts are required to halt this expansion through adoption of preventive technologies and implementing land reclamation programmes.

Table 3.3 Extent and distribution of inland and coastal salinity and mangrove area in various states

State	*Inland saline soils (million ha)*	*Coastal saline soils (million ha)*	*Total saline soils (million ha)* *	*Remark*
Andhra Pradesh	0.510 [1]	0.283[2]	0.793	
Bihar	0.400 [7]	-	0.400	
Chhatishgarh	-	-		In M. .P.
Goa	-	0.018[3]	0.018	
Gujarat	0.661	0.750[10]	1.411 [4]	
Haryana	0.164 [5]	-	0.164	
Jammu and Kashmir	0.009 [6]	-	0.009	
Jharkhand	-	-		In Bihar

Karnataka	0.318 [7]	0.120[11]	0.438
Kerala	-	0.055[12]	0.055
Madhya Pradesh	0.242 [7]	-	0.242
Maharashtra	0.446 [7]	0.070[13]	0.516 [1]
Orissa	-	0.490[14]	0.490
Punjab	0 153 [8]	-	0.153
Rajasthan	1.183 [6]	-	1.183
Tamil Nadu	0.257 [7]	0.204[15]	0.461 [1]
Uttar Pradesh	1.060 [9]	-	1.060
Uttaranchal	-	-	-
West Bengal	-	0.986[11]	0.986
Others Andaman & Nicobar /Pondicherry)	-	0.016[3]	0.016
Union Territories	0.004 [6]	-	0.004
Total	5.407	2.992	8.399

* Total includes inland and coastal saline soils but excludes area under mangrove

[1]Institution of Engineers (AP Chapter) (1999); [2] Singh (1992)

[3] Yadav *et al.* (1979); [4] Dubey *et al.* (1995); Satellite data minus 15 % for errors

[5]Sharma (1999); [6] Ministry of Agriculture (Draft Figure)

[7] Singh (1992); [8]Sharma *et al.* (1998); [9] Anonymous (1998)

[10] Anonymous (1993); [11] NCDBA (1981); [12] Thomas and Mathew (2000)

[13] Chavan and Chavan (1987); [14] Mahapatra and Panda (1994);

[15] Kothandaraman (1987);

The observation that alkali soils occur interspersed with normal soils and commonly in low lying areas has led to the belief that continental cycles have largely influenced the evolution of alkali soils in these plains. The electrolytes present in these soils originate during the course of weathering of alumino-silicate minerals. The heavy rainfall during monsoon facilitates migration, distribution and deposition of these salts through surface and sub-terranean flows. Another observation that alkali soils occupy concave soil scape positions which are about 15-30 cm lower than the adjoining normal lands, led to the belief that alternating wet and dry cycles seem to be one contributing factor. During the wet period the run-off from the surrounding areas collects in the low-lying areas, which upon evaporation gets concentrated. At higher concentrations calcium bicarbonate precipitates resulting in gradual increase in the proportion of sodium in the soil solution and consequently in the exchange complex. These soils have thus, originated through indirect process of sodiumisation commencing initially at the surface.

The highly alkaline environment of these soils brings about degradation of the clay mineral as indicated by the trends of variations of molar ratios of amorphous SiO_2 and Al_2O_3. Degradation has been observed to be maximum in the surface horizon, decreasing with depth in agreement with the degree of sodium saturation.

Yet another view postulated by Gupta (1992) ruled out the formation of alkali soils by weathering of alumino-silicate through carbonation yielding alkali carbonates as has been reported previously. According to this study, inherited (transported) nature of smectites, illites, chlorite and kaolinite has been established through a study of 21 pedons located in different geomorphic locations in Haryana representing various river systems under diverse climatic conditions. Source of salts has been traced to saline series of salt ranges of Himalaya with which the Shali formation of Mandi rock salt is associated and also to Subathu, Jutogh, Tal, Dagshai, and Krol formations of sub-Hiamalaya. Sodium carbonate at low temperatures in these soils is believed to have been formed by a simple reaction between natural salts of sodium and calcium carbonate. These reactants as well other products have been brought down to plains by the ancient river system.

Physico-Chemical Characteristics

The saline and alkali soils can be distinguished from normal soils as well as from each other on the basis of several physical, chemical, biological and mineralogical characteristics and soil-water relationships that gets modified upon chemical degradation. Some of such properties have been discussed in the following sections. The emphasis on the discussions would be on parameters that help differentiate alkali lands from the normal lands.

Physical Characteristics

Effective soil depth

The soil depth that can be effectively exploited by plant roots is an important consideration in plant growth. Generally, excellent yields are produced on normal soils having an effective root zone depth varying from 45 to 90 cm, although shallow-rooted crops do fairly well even in depths up to 30 cm. Root penetration is inhibited seriously in alkali soils due to high ESP and the presence of an impermeable layer caused by *kankar* (impure $CaCO_3$), limiting the effective soil depth to 10-15 cm. Though some crops adapt to edaphic environment by modifying their root system, it is advisable to grow only shallow rooted crops at least in the early phase of reclamation. In saline soils, the zones of *kankar* and gypsum accumulation, if any, restrict the effective soil depth.

Bulk density

This is defined as the dry weight of a unit volume of soil and is usually expressed in g/cm^3 or Mg/m^3. The bulk densities of highly productive normal soils usually range from 1.1 to 1.5 (medium to fine texture) and 1.2 to 1.65 (coarse texture). The alkali and saline soils (medium texture) have a high bulk density (1.5 to 1.65 g/cm^3) inhibiting root penetration and proliferation as well as impede drainage. Because of dispersion effect of sodium, bulk density in top surface layer of alkali soils could go up to 1.7 g/cm^3. The rates of infiltration and permeability are usually low in medium or fine textured soil with bulk densities exceeding 1.65 g/cm^3. The bulk density decreases with application of amendments, tillage and cropping.

Pore space distribution

Pore space and bulk density are closely and inversely related. Soils with a low porosity generally contain little air space at field capacity. In highly productive normal, medium to fine textured soils, the non-capillary porosity, in the plough-zone is usually 10-30%. The alkali soils may have a non-capillary porosity as low as 2% at which the normal aeration of the plants is adversely affected. The optimum values of non-capillary porosity differ for one crop to another. Gupta and Narain (1971) observed that the total porosity and non-capillary porosity in normal soil profile (0-110 cm) varied from 45.8 to 38.5% and 8.6 to 5.7% as compared to 39.5 to 38.9% and 4.9 to 2.5% in saline-alkali soils.

Soil tilth

The soil tilth is a product of the organic matter content, texture, consistency etc., which under good management, combine to form a surface or near-surface physical condition of the soil favourable to plant growth. The highly productive normal soils have a very good tilth. In alkali soils, the soil tilth is very poor because of high pH and ESP. The soils are very hard and compact when dry and very sticky when wet. These soils have, therefore, to be tilled very carefully at optimum moisture content. The saline soils generally have satisfactory tillage properties.

Crust formation

Alkali soils have low stability of structure, disperse and slake when they are wet and may develop a hard crust upon drying. This crust presents a serious barrier to the emergence of seedlings and with some crops it could be the main cause of poor stand. The formation of crust is not only limited to alkali soils but may also occur in normal or saline soils. Typically alkali soil crust having a total salt content of 22.8% was found to contain 48.3% Na_2CO_3, 33.4% $NaHCO_3$, 13.3% Na_2SO_4 and 3.9% NaCl. However, hard surface crusts are typically associated more with high ESP, a characteristic of alkali soils, low organic matter, puddling and wetting the soil to zero tension. Modulus of rupture, a property determined to infer the strength of the crust that is formed on the soil surface upon drying, is found to increase with increasing ESP of the soil as per the following relation (Sandhu *et al.*, 1980):

$$Y = 3.92 + 0.204 \text{ ESP } (r = 0.92) \quad (3.1)$$

Here, Y is the modulus of rupture in bars and ESP is expressed as percent.

Dispersion coefficient

Dispersion coefficient defined as the ratio of water dispersible clay to the total clay expressed as percent, is usually very high in alkali soils and may exceed 90 percent in soils having pH greater than 10.0. The dispersion coefficient increases with increasing ESP (Fig. 3.4) and is usually governed by the ESP of the soil. The dispersion coefficient of normal soils ranges from 20 to 30 percent. This is the main factor,

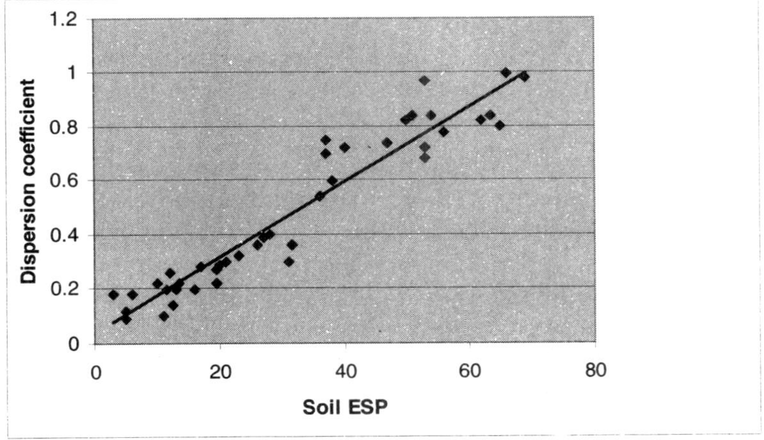

Fig. 3.4 Effect of soil ESP on dispersion coefficient

which causes reduction in the permeability of the alkali soils by sealing the surface pores under the impact of rainfall or when a water of low salinity is applied. It is also one of the major factors in increasing sediment content in the run-off waters from alkali catchment. The formation of a layer of high clay content in the profile at some depth is also attributed to high dispersivity.

Clay swelling and dispersion

Due to its large surface area, the clay content of a soil influences soil hydraulic properties. Exchangeable cations are constrained within the electrical influence of the negatively charged clay particles, which are attracted to the charged surface where their concentration is high into the bulk solution where the concentration is low. As a result, clay particles act as miniature osmometers and imbibe water to lower the ion concentration near charged surfaces. The water uptake is referred to as swelling. Sodium montmorillonite swells freely. Large swelling pressures develop between sodium montmorillonite platelets, and single platelets tend to persist in dilute solutions. Increasing the electrolyte concentration decreases swelling. Divalent calcium ions are more strongly adsorbed to the clay to swell. Individual calcium montmorillonite platelets tend to aggregate into packets or tactoids of several clay platelets with a 0.45 mm film of water on each internal surface.

The soils with illitic clay are more sensitive to dispersion and clay movement than those with montmorillonite clay. The difference in the flocculation value is probably due to a smaller attraction force in Na-illite. Na-illite particles have an average thickness of about 10 mm and the planer surfaces are terraced. Once the particles approach closer to each other, the unavoidable mismatch of the terraces leads to poor contact between the edges and the surfaces leading to smaller edge-to-face attraction forces and consequently, a higher flocculation value for Na-illite than Na-montmorillonite (Oster, 1982).

Shear strength

Shear strength of a soil assumes significance in studies pertaining to construction of buildings and dykes *(bunds)* as well as in studies related to soil erosion. The shear strength decreases with increase in pH and moisture content.

Arubnandam and Heinzer (1977) reported that the critical shear stress which is defined as the stress at which erosion starts, reduces from 25 dyne/cm^2 to 5 dyne/cm^2 as the SAR increases from 5 to 15 for the same CEC of the soils. At still higher SAR, the critical shear stress further reduces and it decreases to 1 dyne/cm^2 at SAR of 60 and at this stage is independent of CEC. As the shear stress caused by rainfall and run-off in a region is similar, alkali lands are likely to be more eroded compared to a normal soil and hence more sediment is likely to occur in the run-off arising from watersheds that have large alkali lands. It is also significant that because of poor shear stress, the dykes cross-section and heights need to be considerably larger than that of normal soils in order to increase the shear strength.

Chemical Characteristics

Soil reaction (pH)

The pH of the saturated soil paste (pH_s) has been widely recognized as an index, distinguishing alkali soils relative to the normal or saline soils. pH of the 1:2 soil water suspension (pH_2) has also been reliably used for the same purpose in specific cases. The appraisal of the soil reaction in saline or alkali soils on the basis of pH_2 is rapid and convenient. It is a useful determination particularly where a large number of soil samples are to be analyzed and where repeated sampling is to be made on the same soil to determine the change in pH with time or treatment. The pH_2 values are usually higher than pH_s, the most striking difference being in alkali soils. In alkali soils, pH_2 values are higher than pH_s by about 1.0 unit while in normal or saline soils, it is higher by 0.2-0.5 units. This could be ascribed to the nature of electrolytes present in alkali and saline soils. Alkali soils contain predominantly Na_2CO_3, a weak electrolyte, whereas the saline soils contain NaCl, a strong electrolyte. On hydrolysis, the pH of weak electrolytes increases sharply with dilution, whereas changes in the pH with dilution are less pronounced in strong electrolytes (Gupta, 1972). The increase in the soil pH values by about 1.0 unit, as the moisture is increased from near saturation to a 1:2 dilution, is useful in identifying alkali soils. The pH_2 value greater than 8.2 corresponds to the ESP value greater than 15 (Agarwal and Yadav, 1956). The pH values for normal, saline and alkali soils reveal that the most productive normal soils have pH in the range of 6 to 8, whereas alkali and inland saline soils have pH_2 in the range of 8-9 for saline and 9-10.8 for alkali soils (Table 3.4).

Table 3.4 The pH values of soils

Nature of the soil	pH_s	pH_2
Normal	< 7.5	< 8.0
Saline	7.5–8.5	8.0–9.0
Alkali	8.2–10.0	9.0–10.8

In addition to dilution, other factors which affect the pH values of the salt affected soils are: the total soluble salt concentration, nature of salts, the composition of exchangeable cations, the nature of cation-exchange materials and the presence or absence of gypsum and alkaline earth carbonates. Sodium carbonate causes strong alkalisation in the soils. Whereas pH of saturated solution of sodium bicarbonate is only 8.4, that of sodium carbonate is as high as 12.0. The excessive soluble salt concentration, particularly those of neutral salts, depresses the soil pH. The highly saline soils having an EC_e of about 100 dS m^{-1} usually have a pH value close to 7.

In soil testing laboratories, the soil is evaluated as 'normal to most of common crops' if pH_2 is 8.5, 'tending to become alkali soil' if pH_2 is between 8.5 and 9.0; and 'alkali soil', harmful for growing crop' if pH_2 is > 9.0; (Muhr *et al.*, 1963). Gupta (1972) suggested that last two limits of pH_2 should be changed to 8.5-9.5 and > 9.5 respectively. Also, in order to relatively distinguish the degree of alkali in the soils, the soils having pH_2 values < 9.3, 9.3-10.0, 10.0-10.5 and > 10.5, may be called low, medium, high and very high alkali soils respectively. From management point of view, a semi or partially reclaimed alkali soil is one whose original pH_2 value > 10 has decreased to < 9.3 in the root zone (0-20 cm) but higher values persist in the lower depth.

Exchangeable Sodium Percentage (ESP)

The sodium adsorption ratio (SAR) and the exchangeable sodium ratio (ESR), which is determined as the cation exchange capacity minus the exchangeable sodium at the saturation percentage of the soil are significantly correlated. Based upon this relationship, ESP is related with SAR by the following equation:

$$ESP = \frac{100\,(-0.0126 + 0.01475\ SAR)}{1 + (-0.0126 + 0.01475\ SAR)} \qquad (3.2)$$

Thus, ESP could be calculated from the SAR of the soil. Either ESP or ES (exchangeable sodium) expressed as me/100g or SAR is usually a good indicator of the structural stability of a soil and of the physical response that might be anticipated when water is applied. The alkali soils containing expanding type 2:1 clay minerals (illite, vermiculite, montmorillonite) exhibit unfavourable physical properties at levels of ESP>15, ES>3.0 me/100g or SAR>15. In general, the physical properties become increasingly unfavourable with increasing ESP. At a given level of ESP, physical properties are usually poor in soils with expanding type 2:1 clay minerals, containing a low electrolyte concentration of salts capable of alkaline hydrolysis, *viz*, sodium carbonate, sodium bicarbonate, silica, etc.. Compared to this, soils with clay minerals of the non-swelling 1:1 type (kaolinite) or mixed types, containing a high electrolyte concentration of salts, viz. sodium chloride or sodium sulphate have better physical properties. ESP or SAR of alkali soils is generally linearly and positively related with pH, whereas there is no such relationship in case of saline soils.

The most productive normal soils have ESP or SAR less than 5 and ES less than 1.0 me/100g. The saline soils have ESP or SAR usually less than 15 but ESP values up to 50 and SAR values up to 100 are not uncommon. The alkali soils have ESP or SAR > 15 but in highly deteriorated soils, ESP may be as high as 100 and SAR may be as high as 500. Qualitatively on the basis of ESP, the alkali hazard could be anticipated as per information provided in Table 3.5. As the ESP of the soil increases from 5-70, the relative productivity of the soil decrease from almost 100 to 0.

Table 3.5. Exchangeable sodium percentage (ESP) and alkali hazard

Approximate ESP	*Alkali hazard*
Up to 15	None to slight
15–30	Slight to moderate
30–50	Moderate to high
50–70	High to very high
> 70	Extremely high

The soil texture and the tolerance of plants to ESP are other two factors, which are of practical importance. The coarse-textured soils exhibit less deterioration in physical properties than the fine-textured soils at a given ESP. Horticultural plants are extremely sensitive (ESP 2-10) followed by pulses (ESP 10-15). Wheat, barley, oats, raya (mustard), *senji, berseem, shaftal, dhaincha,* sugar cane, millets and cotton are semi-tolerant (ESP 15-30), and rice, sugar beet, para grass and Karnal grass are tolerant (ESP 30-60). The crop tolerance to alkali soils has been conventionally expressed with respect to their response to increasing ESP. The appropriateness of this criterion has been questioned because in most of such experiments total salinity tolerances of the crops were often exceeded to obtain high SAR in the soils water or calcium concentrations were insufficient for nutritional balance in low salinity situations. The existing ESP tolerance data should be normalized by associating the adverse effect on crop growth with a minimum calcium concentration (1-2 mmol L^{-1}) required for nutritional balance (Rhoades and Maas, 1979).

Salinity (Soluble salts)

Salinity is most commonly represented by Electrical Conductivity (EC) and is characterized by the presence of excess of soluble salts in the soil. The most productive normal soils have EC_e less than 1 dS m^{-1}. Conventionally, a soil having EC_e more than 4 dS m^{-1} has been designated as saline and less than 4 dS m^{-1} as non–saline. The Soil Science Society of America (1974) has recommended that soils having EC_e greater than 2 dS m^{-1} could be called as saline soils. This seems to be more logical as the growth of most sensitive plants, particularly of the horticultural and pulse crops, begins to experience the adverse effect of salinity at an EC_e of 2 dS m^{-1}. It would be still more appropriate if this limit were further reduced to 1.5 dS m^{-1}, which would roughly correspond with 1000 mg l^{-1} salt concentration.

The saline soils may be associated with high ESP but their physical properties are not affected adversely because of the high electrolyte concentration of the soil solution due to neutral salts. The soluble salts in saline soils mainly comprise the chlorides and sulphates of sodium, though calcium and magnesium are also present in appreciable quantities. The proportion of magnesium is usually higher than that of calcium. Higher concentrations of magnesium than that of calcium cause harmful effects on the physical properties of the soils and crop growth (Yadav and Girdhar, 1980, 1981). Bicarbonates occur in very low amounts and carbonates are usually absent or occur only in traces. Although, sodium salts usually predominate, $CaCl_2$, $MgCl_2$ and $MgSO_4$ are also present. These salts are highly deliquescent and therefore, absorb moisture from the atmosphere, thus, causing the soil to appear moist. Such soils often have a greasy appearance and are almost black in colour. They are likely to be mistaken for alkali soils.

The kind of soluble salts, the texture of the soil and nature of plants are some of the important factors, which determine the plant growth on saline soils. Chloride salts are more harmful than sulphate salts (Table 3.6). As the EC_e of the soil increases from 4 to 20 dS m^{-1} in case of chloride salts and 6 to 40 dS m^{-1} in the case of sulphate salts, the relative productivity of the soil in most cases decreases from almost 100 to 0.

Table 3.6 Relationship between nature of salts in the soil and plant growth

EC_e (dS m^{-1})		*Relative plant growth (%)*
Chlorides	*Sulphate*	
4	6	100
4-8	6-12	80-90
8-12	12-20	50-70
12-20	20-40	20-50
>20	>40	0

Source : Kovda *et al.*, (1973)

At a given salinity, the adverse effects on plant growth are more in fine than in coarse textured soils. The plants also differ widely in their tolerance to salts. The horticultural plants except date palm and pulses are sensitive to salinity (EC_e 1.5–3.0 dS m^{-1}). Sunflower, groundnut, maize, sugarcane and rice comprise the semi-tolerant crops (EC_e 3-5 dS m^{-1}) while cotton, sorghum, pearl millet, wheat, barley, mustard, safflower and sugar beet comprise the tolerant group (EC_e 5-10 dS m^{-1}). Amongst vegetable crops, kale, asparagus, spinach are tolerant; tomato, broccoli, cabbage, cauliflower, lettuce, potato, carrot, onion, pea, squash and cucumber are semi-tolerant; and radish, celery, and green bean are sensitive.

The alkali soils, although relatively low in soluble salts, have a composition that differs considerably from that of normal and saline soils. These soils contain mainly carbonates and bicarbonates of sodium, the alkaline salts capable of hydrolysis. Chlorides and sulphates also occur but in relatively small amounts. The calcium is precipitated in the soil in the presence of bicarbonate ions and therefore, it is commonly deficient in alkali soils. In presence of sodium bicarbonate, calcium bicarbonate still retains some-degree of solubility but in the presence of sodium carbonate even when the total alkalinity level drops to 0.1–0.2 g l^{-1}, calcium ions are virtually eliminated from the solution. Similarly, if concentration of HCO_3 ions exceeds 0.5 gl^{-1}, there would be practically no calcium salts in the soil extract. Absolute concentration of bicarbonate ions in amounts greater than 10.0 mmol l^{-1} may affect mineral nutrition and tend to reduce the availability of iron in many plants, thereby causing chlorosis.

The presence of other salts and the temperature also affect the accumulation of Na_2CO_3. For example; Na_2SO_4 and NaCl depress the solubility of Na_2CO_3 and $NaHCO_3$ and cause them to precipitate. The solubility of the sodium carbonate and bicarbonate at or below 0°C drops to 3-5 g l^{-1} but at temperature of around 30°C, the solubility goes up to 350 g l^{-1}. It is more than that of NaCl at 40°C. Thus, accumulation of Na_2CO_3 and $NaHCO_3$ is generally observed in situations where the salt content is fairly low.

In soil testing laboratories, EC is usually determined in 1:2 soil water extracts. Gupta *et al.* (1969) and Singhla *et al.* (1974) examined the relationships between EC_e and EC_2. It has been observed that EC_2 is highly and significantly correlated with EC_e. The ratio of EC_e/EC_2 decreases with the increase in the saturation percentage of the soil, more conspicuously in alkali soils. On the basis of EC, the soils are evaluated as normal, critical for germination, critical for the growth of salt-sensitive crops and severely injurious to crops if EC_2 is <1, 1-2, 2-3 and > 3 dS m^{-1} (Muhr *et al.*, 1963). In 1:2 soil water suspensions, all soluble salts contribute to the measurement of EC equally whether these are neutral or alkaline salts. On the contrary, in the saturation extract of alkali soils, all the soluble salts are not recovered, resulting in low EC_e values. It is owing to the highly dispersed carbonate system wherein the colloidal particles tend to align themselves and form an impervious layer thereby obstructing the passage of the part of the total soluble salt in the soil solution. On the contrary, chloride salt system facilitates their easy removal in the extract. The salinity appraisal on the basis of EC_2 is very useful particularly when the amount of soil sample is small. It is also useful in cases where large number of soil samples is to be analyzed or where repeated sampling is required to determine the change in salinity with time or treatment. Qualitatively, the soils having EC_e values < 1.5, 1.5-3.0, 3.0-5.0 and 5-10.0 dS m^{-1} may be called as low, medium, high and very high saline soils respectively.

Plant Growth in Salt Affected Soils

Soil Salinity and Plant Growth

Excess salinity affects crop growth in several ways. First and the most important is the less availability of water to the plant and the plant is starved of water even though the soil is moist (physiological drought condition). This is because the osmotic pressure of the soil solution increases with the increase in salt concentration and the plants are unable to extract water as readily as they can from a relatively non-saline soil. In addition to the osmotic effect of salts in the soil solution, at high concentration, absorption of an individual ion may prove toxic to the plants. For example, some constituents of salts e.g. chloride, which at moderate concentration is harmless to most crops, may be toxic at higher concentrations to some crops e.g. citrus and grapes. In addition, some elements like lithium, boron etc. are toxic to citrus and grapes even though they may be present only in very less quantities. Besides, preferential adsorption of one ion may also retard the absorption of other essential plant nutrients necessary for the normal growth of plants. It is believed that the adverse effects are usually due to a combination of these factors although one may be dominating others in many cases.

Soil Alkalinity and Plant Growth

With increasing ESP (or pH), the soil physical properties are adversely affected which results in restricted air and water movement in these soils. Adverse crop growth may also be due to direct toxic effects of Na in many crop plants. The soils, therefore, usually require an amendment so that calcium is made available to replace the excess sodium on the exchange complex. Imbalance in uptake of certain plant nutrients may also occur as a result of excessive uptake of certain other nutrients. Here also, it is hypothesized that the overall adverse effects may be due to interplay of these factors although one or the other factor may dominate in a given situation.

Plant Nutrients

Macro-nutrients

The testing of the soil for major nutrients, *viz.* nitrogen, phosphorus and potassium is a proven, practical method for evaluating the fertility status of the soils. These tests provide a sound basis for making recommendations on fertilizer application. The most productive normal soils are high in organic carbon (above 0.75%), which is used as a measure of available nitrogen, high in available P_2O_5 (above 25 kg ha^{-1}) and high in available K_2O (above 280 kg ha^{-1}). A soil is rated as low in organic carbon, available P_2O_5 and available K_2O if the respective values are below 0.5%, 10 kg ha^{-1} and 110 kg ha^{-1}, respectively. The alkali and saline soils are usually low in nitrogen, medium to high in phosphorus and high in potassium. Barren alkali soils usually have high P and K (available P being 5-10 mgl^{-1}, available K 500-750 mgl^{-1}) and therefore one may not expect any response to the application of P and K fertilizers for few years till the soils are depleted of these nutrients by few crops in succession. Phosphorus retention has been observed to increase with increasing salinity or decreasing SAR (ESP) (Elmahi and Mustafa, 1980).

Micro-nutrients

Deficiency symptoms of zinc, iron and manganese are sometimes seen on plants growing on alkali soils. The content of Zn, Fe, Mn and Cu is usually low in alkali soils (Bhumbla and Dhingra, 1964; Table 3.7). However, the availability of iron and manganese in alkali soils can be increased substantially by submergence and application of FYM (Swarup, 1981, Swarup, 2000). Since zinc deficiency may still persist, it is useful to apply zinc in alkali soils. In saline soils, the content of Cu and Zn is usually less while the Fe and Mn content is generally more than those in alkali soils (Table 3.8).

Table 3.7 Micro-nutrients in normal and alkali soils (mg l^{-1})

Soil	*Zn*	*Fe*	*Mn*	*Cu*
Normal	0.96	15.3	31.7	1.93
Alkali	0.85	4.5	5.5	1.45

Source : Gupta *et al.* (1970)

Table 3.8 Micro-nutrients in saline and alkali soil (mg l^{-1})

Soil	*Zn*	*Fe*	*Mn*	*Cu*
Saline	0.10	67.6	13.2	0.1
Alkali	0.50	2.9	8.0	1.0

Source : Gupta *et al.,* (1970)

The normal soils, saline soils and alkali soils contain boron in the saturation extract in quantities of less than 1.0, 1 to 2 and 2 to 10 mgl^{-1}, respectively (Bhargava *et al.,* 1974). Boron content of 1.0 mg l^{-1} in soils has been considered adequate for the normal growth of most plants. The available molybdenum in normal and alkali soils has been reported to be 0.40 and 0.80 mgl^{-1} respectively (Singh and Singh, 1966).

Toxic Elements

Almost all the essential elements, which are otherwise recognized as micro-nutrients, if present in the soil beyond specific limits, act as toxic elements and adversely affect the growth of certain plants. In addition, some more elements, viz. Al, As, Be, Cl, Cr, F, Pb, Ni, Se and V are also known to cause a toxic effect to plant growth, if present beyond permissible limits. The elements recognized to be of practical importance from the toxicity point of view are B, Li, F, Se and Mo. Out of these five, B, Li and F are phytotoxic. Se and Mo may not adversely affect the plant growth per se but crops, particularly the forages grown on them, may contain an excess of these elements, which cause adverse effects to the animals, which graze on them. The best productive normal soils are generally free of toxic elements or contain less than permissible limits. The saline and alkali soils tend to contain one or more of these elements in toxic amounts.

Biological Characteristics

Organic Matter

Soil organic matter, generally referred to as humus, found in small amounts in productive agricultural soils; generally representing less than 5% of the dry weight, imparts unique and remarkable properties to the inorganic matrix of sand, silt and clay. It is classified as non-humic and humic substances. The non-humic substances are the unaltered remains of plant and animal tissues including the organic compounds. The humic substances are chemically and biologically modified substances and represent the most active fraction of the organic matter in most soils. Humic substances are resistant to microbial degradation. Based on the solubility, these can be separated into four fractions namely (i) fulvic acid, which is soluble in both alkali and acid; (ii) humic acid, soluble in alkali but insoluble in acid and alcohol; (iii) hymatomelanic acid, soluble in alkali and alcohol and (iv) humin, insoluble in both alkali and acid.

In alkali soils, the alkaline solutions of sodium salts being solvents for soil humus, the latter is highly dispersed in the soil solution. On evaporation, a dark coloured residue is left in the form of a thin crust or rings around small depressions, thereby imparting a dark black colour to the surface of the soil. The organic matter content in alkali soils is, therefore, very low, generally in the range of 0.1-0.5%.

Micro-organisms

The physical and chemical properties of a soil determine the nature of the environment in which micro-organisms are found. These environmental characteristics in turn affect the composition of the microbial population both qualitatively and quantitatively. The soil reaction plays a vital role in the growth of microorganisms. The total number of bacteria, actinomycetes and fungi are usually the highest in productive normal soil followed by saline and alkali soil (Table 3.9).

Table 3.9 Microbial counts in different soils

Nature of the soil	*Organisms x 10^5/g soil*		
	Bacteria	*Actinomycetes*	*Fungi*
Normal	96.00	11.6	0.21
Saline (EC_2 6 dS m^{-1})	11.30	0.4	0.045
Alkali (pH_2 10)	2.33	0.04	0.0003

Source : Neelkantan and Pahwa (1977)

Singh (1950) listed the species of blue-green algae found in alkali soils of northern India. Through Nostoc commune, the annual addition of organic matter to the soil is 37-60% and that of nitrogen, 30-38%. Saxena (1960) collected the algal flora of alkali soils and observed that where pH is high (9.0-10.9) and the total nitrogen content of the soil is low (below 0.2%), the population of algal flora is poor. In ditches with stagnant water, where pH varied from 9.0 to 10.2 and total nitrogen content was about 0.03 percent, green and blue algae were in equal proportions. As the pH was lowered (7.9-8.6), the proportion of green algae increased. The development of the algal flora is the most prominent during monsoon.

Total organic carbon (%), dehydrogenase activity (µg TPF/g soil), microbial biomass carbon (mg/kg soil), % microbial biomass carbon and DHA/Misc, all were low in a barren alkali soils. (pH = 10.6, ESP = 95). The values were 0.5 4.5, 56.7, 2.3 and 0.08 respectively (Batra *et al.*, 1997). All values improved to 0.44, 112.1, 203.3, 4.6, 30.55 upon reclamation with Karnal grass and gypsum applied at the rate of 50% GR (pH–9.3, ESP = 40).

Mineralogical Characteristics

Clay Minerals

The kinds of clay minerals present in the soil determine many of the physical and chemical characteristics of a soil. It is well known that the 1:1 layer clay minerals (kaolinite) have only a slight stickiness, a small amount of shrinkage on drying, a small surface area and a low cation exchange capacity. Most 2 : 1 type clay minerals (illite, vermiculite, montmorillonite) have opposite properties. In general, the most productive normal soils, which are dominated with 1: 1 layer clay minerals together with iron and aluminum oxides, have excellent soil-water relationships and easy workability associated with their high degree of aggregation and non-swelling nature. At the same level of ESP, these soils are more permeable than those containing 2 : 1 layer clay minerals. However, 1: 1 layer clays have low cation exchange capacity and a low capacity for moisture retention. The saline soils in India have been identified to contain high amount of muscovite, biotite, hornblende and chlorite. The alkali soils are dominated with illite, mixed layer minerals, vermiculite and chlorite, etc. The normal soils in association contain the same minerals as adjacent saline or alkali soils, but differ in the contents of their constituent minerals and degree of crystallinity (Chatterji and Sachdev, 1979).

Kankar (impure $CaCO_3$) Pan

The *kankar* or impure $CaCO_3$ commonly accumulates in saline or alkali soils developed under arid and semi-arid climates. The accumulation may be diffused throughout the soil profile or may take the form of soft concretions or nodules or may be concentrated in a continuous horizon (caliche, cemented hard clay pan) of different hardness and at different depths below the surface. In alkali soils, a distinct, regular and thick zone of calcium carbonate accumulation, mainly dolomitic exists about 1 m below the surface (Sharma and Bhargava, 1981). The smooth boundary of the calcic horizon, irregular shape of individual concretions and regularity of occurrence underneath vast areas highlight their pedogenic origin (Sehgal and Stoop, 1972). The zone of calcic horizon possibly indicates the zone of shallow water table as the recession of water table causes soil solution to concentrate resulting in precipitation of calcium and magnesium as carbonates. Investigations made at the Usar Reclamation Farm, Chakeri, Kanpur revealed the occurrence of a compact layer 30-40 cm thick and 30-40 cm below the surface, beyond which there is generally a zone of *kankar*, often as a thick pan of 1.2-1.5m depth with typical characteristics (Table 3.10).

The presence of $CaCO_3$ affects both the physical and the chemical properties of a soil. The water movement is restricted and root penetration and proliferation are prevented. The calcareous soils ($CaCO_3$ 2%) usually have pH_s in the range of 7.6-8.4. The presence of $CaCO_3$ in the soil profile in moderate amounts, particularly the root zone depth, prevents excessive deterioration of saline or alkali soils by checking the rise of ESP. The rain water owing to its acidic nature helps in converting $CaCO_3$ to $Ca(HCO_3)_2$ and replace sodium by the calcium released from $Ca(HCO_3)_2$. The most productive normal soils are slightly calcareous. Highly calcareous soils suffer seriously with nutrient and micro-nutrient deficiencies. The plants grown on such soils sometimes suffer with lime induced chlorosis.

Table 3.10 Physical and chemical characteristics of clay pans

Depth (cm)	*Clay (%)*	*Bulk density ($g\ cc^{-1}$)*	*Aeration porosity (%)*	*Hydraulic conductivity ($cm\ hr^{-1}$)*
0-12	18	1.5	5.4	0.039
12-35	22	1.6	3.6	0.014
35-60	25	1.7	2.5	0.004
60-110	24	1.6	2.9	0.009
110-180	19	1.6	-	0.021

Source : Singh (1980)

Gypsum

The small amount (2%) of gypsum ($CaSO_4.2H_2O$) in the soils is considered favourable for crop growth because in such a case calcium replaces sodium on the exchange complex and thereby maintains the soil structure. Excessive gypsum (25%) is harmful to plant growth. Unfortunately, alkali soils do not contain sufficient reserves of gypsum in India. The saline soils, particularly on the Sea coast have been identified to possess gypsum at some depth in the soil profile. Gypsum has also been found to occur in the saline soil profiles of the Rann of Kutch in Gujarat and arid portions of Rajasthan. As much as 0.25-1.0% of $CaSO_4$ is reported to occur in these soils (Satyanarayana,1961).

Soil-Water Relationships

Infiltration Rate

It is defined as the maximum rate at which a soil, in a given condition at a given time, can absorb water. It is also the rate at which a soil will absorb water ponded on the surface as a thin sheet when the ponded area is infinitely large or when adequate precautions are taken to minimize the effect of horizontal flow at the borders. It is the volume of water passing from the soil surface into the soil per unit area per unit time. The initial intake rate rapidly decreases as the soil is wetted and the intake reaches a steady state after some hours, which is known as the basic or equilibrium rate. The most productive normal soils have basic infiltration rates between 1.0 and 3.5 cm hr^{-1}. The alkali soils generally have basic infiltration rate below 0.1 cm hr^{-1} characterizing the soils as non-arable except for rice crop. The initial infiltration rate and the basic infiltration rate decrease with the increase in ESP (Table 3.11). The data on cumulative intake reveals that limited amount of water per irrigation need to be applied to alkali lands to avoid water stagnation for longer periods (Table 3.12).

Table 3.11 Infiltration rate as affected by ESP

Soil ESP	*Initial infiltration rate (cm hr^{-1})*	*Basic infiltration rate (cm hr^{-1})*
5	22.1	3.7
14	20.3	2.7
22	11.9	1.4
30	9.9	1.0
44	8.6	0.7
49	5.9	0.3
62	5.4	0.2
65	2.2	0.1
70	2.0	0.06
72	1.8	0.05
74	1.7	0.04

Source : Singh (1980)

Permeability (Hydraulic conductivity)

Permeability has been defined qualitatively as the quality or state of a porous medium relating to the readiness with which such a medium conducts or transmits fluids. When defined quantitatively, the term hydraulic conductivity is used. It is defined as the constant of proportionality between the flux and the total driving force in Darcy's law or as the flux caused by a unit driving force. The most productive normal soils have reasonably good hydraulic conductivity such that saturated condition, whether from rainfall, irrigation or both, is unlikely to occur for more than 48 hr in the upper root zone. Several factors, viz. texture, structure and structural stability, consistency, $CaCO_3$, cleavage planes, visible pores and depth to impermeable strata such as bedrock or a hardpan influence the hydraulic conductivity of the soils. In soils, hydraulic conductivity primarily depends on the soil texture (Table 3.13).

Table 3.12 Cumulative intake (cm) in a normal and alkali lands amended with different quantities of gypsum

Soil	*Gypsum (t ha^{-1}) added*	*Time (hours)* 1	10	15	20
Normal	-	2.4	7.4	9.1	10.4
Alkali	0	0.6	1.9	2.4	2.8
	7.5	0.8	2.6	3.2	3.7
	15.0	1.1	3.4	4.2	4.8
	22.5	1.2	4.1	5.1	6.0
	30.0	1.2	4.2	5.3	6.2

The hydraulic conductivity also varies with the ESP of the soil. The saturated hydraulic conductivity decreases with increasing ESP. Abrol *et al.* (1978) reported that while an increase in ESP from 5 to 14 resulted in slight decrease in saturated hydraulic conductivity, further increase in ESP brought about a sharp decline (Fig. 3.5). In consequence, the hydraulic conductivity values are lower in alkali soils as compared to normal or saline soils. The unsaturated hydraulic conductivity at 100 cm suction has been observed to be 0.05 cm day^{-1} in alkali soil as compared to 0.6 cm day^{-1} in a normal soil (Acharya and Abrol, 1975). With further increase in suction, the difference in hydraulic conductivity of two soils decreased.

Table 3.13 Permeability of the soil as related to soil texture

Texture	*Hydraulic Conductivity, K (cm hr^{-1})*
Clay	0.13
Clay loam	0.38
Sandy clay-loam	0.50
Sandy loam	4.50
Loamy sand	9.50
Sand	14.00

Source : Hermsmeir (1978)

Redistribution

Redistribution is the process of water movement within the soil profile under the influence of gravity and suction gradients. Properties of the surface and subsurface layers together affect the process of redistribution. The water content in the top 0-15 cm layer sharply decreased over a period following irrigation when the ESP of the soil was 4 compared to when it was 38. It is due to improvement in soil transmission properties following decrease in ESP during reclamation.

Soil water availability

The capacity of a soil to retain water available to plants has a direct bearing on the required depth and the frequency of irrigation. Water retention generally increased with decreasing ESP. At tensions above 300 cm, the differences in moisture retention decrease (Table 3.14). The readily available water is that portion of the water in the soil, which can be readily absorbed by the roots (about 50-75% of the total available moisture). In the case of alkali soils, the moisture holding capacity in the moisture available range of the plants may be 20% less as compared to normal soils. In the case of saline soils, the moisture availability to the plants decreases due to increase in the osmotic pressure of soil water solution. The osmotic pressure increases at the rate of 0.36 bar per unit increase in the electrical conductivity of the soil solution measured in dS m^{-1}.

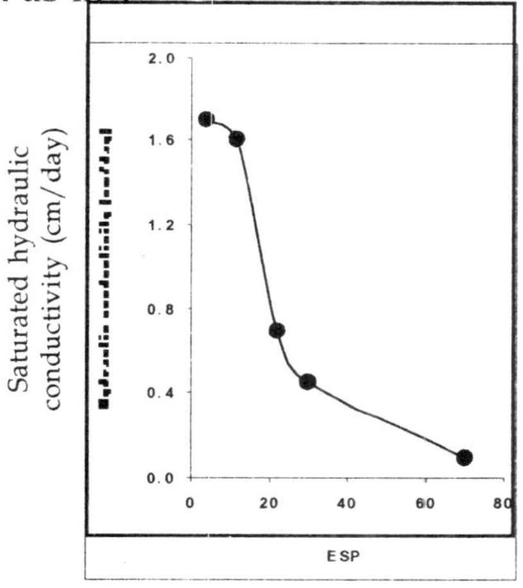

Fig. 3.5 Relationship between saturated hydraulic conductivity and soil ESP

Table 3.14 Soil moisture retention characteristics of an alkali and gypsum treated soil

Soil moisture tension (cm)	*Soil water content (cm^3 cm^{-3})*	
	Gypsum treated soil	*Alkali soil*
50	0.35	0.27
100	0.26	0.24
150	0.24	0.22
200	0.22	0.21
300	0.21	0.20
400	0.20	0.19

Hydrological Properties

The study of the hydrological features of an area is an essential pre-requisite for scientific examination and appraisal of the water resources of an area. Some of the important features relevant to the hydrological studies are; the topography, land use, crops, vegetation and engineering structures. The soils are the topmost medium on earth's surface through which the circulation and distribution of water takes place whether it is through rainfall or any other source. The properties of soil influence the process of run-off generation from rainfall, which in turn affects the formation, reclamation and management of salt affected soils. It may be pertinent to mention that hydrologically speaking a good catchment is defined as the one, which has a good surface water yield potential. On the other hand, for ground water recharge, the same will be designated as bad. For salt affected soils where leaching is one of the most important step in the reclamation and management, it is desirable that the soil surface allows sufficient amount of rainfall to enter and move through the soil profile. Most of the salt affected soils in general and alkali soils in particular are located in flat terrain resulting in restricted drainage. Alkali soils in general occupy lower portions in comparison to the normal soils of the region. They are not only capable of producing high run-off but run-off arising from adjoining areas also collects there so that drainage is impeded. Shallow ground water and poor hydraulic conductivity accentuate the run-off producing potential of these soils. Hydrologically, alkali soils can be included in the Group D soils. These soils have high run-off potential, high water table, clay pan near or at the surface with transmission rates less than 2.5 mm hr^{-1}. However, upon reclamation these soils need to be reclassified under a different group as the infiltration and hydraulic conductivity increase with time.

Bench-mark Soil Series

National Bureau of Soil Survey and Land Use Planning, Nagpur (1986) have identified broadly 64 soil series out of which 3 pertain to alkali soils viz. (1) Zarifa Viran (Established) series, (2) Hirapur series (Tentative) and (3) Sakit series (Tentative). These three series are described in the following sections.

Zarifa Viran Series

The Zarifa Viran series is a member of the fine-loamy, mixed, hyperthermic family of Typic Natrustalfs. Zarifa Viran soils have pale yellow to yellowish brown very strongly alkaline loam to clay loam A horizons, olive brown to light olive brown very strongly alkaline loamy C horizons (Table 3.15 a, b). They have developed in old alluvium in micro depressions on nearly level to flat lands at an elevation of 200 to 250 m above MSL in Karnal district, Haryana and in parts of Uttar Pradesh. The climate is semi-arid sub-tropical with mean annual air temperature of 25°C and mean annual rainfall of 600 to 700 mm (Fig. 3.6)

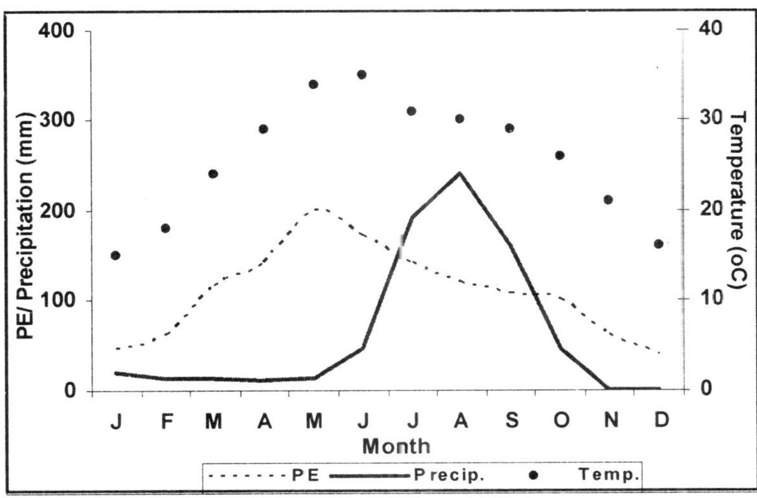

Fig. 3.6 Precipitation, temperature and water balance at Karnal

All 0-5 cm—Pale yellow (2.5 Y 7/4 D) loam, brown to dark brown (10 YR 4/3 M); moderate fine to medium platy structure; slightly plastic; strongly effervescent; few fine roots; many very fine discontinuous vertical and oblique tubular imped pores; pH 10.3; abrupt smooth boundary.

A12 5-24 cm—Yellowish brown (10 YR 5/4 M) clay loam; moderate medium sub-angular blocky structure; firm, sticky and plastic; strongly effervescent; few very fine roots; many very fine discontinuous vertical and oblique tubular imped pores; pH 10.3; clear smooth boundary.

B21t 24-56 cm—Olive brown (2.5 Y 4/4 M) clay; strong medium to coarse angular blocky structure; firm, very sticky and plastic; strongly effervescent; 2 to 3 mm size iron-manganese concretions 5% by volume, few very fine roots; patchy thin cutans; many very fine discontinuous vertical and oblique tubular imped pores; pH 9.8; clear smooth boundary.

B22t 56-85 cm—olive brown (2.5 Y 4/4 M) clay loam; strong coarse angular blocky structure; very firm very sticky and plastic; strongly effervescent; 2 to 3 mm size iron-manganese concentrations 4 to 7% by volume; 5 to 15 mm size lime concretions; patchy thin cutans; many very fine discontinuous vertical and oblique tubular imped pores; pH 9.8; clear wavy boundary.

B3ca 85-118 cm—Light olive brown (2.5 Y 5/4 M) loam; many fine distinct light yellowish brown (10 YR 5/6) mottles; strong coarse angular blocky structure; very firm, very sticky and plastic; strongly effervescent; 50 mm size lime concretions 30% by volume; 5 mm size iron-manganese concretions; patchy thin cutans; many very fine discontinuous vertical and oblique tubular imped pores; pH 9.6; clear smooth boundary.

Cca 118-140 + cm—Light olive brown (2.5 Y 5/4 M) loam; many medium distinct light yellowish brown (10 YR 5/6) mottles; moderate medium to coarse angular blocky structure; very firm, sticky and plastic; violently effervescent; 1 to 3 mm size iron manganese concretions 3 to 5% by volume; many very fine discontinuous vertical and oblique tubular imped pores; pH 9.2.

Table 3.15a Physico-chemical characteristics of Zarifa viran series (Typic Natrustaf)

Horizon	*Depth (cm)*	*Size Class*			*Coares fragments >2 mm, % of whole soil*	*Organic carbon (%)*	*Carbonate as $CaCO_3$ < 2mm (%)*	*pH soil water suspension (1 : 2)*	*Bulk density (g/cc)*	*EC (dS m^{-1})*	*CEC/Clay ratio*
		Sand (2-0.05 mm)	*Silt (0.05-0.002 mm)*	*Clay (<0.002 mm)*							
A11	0-5	43.4	34.6	22.0	-	0.30	0.5	10.3	-	8.2	0.46
A12	5-24	33.4	37.6	29.0	-	0.30	0.9	10.3	1.48	8.0	0.44
B21t	24-56	30.6	36.2	33.2	-	0.20	1.4	9.8	-	1.9	0.45
B22t	56-85	26.0	42.6	31.0	4	0.20	3.3	9.8	1.63	1.4	0.46
B3ca	85-118	33.2	40.0	26.8	10	0.10	12.4	9.6	1.47	1.0	0.41
Cca	118-140	45.0	32.0	23.0	-	0.10	20.5	9.2	-	0.9	0.41

Table 3.15b Physico-chemical characteristics of Zarifa viran series (Typic Natrustaf)

Depth	*Exchangeable bases (c mol (p⁺) kg⁻¹)*			*Exchangeable Na%*		*Water at saturation (%)*	*Water extract from saturation paste (m mol 1⁻¹)*							*DTPA extractable micronutrients (mg l⁻¹)*			
	Ca+Mg	Na	K		CEC NH_4 OAC		Ca+Mg	Na	K	CO3	HCO3	Cl	SO4	Zn	Cu	Mn	Fe
0-5	0.2	9.9	0.1	97	10.2	33	0.4	85.3	0.2	30.0	36.5	12.2	5.5	0.36	2.01	12	9
5-24	0.3	12.1	0.4	94	12.8	39	0.4	83.9	0.1	27.0	40.5	14.5	5.5	0.36	2.32	9	16
24-56	0.8	13.4	0.6	90	14.8	32	0.6	18.0	0.1	2.5	8.5	5.5	3.0	0.34	1.38	11	6
56-85	1.8	12.4	0.4	85	14.6	40	0.5	13.5	0.1	2.2	7.6	2.5	2.0	0.21	0.80	8	5
85-118	3.1	7.6	0.5	68	11.2	40	0.8	10.0	0.1	2.2	4.5	2.5	1.0	0.21	0.50	6	4
118-140	5.6	3.8	0.4	39	9.8	44	1.0	9.2	0.1	1.5	5.0	2.5	1.0	-	-	-	-

Micromorphology: The high sodium saturation causes peptization of the soil material when wet. Clay is released with drainage of the water and sorting of grain sizes occurs. Over the depth of 85 cm studied few to common cutans and common complete infillings of voids composed of clay (eg. Argillans) and/or clay sized material and/or silt-sized material occur. Often, the cutans and complete infillings are laminated. Carbonates are accumulating over the studied depth. In the A horizon they occur to a minor extent, mainly as neocalcans or calcans. In the B horizon, the quantity increases rapidly and nodules of increasing diameters are found. Micas are under alteration in this soil. Some sesquioxides have been released and accumulate to a minor extent in the ground mass.

Range in characteristics : The thickness of the solum is more than 100 cm. The estimated MAST is 26°C. MSST is 30.7°C and MWST is 14.0°C. The moisture regime is ustic.

The A horizon is about 25 cm thick. Its colour is in hue 2.5 Y and 10 YR, value 5 to 7 and chroma 3 to 4. The texture is loam to clay loam. The Bt horizon is 50 to 60 cm thick. Its colour is in hue 2.5 Y and 10 YR. value 3 to 4 and chroma 4. The texture is clay loam. Iron-manganese concretions are present. The B3ca horizon is about 30 cm thick with the same colour and texture as in Bt. It has light yellowish brown mottles. The Cca horizon has iron-manganese concretions and light yellowish brown mottles. It has more lime than the overlying horizon.

Drainage and permeability: Imperfectly drained with moderately slow permeability.

Use and vegetation : Mostly barren with salt-loving grasses.

Distribution and extent : Extensive in alluvial plains in Karnal and adjoining districts of Haryana and parts of Uttar Pradesh.

Type location : Village Gudha, Tehsil and District Karnal, Haryana; CSSRI Farm, about 200 m south-west of tube well No. 1. 29° 25′N 76° 55′ E.

Series proposed : Central Soil Salinity Research Institute, Karnal.

Interpretation: Zarifa Viran soils are saline and highly alkali with moderately slow permeability. Due to their location in depressions, water stagnates during rainy season. The soils need to be reclaimed to bring it under cultivation. The soils of this series are grouped as:

(i)	Land capability sub-class	IIIs
(ii)	Irrigability sub-class	3d
(iii)	Productivity potential	Low

Hirapur Series

The Hirapur series is a member of the fine-loamy, mixed, hyperthermic family of Aeric Halaquepts. Hirapur soils have light olive brown to olive brown very strongly alkaline very fine sandy loam A horizons, olive brown very strongly alkaline sandy clay loam B horizons and olive brown to light olive brown very strongly alkaline sandy clay loam C horizons (Table 3.16a, b). They have developed in alluvium in Aligarh district of Uttar Pradesh on nearly level to gently sloping lands of 1 to 3 percent slopes at an elevation of 150 to 200 m above MSL. The climate is semi-arid sub-tropical with mean annual air temperature of 26.7°C and mean annual rainfall of 775 mm (Fig. 3.7). A fluffy layer of salts, about 2.5 cm thick, is observed on the surface during dry months. Water table fluctuates between 0.2 and 2 m depth.

A1 0-10 cm—Light olive brown (2.5 Y 5/4 M) very fine sandy loam; moderate medium platy structure; friable and slightly plastic; strongly effervescent; salt cutans present;

many fine and medium fibrous roots; pH 10.4; abrupt wavy boundary.

A3 10-42 cm—Olive brown (2.5 Y 4/4 M) sandy clay loam; moderate fine to medium sub-angular blocky structure; friable and slightly plastic; strongly effervescent; salt cutans present; 0.5 mm size iron-manganese concretions 1 to 2% by volume; irregularly scattered sand pockets, stratified; common fine and medium fibrous roots; many very fine to fine discontinuous vertical tubular imped pores; pH 10.3; clear smooth boundary.

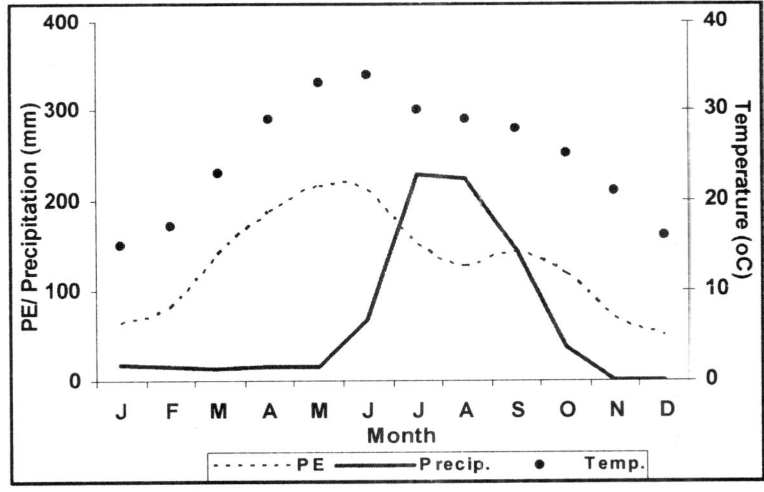

Fig. 3.7 Precipitation, temperature and water balance at Hirapur

B2 42-71 cm—Variegated colours–olive brown and very dark greyish brown (2.5 Y 4/4, 3/2 M) sandy clay loam; moderate fine to medium sub-angular blocky structure; friable and slightly plastic; strongly effervescent; 35 mm size iron-manganese concretions about 7 to 10% by volume; irregularly scattered sand pockets, stratified; common fine and medium fibrous roots; many very fine to fine continuous vertical tubular imped pores; pH 10.2; diffuse smooth boundary.

Table 3.16a Physico-chemical characteristics of Hirapur series (Aeric Halaquept)

Horizon	*Depth (cm)*	*Size Class*			*Coares fragments >2 mm, % of whole soil*	*Organic carbon (%)*	*Carbonate as $CaCO_3$ < 2mm (%)*	*pH (1:2.5 soil water suspension)*	*DTPA extractable micronutrients (mg l^{-1})*			
		Sand (2-0.05 mm)	*Silt (0.05-0.002 mm)*	*Clay (<0.002 mm)*					*Zn*	*Cu*	*Mn*	*Fe*
A1	0-10	65.4	19.8	14.8	-	0.30	2	10.4	0.27	0.94	4	10
A3	10-42	56.9	20.1	23.0	-	0.20	2	10.3	0.15	1.42	9	20
B2	42-71	54.0	20.8	25.2	-	0.20	2	10.2	0.07	0.58	10	7
B3	71-106	50.2	22.6	27.2	-	0.10	3	9.8	0.07	0.27	6	4
C1ca	106-122	53.0	20.6	26.4	-	0.10	8	9.7	-	-	-	-
C2ca	122-150	57.0	22.6	20.4	-	0.10	7	9.3	-	-	-	-

Table 3.16b Physico-chemical characteristics of Hirapur series (Aeric Halaquept)

Depth	*Exchangeable bases (c mol (p⁺) kg⁻¹*			*Exchangeable Na%*	*CEC NH$_4$OAC*	*Water at saturation (%)*	*Water extract from saturation (paste (m mol 1⁻¹)*							*EC (dS m⁻¹)*	*Clay fraction mineralogy*
	Ca+Mg	*Na*	*K*				*Ca+Mg*	*Na*	*K*	*CO_3*	*HCO_3*	*Cl*	*SO_4*		
0-11	0.1	7.9	0.3	95	8.3	47	0.4	225.2	0.5	101.0	114.0	15.0	14.0	24.0	MI5 CH2
11-38	0.4	11.8	0.4	94	12.6	46	0.5	115.3	0.4	38.5	51.5	9.5	13.5	11.1	
38-48	0.9	12.8	0.4	89	14.1	62	0.6	95.0	0.2	30.5	50.5	6.5	8.0	8.7	MI4 SM2 VM 2
48-69	1.4	13.2	0.6	89	15.2	56	0.5	74.2	0.4	12.5	45.2	6.5	9.5	6.5	VM2
69-94	2.2	10.2	0.4	80	12.8	53	0.8	34.7	0.2	5.5	20.5	4.5	4.2	3.2	
94-121	3.9	4.5	0.6	50	9.0	47	1.2	19.1	0.2	4.2	9.5	5.0	3.5	1.8	
121-142	5.8	2.5	0.5	28	8.8	57	1.2	13.2	0.2	2.2	6.6	4.0	2.2	1.3	

MI=mica, SM= Smectite, VM= Vermiculite, CH= Chlotite (5 means more than half, 4 means half to one third and 2 means one fifth to one

B3 71-106 cm—Olive brown (2.5 Y 4/4 M) sandy clay loam; massive tending to form weak fine sub-angular blocky structure; firm and slightly plastic; strongly effervescent; 2 mm size iron-manganese concretions about 1% by volume; few fine and medium fibrous roots; many very fine to fine continuous vertical tubular imped pores; pH 9.8; abrupt smooth boundary.

Clca 106-122cm—Variegated colours-olive brown and dark greyish brown (2.5 Y 4/4, 4/2 M) sandy clay loam; massive; friable; strongly effervescent; 2 to 7 cm size calcium carbonate concretions about 5 to 6% by volume; few fine fibrous roots; pH 9.7; abrupt smooth boundary.

C2ca 122-150+ cm—Light olive brown (2.5 Y 5/4 M) sandy clay loam; massive; friable; strongly effervescent; 3 to 4 cm size calcium carbonate concretions about 5 to 6% by volume; pH 9.3.

Micromorphology: The fauna have played an important role in producing most of the voids and causing homogenization of the soil material. The soil material is very unstable when wet. Micas are altering and part of the micas has been completely altered to clay minerals. High sodium saturation causes peptization of clay. This material flows into voids where sorting of grain sizes occurs whereby few fine clay cutans and common infillings are observed. The quantity of cutans and laminae composed of clay is relatively high and is probably due to the addition of clays derived from altered mica. No change in occurrence of cutans and infilling is observed with depth. Carbonates, accumulated in thin calcans and neocalcans, increase with depth. Similarly, sesquioxides are accumulating in nodules and increase with depth.

Range in characteristics : The thickness of the solum is 100 to 110 cm. The estimated MAST is 26.6°C. The MSST is 29.9°C and MWST is 16.0°C. Moisture regime is aquic, with water table within 0.2 m depth during some part of the year.

The A horizon is 30 to 45 cm thick. The colour is in hue 2.5 Y, value 4 to 5 and chroma 3 to 4. The texture is fine sandy loam to loam. Thick salt fluffy encrustation is noticed on the surface in dry season. The B horizon is 60 to 70 cm thick. Its colour is in hue 2.5 Y, value 3 to 4 and chroma 2 to 4. The texture is sandy clay loam to clay loam. Few fine mottles are occasionally present but iron-manganese concretions are invariably present.

Drainage and permeability: Imperfectly drained with moderately slow permeability.

Use and vegetation: Mostly barren with sparse thorny vegetation and grasses.

Distribution and extent: Extensive in Aligarh and adjoining districts of Uttar Pradesh.

Type location: Village Hirapur, tehsil Sikandararao, District Aligarh, U.P.; about 1.5 km south-west of Hirapur and 7 km from Akbarabad on the left of Aligarh-Etah road, 27° 45 N 78° 20 E.

Series proposed: Central Soil Salinity Research Institute, Karnal

Interpretation: Hirapur soils are imperfectly drained and are saline-alkali. Water table fluctuates between 0.2 and 2 m depth indicating the need for surface drainage. These soils can be grouped as:

(i)	Land capability sub-class	IIIs
(ii)	Irrigability sub-class	3d
(iii)	Productivity potential	Low

Sakit Series

The sakit series is a member of the fine-loamy, mixed, hyperthermic family of Typic Natrustalfs. Sakit soils have light brownish grey to light olive brown very strongly alkaline fine sandy loam to sandy clay loam A horizons, variegated coloured dark brown to dark yellowish brown very strongly alkaline clay loam Bt horizons, yellowish brown to dark greyish brown mottled very strongly alkaline gravelly sandy clay loam to clay loam C horizons (Table 3.17a, b). They have developed in old alluvium on flat terraces in Etah and adjoining districts of Uttar Pradesh at an elevation of 150 to 200 m above MSL. The climate is semi-arid sub-tropical with mean annual air temperature of 26.0°C and mean annual rainfall of 675 mm (Fig. 3.8). Principal associated soils are Hasanpura series, which is a Halaquept, and Kazi Nagla series a Haplustalf.

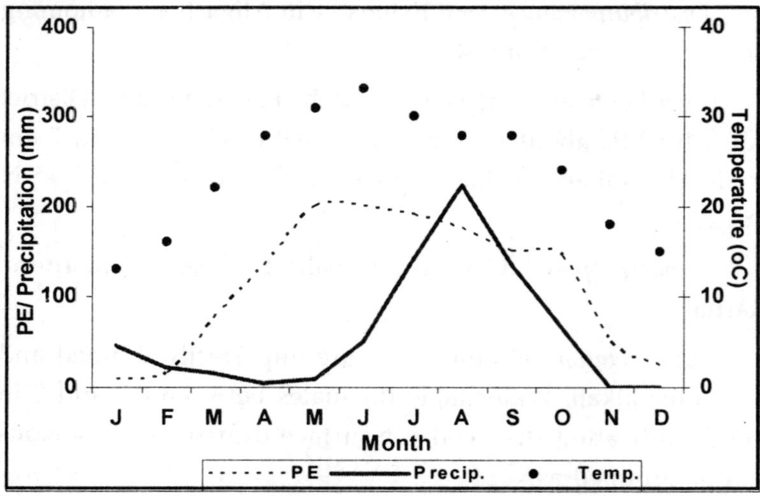

Fig. 3.8 Precipitation, temperature and water balance at Sakit

Typifying pedon:

Sakit very fine sandy loam–saline waste.

A11 0-11 cm—Light brownish grey (2.5 Y 6/2 D) very fine sandy loam, greyish brown (2.5 Y 5/2 M); moderate fine to medium platy structure; hard, friable; strongly effervescent; salt cutans; common fine roots; pH 10.5; abrupt wavy boundary.

A12 11-38 cm—Light olive (2 5 Y 5/4 M) sandy clay loam; weak to moderate medium sub-angular blocky structure; friable, slightly sticky and slightly plastic; strongly effervescent; few 1 to 2 mm size iron-manganese concretions 1 to 2% by volume; salt cutans; few fine fibrous roots; common very fine discontinuous vertical tubular imped pores; pH 10.4; clear wavy boundary.

B21t 38-48 cm—Variegated colours–dark brown (10 YR 3/3 M) and dark greyish brown (2.5 Y 4/2 M) clay loam; moderate medium columnar structure; firm, slightly sticky and slightly plastic; strongly effervescent; 1 to 2 mm size iron-manganese concretions 1 to 2% by volume; salt cutans; few fine fibrous roots; many very fine discontinuous vertical tubular imped pores; pH 10.2; abrupt wavy boundary.

B22t 48-69 cm—Variegated colours–dark yellowish brown (10 YR 4/4 M) and dark greyish brown (2.5 Y 4/2 M) clay loam; strong medium columnar structure; firm, sticky and plastic; very strongly effervescent; 2 to 5 mm size calcium carbonate concretions about 5% by volume; common fine distinct strong brown (7.5 YR 5/6) mottles; very few thin clay cutans in pores and on ped faces; few fine fibrous roots; many very fine discontinuous vertical tubular imped pores; pH 10.1; clear wavy boundary.

B23t 69-94 cm—Variegated colours–mainly dark brown (10 YR 3/3 M) and dark yellowish brown (10 YR 4/4 M) clay loam; moderate coarse columnar structure; firm, sticky and plastic, strongly effervescent; 2 to 5 mm size calcium carbonate concretions 1 to 3% by volume; common fine distinct strong brown (7.5 YR 5/8) mottles; patchy thin clay cutans in pores and on ped faces; few fine fibrous roots; many very fine discontinuous vertical tubular imped pores; pH 10.0; abrupt wavy boundary.

C1ca 94-121 cm—Variegated colours–mainly light yellowish brown (10 YR 6/4 D), brownish yellow (10 YR 6/6 M) and light brownish grey (10 YR 6/2 M) gravelly sandy clay loam; moderate coarse angular blocky structure tending to be massive; very firm, slightly sticky and plastic; violently effervescent; calcium carbonate concretions about 50% by volume; pH 9.6; abrupt wavy boundary.

IIC2ca 121-142 + cm—Variegated colours–mainly dark greyish brown (2.5 Y 4/2 M) and light olive brown angular blocky structure tending to be massive; friable to firm, sticky and very plastic; violently effervescent; 5 to 20 mm size calcium carbonate concretions 1 to 2% by volume; few fine brown fibrous roots; pH 9.0.

Micromorphology: The fauna are responsible for most of the recent and former voids. The soil material is unstable when wet. High sodium saturation causes peptization releasing clay which moves down, fills the voids and forms cutans. The composition of the cutans and infillings become finer grained with increasing depth. In the B21t horizon the former fine to medium prismatic structure elements are embedded in infilled, often coarser grained zones about 10 mm wide. Carbonates are accumulating throughout the B horizon. Carbonate and sesquioxide nodules also occur.

Range in characteristics: The thickness of the solum is 85 to 100 cm. The estimated MAST is 27°C, MSST is 30.7°C and MWST is 17.5°C. The moisture regime is ustic.

Table 3.17a Physico-chemical characteristics of Sakit series (Typic Natrustalf)

Horizon	Depth (cm)	Sand (2-0.05 mm)	Size Class Silt (0.05-0.002 mm)	Clay (<0.002 mm)	Coares fragments >2 mm, % of whole soil	Organic carbon (%)	Carbonate as $CaCO_3$ < 2mm (%)	pH (1:2.5 soil water suspension)	DTPA extractable micronutrients (mg l^{-1})			
									Zn	Cu	Mn	Fe
A11	0-11	64.6	17.2	18.2	-	0.40	0.8	10.5	0.58	0.81	7	30
A12	11-38	52.4	22.4	25.2	-	0.30	1.0	10.4	0.31	2.56	8	24
B21t	38-48	41.0	25.4	33.6	-	0.30	0.9	10.2	0.30	1.47	5	15
B22t	48-69	41.2	27.4	31.6	-	0.20	0.9	10.1	0.12	0.59	4	11
B23t	69-94	42.8	29.4	27.8	-	0.20	3.0	10.0	0.15	0.30	3	7
C1Ca	94-121	47.6	25.0	27.4	-	0.10	20.1	9.6	-	-	-	-
IIc2Ca	121-142	50.2	25.2	24.6		0.10	21.6	9.0				

Table 3.17b Physico-chemical characteristics of Sakit series (Typic Natrustalf)

Depth	*Exchangeable bases (c mol (p^+) kg^{-1}*					*Water at saturation (%)*	*Water extract from saturation paste (m mol 1^{-1})*							*EC (dS m^{-1})*	*Clay fraction mineralogy*
	Ca+Mg	*Na*	K	*Exchangeable Na(%)*	*CEC NH_4 OAC*		*Ca+Mg*	*Na*	K	CO_3	HCO_3	*Cl*	SO_4		
0-10	0.1	6.5	0.2	96	6.8	39	0.4	460.1	0.2	226.5	200.5	22.0	12.0	44.4	MI5 VM2
10-42	0.4	9.1	0.3	93	9.8	38	0.4	147.5	0.2	48.5	72.5	17.5	11.5	13.9	
42-71	0.9	9.0	0.5	86	10.4	35	0.2	29.6	0.2	7.0	14.0	6.0	5.0	3.3	
71-106	1.6	10.0	0.6	82	12.2	35	0.4	20.1	0.1	3.0	12.0	3.0	3.0	2.1	
106-122	2.8	7.2	0.5	68	10.5	40	0.5	19.2	0.2	2.5	7.5	6.0	3.7	1.6	MI4CH 2IT2
122-150	04.3	3.1	0.4	39	7.8	37	0.6	12.5	0.2	2.0	4.5	3.8	1.9	1.0	

MI=mica, VM= Vermiculite, CH= Chlotite and It = Interstratified (5 means more than half, 4 means half to one third and 2 means one fifth to one twentieth

The A horizon is 30 to 40 cm thick. Its colour is in hue 2.5 Y, value 5 to 6 and chroma 2 to 4. The texture varies from sandy loam to clay loam. Salt incrustations at the surface and salt cutans in lower part of the A horizon are common. The Bt horizon is 50 to 60 cm thick. It has variegated colours in hues 10 YR and 2.5 Y, value 3 to 4 and chroma 2 to 4. Texture is dominantly clay loam. Clay cutans and distinct mottles are present. The Cca horizon, which is more than 50 cm thick is of variegated colours, and mottled.

Drainage and permeability: Imperfectly drained with slow permeability.

Use and vegetation: Mostly barren with salt-loving grasses.

Distribution and extent: Extensive in Etah and adjoining districts of Uttar Pradesh.

Typical location: Village Ramgarhi–Hasanpur, Tehsil Jalesar, District Etah, Uttar Pradesh 27° 29′ N 78° 18′ E.

Series proposed: All India Soil and Land Use Survey, Regional Centre, Delhi.

Interpretation: Sakit soils are highly saline and alkali. These have drainage problems and are subject to water stagnation during monsoon. Ground water rises to within 2 m from the surface. These soils need to be reclaimed to bring under cultivation. The soils can be grouped as:

(i) Land capability sub-class IIIs

(ii) Irrigability sub-class 3d

(iii) Productivity potential Low

REFERENCES

Abrol, I. P., Saha, A. K. and Acharya, C. L. 1978. Effect of exchangeable sodium on some physical properties. J. Indian Society Soil Sci. 26: 98-105.

Acharya C.L. and Abrol, I.P. 1975. Comparative study of soil water behaviour in a sodic and adjacent normal soil. J. Indian Soc. Soil Sci. 23 : 391-400.

Agarwal R.R. and Yadav J.S.P. 1956. Diagnostic techniques for the saline and alkali soils of the Gangetic alluvium in Uttar Pradesh. J. Soil Sci. 7 : 109-21.

Agarwal R.R., Yadav, J.S.P. and Gupta, R.N. 1979. Saline and Alkali Soils of India. ICAR, New Delhi, 286 p.

Anonymous. 1993. Proposal for Technology Research in Irrigation and Drainage. International Program for Technology Research in Irrigation and Drainage. IPTRID. World Bank.

Anonymous, 1998. UP Sodic Land Reclamation Project: Special Study On Drainage (Final Report). Mott MacDonald Limited and Ecotech Services Limited. Lucknow. 97 p.

Arubnandam, K. and heinzer R.T. 1977. Factors influencing erosion in dispersive clays and methods of identification. Proc. Paris Sem. Erosion and solid Matter Transport in Inland Waters. IAHS–Alsh. Publ. 122, 75-88.

Bandyopadhya, A.K. 1971. Effect of rainfall on calcareous saline sodic soils in India. Agroem Talajt. 20 : 511-514.

Batra, L., Kumar, A. and Manna, M. C. 1997. Microbiological and chemical amelioration of alkaline soils by growing karnal grass and gypsum application. Experimental Agriculture. 33: 389-94.

Bhargava, G.P., Pal D.K., Kapoor B.S. and Goswami S.C. 1981. Characteristics and genesis of some sodic soils in Indo-Gangetic alluvial plains of Haryana and Uttar Pradesh. J. Indian Soc. Soil Sci. 29 : 61-70.

Bhargava, G.P., Singhla S.K. and Gupta I.C. 1974. Distribution of boron in a salt affected and contiguous normal soils. Ann. Arid Zone 13 : 32-8.

Bhumbla D.R. and Dhingra D.R. 1964. Micro-nutrient status of saline and alkali soils of the Punjab. J. Indian Soc. Soil Sci. 12 : 255-60.

Chatterji R.K. and Sachdev C.B. 1979. Mineralogical characteristics of salt affected and adjacent normal soils. Curr. Agric. 3 : 43-52.

Chavan, K. N. and Chavan, A. S. Problems and prospects of agriculture in coastal areas of Maharashtra. 1987. J. Ind. Soc. Coastal agric. Res. 5 (1): 101-106.

Dubey, D. D., Sharma, O.P., Madhurama, S. and Gupta, Raj K 1995. Salt Affected Soils of Gujarat: Extent, Nature and Management. CSSRI, Karnal.

Elmahi Y.E. and Mustafa M.A. 1980. The effect of electrolyte concentration and sodium adsorption ratio on phosphate retention by soils. Soil Sci. 130 : 321-325.

Gupta I.C. 1972. Note on relationship between pH of saturated soil paste and 1:2 soil water suspension. Indian J. Agric. Sci. 42 : 962-963.

Gupta I.C. 1979. Note on the effect of leaching and gypsum application on the detoxification of boron in a saline sodic soil. Curr. Agric. 3 : 231-234.

Gupta I.C., Bohra R.K. and Abichandani C.T. 1969. Relationships between certain indices of saline water irrigated soils of western Rajasthan. Ann. Arid Zone. 8 : 27-32.

Gupta I.C., Singhla S.K. and Bhargava G.P. 1974. Distribution of lithium in some salt affected soil profiles. J. Indian Soc. Soil Sci. 22 : 88-89.

Gupta, S. K. 2002. Extent and distribution of salt affected soils in India. Lecture delivered to the participants of Training Programme. CSSRI, Karnal.

Gupta S. K., Bansal K.N. and Verma G.P. 1970. Distribution of nutrient cations in saline and sodic soils of Chambal commanded area of Madhya Pradesh. J. Indian Soc. Soil Sci. 18 : 77-81.

Gupta S.K. and Gupta I.C. 1987. Management of Saline Soils and Waters. Oxford and IBH Publishig Co., New Delhi. 339p.

Gupta V.K. and Dabas D.S. 1980. Distribution of molybdenum in some saline sodic soils from Haryana. J. Indian Soc. Soil Sci. 28 : 28-30.

Gupta R.N. and Narain B. 1971. Investigations on some physical properties of alluvial soils of Uttar Pradesh related to conservation and management. J. Indian Soc. Soil Sci. 19 : 1-9.

Gupta R.N. and Singh, N. 1971. Some physical and physico-chemical investigations on clay pan formation in the saline-alkali soils of Gangetic basin of Uttar Pradesh. Proc. All India Symp. Soil Salinity, Kanpur. 73-77.

Hermsmeirr, L.E;. 1978. Drainage practice in Imperial valley. Trans. ASAE. 21 : 105-109.

Institution of Engineers India (1999). Institution of Engineers India, Andhra Pradesh Chapter.

Kothandaraman, G. V. 1987. Problems and prospects of agriculture in Coastal areas of Tamil Nadu. 1987. J. Ind. Soc. Coastal agric. Res. 5(1):117-122.

Kovda V.A., Van den Berg C. and Hagan, R.M. (Ed.) 1973. Irrigation, Drainage/Salinity. FAO, Rome.

Lavado R.S., Gonzalez Quintana J.A. and Hevia G.G. 1978. Content and distribution of lithium in Lapampa soils. Commun Soil sci. PI. Analy. 9 : 299-310.

Mahapatra, I. C. and Panda, M. 1994. Farming systems research and development in eastern coast of India. J. Ind. Soc. Coastal agric. Res. 12: 67-77.

Ministry of Agriculture. 1994. Draft Report on Status of Land Degradation in India. Min. of Agriculture. New Delhi. 102 p.

Mushr R.G. et al., 1963. Soil Testing in India. USAID, New Delhi.

Narwal R.P., Singh M. and Singla J.P. 1979. Selenium distribution in some salt affected and normal soils of Haryana. Curr. Agric. 3 : 59-62.

Nayyar V.K. et al., 1990. Micro-nutrients in soils and crops of Punjab. Res. Bull. Deptt. of Soils, PAU, Ludhiana, 148 p.

NBSS & LUP 1986. Benchmark Soils of India (Murthy R.S. et al., Ed.). NBSS&LUP, Nagpur.

NCDBA (1981). Report of the National Commission on Development of Backward Areas. In Report of the Working Group (1991). Ministry of Water Resources. Govt. Of India, New Delhi.

Neelakantan S. and Pahwa, M.R. 1977. Note on the distribution of micro-organisms in normal, saline and alkali soils. Curr. Agric. 1 : 77-78.

Oster, J. D. 1982. Gypsum usage in irrigation agriculture: a review. Fertil. Res. 3:73-89.

Poonia S.R. and Bhumbla D.R. 1973. Effect of gypsum and calcium carbonate on plant yield and chemical composition and calcium availability in a non-saline sodic soil. Pl. Soil. 38 : 71-80.

Rhoades, J.D. and Maas E.V. 1974. Response of crops to sodicity and calcium concentration. Ann. Rep. U.S. Salinity Laboratory, California.

Richards, L.A. (Ed.). 1954. Diagnosis and Improvement of Saline and Alkali Soils. USDA Hbk 60. U. S. Salinity Laboratory, Riverside, USA. : 160p.

Sandhu, S. S. , Acharya, C. L. and Abrol, I. P. 1980. The effect of exchangeable sodium on the water retention, transmission and modulus of rupture of a soil. Proc. Int. Symp. On Salt Affected Soils, Karnal. 185-194.

Satynarayana K.V.S. 1961. Studies on the soils of Rann of Kutch I. Description of some profiles and the distribution of salts and gypsum in the profiles. Bull. Indian Soc. Soil Sci. 6 : 125-133.

Saxena P.N. 1960. Algal flora of usar lands in Uttar Pradesh. Sci. Cult. 25 : 542-543.

Sehgal, J.L. and Stoop, G. 1972. Pedogenic calcite accumulation in arid and semi-arid regions of the Indo-Gangetic plains of Punjab. Geoderma. 8 : 59.

Sharma, P. K., Singh, Charan jit, Verma, V. K. , Chopra, R. and Minakshi. 1998. Mapping and monitoring of salt affected soils in Punjab using remote sensing technology. Tech. Rep. PRSC-98/1. Punjab Remote Sensing Center, Ludhiana. 75+xvii p.

Sharma, R. C. 1999. Extent and nature of problems for managing natural resources in Haryana. Paper Presented at Sensitization Workshop on Subsurface Drainage. CSSRI, Karnal. 3-6 (Unpublished)

Sharma, R.C. and Bhargava, G.P. 1981. Morphogenic changes in an alkali soil pedon during amelioration through gypsum application. J. Ind. Soc. Soil Sci. 29 : 274-75.

Sharma, R. C., Rao, B. R. M. and Saxena, R. K. 2004. Salt affected soils in India-current assessment. In. Advances of Sodic land

Reclamation. Pub. International Conf Sustainable Management of Sodic Lands, Lucknow. 1-27.

Sharma, S.K. and Gupta, I.C. 1986. Saline Environment and Plant Growth. Agro Botanical publishers, Bikaner, 172 p.

Singh, N. T. 1992. Land degradation and remedial measures with reference to salinity, alkalinity, water logging and acidity. In Natural Resources Management for Sustainable Agriculture and Environment. (Deb, D. L. Ed.) Angkor Publication, New Delhi.

Singh, O.P. 1980. Analysis of the hydologic changes taking place in alkali soil watersheds during reclamation. Ph.D. Thesis, JNTU, Hyderabad.

Singh, R.N. 1950. Reclamation of usar lands in India through blue green algae, Nature (London) 165 : 325-326.

Singh, S. and Singh B. 1966. Trace elements studies on some alkali and adjoining soils of Uttar Pradesh II-Profile distribution of cobalt. J. Indian Soc. Soil Sci. 14 : 177-181.

Single, N. and Singh, M. 1980. Effect of sulphur and selenium on nitrogen, sulphur, selenium and phosphorus in raya grown in some soils. J. Indian Soc. Soil Sci. 28 : 491-500.

Singhla, S.K., Bhargava, G.P. and Gupta, I.C. 1974. Relationships between certain diagnostic indices of salt affected soils of Indo-Gangetic alluvial region. Ann. Arid Zone. 13 : 218-23.

Soil Science Society of America 1974. Glossary of Soil Science Terms. Soil Science Society of America Madison. USA.

Swarup, A. 1981. Effect of flooding on physico-chemical changes in sodic soils. Z. Pflanzen Bodenk. 144 : 136-42.

Swarup, A. 2000. Nutrient management for crop production in alkali lands. In. Salinity Management in Agriculture .Gupta et al. Eds.). CSSRI, Karnal. 99-108.

Szaboles, I. 1974. Salt Affected Soils in Europe. Martinus Nijh off-The Hague & Research Institute for Soil Science & Agricultural Chemistry, Budapest.

Yadav, J.S.P. and Girdhar, I.K. 1980. Effect of varying Mg/Ca ratios and electrolyte concentrations in the irrigation water on the soil properties and wheat crop. Pl. Soil. 56 : 413-428.

Yadav, J. S. P., Bandyopadhayay, A. K. , Rao, K. V. HG. K., Sinha, T. S. and Biswas, C. R. 1979. Coastal Saline Soils of India. RRS, CSSRI, Canning (WB). 30 p.

Yadav, J.S.P. and Girdhar, I.K. 1981. The effect of different magnesium : calcium ratios and sodium adsorption ratio values of leaching water on the properties of calcareous versus non-calcareous soils. Soil Sci. 131 : 144-158.

4

LAND DEVELOPMENT AND LEACHING

The demand for the land is increasing at a very fast pace. There is keen competition among demands for various purposes notably for industry, housing and recreation. It is the prime agriculturally productive lands that are taken over to meet these demands. Therefore, to increase agricultural production not only crop yields per unit land need to be increased but attempt should also be made to bring all lands under plough which till now are considered unproductive and waste. It seems that any horizontal expansion in agriculture would come through the reclamation of degraded lands. The technology to bring such lands under plough is now available and if cultivated, these lands can contribute a tidy sum to the total agricultural production of the country. This chapter addresses to one of key component of a reclamation plan that is land development and leaching.

Land Development

Alkali soils are usually barren and land development for these soils consist of a package that clears the land to make it fit for cultivation and allows improved water management and facilitates unrestricted drainage.

Reconnaissance Survey

First and foremost step to reclaim the land is to carry out a reconnaissance survey of the area which should be followed up with a topographic and soil survey. The reconnaissance survey helps in identifying the location of the farm boundaries, necessity and extent of the land clearing operation, extent and type of problem and position of the water table. Usually, much larger area is included in this kind of survey compared to the area that is proposed for reclamation. It helps to know the area for locating possible outlets or to assess the possibility of the run-off from the adjoining lands to enter the area.

Land Clearing

Prior to making a detailed survey of the area, it is essential to remove undesirable vegetative growth from the land. In this process, some or all the trees, bushes, vegetation, trash and boulders are cleared from the area. In alkali lands, fields are usually barren and land clearing operation may not be needed except for the normal lands, which may be included in the project because of contiguity. Rarely, machine like root rakers, stumpers, root cutters etc., would be required. Most operations can be completed manually. In case there are large levelling differences, only then a bulldozer may be required to carry out rough land levelling operation. The operation can also be carried out with a 30-50 HP tractor. For initial breaking of the soil a mould board plough, a disc plough or a sub-soiler could be used.

Topographic and Soil Survey

After the clearing operation, topographic survey of the area is carried out to draw a topographic map. Such maps indicate all the permanent structures in the area. The map is used to prepare levelling design, to design the irrigation and drainage systems, and to prepare fields layout. Soil survey reveals the true nature of the problem and helps delineate normal lands from the alkali lands. Severity and kind of the alkali problem, soil texture, depth of the soil, depth to water table and depth to impermeable layer all could be investigated at this stage.

Land Levelling

In its natural state, ground surface can seldom be suited for efficient and uniform application of water. In case of alkali soils, because too little water would reach the high spots, leaching may be distinctly less than the low spots causing non-uniformity in leaching and hence, patchy crop stand. Too much and too little water is likely to result in uneven crop, reduced yield and loss of water and nutrients. Therefore, land levelling must precede any reclamation programme.

Land levelling, which is misunderstood as the table-top levelling of the fields is usually due to mistaken belief. The levelling in the real sense of this purpose means to provide a gentle slope to the land surface along the length with nil or too little slope along the width. This would allow the water to move along the length as a uniform sheet. This would also allow to control the depth of water per irrigation. Optimum longitudinal and cross slopes for the borders and furrow methods of irrigation should be selected (Table 4.1). For small areas, levelling operation is usually done by the tractors and the driver's judgement is sufficient to achieve the desired level. In large area planning, however, a complete design of the land levellling operation in blocks of economically feasible sizes is necessary. Before doing so, it is beneficial to complete rough grading with the help of bulldozer. For hauls exceeding 100 m, the efficiency of a bulldozer is reduced significantly. In such cases, use of scraper with a pick up and carry operation could be employed.

Degree of land levelling

Coefficient of land uniformity, an index of the effectiveness with which land levelling operation has been carried out, has been defined as follows (Tyagi and Singh, 1979).

$$LUC = \left[1 - \frac{1/n \left| \Sigma \, (LD - LE) \right|}{LD} \right] \tag{3.1}$$

Table 4.1 Desirable slopes for surface irrigation methods

Methods of irrigation	*Slope*	*Soil type*	*Slope (%)*
Border	Longitudinal	Heavy (clay)	0.05-0.25
		Medium (loam)	0.20-0.40
		Light (sandy)	0.25-0.65
	Cross	For all soils	Zero or as minimum as possible
			Maximum permissible
Furrow	Longitudinal	Sand	0.25
		Sandy loam	0.40
		Fine sandy loam	0.50
		Clay	2.50
		Loam	6.25
	Cross	For all soils	Not exceeding 2.0

Here LUC is the coefficient of land uniformity, LD is the desired elevation at a grid point and LE is the existing elevation at the grid point. Agarwal and Goel (1982) used another index to define the accuracy of land levelling. According to them, levelling index L, is written as

$$L = \frac{|\Sigma \text{ Difference in designed and existing grid levels}|}{\text{Number of grid points}} \qquad (3.2)$$

Tyagi (1982) reported that to apply a recommended depth of 4 cm of water per irrigation in alkali soils, the levelling index should be 1.5 or less. Tyagi and Singh (1979) also evaluated 3 secondary land levelling implements to assess the cost of land levelling and to compare the attainable LUC. With the Super Leveller a LUC of 0.96 could be obtained and therefore, this implement has been considered as the most precise followed by a combination of blade and float (Table 4.2).

Table 4.2. Time, cost and land uniformity coefficient for different levelling implements

Implement	Time for common operation (hr) Ploughing	Discing	Time for land shaping operation (hr)	Cost for common operations (Rs. ha^{-1})	Cost of land shaping operation (Rs. ha^{-1})	Total cost (Rs. ha^{-1})	LUC
Levelling blade	10	10	26.4	500	660	1160	0.72
Levelling float	10	10	15.0	500	376	875	0.63
Levelling blade and float	10	10	18.5	500	463	963	0.90
Super leveller	10	12	19.5	550	487	1037	0.96

With the popularization of laser land levelling more precise results could be obtained. With laser land leveling, skill of the operator becomes immaterial to the leveling operation. It to a great extent would help in irrigation water management.

Cost of land levelling

The cost of land levelling depends upon the soil type, initial undulations, field size, type of machinery used and the skill of the person carrying out the operation. Land levelling cost is not proportional to the differences in the initial and final levels. With increase in precision, cost of land levelling increases almost exponentially. The cost may vary from a few hundred rupees to several thousands rupees and therefore, it is necessary to plan and economize on its cost.

Other Mechanical Treatments

Some of the mechanical treatments that help to improve the physical conditions of alkali lands are the deep ploughing, sub-soiling and the profile inversion. These operations singly or in combination result in a loosened soil mass with improved infiltration rate and hydraulic conductivity. The profile inversion aims to cover an undesirable soil layer with better material from a lower layer or to utilize gypsiferous sub-soil for amelioration of the top layer of the alkali soils. Ramamoorthy (1968) reported that in case of soil having a high concentration of salts on the soil surface and relatively lesser amounts of salts below, soil inversion could be effective.

Field Arrangement

Laying out fields of workable sizes and shapes is essential for successful irrigated farming. Length and width of the plots are usually decided on the basis of irrigation method to be used. For example, in the case of border irrigation, width of plots may be a multiple of the width of a single border. Although, for the operation of leaching, it is desirable to have small sized plots, yet leaching being a one-time operation, field layout on this basis may be costly and undesirable. The common practice then could be to make temporary dykes (*bunds*) to accomplish leaching.

A well designed irrigation system, which can deliver the required amount of water to all the parts of the area at the required time and in desired amounts should be established. In alkali soils, it is desirable that each field is provided with a drainage channel at the tail end. If the lands are waterlogged and subsurface drainage is to be implemented then more rigorous investigations and design practices need to be adopted.

Installation of Tube Well for Assured Supply of Good Quality Water

Timely application of good quality canal or tube well water in adequate quantities is an essential input to any reclamation program. Since water supply both from the rainfall and canals is inadequate and unreliable, it is necessary to have a source of water, which is under the control of the farmers. A tube well for that purpose seems to be the only alternative. Since alkali areas in general are underlain by good quality water and the aquifer characteristic are favourable for the installation of a tube well, this activity could be taken up as a part of the land development. Besides meeting the irrigation needs of the land reclamation programme, it would also help in lowering the water table.

Physical Activities for Reclamation of Alkali Lands

Some of the on-farm activities that need to be undertaken have been estimated on the basis of experimental and field experiences (Table 4.3). It may also help to understand the components of cost in an alkali land reclamation programme.

Table 4.3. Work components as envisaged in reclamation of alkali soil

Sr. No.	*Kind of work*	*Amount of work*
1	*Bunding* (m ha^{-1})	470
2	Irrigation channels (m ha^{-1})	100
3	Drainage channels (m ha^{-1})	100
4	Outlet (small)	1
5	Land levelling (Tractor/hrs)	10
6	Tube well (number)	1 per 4 ha
7	Pump set (number per tube well) or sump	1
8	Soil amendment (t ha^{-1})	8-12
9	Subsurface drainage (m ha^{-1})	*

Note: Items 1-7 as per UPLDC norms

* Required only if the ground water quality is poor and water table is at shallow depth

Leaching

The only practical way to reduce the salts to an acceptable level is to leach the excess salts out by passage of low salinity water through the active root zone. Without drainage, to provide for adequate leaching, salinization is a foregone conclusion and leaching is bound to fail. One can identify 5 critical stages in any reclamation programme. These are preparatory stage, construction stage, leaching stage, leaching-cropping stage and normal cropping stage (Elagabaly, 1971). This section would deal with leaching and leaching-cropping stages.

Leaching : Definition and Objectives

Leaching is essentially a process whereby water of low concentration is applied to displace the soil solution of relatively high concentration. The application of the excess water to pass through the root zone with the aim of pushing the salts below the root zone is defined as leaching. The leaching of salts is carried out to meet one of the following objectives:

(i) To remove or to reduce the salts in the root zone commonly known as one time leaching for reclamation. In alkali soils leaching also helps in transporting the exchanged ions below the root zone.

(ii) To maintain the salt balance in the reclaimed or irrigated lands so that crops do not suffer due to excess salts at any time in future.

Time of Leaching

Availability of sufficient water at a particular time appears to be the major factor that determines the appropriate time of leaching. In case there is no constraint of water, the best time for efficient leaching is when the water table is deepest and evaporation is minimum. Leaching of sodium sulphate may, however, be retarded during winter season when evaporation is minimum. If water table were at shallow depth during the whole year, it would be appropriate to choose a period when water table is at least a meter deep below the soil surface. In case leaching is to be accomplished through rainfall, it is natural that one has to wait for a period when excess rainfall is expected. For example, in the Indian context, at most places in arid and semi-arid zones, excess rainfall is only experienced during the monsoon season. Therefore, month of July appears to be the best time for leaching. If, some water is available towards the beginning of this period, it could be used for pre-monsoon leaching. It would enhance the efficiency of leaching through rainfall. If it is proposed to grow rice, it is necessary to start reclamation in the month of June such that fields are ready for the sowing of the crop in the first week of July.

Depth of Reclamation

The depth of land reclamation depends largely upon the potential land use. For shallow rooted crops leaching of at least top 15 cm is essential. In other cases, it could vary from 60 cm for arable crops or pastures to more than 2 m for trees. For diversified cropping, the depth of reclamation usually varies from 1 to 1.5 m. It may be noted that these are the minimum recommended depths and appropriate measures against resalinization should be adopted.

How Much to Leach

The level to which salt should be brought down during leaching is normally determined by the crops to be grown following reclamation. The level of salts should be such that for the planned crop and management strategies, salt constituents of concern (salinity, specific ion concentration or alkali) should not exceed the permissible limit during the crop growth season. If the level achieved after leaching does not permit cultivation of the proposed crop, either a more tolerant crop should be selected or additional leaching water must be applied. Most comprehensive data on salinity tolerance of crops have been published and often this data form the guidelines for crop selection in reclaimed lands (Maas and Hoffman, 1977; Maas, 1980, Gupta and Sharma, 1990). Detailed discussions on this subject are included in Chapter 8.

Leaching Curves

In planning reclamation of alkali soils, the leaching curve is a useful tool to decide whether desalinization or reduction in alkalization is technically and economically feasible. It also helps to decide the most suitable reclamation methods. Leaching curves could be developed with sufficient accuracy on the basis of results from simple and rapid leaching tests provided the same method of leaching is followed for preparing the curves as is intended under field condition. A simple, straightforward way to prepare leaching curve is by running a test similar to the one used for the evaluation of the infiltration rate. Two concentric cylinders are used in such tests (Fig. 4.1). The water level in the inner cylinder is kept at a constant level and water that infiltrates is measured till the pre-determined amount of water has entered the soil. The experiment is usually a replicated trail. In these experiments, 3-4 depths of water are passed and are taken to be the treatments. Soil samples in the inner cylinder are taken before and after the completion of the test for evaluating moisture content and salt status in different layers. For salt status appraisal, the most convenient approach is to measure the bulk soil EC, SAR or ESP.

The amount of water drained below a given depth D_w, is found by subtracting from the total depth infiltrated, the amount of water evaporated and the amount of water needed to moisten the soil. The EC_{eq} is commonly used to make the leaching curve independent of the salinity of irrigation water and the existing evaporation and drainage condition. It is obtained by measuring the soil salinity of the 0-2 cm layer in a treatment where maximum amount of water has entered the profile. It is expected that the salinity in this layer attain a practically constant minimum soon after the leaching commences.

Fig. 4.1 A view of the experimental set-up to prepare leaching curves

The dimensionless plot of $EC-EC_{eq}$ / EC_e-EC_{eq} (EC_e is the initial soil EC) versus D_w /D_s (D_s is the depth of the soil) will provide the desired leaching curve (Fig. 4.2). This curve could be made use of in future for the test soil and conditions under which leaching test has been conducted. Similar curves could be prepared for SAR (Fig. 4.2). The main limitation of the leaching curve in subsurface drained lands relates to the type of flow. In leaching curves, flow is vertical and therefore such curves will be applicable to soil depths at which water movement is vertical or practically vertical. Thus, the leaching curves prepared with this method may not be applicable to strips near the drains or 1m below the soil surface in widely spaced laterals with lateral drain depth of 1.5 m or more.

Leaching of Amended Alkali Soils

While saline soils could be reclaimed through leaching alone, alkali soils require application of an amendment to replace Na ions by a more favorable ion, the Ca on the exchange complex. Therefore, leaching in amended alkali soils is not only required to transport the applied chemical constituents of the amendment to the site of exchange, but also to transport the exchanged ion and soluble salts below the root zone. Commonly, gypsum or pyrites is applied as an amendment to reclaim alkali soils.

Leaching of gypsum amended soils

It is believed that gypsum is sparingly soluble in water and therefore, requires huge quantities of water for leaching. Recent studies have revealed that water requirement for leaching gypsum-amended soils may not be more than what is necessary for removing soluble salts in a saline soil. A good field practice for leaching gypsum-amended soils is to continuously pond the fields for about a week after gypsum has been applied and transplant the rice crop thereafter. Remaining requirement of water for leaching could be met through deep percolation losses from the rice fields. The application of this technique has been demonstrated on a field scale at CSSRI, Karnal. It has been reported that percolation rate in plots with rice plants increased and was 20 times more after 65 days compared to plots where no rice crop was grown (Chhabra and Abrol, 1977).

Leaching pyrite amended soils

Pyrite is applied to the soil when the moisture content is slightly more. Once the amendment has been applied, fields are left as such for about a week. No latching is carried out during this period to allow time for the pyrite to oxidize. After this, water is ponded on the soil surface for about a week either in the continuous ponded mode or in intermittent ponding mode. Total time required for leaching would be slightly more in the later case. The leaching in this fashion should be followed by rice transplanting as in the case of gypsum amended soils. It should takes care of the remaining water requirement for leaching. In view of this, it is advisable to start a reclamation programme slightly in advance in case pyrite is used as an amendment.

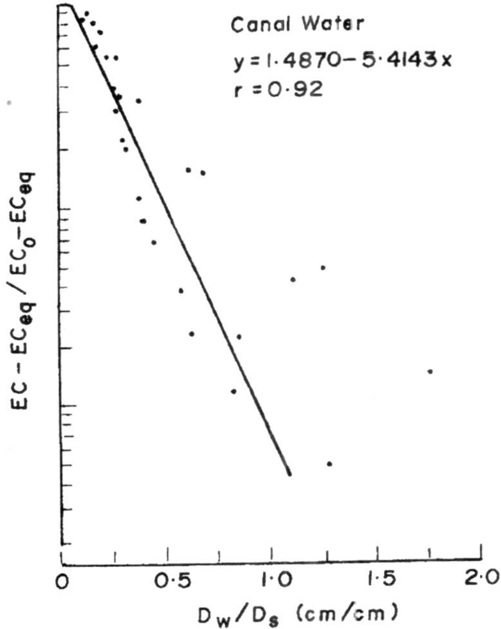

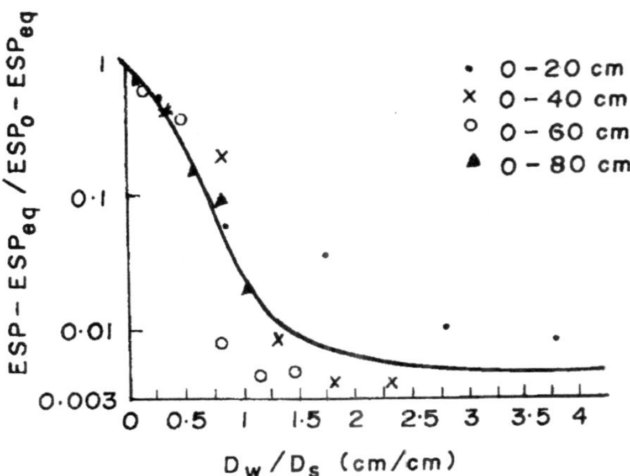

Fig. 4.2 Leaching curve (upper) for a saline soil (Sampla) and (lower) for a saline-alkali soil (Hansi)

Amount of Water Required for Leaching

In an ideal soil system without bypass, dissolution of precipitated salts, salt diffusion constraints or hydrodynamic dispersion, the salt concentration of the soil water present in a given depth of the soil profile should drop to the concentration of the applied water when one pore volume (1 PV) of the water has passed through the profile. The actual amount of water required under practical leaching, however, depends mainly upon the following factors:

(i) Amount of salt initially present in the profile

(ii) Desired level of salt in the root zone

(iii) Soil texture

(iv) Type of salts

(v) Soil depth to be reclaimed

(vi) Efficiency of the drainage system

(vii) Method of leaching.

The amount of water required to reclaim is less in intermittent than in continuous leaching or in unsaturated than in saturated leaching. It is mainly because efficiency of leaching is higher under intermittent and unsaturated leaching. A unit depth of water was reported in the past to remove about 80 percent of the salts from a unit depth of the soil (Reeve *et al.*, 1955). Field data with continuous leaching, however, show a wide range varying from a low value of 0.3 cm to a high value of 2.58 cm.

Amount of water required for leaching alkali soils is usually based on the solubility of gypsum in water. Accordingly, it was estimated that 150 cm of water must be passed through the root zone to dissolve 10 tons of gypsum per ha usually applied to reclaim the lands. This amount was viewed as very high and Jury *et al.* (1979) refined this estimate. The authors derived an equation to estimate water required to achieve desired reduction in the exchangeable sodium. The major difficulty with this equation has been to estimate the effective concentration of (Ca^{++} + Mg^{++}) ions in the leaching solution. Hira *et al.* (1981) developed an equation, which can be used to find out dissolution of gypsum particles of different diameters, and therefore can be effectively used to find out the leaching requirement of gypsum-amended soils. This equation is written as follows:

$$Z^{1/3} = I + K A_{Nai} \sqrt{21//3}\ D_0\ m\ p \qquad (3.3)$$

where z is (m_o–m/m_o), m is the gypsum (gram equivalent) dissolved, m_o is the initial gypsum added per unit surface area, I is the depth of irrigation water (cm), p is the density of gypsum (Mg m^{-3}) and D_o is the initial diameter (cm) of the gypsum particles. A_{Nai} is the initial amount of exchangeable sodium per unit surface area of soil (gram equivalent) and K is an empirical constant (cm^{-2}).

To dissolve 99 percent of the gypsum in the top 30 cm soil layer and to remove soluble salts, only 36 cm of water is required for gypsum particle of sizes ranging from 0.5 to 2.0 mm. For lower size, even lesser amounts will serve the purpose. Results from recent studies indicate that amount of water necessary to leach gypsum amended soils may not be more than that required to remove soluble surface concentrated solutes.

Continuous and Intermittent Leaching

Leaching efficiency could be improved by creating unsaturated conditions during leaching and by reducing the average rate of water movement. This can be achieved through intermittent ponding of water on the soil surface. Intermittent leaching minimizes loss of water through large pores and provides greater opportunities for diffusion of salts from immobile pockets to the mobile zone. Intermittent leaching has been found to be useful in field trials and is reported that as much as 30 to 70 percent water required for leaching in continuous ponding could be saved (Nielsen *et al.*, 1966; Elgabaly, 1971; Hoffman, 1980). Nielsen *et al.* (1966) reported that intermittent ponding might not be useful in cases where surface layer is more restrictive than the lower layers. In such cases, even during continuous ponding, unsaturated condition will prevail in the profile. Intermittent ponding has not been found superior to continuous ponding in alkali soils (Abrol and Bhumbla, 1973), sandy loam soil (Leffelaar and sharma, 1977) and for reclamation of saline soils formed as a result of 2-5 years of application of saline water (Jury *et al.* 1979). Similar results were reported for leaching of boron (Beyce, 1972). Hoffman (1980) reported an empirical equation to work out amount of water required for initial leaching. It revealed that intermittent ponding may be useful for clay loam and peat soils but for sandy loam it may not result in any saving of water. Surface evaporation of water occurring between leaching may sometimes overshadow the increased leaching efficiency brought about by intermittent leaching. For example, Elgabaly (1971) reported that time gap between two ponding should not exceed 10 days in summer and 20 days in winter to keep the upward flux of salts within reasonable limit. Synthesis of present day data reveals that intermittent leaching may be useful in soils with large bypass (with cracks or structured soils), poor soil permeability, deep ground water table and during periods of low evaporative demand. On the other hand continuous ponding may give reasonably good results in soils with good permeability, unstructured soils, areas with shallow saline ground water and during periods of high evaporative demand.

Modelling Leaching

Empirical Equations

Although several theoretically elegant mathematical models are available to estimate water required for leaching, yet a number of empirical equations have been proposed (Table 4.4). These equations are based on site-specific investigations and are used as a practical approach for this purpose. In utilizing these equations, field parameters would not be needed and therefore, application of these equations will be restricted to the sites for which experimental data have been used in preparing the equation. Few of the equations have been generalized and extensively used (Dieleman, 1963; Hoffman,

1980). In equations reported in Table 4.4 'a' and 'b' are constants but may not necessarily have the same meaning. The other parameters are, D_1, D_c and D_s which stand for depth of water applied, depth of water drained and depth of the soil, respectively. The simplest equation is that of the Reeve (1957) which has been widely used (Dahiya *et al.*, 1981; Leffelaar and Sharma, 1977; Jury *et al.*, 1979). A critical analysis will reveal that equations proposed by Khosla *et al.*, (1979) and Chawla (1985) are similar to the single layer models derived on the basis of layer-wise equilibrium theory with q = 1/b and a = 1. In the study by Khosla *et al.* (1979), it was observed that q was 0.274 as against the moisture content of 0.35 % after 24 hr of termination of the experiment. The difference could due to the fact that leaching occurred at moisture content lower than what has been attained finally.

Table 4.4 Commonly used empirical equations for calculating leaching

Equations	*Proposed and used by*	*Parameter*
$(D_1/D_s) = a.\exp(-b(1-f))$	Beyce (1972)	EC
$(D_1/D_s) = a-b(1-f)$	Beyce (1972)	Boron
$(1-f) = a.\exp(-b(D_d/D_s))$	Khosla *et al.* (1979), Chawla (1985)	Chloride, EC, SAR
$(1-f)(D_d/D_s) = a$	Hoffman (1980), Jury *et al.* (1979)	EC
$(1-f) = a.\exp(b.D_s/D_1)$	Raj and Nath (1984)	EC
$(L-f) = a(D_s/D_1) + b$	Reeve (1957); Leffelaar and Sharma (1977); Dahiya *et al.* (1981)	EC, ESP
$\log\frac{(ESP-ESP_{eq})}{(ESP-ESP)} = -a(D_d/D_s)$	Leffelaar & Sharma (1977)	ESP
$D_1 = a.\log(1/(1-f)^{-b})$	Agarwal *et al.* (1982)	Salt content (%)

The value of 'a' in fact should be close to 1.0. The minor difference in the value of this parameter should not be viewed seriously. Similarly, the equation proposed by Raj and Nath (1984) can also be shown to conform to the single layer model of Burns (1976). When compared with this model, value of 'a' should be 0.0 and b should be equal to q/2. Although other equations cannot be compared easily, it appears that to many field situations, single layer models could be fitted with convenience instead of trying empirical equations. Khosla *et al.* (1979) showed that Dielman's and Burns model fitted well to his data set (r = 0.92 and r = 0.91). These values are comparable to the empirical equation (r = 0.96).

Layer-wise Equilibrium Theory

The approach based on layer-wise equilibrium theory has been put to practice for simulating leaching of saline soils (van Der Molen, 1956; Levin, 1964). The approach is based on mass conservation in respect of both the solute and water. Basically, the models based on this concept divide the soil into several layers and applied water into several pulses. After each addition, the increment of water is assumed to mix completely with the soil solution in that layer. A new equilibrium is assumed to occur between the absorbed ion or that in the solution. If the field capacity is exceeded, the excess water is assumed to move into the next layer where it again mixes with the soil water in that layer. The solution in excess of field capacity is thus, assumed to move into subsequent layers until either downward percolation ceases or the required depth is reached. For some situations, analytical models could be developed but for others listing of a computer programme would be required. In both cases mathematical treatment remains simple. Mathematically, all the models could be described by an equation of the form as given below.

$$C_{I'}J = \frac{C_{I',\,j-1}\,\theta_{I',\,j-1} + C_{I-1,\,j}\,Hi\,(D_j \Sigma H_{I-1}(\theta_{I-1',\,j}\,\theta_{I-1,\,j-1}))}{\theta_{I',\,j-1}\,H_I + (D_j \Sigma H_{I-1}\,(\theta_{I-1',\,j}\,\theta_{I-1,\,j-1}))} \quad (3.4)$$

It means, the salt concentration in the layer following application of a pulse of water each of some known depth will be equal to the concentration after the j-1_{th} pulse times the amount of water at the end of j-1_{th} application plus the concentration of the effluent from I-1$_{th}$ layer times the depth of water drained below I-1$_{th}$ layer divided by the total water. Here C_{ij} is the concentration of the I_{th} layer after j_{th} pulse, q_{ij} is the moisture content of the Ith layer after jth pulse, H_{i} is the depth of the Ith layer and D_j is the depth of water applied in j_{th} pulse.

The moisture content in this formulation could also be varied. If it is taken as constant and equal to the final moisture content then each pulse of water applied will move to the next layer without any change in the moisture content of the layer through which it passes. It is also possible to incorporate that following the water application, the water from the upper layer will move to the next layer only if the water content in the upper layer exceeds field capacity or some pre-decided level (Bresler, 1967; Terkeltoub and Babcock, 1971; Burns, 1974). The model could be coupled with other models that simulate interactions of ions between the soil and the solution phase. Such interactions would be relevant to problems related with alkalinity (Tanji *et al.*, 1972; Gupta and Pandey, 1979). Burns (1974) incorporated the effect of evaporation and redistribution on solute transport using the evaporation limit concept, which was later improved by Kapoor and Pal (1986).

Hydrodynamic Dispersion Theory

Convective dispersive equation by far is the most commonly used equation for evaluating steady state one-dimensional salt transport in a homogenous soil. Analytical and numerical solutions of the hydrodynamic dispersion equations are available or could be developed. However, leaching of alkali soils would require numerical techniques to solve the equation.

Leaching Efficiency

The experience of leaching trials carried out world over testifies that leaching does not take place by simple piston flow displacement as postulated initially (Rouselle, 1913). If that were the case, one would need to apply only an amount equal to one pore volume to obtain complete leaching of salts present in the root zone. Several factors such as diffusion, dispersion and variation in localized flow velocities in the soil pores tend to reduce the effectiveness of leaching. Boumans and van Der Molen (1964) introduced the concept of leaching efficiency, which says that part of the water used for leaching bypasses the zone of reclamation without contributing to salt removal resulting in leaching efficiencies lower than unity. It might happen due to incomplete mixing or due to movement of water through the large pores (cracks, root or rat holes). The concept could be mathematically written as:

$$C_d = L_e\, C_s + (1\text{-}L_e)\, C_I \qquad (3.5)$$

such that

$$C_d = C_I + (C_s\text{-}C_I)\, L_e \qquad (3.6)$$

It states that concentration of drainage water, C_d, consists of a fraction, L_e of the incoming water that will flow out of root zone with the concentration C_s of the soil solution, and a fraction (1-L_e) that will have its original concentration C_i. The part that has the same concentration as C_s i.e. L_e could be defined as leaching efficiency. Miscible displacement theory as verified in field and laboratory trials indicates that leaching efficiency is well below 100 percent as might be expected in case of piston displacement. Initially, it is relatively high and decreases as the amount of water drained increases or the reclamation proceeds. Thus, in practice leaching efficiency is dynamic term and cannot be treated as a constant (Bouwer, 1969). The assertion of Bouwer (1969) that leaching efficiency can be assigned numeric values based on soil texture appears unreasonable (Schilfgaarde van, 1976; Pandey and Gupta, 1981).

Leaching efficiency would also depend upon the method of water application and initial distribution of salts in the profile. It would also be affected by the presence of cracks, root holes, animal burrows in the surface layers and continuous large pores in the profile. As such substantial amount of water could bypass the zone of reclamation. It appears that in the original formulation of Boumans and van Der Molen (1964), only the last component has been considered towards leaching efficiency, which may to some extent depend upon soil texture for many practical situations. However, the formulation does not appear logical as far as definition of the leaching efficiency is concerned. It appears at this stage that a distinction be made between the bypass factor or mixing efficiency and leaching efficiency. The leaching efficiency could be defined as the amount of salt drained as a fraction of the amount of salt present in the profile per unit pore volume after pre-decided pore volumes of water have been drained.

Conjunctive Use of Saline and Good Quality Waters

In many salts affected areas in the country, good quality water, which is a pre-requisite for reclamation, is either limited or is not available at the desired time. Semi-arid regions where large quantities of underground saline water are available at shallow depth, offer the greatest potential for the conjunctive use of saline and good quality waters for leaching. The following conditions should be helpful for making efficient use of this technique.

(i) The salinity and SAR of the saline water should be less than the salinity and SAR of the soil.

(ii) Gradually, the water of lower concentration / SAR is used for leaching such that finally fresh water is used. To implement this strategy, good quality water in right quantities and at the right time should be available.

Elgabaly (1971) recommended that ratio of the divalent cations to the total cations in the saline water used for leaching should be more than 0.30. Robochev (1977) reported that saline soils of Turkmenia could be reclaimed with Caspian Sea water followed by fresh water. Alzubaichi and Hassan (1978 a,b) reported that use of drainage water resulted in saving of 14-33 percent of fresh water depending upon soil texture in laboratory soil columns and the saving increased to 62 percent in field soils. Several studies carried out in India establish that saline ground or drainage waters could be effectively used for leaching saline/alkali soils. This practice should help to minimize the problem of water logging as well as problems related to disposal of saline water. Such problems are commonly experienced in areas drained by subsurface drainage systems.

Taylor *et al.* (1964) established that highly saline water could be used for reclamation of alkali soils provided requisite quantity of calcium salts are present and subsequent leaching is done with water of low salt concentrations. Quirk and Schofield (1955) observed that electrolyte concentration of leaching water that need to be used for leaching is closely related to the exchangeable sodium percentage of the soil to maintain stable permeability. For every level of exchangeable sodium percentage, there is a corresponding range of electrolyte concentration of leaching water, which can be used without any fear of appreciable reduction in the permeability of the soil. Use of properly balanced saline water as a source of divalent cations for reclaiming alkali soils is a feasible proposition. It does not require application of any extra amendment and holds great promise in India.

Leaching for Salt Balance

Salts are added to the soil through the application of irrigation water. The long-term viability of irrigated agriculture requires that amount of salts brought into the soil must not be allowed to accumulate beyond certain limit. The drainage water that percolates beyond the root zone should remove salts added beyond this limit. For mass balance of salts in the root zone, following relation must hold true:

$$D_I C_I = D_d C_d \tag{3.7}$$

Here D_I and D_d stand for the amount of irrigation and drainage water and C_i and C_d are the salt concentration of these waters.

In this formulation, mass of salts added from weathering of minerals or dissolution of salt deposits, mass of salts added as fertilizers or mass of salts lost as precipitation and mass of salts taken up by crops are neglected. It is also assumed that under steady state conditions, there is no build-up of salinity.

From eq. (3.7), it immediately follows that.

$$\frac{D_d}{D_i} = \frac{C_i}{C_d} \quad (3.8)$$

The leaching requirement, LR, was originally defined as the fraction of the irrigation water that must pass through the root zone to maintain soil salinity at some pre-decided level. Mathematically,

$$LR = D_d/D_i \text{ or } C_i/C_d \quad (3.9)$$

As EC of the solution is a good index of the solution concentration, the later is often replaced by EC such that

$$LR = EC_i/EC_d \quad (3.10)$$

Here EC_i and EC_d are the electrical conductivity of the irrigation and drainage water, respectively. Recent literature makes distinction between, LR, which is the theoretically average requirement of water for leaching, and LF, which is the actual fraction of the applied water that passes through the root zone. Similarly, distinction is also made between LR calculated from solution concentration (eq. (3.9)) and LR calculated from solution EC (eq. (3.10)). Smith and Hancock (1986) have shown that universal substitution of electrical conductivity for salt concentration is objectionable as LR estimated from C_i/C_d or EC_i/EC_d may not be equivalent. In order to estimate LR one must know the concentration of the drainage water. For this purpose information on tolerance of crops to soil salinity will be required.

Alkalinity Hazard and Leaching Requirement

Sodium is one of the most hazardous chemical constituents of irrigation water. An otherwise suitable, saline water may become unfit for irrigation if sodium predominates. The effect of sodium in irrigation water is either because of its consequences on the plant or though the deterioration in soil physical condition. High SAR or RSC of the irrigation water generally indicates the alkali hazard. The exchangeable sodium percentage of the soil is related to SAR by the relationship:

$$ESP = SAR_{dw} = m\ SAR_{iw} \quad (3.11)$$

here, m is an empirical constant.

This relationship is true for bicarbonate-free waters used on non-calcareous soils. U.S. Salinity Laboratory Staff (1954) indicated that SAR of the water is a good indication of the ESP of the soil though in recent times some question marks have been put on this relationship mainly in case of water having Mg/Ca exceeding unity (Gupta, 1984a). For waters containing bicarbonate, the relationship between the SAR of the drainage water (SAR_{dw} which is assumed equivalent to the SAR of the bottom of the root zone) and that of the SAR of the irrigation water is as below (Rhoades, 1974):

$$SAR_{dw} = m\ SAR_{iw}\ [1 + (8.4 - pH_c)] \quad (3.12)$$

The pH_c is the theoretical pH at which the water of a given (Ca^{++} + Mg^{++}) and (CO_3^{--}+ HCO_3^-) will have an equilibrium with solid lime. With the values of SAR_{dw} and pH_c known, the value of SAR_{dw}, which can be tolerated by a crop is incorporated in either Eq. (3.11) or Eq. (3.12). Solving these equations for m and with the following relationship:

$$m = \frac{Y(1 + 2\ LR)}{LR} \quad (3.13)$$

in which LR is the leaching requirement for SAR control and Y is a mineral weathering coefficient. When m is known, it is easy to evaluate LR for calcareous soils with the help of Fig. 4.3. It is necessary that for each water, LR for salinity as well as SAR control should be determined. The higher value should be used to achieve good crop yield and to maintain good soil physical environment.

Cropping During Leaching

In most barren salt affected soils, salinity/alkalinity of the soil is too high to grow any crop from the beginning. It usually takes over two to six years to fully reclaim the soil. In order to utilize the land, suitable crops should be identified and grown during this period. This state is usually referred to as the leaching-cropping stage. During this period, crops are selected on the basis of salt tolerance, tolerance to alkali, tolerance to water logging, water required to grow the crop viz.-α-viz. the availability of water in the region and economic value of the crop. The cropping of the virgin alkali lands should usually begin from *kharif* (monsoon) season. As transplanted rice is tolerant to high ESP, the crop can be grown right in the first year of reclamation after about a week of leaching. It has been shown that wheat is more tolerant to alkali than barley. In the case of salinity, the reverse is true. Experimental evidence at the Central Soil Salinity Research Institute, Karnal revealed the rice-wheat is an economically viable crop rotation for the reclamation and management of alkali soils.

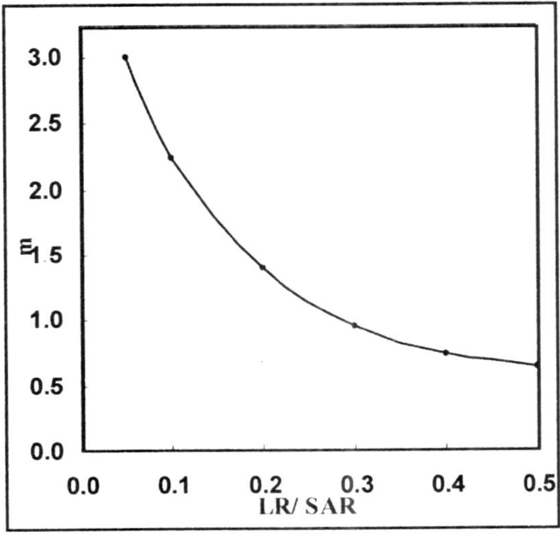

Fig 4.3 Evaluation of leaching requirement for SAR control

Pitfalls

Quite often, leaching is considered as simple application of excess amount of water before a crop is sown. In practice, such simple interpretation of the technique has resulted in delays or even complete failure of the reclamation programs. Practically speaking, leaching is beneficial only when applied as a package. One or more of the following pitfalls are very often identified in the design of reclamation programs:

(1) Leaching without adequate drainage is often undertaken leading to severe problem of water logging and soil salinization. Right type of drainage system with appropriate capacity must be installed at the right depth before starting a reclamation programme including leaching.

(2) Inadequate dyking (*bunding*), levelling, field layout and slope often result in spotted leaching.

(3) In many cases, availability of water in right quantities and at the right time is not ensured. In these circumstances partial leaching may lead to failure of the whole programme.

(4) If delay due to low permeability of soils is feared, then cultural practices, which enhance infiltration rate and/ or suitable amendments, need to be applied at the right moment. Many times this aspect is ignored.

(5) Steps are not taken to minimize salinization, which in most cases is the principal mechanism leading to delay/failure of a leaching programme.

REFERENCES

Abrol, I. P. and Bhumbla, D. R. 1973. Field studies on salt leaching in a highly saline-sodic soil. Soil Sci. 15: 429-33.

Agarwal M.C. and Goel, A. C. 1982. Effect of field levelling quality on irrigation efficiency and crop yield. Agric. Water Mgmt. 4: 457-64.

Agarwal, R.R., Yadav, J.S.P., and Gupta, R.N. 1982. Saline and Alkali Soils of India. Indian Council of Agricultural Research, New Delhi. 286 pp.

Alzubaichi, A. and Hassan, K.M., 1978a. Leaching of some salt affected soils in Iraq using drainage water. I: Leaching of some salt affected soils of different textures by drainage water under laboratory conditions. Iraqi J. Agric. Sci. 13: 199-218.

Alzubaichi, A. and Hassan, K. M. 1978b. Leaching of some salt affected soils in Iraq using drainage water II: Leaching of saline alkali soils from Abu-Ghaib by drainage water under field conditions. Iraqi J. Agric. Sci. 13: 219-34.

Beyce, O. 1972. Drainage of salty soils. Irrigation and Drainage Paper 16, FAO Rome, 63-7.

Boumans, J. H. and van Der Molen, W.H. 1964. Out watering behoefts can be volede gronden in verband met hun Zoultuishouding and Landic Ty drschu ft. 76: 880-7.

Bouwer, H. 1969. Salt balance, irrigation efficiency and drainage design. ASCE Proc. 95(IRI): 121-44.

Bresler, E. 1967. A model for tracing salt distribution in the soil profile and estimating the efficient combination of water quality and quantity under varying field conditions. Soil Sci. 104: 227-33.

Burns, I.G. 1974. A model for predicting the redistribution of salts applied to fallow soils after excess rainfall or evaporation. J. Soil. Sci. 25: 165-78.

Burns, I.G. 1976. Equation to predict the leaching of nitrate incorporated to a known depth or uniformly distributed throughout soil profile. J.Agric. Sci. Camb. 86: 305-11.

Chawla, K. L. 1985. Salt and water transport under high water table conditions. Ph. D. Thesis. Kurukshetra University, Kurukshetra.

Chhabra, R. and Abrol, I. P. 1977. Reclaiming effect of rice grown in sodic soil. Soil Sci. 124: 49-55.

Dahiya, I.S., Malik, R.S. and Singh, M. 1981. Field studies on leaching behaviour of highly saline sodic soil under two modes of water application in presence of crops. J. Agric. Aci. Camb. 97: 383-9.

Dahiya, I.S., Singh, M. and Hajrasuliha, S. 1980. Simultaneous transport of surface applied salts and water through unsaturated soils as affected by infiltration, redistribution and evaporation. Soil. Sci. Soc. Am. J. 44: 223.

Dieleman, P.J. 1963. Reclamation of salt affected soils in Iraq. Voenman Wageningen. 175-90.

Elgabaly, M. M. 1971. Reclamation and management of salt affected soils. Salinity Seminar, Baghdad. FAO Irrigation and Drainage Paper 7: 50-79.

Elgabaly, M. M. 1971. Problems of sampling, analysis and mapping of salt affected soils. Soil Bull. 31, FAO Rome, 30-8.

Gupta, S. K. and Pandey, R.N. 1979. A simplified equation of reactive solute transport in soils. J. Agric. Sci. Camb. 92: 587-9.

Gupta, S.K. and Sharma, S.K. 1990. Response of crops to high exchangeable sodium percentage. Irrigation Science. 11:173-9.

Gupta, S.K. 1984. A Mathematical model for evaluating leaching and its parameter identification under laboratory and field conditions. J. Institution of Engineers. India. 64(AG-2): 68-71.

Hira, G. S., Bajwa M.S. and Singh N.T. 1981. Prediction of water requirement for gypsum dissolution in sodic soils. Soil Sci. 131: 353-8.

Hoffman, G.J. 1980. Guidelines for reclamation of salt affected soils. Proc. Inter-American Salinity and Water Mgmt. Tech, Conf. Juarez, Mexico. 49-64.

Jury, W.A., Jarrell, W. M. and Devitt, D. 1979. Reclamation of saline-sodic soil by leaching. Soil Sci. Soc. Am. J. 43: 1100-6.

Kapoor, A. K. and Pal, R. 1986. Predicting salinization and sodification of bare sandy loam soil after irrigation with poor quality water interspersed with rain. Soil Sci. 141: 281-8.

Khosla, B. K., Gupta, R. K. and Abrol, I.P. 1979. Salt leaching and the effect of gypsum application in a saline-sodic soil. Agric. Water Mgmt. 2: 193-202.

Leffelaar, P.A. and Sharma, R.P. 1977. Leaching of a highly saline sodic soil. J. Hydrol. 32: 203-18.

Levin, I. 1964. Movement of added nitrates through soil columns and undisturbed soil profile. Trans. 8th Intern. Congr. Soil Sci. Bucharest, IV: 1011-22.

Mass, E.V. 1980. Crop tolerance to saline soil and water. In: Prospects for Bio-saline Research. Proc. US-Pak Bio-saline Res. Workshop, Karachi, Pakistan. 205-11.

Mass, E. V. and Hoffman G.J. 1977. Crop salt tolerance: Current assessment. J. Irrig. Drain. Div. 103 (IR 2): 115-34.

Nielsen, D.R., Biggar, J.W. and Luthin, J.N. 1966. Desalinization of soil under controlled unsaturated flow conditions. 6th Int. Congr. Irrig. and Drain. New Delhi. II: 15-24.

Pandey, R. N. and Gupta, S. K. 1981. Salt balance and leaching efficiency in farm irrigation system. J. Indian Soc. Soil Sci. 29: 50-4.

Quirk, J.P. and Schofield, R.K. 1955. The effect of electrolyte concentration on soil permeability. J. Soil. Sci. 6: 163-78.

Raj, M. and Nath, J. 1984. Estimation of water requirement for reclaiming saline soils. J. Indian Soc. Soil. Sci. 32: 249-52.

Ramamoorthy, B. 1968. The scope for living with soil salinity and alkali conditions in India. Proc. 7th NESA Irrig Pract. Sem. Lahore. 345-60.

Reeve, R.C. 1957. The relation of salinity to irrigation and drainage requirements. 3rd Congr. on Irrrig. and Drain.5: 10.175-10.187.

Reeve, R.C., Pillsbury, A.F. and Wilcox, L.V. 1955. Reclamation of a saline and high boron soil in the Coachella Valley of California. Hilgardia. 24: 69-91.

Rhoades, J.D. 1974. Drainage for salinity control. In: Drainage for Agriculture. (Ed. J. van Schilfgaarde). Agronomy Monograph 17. Am. Soc. Agron. Wisconsin, U.S.A. 433-61.

Robochev, I. S. 1977. Kinetics of the movement of salts during washing of soils with Sea water. Dokl. Vses. Orolena Lenina Akad. S. kh. Nauk. Irri. V.I. Leniana. 5: 33-5.

Rouselle, V. 1913. Le mouvement des nitrate dans le solet ses consequences relative a l'emploi du nitrate de soude. Annanles de Science Agronomique 4th series.

Schilfgaarde, van J. 1976. Water management and salinity. In: Prognosis of Salinity and Alkalinity. Soil Bull. 31. FAO Rome. 53-68.

Smith, R.J. and Hancock, N. H. 1986. Leaching requirement of irrigated soils. Agric. Wat. Mgmt. 11: 13-22.

Tanji, K.K., Doneen, L.D., Ferry G.V. and Ayers R.S. 1972. Computer simulation analysis on reclamation of salt-affected soils in San Joaquin Valley, California. Soil Sci. Soc. Am. Proc. 36: 127-33.

Taylor, E .M., Puri, A. N. and Asghar A. G. 1964. Soil deterioration in the canal-irrigated areas of the Punjab. I. Equilibrium between

Ca and Na ions in base exchange reaction. Indian J. Agric. Sci. 4(7): 8.

Taylor, E .M., Puri, A. N. and Asghar A. G. 1964. Soil deterioration in the canal-irrigated areas of the Punjab. II. Relation between degree of alkalization and dispersion coefficient in deteriorated soil. Indian J. Agric. Sci. 4(15): 7.

Terkeltoub, R. W. and Babcock, K. L. 1971. A simplified model for predicting salt movement through soils. Soil Sci. 111: 182-7.

Tyagi, N. K. 1982. Kallar bhumi mein sinchai karein (Hindi). Kheti. 35(3):17-8.

Tyagi, N. K. and Singh, O. P. 1979. Investigations on effect of soil moisture on performance of land levelling implements. J. Agric. Engg. 15:67-72.

U. S. Laboratory Staff. 1954. Diagnosis and Improvement of Saline and Alkali Soils. U. S. Deptt. Agric. Handbook 60. 160pp.

van Der Molen, W. H. 1956. Desalinization of saline soils as a column process. Soil Sci. 81:19-27.

van Der Molen, W. H. 1973. Salt balance and leaching requirement. In. Drainage Principles and Applications: Theories of Field Drainage and Watershed Runoff. Int. Instt. Land Reclam. And Improve. Wageningen. 11:62-99.

5

DRAINAGE METHODS

Alkali soils that occur extensively in the Indo-Gangetic plains of India have developed as a result of impeded drainage. Because of flat topography and relatively low micro-relief in relation to adjoining normal soils of the area, surface drainage is inadequate and inefficient. It results in prolonged stagnation of water following rainfall. Because of poor hydraulic conductivity, internal drainage is also restricted. Artificial drainage, therefore, is an essential pre-requisite for the reclamation and management of alkali lands. Surface, subsurface or a system that integrates the two kinds of drainage can solve the twin problems of water stagnation and high water table. With improved drainage and appropriate management techniques, it is possible to create an environment, which is conducive to human settlement, economic development and social progress.

Drainage: Definition and Types

Removal of excess water whether at the soil surface or in the root zone through surface or subsurface means to improve soil environment with the objective to increase agricultural production is known as drainage. Various means of drainage help in converting swamps, bogs, deltas and other waterlogged soils, too wet for crop production, into areas of high productivity. As for humid regions, drainage for alkali lands too could be grouped into the following four categories:

1. Surface drainage
2. Horizontal subsurface drainage (Tile or pipe drainage)
3. Vertical drainage (Tube well drainage)
4. Bio-drainage

Drainage Coefficient

The purpose of drainage is to prevent the adverse effects of water logging on crops. Design of run-off disposal network for a region will depend upon soil, climate, land use, topography, engineering feasibility and economic viability. It is necessary to remove the excess water before the crop is adversely affected or completely damaged. As the crops differ in their tolerance to water stagnation or the high water table, the design rate will be more for some crops than for others. Technically speaking, drainage coefficient is defined as the rate of water removal from the cropland and is usually expressed in terms of depth of water over the drainage area to be removed in 24 hr. The drainage coefficient should be worked out for each season and crop combination. The most critical values should be used in drainage design.

Drainage coefficient for surface drainage

Alkali soils have a high run-off generating capacity. The drainage coefficient of these lands decreases upon reclamation and it continues to decrease with number of years of reclamation until it stabilizes. The major reduction, however, occurs right in first year of reclamation. For the same crop, the drainage coefficient will be more in alkali soils. But it should be clear that, to design a surface drainage system on the basis of original soil properties would lead to over design. Thus, with imaginative planning, cost of drainage could be reduced and land under drainage channels could be saved.

Surface drainage in India is mostly required during the monsoon season. The simplest method for evaluating surface drainage coefficients for an area under different crops is described in the following steps.

1. Evaluate maximum rainfall depth for different duration (generally one to seven days), which may occur with a probability of 20 percent. Some times a probability of 10 percent is also used. It means that a recurrence interval of 5-10 years should be used.
2. Evaluate the basic infiltration rate and average potential evapotranspiration rate.
3. Estimates the tolerance of crop to the surface inundation. For example say two days. Multiply infiltration rate and evapo-transpiration rate by this period.
4. Once these values have been calculated, surface drainage requirement is calculated by the equation.

$$D = 1/n\,[R_n-(I + P)n] \qquad (4.1)$$

Here D, is the drainage rate in mm day^{-1}, R_n is the rainfall for n days duration in mm; n is period for which crop could tolerate surface stagnation of water; I and P are the basic infiltration and potential evapotranspiration rates in mm/day. This method is recommended for the design of field drains.

Another method for estimating drainage coefficient is Curve Number (CN) technique, which has been largely used by USDA, SCS and has been adopted for similar conditions in India. The method is quite popular among state agencies. Complete details of this method are beyond the scope of this book. Readers may refer any book of Hydrology for the detailed evaluation procedure. This method is useful for design of collectors, sub-mains and main drains.

Drainage coefficient for subsurface drainage

For waterlogged soils with high water table, three periods of excess water should form the basis of calculations:

1. Period of leaching for reclamation

2. Water table rise and its control during the irrigation season
3. Water table rise and its control during the monsoon season

In most cases, period of the monsoon season is most critical. Design subsurface drainage coefficients vary from 5 mm/day to 100 mm/day. In most salt affected soils, lowering of the water table from the soil surface to 30 cm below the surface in two days is adequate. This criterion could be directly applied for drainage design based on unsteady state design equations. This criterion on an average would yield a drainage rate of 10 mm/day for medium textured soils when water table is to be controlled at 1m below the soil surface with drains installed at a depth of 1.5 to 1.75m. Recent experiences reveal that for arid and semi-arid regions, a drainage coefficient of less than 5 mm/day would be adequate (Table 5.1). The drainage design for medium textured soils in semi-arid regions would be adequate, if the water table is lowered to 30 cm below the soil surface in about 2.5 days instead of a 2 days as per prevailing design criterion.

Table 5.1. Subsurface drainage coefficients from different locations (as observed from test plots)

Site	*Rainfall (mm)*	*Rate (mm/day)*	*Recommended ranges (mm/day)*
Chambal (Rajasthan)	850*	3.0	2.5-3.5
Sampla (Haryana)	600	2.5	2.0-3.0
Hisar (Haryana)	400	2.0	1.5-2.5
Dabhou (Gujarat)	800	4.0	3.0-5.0
Mundlana (Haryana)	500	5.0	5.0
Kailanakhas (Haryana)	500	6.8	5.0-7.0
Muraj (Gujarat)	500	2.8	2.0-4.0

*Variation in the range of 600-1400 mm.

Source: Gupta and Gupta (1997)

Surface Drainage

Surface drainage in India is mainly treated as a flood control measure. Farm drainage is often a neglected component. The basic requirement for the design of surface drainage system is to provide sufficient capacity drains to carry out the designed run-off with an adequate degree of protection. But at times, this condition is not met by the design. Thus, large areas are seen as pool of water during the monsoon season. Because of low infiltration rates, water on alkali lands stagnates more often and it continues for a longer duration. For medium textured alluvial soils, a surface drainage methodology has been tested for alkali lands, which constitutes mainly of the following two steps:

1. Land grading or smoothening
2. Disposal of monsoon season rainfall appropriately referred to as management of rain water

Land Grading or Smoothening

To remove excess water from the soil surface, which accumulates either due to excess rainfall or due to excess irrigation water, the land must be properly graded and smoothened. Land grading or smoothening, besides helping in efficient drainage, also helps in the following manner:

1. It permits uniform distribution of water so as to have uniform leaching of salts
2. It permits application of low depths of water during each irrigation such that to apply same amount of water, frequency of irrigation could be increased

A more detailed discussion on this aspect has been included in Chapter 3. For more information readers may turn to this chapter.

Disposal of Monsoon Season Rainfall

A major fraction of the alkali lands in the country is found in semi-arid regions where annual average rainfall is in the range of 550 mm to 950 mm. The major portion (75-80 percent) of this rainfall occurs during the monsoon season i.e. from June to September. Another significant aspect of this rainfall is that a major portion (50%) occurs in few heavy storms with long intervening dry spells. In the absence of one or more rainfall storms, the rainfall is reduced to that extent. The data highlighting these characteristics of the rainfall at Karnal are reported in Table 5.2. It shows that at probabilities of 10 and 20 percent, one-day rainfall is 183 mm and 152 mm, respectively and a continuous dry spell of 34 to 39 days could occur during the season. The probability of continuous dry spell exceeding 10 days (also referred to as critical dry spell) is more than 30 percent in each month of the monsoon season (Table 5.3).

Table 5.2 Maximum storm rainfall and dry spell of different return periods (Gauging station, Karnal)

Rainfall duration	*Rainfall (mm) for return periods of years*					
(day)	*1.01*	*2.33*	*5*	*10*	*25*	*100*
1	41	120	152	183	221	289
2	51	155	201	238	285	335
3	61	171	219	258	307	381
4	67	179	228	268	318	394
5	69	185	241	285	340	419
Mds (day)	15	28	34	39	45	54

Mds = Maximum continuous dry spell in the monsoon season

The probability of storm exceeding 30 mm in the winter months is also quite high (Table 5.4). When storms of 30 mm or higher magnitude occur following irrigation, acute drainage problem could occur even during the *rabi* season. Probability of 20 mm rainfall to occur in the month of November is only 4.0 percent. It means, sowing of wheat crop in the month of November is highly dependent on the availability of irrigation water from other sources. The water may be supplied either through a surface irrigation system or ground water resource.

Storing short-term excess rainfall in farm ponds or regional depressions during the monsoon season could also create an equally effective source of water. The stored water could be recycled for irrigation during dry spells and to provide water for pre-sowing irrigation to wheat crop.

Ground Water Table Fluctuation

Depth to the ground water table varies from year to year and has a seasonal fluctuation largely depending upon the rainfall. The highest and lowest peaks occur during September/October and May/June, respectively. Water table in several areas remains high for longer periods. On the other hand, in another areas, it remains high only during the monsoon season. At many places, water table is declining as is being

Table 5.3 Probability of occurrence of dry spells of various duration

continuous dry spell greater than or equal to (day)	*Probability (%) of occurrence in the month of*			
	June	*July*	*August*	*September*
10	92.5	45.1	32.1	71.8
15	60.0	15.0	9.1	39.4
20	29.6	4.3	2.4	17.9
25	11.1	1.2	0.6	7.5

Table 5.4 Recurrence interval of heavy storms during winter at Karnal (November-March)

Rainfall storm equal to or more than (mm)	*Return period (years)*
30	2.18
40	2.66
50	6.00

experienced in Kurukshetra/Kaithal (Fig. 5.1) and other districts of Haryana (Table 5.5). Although this situation has greatly facilitated the reclamation and management of alkali lands in the region; further decline is likely to affect crop production in general unless, measures are taken to reverse this trend.

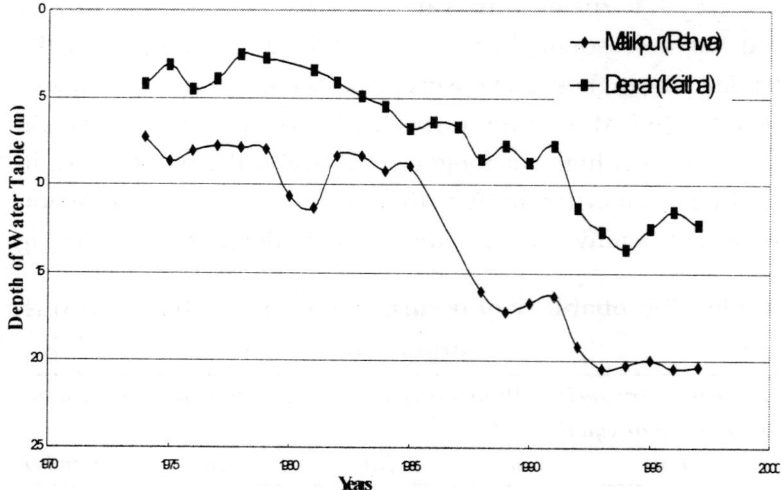

Fig. 5.1 Declining water table behaviour in Kurukshetra and Kaithal districts of Haryana

From the analysis and statements made in this section; following drainage problems can be formulated.

1. Alkali soils are prone to surface congestion of the rainwater both during the monsoon and winter seasons. Timely removal of excess water, therefore, is essential.

2. The ground water table fluctuates during the year and the highest peak occurs in the month of September/October. The peak used to be close to the soil surface in sixties and remained within reasonable limits up to 1975. With further decline in

the peak level, it is now paramount to take steps for stabilizing the water table.

Table 5.5 Declining water table in various districts of Haryana

District	*Depth to water table (m)*		*Fall in water table (m)*
	1974	*1998*	
Mohindergarh	20	32	12
Kurukshetra	08	18	10
Rewari	12	16	04
Gurgaon	05	11	06
Panipat	05	08	03
Karnal	05	08	03
Kaithal	06	08	02
Faridabad	05	07	02
Sonipat	04	05	01

3. The dilemma of excess and deficit water haunts the region many times during the same monsoon. Rainstorms of 150 mm in two days could be expected in alternate years, whereas a dry spell of 28 days could also be expected at the same probability, necessitating the need for extra irrigation water during such period.

Rain Water Management and Surface Drainage

Because of the erratic nature of rainfall, its distribution pattern and poor infiltration rates, the problem of surface drainage in alkali lands is really acute. Whereas drainage is commonly understood as the quick removal of surface water from the fields, in general, it may be difficult to achieve the same in alkali soils even with drainage rates of 20-25 mm/day (Table 5.6). In the first year of reclamation water at this rate could be removed on the 5th day. Even in the 5th year of reclamation, at this rate, water from the fields can only be removed on the 3rd day. In view of such insurmountable problems, the purpose of drainage in case of alkali lands should not be to speedily remove the water; instead, the objective should be the best possible utilization of the rainfall within the catchment. As a matter of fact, rainwater is the best quality water available for utilization. A three-tier system of surface drainage has been developed at the Central Soil Salinity Research Institute, Karnal, which consists of storage, detention and let off (Gupta and Dhruva Narayana, 1972). Briefly, the 3 tiers of the system are:

1. Rainwater is allowed to accumulate and remain on the cropland till such time and extent as will not be harmful to crops (Fig. 5.2).
2. Excess water from the fields is led to the dugout ponds of sufficient capacity. The stored water can be utilized subsequently during dry spells or for irrigating winter season crops.
3. Rainwater in excess of these two components of storage is led out of the area to the natural drainage system through tertiary and main drains.

The first component of this drainage system is a crop based component and requires extensive location specific testing. Rice crop, which is the recommended crop in the summer season for alkali lands, could be used as the test crop. It is known the depth of the stored water as well as the time for which such depths of water are stored in the rice fields affects the rice yield. The interaction of storage depth and time of storage on rice yield was studies for a 5 years period in an alkali soil under reclamation at Karnal. The rainwater storage not only reduced the irrigation water requirement but also increased the ground water recharge (Table 5.7). In four out of five years, yields from undrained plots were at par with those where instantaneous drainage was provided (Gupta and Pandey, 1979). Only in one year, when total rainfall as well as one day and two day storms was equal to 5 year return period values, the effect of drainage was observed.

Fig. 5.2 A view of the rain water storage in rice fields

Table 5.6. Dynamic of drainage coefficient in alkali soils under reclamation for rainfall storms of various duration and 5 year return period (Karnal)

Year of reclamation	*Basic infiltration rate (mm/day)*	*Drainage coefficient (mm/day) for different consecutive days* 1	2	3	4
Unreclaimed	12	140.0	88.5	61.0	45.0
1st	30	112.0	70.0	43.0	27.0
3rd	47	105.0	53.5	26.0	10.0
5th	51	101.0	46.0	22.0	6.0

Though yield increased with drainage, but irrigation water requirement also increased due to increased drainage. The overall analysis suggested that for such years also, only 20-25 percent of total growth period rainfall should be drained (Fig. 5.3). The irrigation water use efficiency is high in undrained than drained plots (Fig. 5.4). It was concluded that surface drainage requirement of alkali soils can be reduced to a greater extent by storing rainwater in rice fields. These rice fields then serve as ground water recharge basin.

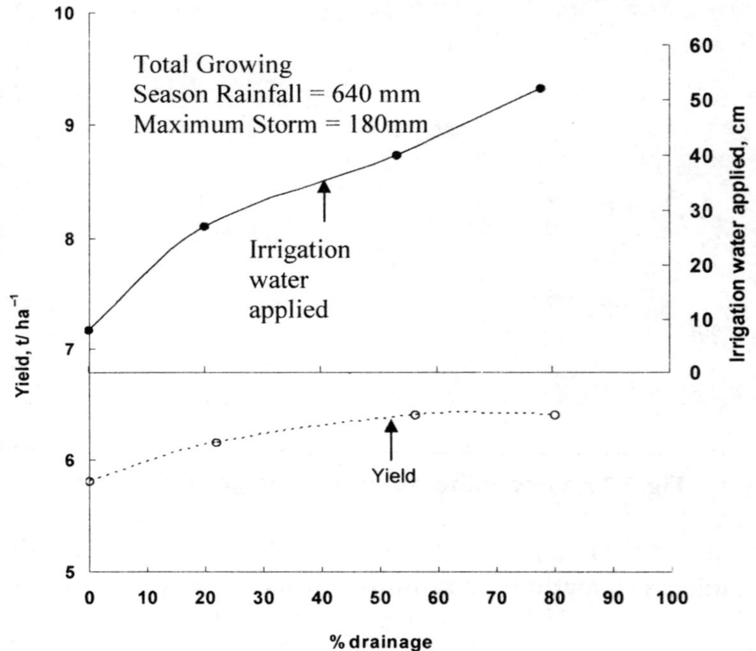

Fig. 5.3 Irrigation requirement and rice crop yield in relation to different levels of drainage

Based upon this study, a strategy for rainwater management (drainage in flat lands) is proposed, which makes use of dugout ponds as the storage structure. This strategy calls for growing of crops, which require less water in uplands. The rainwater drained from these cropped areas is stored in the dugout pond and the water stored is used in low lands, which are generally alkali and are cropped with rice. With this technology drainage problem of flat terrain is solved and rainwater is conserved within the catchment. Only a minor fraction of the rainfall is released to the drainage system. The peak of the run-off hydrograph would also be substantially reduced.

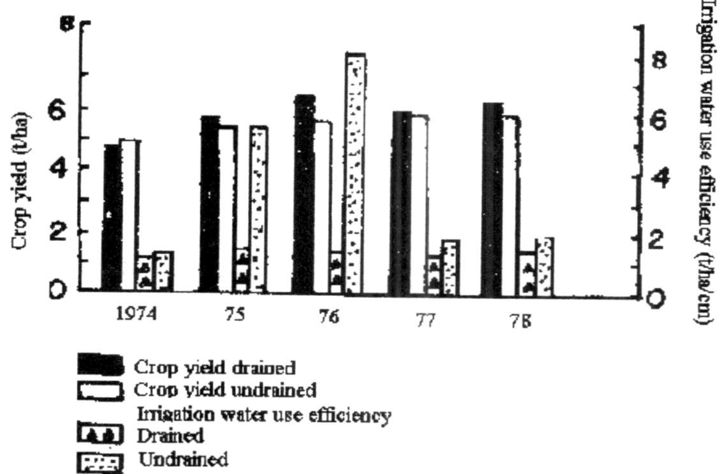

Fig. 5.4 Crop yield and water use efficiency as influenced by rainwater management

Table 5.7. Irrigation water requirement and benefit to ground water due to rainwater storage in rice fields

Year	*Irrigation and rain water used (cm) Complete Storage of rain water*	*Removal of rain water above 5cm 24 hr after the storm*	*Reduction in ground water load (cm)*	*Drainage need for optimum crop yield (cm)*	*Extra recharge (cm)*	*Net benefit to ground water (cm)*
1974	35.0 (37.1)*	40.0 (29.1)	5.0	0	3.2	8.3
1975	10.0 (60.5)	30.0 (20.8)	40.0	0	9.7	39.7
1975	7.2 (64.0)	49.7 (11.4)	42.5	16.0	10.1	36.6
1977	33.0 (47.9)	46.1 (27.9)	13.1	0	6.9	20.3
1978	27.7 (39.8)	43.2 (20.5)	15.5	0	2.8	18.3

*Figures in parenthesis indicate amount of irrigation water used

Depth Day Index

In order to combine the effect of storage depth and the duration for which such depths are allowed to remain in the fields, an index designated as 'Depth Day Index' (DDI), has been proposed (Gupta and Pandey 1983). Mathematically, the index could be evaluated as per the following relationship:

$$DDI = \sum_{j=1}^{m} \sum_{i=1}^{n} (D_{ij} - d)\, P_{ij}\, f_i; \text{ for all } D_{ij} > d \qquad (4.2)$$

Here,

D_{ij} = average depth of ponding at jth crop stage and ith water depth range

d = optimum depth of ponding (generally assumed as 10 cm)

P_{ij} = number of days for which P_i depth of ponding is maintained

i = dummy variable indicating the stage

j = number of depth ranges

m = number of crop growth stages

f_j = constant, depends upon the adverse effects at a given crop growth stage of a variety

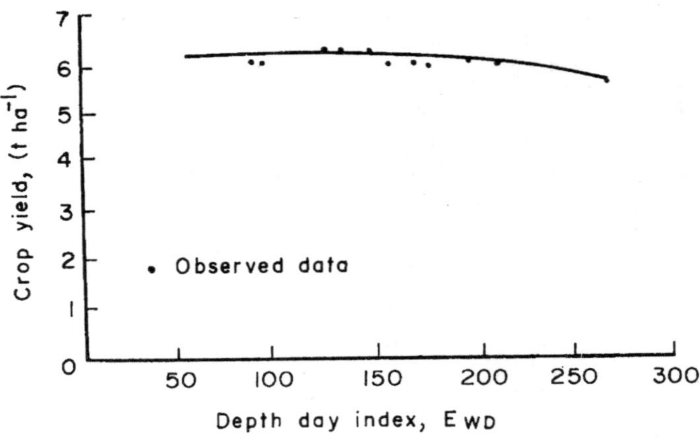

Fig. 5.5. Influence of depth day index on rice yield

Analysis of data indicated that actual yield starts declining only after the index has reached 150 (Fig. 5.5). The maximum yield reduction of 6.4 percent occurred at an index of 250. Thus, if daily depths of ponding are monitored after each storm, it is possible to determine when to drain the rain water from the fields. Greater caution is needed while index approaches 150. At the initial stage, when the crop is more likely to be submerged after heavy storms, drainage will be necessary to avoid complete submergence of transplanted seedlings.

Overall Performance of Three Tier System

The overall performance of the three-tier system of drainage at Karnal is presented in Table 5.8. This shows that more than 90 percent of the rainfall can be stored within the catchments.

Table 5.8. Performance of three-tier system of drainage at Central Soil Salinity Research Institute, Karnal farm

Year	*Rainfall (cm)*		*Tier*		*Total water stored in study area (% of total rainfall)*
		I	*II*	*III*	
1972	69.5	49.4	8.0	12.1	82.5
1973	58.9	39.4	10.0	9.4	84.5
1974	37.3	35.8	1.6	0.5	99.0
1975	60.5	54.0	5.2	1.2	98.5

Alternative to Dugout Ponds

The proposed rainwater management technology drastically reduces the drainage volume to be stored in the dugout ponds. In winter season also drainage amounts are not large and drainage may be required only once in 3 to 5 years. As the amount of drainage with rice is less, questions about the utility of dugout ponds have been raised. Therefore, use of alternative drainage structures has been investigated. One of such structures is cavity well, which is commonly installed in many areas for ground water development. For land locked fields, cavity wells could be only alternative for the disposal of surplus water. In short-term trials, the system has worked successfully. As a precaution to maintain the cavity in proper form, following suggestions are made:

1. Construct a separate cavity for drainage at the lowest portion of the farm.
2. Construct a sediment trap before the water is led into the cavity.
3. Run this cavity intermittently such that the aquifer pores remain in good condition. The water thus, withdrawn can be used for irrigation around the cavity well. This system of drainage is similar to down wells commonly used and referred to as vertical outlet.

Surface Drainage for Black Soils (Vertisols)

Vertisols and associated soils occur in Peninsular India between 8°45′and 26°0′ N latitude and 66° 0′ and 83° 45′ E longitude and occupy about 72.9 million ha area (Murthy *et al.* 1982). It makes about 23.2 % of the geographical area of the country. These soils are mainly distributed in the states of Maharashtra, Madhya Pradesh, Gujarat, Andhra Pradesh, Karnataka, Tamil Nadu, Rajasthan, Orissa and Bihar (Table 5.9). The problems of water stagnation and moisture stress are common features of the Vertisols of the semi-arid regions, which is further intensified on sodication. Thus, the crops suffer due to poor aeration in the initial stage and moisture stress during dry spells or after the withdrawal of monsoon or delay in irrigation.

Although the Vertisols have high potential productivity, the soils remain under utilized owing to number of water management problems. Low water infiltration rate, narrow workable moisture range, poor soil tilth and low hydraulic conductivity leading to poor internal drainage are some of the problems associated with such soils. Contrary to recommended ESP of 15 at which structural degradation of lands is anticipated, in these soils ESP beyond 10 also causes structural breakdown because of high degree of clay dispersion.

Surface drainage seems to one of the economically viable options for minimizing surface stagnation as well as for improving aeration. Some of the systems that have been success fully tried are as follows.

Table 5.9 Distribution of Vertisols in India (Murthy *et al.* 1982)

State	*Area (million ha)*	*% of total Vertisol area of the country*	*% of the geographical area of the country*
Maharashtra	29.9	39.1	9.1
Madhya Pradesh	16.7	21.8	5.0
Gujarat	8.2	10.6	2.5
Andhra Pradesh	7.2	9.4	2.2
Karnataka	6.9	9.0	2.1
Tamil Nadu	3.2	4.2	1.0
Rajasthan	2.3	3.0	0.7
Orissa	1.3	2.0	0.4
Bihar	0.7	0.9	0.2
Total	76.4	100.0	23.2

Raised and Sunken Bed System

The system consists of an array of raised and sunken beds running parallel to each other. The run-off from raised beds having an upland crop is collected in the sunken beds, which have rice crop (Fig. 5.6). Verma and Sharma (1998) reported that in black alkali soils bed width of 6-7.5 m in 1:1

raised and sunken bed system with a difference of about 40 cm would serve the purpose in an area receiving monsoon rains in the range of 600-800 mm.

Moderate Slopes and Furrow System

Provision of moderate slope along the furrow across the slope at a suitable spacing can provide enough drainage to support good crops. Verma *et al.* (1986, 1987) found that out of the three slopes tried (1.00, 0.65 and 0.30), 0.65 % slope provided most efficient drainage for sorghum and cotton in moderately sodic soils and lead to highest yield of these crops.

Ridge and furrow systems and parallel open ditch systems have also been found effective. For example, it has been shown that open ditches of 0.10 to 0.15 m^2 cross section spaced at 8-10 m interval helps in increasing crop yield in areas with rainfall of about 1000 mm.

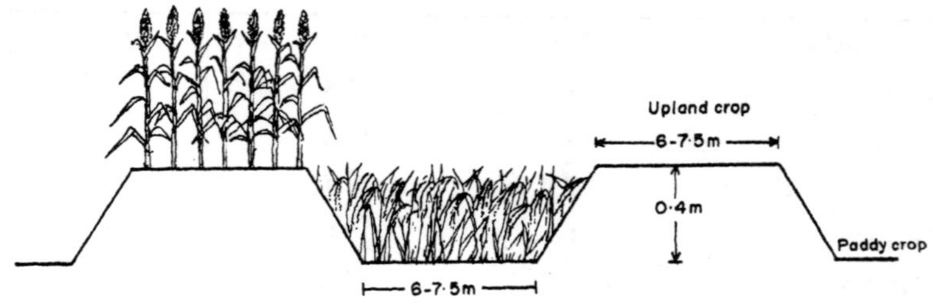

Figure 5.6. A scematic view of the raised and sunken beds for surface drainage

Subsurface Drainage

In areas where water table is high, it is necessary to install subsurface drainage system to control the ground water table at some reasonable depth. It can be accomplished either by horizontal tile (pipe) drainage or by tube well drainage (vertical drainage). In the construction of a cost effective subsurface drainage system, a logical sequence of investigations and design should be followed. For a pipe drainage system following sequence is suggested:

1. *Preliminary survey*: This survey generally examines the drainage limitations and possible economic benefits. This should help in arriving at a decision on the feasibility of taking up further investigations.
2. *Reconnaissance survey*: In this survey, planner or designer tries to get as much data as possible by going around the area mainly to familiarize himself with the tasks ahead and possible solutions.
3. *Detailed survey*: This is the main component of the drainage investigations where information on soils, sub-soils, ground water table behaviour, existing drainage, outlet conditions and gradients available, crop rotation, depth to impermeable layer, infiltration rates, hydraulic conductivity and drainable pore space etc. are obtained.
4. *Analysis* of data: All the evidence and data collected are analyzed to find out the main and/ or secondary drainage problems. The actual design parameters are calculated from the data. Drain depth is selected on the basis of crop root zone and/ or salinization hazard. Normal depth is in the range of 1.2-3.0 m. For manual installation, the depth may not exceed 1.8 m in most cases.
5. *Drainage design*: Once the design parameters are in hand, lateral drain spacing is calculated by one of the several steady or unsteady state drainage design equations.

Steady State Theory

Although a number of equations are available, yet the most important and widely used equation is that of Hooghoudt. The equation for a two-layered soil profile is written as:

$$L^2 = \frac{8\ K_2\ dH + 4\ K_1 H^2}{R} \qquad (4.3)$$

Where L, is the drain spacing in m; K_1 and K_2 are the hydraulic conductivity of the soil layers above and below and drain respectively, mm day^{-1}; H is the ground water table height above drain, m; d is the equivalent depth to impermeable layer and R is the recharge or the discharge rate. A definition sketch illustrates these parameters and variables more effectively and clearly (Fig. 5.7). The equivalent depth is a function of the actual depth of impermeable layer, D; the drain radius and the drain spacing. Because of its dependence on drain spacing eq. (4.3) can only be solved through trial and error. In a homogenous profile $K_1 = K_2$ for which eq. (4.4) reduces to:

$$L^2 = \frac{K}{R}\ (8\ dH + 4\ H^2) \qquad (4.4)$$

Under most practical condition, most steady state equations yield similar design spacing.

Unsteady State Theory

In case of unsteady state theory, Glover-Dumn equation is most commonly used for design (Dumm, 1969). The equation in its most familiar form is:

$$L^2 = \frac{8\ K\ dt}{4\ H_o} \qquad (4.5)$$

$$f \ln (---)$$
$$\pi H_t$$

Here, f is the drainable pore space in fraction and H_o and H_t are the heights of water table above drains before and after t, days of drainage. For semi-arid regions where most of the alkali lands in India are situated, it is recommended that water table should be lowered from the soil surface to 30 cm below the soil surface in 2.5 days. Location specific modifications to this criterion can, however, be made.

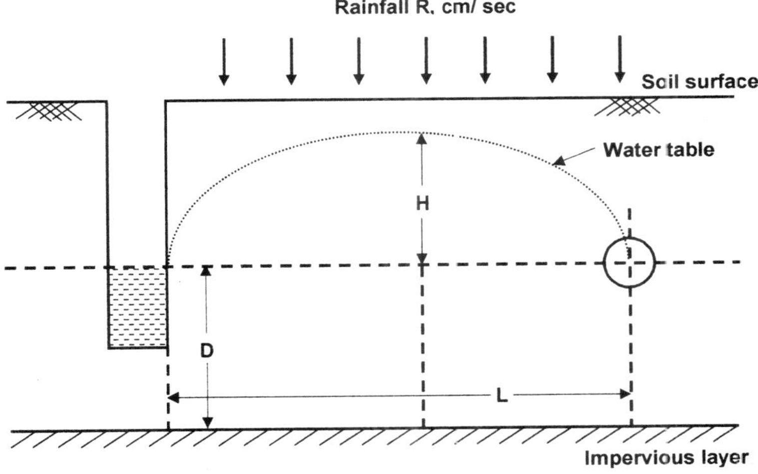

Fig. 5.7 Definition sketch of subsurface drainage in the case of steady state drainage

Eq. (4.5) is applicable when D >> H_o /2. If this condition is not met with then d in eq. (4.5) is replaced by d_1 such that $d_1 = d + H_o /2$

With this modification eq. (4.5) calculates drain spacing that is nearly similar to the one given by van Schilfgaarde's equation.

Pandey and Gupta (1990) modified Hooghoudt equation following Bouwer and van Schilfgaarde (1963) approach. They suggested that in arid and semi-arid regions, contribution of evaporation is significant and should be taken into account in drainage design. These calculations revealed that for the Indo-Gangetic plains, when evaporation is considered, drain spacing should be increased over and above the spacing calculated for a case in which evaporation is neglected.

Tile Drainage : A Case Study

The performance of tile drainage system to control water table and for reclamation of alkali soils was studied in a replicated experimental trial at Karnal (Jaiswal and Dhruva narayana, 1972). The hydraulic conductivity of the soil as measured by auger hole method for the area is given in Table 5.10. The design spacing for these conditions was worked out to be 20m for a drain depth of 1.2 m. In order to test the design equation and for economic considerations, two additional spacing of 10 m and 30 m were also tried. Both open and closed drains were installed. The performance of open drains was unsatisfactory because of unstable slopes and high maintenance cost. Performance of subsurface drains is reported in Table 5.11 (Jaiswal and Pandey, 1973). The drainage volume and amount of salts removed from various spacing were less than 0.63 cm and 54 kg ha^{-1}, respectively. Even when subjected to continuos leaching for more than 90 days, there

Table 5.10. Hydraulic conductivity of alkali soils as measured is situ using auger hole method

Average depth of bore (m)	*Hydraulic conductivity in m day^{-1}*
1.02	0.26
1.08	0.41
1.10	0.31
1.20	0.33
1.50	0.23

was no flow from the drains. During this period, soil moisture profile was well below the drain level. The following are the reasons for non-functioning of drains:

1. Hydraulic conductivity of the surface layer of alkali soils is poor resulting in unsaturated flow in sub-surface layers. The hydraulic gradient in the vertical direction between the wetting front and the water table is of much larger magnitude than the horizontal direction in the vicinity of drains, which would have helped the water to move to the drains.
2. The water level at the time of ponding was below 150 cm and the additional amount of water being added to the water table was not sufficient to meet the natural drainage capability of the aquifer in the post monsoon season. Thus, it did not allow build-up of the water table up to the drain level, which could have allowed the drain to function.

The overall performance of subsurface drains has been poor. In view of poor infiltration rates and hydraulic conductivity, extensive network of shallow and deep tube wells and good quality ground water rising only during few months of the monsoon season; it is reasoned out that horizontal subsurface drainage may not be required in major parts of alkali lands in India. However, around 10 percent of the areas existing in a thin transition belt where category of salt-affected lands changes from alkali to saline; subsurface drainage could be required and seems to be feasible. Poor quality of ground water under these conditions improves hydraulic conductivity. The lowering of the water table would be essentially needed to control secondary soil salinization. The field results revealed that the water table could be effectively controlled with a drain spacing of 67 m. The drains in this case were placed at a depth of 1.75 m. The crop rotation in these soils should be the same as in the case of alkali soils i. e. rice during summer and wheat during winter.

Improving Performance of Subsurface Drainage

Performance of subsurface drainage can be enhanced by application of gypsum or by sub-soiling. A combination of the two could also be used if required.

Table 5.11. Performance of subsurface drains in alkali soils

Particulars	*Spacing (m)*			
	Open ditch	*Tile drainage*		
	10m	*10 m*	*20 m*	*30 m*
No. of days the drain functioned	37	37	37	25
Maximum rate of fall of water table (cm/day)	0.68	0.64	0.41	0.08
Total depth of drainage water removed (mm)	6.0	6.3	4.0	0.5
Electrical conductivity of drainage water (dS m^{-1})	1.40	1.40	1.55	1.60
Total amount of salt removed from 150 cm profile (kg/ha)	53	54	27	5
pH of drainage water	9.1	9.0	9.2	9.2

Application of gypsum

Gypsum is a chemical amendment, which improves infiltration rate and the hydraulic conductivity. Although application of gypsum is necessary to lower soil ESP, additional gypsum should be added to the backfill material to improve its hydraulic conductivity and to minimize dispersion on wetting. It will provide a connection to the drain through a high hydraulic conductivity column, which should improve the performance of the drains.

Sub-soiling

Sub-soiling is a general term describing a soil cultivation practice that is intended to break up the soil horizons beneath the cultivated top soil. The basic function is to disrupt any layer of compaction or induration and improve the permeability of the soil by creating a network of fissures all the way to the sub-surface layers. The sub-soiling is generally carried out at a spacing of 1.0-1.5 times the depth of sub-soiling. It is intended to be a one-time operation, although its effectiveness is reduced with time. Therefore, it is generally advised to repeat the process after 4-5 years or earlier, if necessary.

Vertical Drainage

Vertical drainage also popularly known as tube well drainage is accomplished through a borehole from which under ground water is extracted to lower the water table. For lowering the water table necessary condition is that total discharge (draft of wells) over the region should be more than the total recharge to the aquifer. For a successful tube well drainage scheme, following conditions should be met with:

1. The water bearing aquifer should be at a shallow depth such that water can be pumped economically.
2. Water bearing horizons that are to be pumped should be connected to the water table.
3. The effluent disposal system should be constructed to facilitate disposal of the water.

Excellent conditions exist for vertical drainage to be successful in the Western Yamuna Command of Haryana, especially, under the alkali soil regions. The transmissibility coefficients for the shallow aquifer range form 144 to 360 m^2/day, whereas for the deeper aquifers, it is in the range of 400-4000 m^2/day. Such transmissibility values permit successful installation of tube wells. Because of this reason as well as to assure supply of irrigation water, farmers in this area have gone for shallow tube wells in a large number. This has resulted in arresting the rising trend of groundwater table in most severely waterlogged areas (Gupta, 2000). A statement of the falling ground water table in several districts of Haryana reveals that water table rise can be arrested by tube wells (Table 5.5, Fig. 5. 1). It may be pertinent to note that tube well density in Karnal and Kurukshetra districts almost doubled from 9 wells/ sq km in the year 1969 to 19 wells/sq km in 1982. On the other hand, the water table continues to rise in areas where tube wells are not installed in sufficient number mainly because of poor ground water quality. As a result, substantial area is affected by water logging in the state of Haryana (Table 5.12). Similar situation also happens to be in the southwest Punjab where water table is rising (Fig. 5.8). It is now understood that in areas where ground water is saline but good aquifers are available, farmers should be advised to install tube wells to exploit ground water. It is now possible to usefully employ saline waters if the EC of the ground water is < 6 dS m^{-1}. The modern techniques of use of saline water in agriculture should be taught to the farmers and incentives should be given to encourage them for adoption of these techniques. The waters with still higher EC could be pumped out by some government agency provided a proper disposal system could be constructed. In order to encourage the ground water development, following policies and incentives could be considered in areas where alkali land reclamation programmes are undertaken.

- Subsidy on tube well construction,
- On-demand fresh water supply to leach down the salt or for cyclic/blending strategies
- Compensation in canal water rates in lieu of use of ground water.

On this basis it is now confirmed that in alkali lands where good quality ground water is available, vertical drainage would continue to be the preferred practice for subsurface drainage. Even in areas where ground water may contain some Residual Sodium Carbonate (RSC), vertical drainage may get preference over the conventional horizontal drainage since adding limited quantities of gypsum to neutralize the RSC would effectively help in the use of ground water.

Table 5.12. Waterlogged and potentially waterlogged areas (sq.km.) in Haryana

District	*Waterlogged area (0-1.5m)*	*Potentially water-logged area (3m)*
Ambala	75 (5)*	271 (17)
Panchkula	–	12 (1)
Yamunanagar	16 (1)	340 (19)
Kurukshetra	–	–
Kaithal	74 (3)	561 (20)
Karnal	20 (1)	69 (3)
Panipat	9 (1)	94 (9)
Sonepat	247 (11)	779 (34)
Rohtak	364 (22)	733 (44)
Jhajjar	365 (20)	732 (39)
Faridabad	73 (3)	288 (4)
Sirsa	119 (3)	271 (17)
Fatehabad	241 (10)	390 (16)
Hisar	360 (10)	583 (15)
Jind	258 (9)	590 (22)
Bhiwani	41 (1)	476 (9)
Mahendragarh	–	13 (1)
Riwari	–	7
Gurgaon	236 (9)	416 (15)
Total	2498 (6)	6625 (15)

* Figures in parenthesis show the percentage of total area.

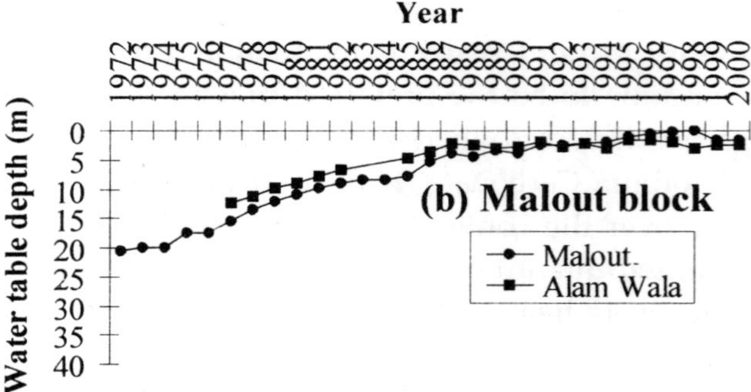

Fig. 5.8 Hydrographs showing rise in water table in Malout block in southwest Punjab

Bio-drainage

This method is called bio-drainage because in this technique a biotic material is used for drainage. A quick growing plant, which exhibits luxury consumption of water, if freely available, is grown over waterlogged marshy areas to reclaim them and to reduce drainage requirement of the region. Though a detailed discussion on plants suitable for growing in alkali soils will be taken up in Chapter 5, it is now well known that eucalyptus, a exotic plant can be successfully grown in these soils. Although opinions widely diverge on the exact amounts of ground water utilization by this plant yet it has found favor with farmers because it is quite sturdy and can tolerate adverse conditions. Eucalyptus plantations are often held responsible for the depletion of ground water in several areas of Punjab, Haryana, Uttar Pradesh and Gujarat, yet sufficient data are not available which may confirm or contradict this accusation.

Limited data on the water requirement of this plant to some extent confirm the belief that this plant utilizes large quantities of water in case water is freely available (Table 5.13 and 5.14). In spite of this a simple calculation by the authors revealed that this plant has limited capability as bio-drain material, because of the following factors:

1. The one-hectare plantation of this crop cannot transpire more water than a shallow tube well of 10-12 l/sec.
2. Because of almost zero evapotranspiration during night, the system does not create water table draw down such that additional land could be reclaimed. Only the land, which has been planted, will be put to use. Thus, there is no reclamation of land for additional use.

Table 5.13 Potential water consumption of four plant species during seedling stage

Species	*Potential water consumption per seedling (mm)*
Delbergia latiflora	1,143
Eucalyptus ciltridora	5,526
Pinus roxburghii	936
Populus casale (488)	2,704

Source: Dabral (1970)

Table 5.14 Evapotranspiration (mm) of Eucalyptus forested catchment near Collie, Western Australia

Year	*Period* +	*ET*	*ET/day*	*EP/day*	*ET/EP*
1974	(1)	360	2.0	6.4	0.31
	(2)	395	3.8	2.4	1.56
1975	(1)	353	1.9	6.6	0.30
	(2)	579	3.2	2.6	1.21
1976	(1)	492	2.7	6.2	0.43
	(2)	455	2.5	2.6	0.97
1977	(1)	335	2.1	6.4	0.33
	(2)	486	2.7	2.5	1.05
1978	(1)	417	2.3	6.3	0.36
	(2)	396	2.2	2.3	0.94
Mean	(1)	401 ± 25		6.4 ± 0.1	0.35 ± 0.02
	(2)	522 ± 52		2.5 ± 0.1	1.15 ± 0.1

+ (1) Oct.-March; (2) Aug.-Sep., EP = Pan evaporation, ET = Actual evpotranspiration; Source: Sharma (1984)

It is therefore, concluded that some kind of subsurface drainage is essentially required to reclaim alkali lands. The integrated drainage consisting of surface and vertical drainage can be more effective and would require less financial investments. It is believed that conventional horizontal drainage may have limited application for alkali lands but would be suitable for areas where groundwater is shallow and saline. Such areas may be found in transition zones i.e. where areas dominated by alkali problems merge with areas dominated by problems of salinity.

REFERENCES

Bouwer. H. and Van Schilfgaarde J. 1963. Simplified method for predicting fall of water table in drained lands. Trans. ASAE 6: 288-96.

Dabral, B.G. 1970. Preliminary observation on potential water requirement in Pinus roxburghii, Escalyptus citridora, Populus casale (488) and Delbergia latifolia. Indian Forestry, 98: 733-8.

Dumm, L.D. 1964. Validity and use of transient flow concept in subsurface drainage. Trans ASAE. 7: 142-6, 151

Gupta, S.K. and Dhruva Narayana, V.V. 1972. Surface drainage methods for saline alkali soils. Proc. Symp. Waterlogging Causes and Measures for Prevention. CBIP, New Delhi, 118 (2): 129-34.

Gupta, S.K. and Pandey, R.N. 1979. Crop and water yield as affected by rain water storage in rice field-a field evaluation. Field Crop Res. 2: 365-71.

Gupta, S.K. and Pandey, R.N. 1983. Effect of depth and time of rain-water storage in the field on the yield of rice during the monsoon. Indian J. Agric. Sci. 53: 8.4-6.

Gupta, S.K. 2000. Reclamation of waterlogged salt affected lands: An overview of various drainage systems. Proc. 8th ICID Int. Drainage Workshop. New Delhi. Vol II: 261-276.

Jaiswal, S. R. and Dhruva Narayana, V.V. 1972. Design of subsurface drainage systems. Proc. Intern. Symp. Develop. of Ground Water Resource Madras. I (II-b): 29-36.

Murthy, R. S., Bhattacharjee, J. C., Lande, R. J. and Pofali, R. M. 1982. Distribution, characteristics and classification of Vetisols. Trans. 12th Int. Cong. Soil Sci., New Delhi. Symp. Pap II. 3-22.

Pandey, R. S. and Gupta, S. K. 1990. Drainage design equation with simultaneous evaporation from soil surface. ICID Bull. 39: 19-25.

Sharma, M. L. 1984. Evapotranspiration from a Eucalyptus community (Wembely, Australia). Agric. Water Mgmt. 18: 41-56.

Verma, S. K. and Sharma, O. P. 1998. Reclamation of sodic Vertisols under rainfed conditions Through rain water conservation practices. Proc. Nat. Symp. Technological Advances in Agric. And Livestoock Production in MP. Jabalpur.

Verma, S. K., Gupta, R. K. and Paradkar, V. K. 1986. Adequate surface drainage boosts sorghum and cotton yield in sodic clay soils. Ind. Farming. 37(1). 13.

Verma, S. K., Paradkar, V. K. and Gupta, R. K. 1987. Effect of method of plantation on yield of cotton in sodic Vertisols. Ind. J. Soil Cons. 14: 36-38.

6

CHEMICAL AMENDMENTS

The chemical amendments are primarily used for the reclamation of alkali soils. These amendments neutralize the pH of the soil, react on the free sodium carbonate, and replace the exchangeable sodium by calcium. The degree of soil alkali (ESP) and the availability of *Kankar* (impure $CaCO_3$) in the soil help to decide the kind of amendment to be applied as well as determine the effectiveness of the chemical amendments.

Chemical Amendments

The chemical amendments may broadly be classified in two categories:

1. Soluble calcium salts, viz. Calcium chloride, Gypsum and phospho-gypsum, and
2. Acidifying materials, viz. Pyrites, sulphuric acid, and industrial wastes (spent wash, dairy waste).

Besides some organic substances could also be used as amendments.

The success of a chemical reclamation programme is linked to the availability of water in adequate quantities, its quality and depth to water table. The quality of surface and/

or ground water should be good and the water table should be below the permissible limits.

The alkali soils have been commonly found to contain *Kankar* ($CaCO_3$ concretions) in sufficient amount in the root zone depth. The solubility of slowly soluble $CaCO_3$ concretions (13.1 mg l^{-1}) could be increased through increase in the concentration of CO_2 and/or lowering the soil pH (Table 6.1). In the presence of CO_2 , $CaCO_3$ is converted into calcium bicarbonate whose solubility varies between 60 and 140 mg 1^{-1}. The calcium from the calcium bicarbonate helps the replacement of the exchangeable sodium from the exchange complex of the soil. Thus, if by any means, CO_2 concentration in the soil could be increased or the pH of the soil could be decreased, the alkali soils of low and medium degree could be reclaimed naturally. Since almost all alkali soils contain $CaCO_3$, there is no point in adding this to the soil for reclamation as an amendment. Efforts are however, needed to increase its solubility. The most practical means of reducing pH and permanently increasing the CO_2 concentration in the soil is to intensify the microbiological process of decomposition of organic substances ploughed into the soil in the form of green or farm yard manure. The application of small amounts of gypsum or other acidifying materials and the conservation of rain water during the monsoon season can also help to speed up the process of the natural reclamation.

Gupta and Abichandani (1970) reported that in highly calcareous alkali soils, the high ESP was reduced from 59.5 to 18.0 and from 34.9 to 11.0 due to leaching alone caused by the rainfall (350 to 450 mm) in Western Rajasthan. The soils had pH_2 values lower than 9.0. In addition to the remarkable changes in ESP, the total concentration and composition of the soluble salts was also changed favourably. EC_e in the top 0-20cm decreased from 11.8 to 2.6 and 22.2 to 2.1 dS m^{-1} in two soils, respectively.

Table 6.1 Solubility of $CaCO_3$ (mg/l) as affected by the CO_2 content and pH of the soil

Content of CO_2 in air (% by volume)	*pH*	*Solubility of $CaCO_3$*
0.00	10.23	13.1
0.03	8.48	63.4
0.30	7.81	133.4
1.00	7.47	202.9
10.00	6.80	470.0
100.00	6.13	1098.6

Source: Kovda *et al.* (1973)

Gypsum is by far, the most common amendment used in the reclamation of alkali soils. In India, this has been used for about one century. Leather (1897) reported for the first time that, the addition of small amounts of gypsum to reduce Na_2CO_3 to 0.1 percent, in the fine size, applied at the surface of alkali soils, was very beneficial.

Pyrites has recently come in use and is becoming an increasingly popular amendment.

Sulphuric acid seems to be the most effective chemical amendment but because of its prohibitive cost and operational difficulties, has not become very popular in India although it is commonly used in U.S.S.R and U.S.A.

Gypsum

There are three main commercial forms of calcium sulphate, viz. (i) anhydrite form, land plaster ($CaSO_4$); (ii) semi-hydrate form, commonly called plaster of Paris ($CaCO_4.1/2 H_2O$); and (iii) di-hydrate form, generally known as gypsum ($CaSO_4.2H_2O$). It is di-hydrate kind of gypsum that is commonly used in agriculture.

Occurrence of gypsum

Gypsum occurs extensively in natural deposits as a white coloured secondary mineral. In India, rich deposits of gypsum are found in Rajasthan. It also occurs in appreciable quantities in Tamil Nadu, Gujarat and Himachal Pradesh. The resources of gypsum in India are estimated to be about 100.4 x 10^7 tonnes, 90 percent of which are located in the mines of Rajasthan only. Besides the gypsum from mines, it is also available as a by-product from some chemical industries manufacturing phosphoric acid, tartaric acid, formic acid, oxalic acid, citric acid and common salt. Major quantities of by-product gypsum, commonly known as phospho-gypsum, are produced during the manufacture of phosphoric acid by wet process in which rock phosphate is treated with sulphuric acid. For every tonne of P_2O_5 produced, 5.5 tonnes of phospho-gypsum containing 25 percent water is produced. More than 10.0 lakh tonnes of by-product gypsum is available from industries manufacturing chemical fertilizers in India.

Quality

Purity

Mines of the Fertilizer Corporation of India Ltd. (FCI) contain three grades of gypsum having different purity levels: (i) Grade I: 85-90% $CaSO_4.2H_2O$, (ii) Grade II: 80-85% $CaSO_4.2H_2O$, and (iii) Grade III: 70-80% $CaSO_4.2H_2O$. The chemical analysis of various grades of gypsum is reported in Table 6.2.

Table 6.2 Chemical analysis of gypsum mined by the FCI

Constituents (%)	*Gypsum grade*		
	I	*II*	*III*
$CaSO_4.2H_2O$	88.67	83.32	77.56
SiO_2	4.84	9.75	12.37
Mixed oxides (R_2O_3)	0.68	0.85	1.59
MgO	1.12	0.88	0.81
CaO	30.59	28.08	28.56
Loss on ignition	21.17	20.40	20.44
Chlorides as NaCl	0.008	0.014	0.016

Bureau of Indian Standards (BIS) specifications

According to the revised specifications as per IS:1290-1965, the mined gypsum is divided in five grades, viz. (i) Grade I for use in surgical plaster industry; (ii) Grade II for ammonium sulphate industry; (iii) Grade III for pottery industry; (iv) Grade IV for cement industry, and (V) Grade V for land reclamation programmes. The specifications for different grades of gypsum are reported in Table 6.3.

The gypsum of grade III mined by the FCI conforms to the ISI specifications for grade V gypsum, suitable for reclamation of alkali soils. The gypsum to be used in the reclamation should not contain more than 1.0% of Na_2O.

Table 6.3 BIS specifications for gypsum of different grades

Constituents	*Gypsum grade*				
	I	*II*	*III*	*IV*	*V*
Free water, maximum	1.0	–	1.0	–	–
CO_2, maximum	1.0	–	3.0	–	–
Silica and insolubles	1.0	0.5	6.5	–	–
Fe_2O_3 and Al_2O_3, maximum	1.0	1.5	1.0	–	–
MgO, maximum	0.5	1.0	1.5	3.0	–
$CaSO_4$, minimum	96.0	86.0	83.8	80-85	70-80
Chlorides (as NaCl) maximum	0.1	0.01	0.01	0.5	–

Solubility

Gypsum is soluble in water to the extent of about 0.25 percent and is, therefore, a direct source of soluble calcium. Obviously, the rate of reaction of gypsum is limited only by its moderate solubility. It has been conventionally recognized that an application of 90 to 120 cm of irrigation water is required to dissolve 10 to 12 t ha^{-1} of high-grade gypsum (Richards *et al.*, 1954). It is true only for normal soils. The solubility of gypsum in alkali soil on the other hand also depends upon pH, ESP and type of salts in the soil. In the case of alkali soil the solubility of gypsum is ten times more (Oster and Halvorson, 1978). It is also reported that the amount of water required to dissolve the added gypsum to reclaim alkali soils does not increase with the amount of gypsum added provided it equals the gypsum requirement (Hira and Singh, 1980).

In the case of mixtures of salts with dissimilar ions, usually found in saline soils, the solubility of gypsum changes when combined with chlorides (Table 6.4). The actual solubility increase is due to the effect of Na^+ and Cl^- in solution so that the concentration of the ions must increase to maintain the constancy of the solubility product.

Table 6.4 Solubility of gypsum in water in the presence of NaCl and $CaCl_2$ (in g per 100g of water)

Chlorides (mmol l^{-1})		*Solubility of $CaSO_4$*
NaCl	0	0.204
	17.2	0.787
	20.2	0.823
	24.4	0.820
	29.3	0.614
	35.8	0.709
$CaCl_2$	0	0.204
	5.2	0.103
	9.9	0.086
	18.9	0.077
	40.8	0.035

Redly *et al.* (1980) studied the solubility of $CaSO_4$ containing chemical amendments, semi-hydrates and mechanically activated anhydrites, in the saturation extracts of alkali soils differing in the concentration and composition of water-soluble salts and the degree of sodium saturation.

The equilibrium concentration of Ca ions in the soil extracts saturated with these materials exceeded 10-50 times the Ca ion concentration in the original solution (Table 6.5). It increased with the increase in the ionic strength in the case of solutions poor in sulphates. On the other hand, the relatively stable Ca ion concentration was found in the studied concentration range with the increasing ionic strength in solutions, where sulphates dominated. The thermodynamic solubility product of $CaSO_4$ calculated from the reduced activates of Ca and SO_4 ions is practically independent of the ionic strength of the solution but it depends on the kind of material, the average being as follows:

Analytical $CaSO_4$ ½ H_2O	3.03×10^{-5}
Fine grained $CaSO_4$	4.23×10^{-5}
Coarse grained $CaSO_4$	4.78×10^{-5}

Table 6.5 The average values of Ca^{++} and SO_4^- concentration (mmol l^{-1}) in the saturation extract of soil profiles

Soil characteristics					
pH	*EC_e (dS m^{-1})*	*ESP*	*Treatments**	*Ca^{++}*	*SO_4^-*
5.9-9.6	3.0-10.7	30-75	0	3.4	84.8
			1	29.8	107.1
			2	32.6	115.7
			3	38.7	119.8
7.4–9.5	0.4-1.8	8-29	0	1.8	5.8
			1	31.4	42.5
			2	36.6	43.5
			3	43.5	49.7
6.6–8.7	1.8–9.9	2–32	0	3.0	44.0
			2	46.7	87.5
			3	48.8	92.4
7.5–8.9	0.9–1.3	3–12	0	1.2	5.2
			2	66.5	74.5
			3	67.3	72.7

*Treatments: 0 = Original soil, 1 = Analytical $CaSO_4$ semi-hydrate
2 = Fine grained $CaSO_4$ 3 = Coarse grained $CaSO_4$

The pH value and the SAR/ESP of the soils are usually lower after saturation with $CaSO_4$. The amount of cations from the dissolution of $CaSO_4$ (given in $CaSO_4$ g/kg soil), resulting in the change of a unit value of ESP (in the range of 5–40) is 0.15 and 0.26 for samples with low and high SO_4^- content, respectively.

The solubility of gypsum increases if it is applied in conjunction with farmyard manure or green manure (Maharudrappa *et al.* 1972). Dargan *et al.* (1976 a,b) also observed that the use of FYM in conjunction with gypsum resulted in higher yield of the first crop of berseem, sugarcane and rice grown in separate fields (Table 6.6). There was a high order of interaction of the combined application of FYM and gypsum.

Table 6.6 Effect of FYM and gypsum on the yield of crops ($t\ ha^{-1}$)

Treatment	*Berseem fodder*	*Sugarcane (Stripped cane)*	*Rice*
Control	0.15	-	2.45
FYM 25 t/ha	0.83	0.49	3.59
FYM 50 t/ha	1.74	0.47	3.74
Gypsum 25% GR	–	14.32	4.23
FYM 25 t/ha + Gypsum 25% GR	–	21.37	5.29
FYM 50 t/ha + Gypsum 25% GR	–	35.77	5.46
Gypsum 50% GR	9.49	28.65	5.70
FYM 25 t/ha + Gypsum 25% GR	29.48	37.46	5.76
FYM 50 t/ha + Gypsum 50% GR	31.89	39.11	6.89
C.D. at p = 0.05	4.77	9.29	0.89
Soil pH_2 at start	10.5	10.6	10.6

Source: Dargan (1979)

Chemical reaction

Gypsum reacts with sodium on the exchange complex as per the following reaction:

$$2\ \text{Na-soil} + 2CaSO_4 \rightarrow \text{Ca-soil} + Na_2SO_4 \quad (6.1)$$

Alkali soil Normal soil

Fineness

Conventionally, gypsum of about 2 mm particle size (10 mesh) has been used for the reclamation of alkali soils (Kovda *et al.*, 1973). According to the ISI specification, the whole of the material must pass through 10 mesh and at least 50 percent of it must pass through 60 mesh (0.25mm) sieve. These standards pertain to 30 mesh fineness. Gypsum is very cheap, as its cost at the mine site is almost negligible. The degree of fineness to which gypsum need to be ground assumes significance since it would determine the cost of gypsum to the farmer and hence the economics of land reclamation. About 15 percent of the total cost of gypsum could be on account of grinding to a fineness of 30 mesh. The cost could be reduced provided we adopt a standard in which gypsum fineness of 10 mesh is used in reclamation programmes.

Quantity of gypsum

The quantity of gypsum that has to be applied obviously depends upon the initial exchangeable sodium content of the soil and the level to which it has to be reduced, presuming that the irrigation water is of good quality. The levels to which the exchangeable sodium content of the soil is to be reduced depends upon the texture of the soil and the first crop to be grown following land reclamation. For example, if the soil is initially fully saturated with the exchangeable sodium (ES = 10 to 15 me/100g, ESP = 95 to 100), it may suffice the purpose to reduce the ESP to about 50 if tolerant crop like rice is to be grown. Likewise, ESP has to be reduced to 30 if semi-tolerant crops like wheat, or to 10 if sensitive crops like gram, are to be cultivated. Similarly, for the same crop, coarse-textured soils can support optimum growth at relatively higher ESP than fine-textured soils. Bhumbla and Abrol (1975) reported that satisfactory yield of rice, wheat and barley can be obtained by adding gypsum @ 50 percent of gypsum requirement as determined in the laboratory by Schoonover's method (Fig. 6.1 and 6.2).

The quantity of gypsum also depends upon the depth of the soil to be reclaimed. It is not practical or even necessary, to remove all of the exchangeable sodium from the entire soil profile by the application of gypsum. A common practice is to apply sufficient gypsum to remove sodium from the top 10-20 cm of the soil. This improves the physical condition of the surface soil quickly and permits the growth of shallow rooted crops. The shallower application of gypsum @ 50% GR (calculated for 0-15 cm soil depth), up to 10 cm depth has been reported to be superior to the application in the 0-30 cm depth (Table 6.7).

Table 6.7 Effect of depth of mixing gypsum on the yield of crops (t ha^{-1})*

Gypsum (t ha^{-1})	*Depth of mixing (cm)*	*Barley 1970-71*	*Rice 1971*	*Wheat 1971-72*
0	10	0.00	5.18	2.04
	20	0.00	5.69	1.77
	30	0.00	4.62	0.93
13.5	10	2.64	7.02	3.28
	20	2.46	6.05	3.16
	30	0.53	5.64	2.06
27.0	10	2.83	6.71	3.67
	20	3.22	6.28	3.67
	30	2.30	5.98	3.53
C.D. at p = 0.5 for Gypsum and depth		0.35	0.73	0.41

* Initial soil pH_2 = 10.5
Source: Khosla *et al.* (1973)

Frequency of application

Single application of gypsum at the rate of 25% GR (6.5 t ha^{-1}), before the first crop of rice, has proved as effective as the higher and repeated doses in subsequent years, in respect of crop yields on a highly alkali soil (Table 6.8). The pH_2 came

Fig. 6.1 Rice crop in a gypsum treated plot

Fig. 6.2 Rice crop in a plot without application of gypsum

down from 10.7 in the first year before the rice crop to 9.5, 8.6 and 8.4 after the wheat crop in the first, second and third year, respectively. It shows therefore, that if reclamation has to proceed with the rice as the first crop, application of gypsum @ 25% GR would be enough, if average yield for 3 or more years is taken as the basis. However, the yields may be low in the first year by applying gypsum at the rate of 25% GR as compared to 50% GR.

Table 6.8 Effect of gypsum doses applied over three years on crop yields (t ha^{-1})

Gypsum (t ha^{-1})			*Grain yield*	
1st year	*2nd year*	*3rd year*	*Rice*	*Wheat*
6.5	–	–	7.01	4.33
6.5	6.5	–	6.40	3.98
6.5	6.5	6.5	7.46	4.16
13.0	–	–	6.64	4.51
13.0	6.5	–	7.04	4.35
13.0	6.5	6.5	7.24	4.50
19.5	–	–	6.92	4.62
19.5	6.5	–	7.31	4.72
19.5	6.5	6.5	6.96	4.57
26.0	–	–	7.20	4.69
26.0	6.5	–	7.24	4.89
26.0	6.5	6.5	7.14	4.17

With continuous use of high quality irrigation water following good irrigation and cropping practices, reclamation in the sub-soil usually proceeds with time because of the following factors:

(i) Almost all alkali soils contain sufficient reserves of *Kankar*

(ii) The irrigation water of high quality, usually available from the canals carrying fresh water contains Ca, eight to ten times higher than Na and this leads to constant replacement of Na with Ca on the exchange complex particularly after the application of gypsum

(iii) The use of nitrogenous fertilizers, particularly $(NH_4)_2SO_4$, is very effective in lowering down the soil pH. This also exerts a marked influence in releasing more calcium from $CaCO_3$

(iv) Consequent upon the start of the process of reclamation through cultivation of crops, the plant roots evolve CO_2 which helps in the conversion of $CaCO_3$ into $Ca(HCO_3)_2$. The solubility of Ca is more in the latter form.

(v) Because of the rainwater being acidic in nature due to its CO_2 content, the natural reclamation of the soil also takes place to some extent.

In view of the foregoing analysis, it can be generalized that in a particular situation small amounts of gypsum (25%GR) can help to initiate the process of reclamation of alkali soils provided

- good quality water is available for irrigation
- the rains are appreciable and effective
- the soils contain sufficient reserves of $CaCO_3$
- adequate amount of nitrogenous fertilizers are used
- rice is grown as the first crop.

The process of reclamation would proceed with time, provided the land is cropped continuously with out leaving it fallow.

Phospho-gypsum

In addition to the mined gypsum, large quantities of by-product gypsum, commonly known as phospho-gypsum are available. The phospho-gypsum is reported to contain about 90 percent $CaSO_4$ and 1 and 2 percent fluorine. The detailed composition of phospho-gypsum as available from different industries is given in Table 6.9.

Table 6.9 Chemical composition of phospho-gypsum

Characteristics	*Albright Morarji and Pandit Ltd., Ambernath*	*FCI, Trombay*	*Coromandel Fertilizer Ltd., Visakhapatnanm*	*FCI, Haldia*	*SPIC, Madras*
Combined water	19.5	20.2	–	–	–
Total P_2O_5	1.0	0.15-1.0	0.8-1.0	–	–
CaO	31.1	30-52	30.8	–	32.0
Mixed oxides	0.9	–	0.45	–	0.5
SIO_2 and other insolubles	1.8	–	4.6	0.7	0.9
F	1.52	–	0.6	0.35	1.1
Na_2O	0.56	–	1.3	–	–
K_2O	0.06	–	–	–	–
Equivalent $CaSO_4 . 2H_2O$	-	95-98	90.2	70.2	–

Source: Rohtagi *et al.* (1977)

Mehta and Yadav (1977) reported that phospho-gypsum is a promising chemical amendment and can be used effectively for the reclamation of alkali soils. Reclaimed lands support good crop stand. Singh *et al.* (1980) conducted detailed studies on the phospho-gypsum and its effect on the soil properties and crop growth. This study discounted the adverse effects of fluorine in the phospho-gypsum and explained that the adverse effects of fluorine are nullified because of the phosphorus contained in this amendment.

Pyrites

Pyrite is a mineral containing iron and sulphur having generally the chemical composition as FeS_2. There are two main commercial grades of pyrites, viz. (i) low grade pyrite shales, which contains 10% sulphur and (ii) high grade pyrites, which contain 40% sulphur.

Occurrence

Pyrites occur extensively in natural deposits as black coloured sediment. In India, rich deposits of pyrites are found in Bihar located in the Vindhya hills at Amjhore in Rohtas district in Jharkhand state. The pyrite bed has a thickness of about 0.6 m and is overlaid by 5-6 m thick pyrites ferrous shales, covering an area of 48 sq km. The resources of pyrites in India are estimated to be 1500 million tonnes (10 percent S) plus 350 million tonnes (40 percent S), available exclusively in Jharkhand.

Quality

Pyrites Phosphates and Chemicals Ltd. are intensively exploring and exploiting the deposit in Amjhore block. As a result, a reserve of 24 million tonnes of 40 percent 'S' grade and 150 million tonnes of 10 percent 'S' grade have been brought under the proved category. In the present method of mining, 0.6 MT of pyrites (40 percent S) and 1 MT of pyrite ferrous shale (10 percent S) are being mined simultaneously. The run-off mine thus obtained contains 22 percent sulphur. As a result of beneficiation, high grade pyrites containing 38-40 percent 'S' are to be supplied to the Fertiliser Corporation of India, Sindri, for the manufacture of sulphuric acid and the residual product is left over as rejects containing about 10-12 percent 'S' (Jaggi, 1978). The low-grade pyrites available for agricultural use contains 22 percent 'S'.

Chemical Composition

The pyrites are highly pyrophoric in nature and immediately react with air and water to form sulphuric acid and iron sulphate. The mineral pyrites occur in various physical forms, viz. crystalline, amorphous and powdery. The powdery form is the most reactive and contains about 22-24 percent sulphur. The pyrite ferrous shale lying on the top of the pyrites bed contains, on an average about 10 percent sulphur. The chemical composition of the pyrites of the two grades is given in Table 6.10. The shale lying below the pyrites bed does not contain any sulphur. Due to pyrophoric nature of the pyrites, the mine water becomes acidic with a pH around 3.

Table 6.10 Chemical composition of pyrites (percent)

Constituent	*Pyrites (powder)*	*Pyrites (shales)*
Sulphur	22-24	11.7
Iron	20-22	11.7
Al_2O_3	6-8	11.3
SiO_2	35-40	46.9
CaO	0.1	4.3
MgO	0.5-0.6	0.9
Cu	0.05	–
Mn	0.01	–
C	–	3.2
Moisture	–	14.7

Chemical Reaction

The low quality pyrites having different percentage of sulphur (15-30 percent) classified as agricultural grade is normally used in the reclamation of alkali soils. Pyrites per se do not react with the soil directly and therefore, its mode of reaction in alkali soils must be clearly distinguished from that of elemental sulphur. The elemental sulphur has to be oxidised to sulphuric acid through sulphur oxidising bacteria like *Thiobacillus thiooxidans*, etc. Sulphur oxidation is therefore, slow in alkali soils. The sulphur present in the pyrites is a highly reduced compound of a higher oxidation state. The rate of reaction depends upon several factors, viz. moisture content, availability of oxygen, temperature and presence of toxic constituents around the granules. The biological oxidation of sulphur in the amendment is carried out mainly by *Thiobacillus ferrooxidans* but only at a specific pH range normally obtainable in rice crop fields (Singh *et al.*, 1978). In buffer suspensions, it has been found that the oxidation of pyrites is maximum at pH 5.0. At a pH 2.5, oxidation is low and at pH 8.0 it is negligible (Venkat Krishnan, 1980).

The oxidation of pyrites starts as soon as the material is mixed, exposed to the air and ground to a finer state. The reaction, even though slow, is wasteful as some of the sulphur may escape to the atmosphere as follows:

$$FeS_2 + 3O_2 \rightarrow FeSO_4 + SO_2 \tag{6.2}$$

The dominant reaction occurs in the presence of water and both the products formed as below directly or indirectly react with the soil.

$$2\,FeS_2 + 7O_2 + 2H_2O \rightarrow 2FeSO_4 + 2H_2SO_4 \tag{6.3}$$

$$CaCO_3 + H_2SO_4 \rightarrow CaSO_4 + CO_2 + H_2O \tag{6.4}$$

$$2\text{ Na–Soil} + CaSO_4 \rightarrow \text{Ca–Soil} + Na_2SO_4 \tag{6.5}$$

It is seen that the immediate effectiveness of pyrites in alkali soils would vary with the date of mining of the material and storage conditions. Singh *et al.* (1978) observed that more than 36 percent of the sulphur is extracted in water in the first two days from the pyrites containing 30 percent sulphur. Later on, the oxidation is slow. This aspect has to be kept in mind while judging the effectiveness of sulphuric acid produced due to the oxidation of pyrites in the reclamation of alkali soils, containing sufficient reserves of $CaCO_3$.

Simple test for quality

As a thumb rule, pyrites to be effective for reclamation must contain at least 5 to 6 percent soluble S at the time of its application in the field. A simple field test to test the pyrite quality is to measure the pH of the pyrite dissolved in water. For this purpose dissolve one-gram pyrite in 100 ml distilled water and check the pH using a pH meter or litmus paper. If the pH is more than 2.5, the pyrite must be stored, moisten by sprinkling water over the bags periodically till its pH decreases to 2.5 or less (Sharma and Swarup, 1990).

Method of Application

Not much information is available as to what is the appropriate method of pyrite application for its optimum efficacy. Singh *et al.* (1978) observed that the surface application of pyrites lowered pH and ESP of the soil to a greater extent as compared with its mixing in the surface 10 cm of the soil. The efficiency of the amendment was lowered when soil water content was decreased from full saturation to one-fourth saturation.

Venkat Krishnan (1979) reported that mixing of the pyrites in the whole soil column was inferior to surface placement. Mixing the surface pyrites with the rest of the soil after 12 and 18 days of surface application performed comparably and resulted in better and more uniform improvement of the soil than retaining the pyrites on the surface unmixed. Mixing of the pyrites after 6 days of application led to very poor improvement. Higher amounts of leachates were collected from column when pyrites was surface placed. Pyrites showed signs of appreciable oxidation forming a rusty coloration after about 15 days.

Guidelines for increasing the pyrite efficiency are as follows:

- The pyrite must be crushed properly before use. Its soluble S content should be more than 5 per cent.
- Apply pyrite only when the field moisture content is near the field capacity.
- To facilitate proper oxidation of pyrite, it should be applied on the moist surface as thinly as possible. Sufficient time should be allowed for it to oxidize on the surface of the soil.
- Water should be kept ponded in the field for 7-15 days to achieve leaching before transplanting the first rice crop.

Since pyrite as such contains free H_2SO_4, gloves and gumboots should be used during its handling and application to avoid the acid injury.

Sulphuric acid

The farmers in the Western States of U.S.A. (California, Arizona etc.), U.S.S.R and Central Asian Countries have been using concentrated sulphuric acid as a means of reclaiming the calcareous alkali soil under irrigated farming.

The reclamation is based upon the following chemical reactions:

$$H_2SO_4 + CaCO_3 \rightarrow CaSO_4 + CO_2 + H_2O \quad (6.6)$$

$$2Na\text{-clay} + CaSO_4 \rightarrow Ca\text{-clay} + Na_2SO_4 \quad (6.7)$$

but if the soil is non-calcareous,

$$2Na\text{-clay} + H_2SO_4 \rightarrow 2H\text{-clay} + Na_2SO_4 \quad (6.8)$$

The sulphuric acid, obviously, react very quickly with alkali soils. Since on equivalent basis, only half of the quantity as that of gypsum is required for use, its cost of transport is much lower than gypsum. The initial cost of the sulphuric acid is apparently very high. If the time taken to reclaim the soil is any criterion then it may not be costlier than gypsum, since expenses only begin to be defrayed when the exploitation period is reached, i.e. when the crops can be cultivated in the area (Kovda *et al.*, 1973). By any standard, sulphuric acid is more efficacious and economical than gypsum in the highly calcareous alkali soils, provided calcium and organic matter are not depleted completely, for the simple reason that after complete reclamation there is no restriction in the choice of crops. Even the most sensitive crops comprising horticulture plants can be established well because the soil profile is reclaimed through a deeper depth, whereas, with gypsum, reclamation is a slow and proceeds only gradually with time through small depths.

Overstreet *et al.* (1951) compared the effectiveness of gypsum, sulphur and sulphuric acid on a highly alkali soil (ESP 60-100). After seven months of experimentation, including leaching of the soils, sulphuric acid reduced soil ESP to 10, more effectively than gypsum.

Large scale reclamation programmes of alkali soils are being executed in Armenia by the application of 1 percent sulphuric acid solution, heavy leaching (1500-30,000 m^3ha^{-1})

sometimes combined with rice cultivation, and extensive deep drainage (horizontal drains combined with tube wells). Since the alkali horizons of these soils are very thick (as much as 60-100 cm), the sulphuric acid is applied layer by layer, with multi-tier ploughs or using a special ripper. The standard application of sulphuric acid is 30 t/ha (expressed as 80 percent acid), and the crop (cotton, fruits and vines) yields for the first two years are sufficient to pay for the reclamation cost.

In the Indian context, where farmers are more dependent upon subsidies, and where adequate machinery for transport and application of H_2SO_4 are yet not available, probably use of sulphuric acid cannot become popular. Gypsum and pyrite would continue to dominate as amendments in land reclamation programmes.

Organic Amendments

Alkali soils are generally deficient in organic matter. Thus, addition of crop residues and other organic materials in the soil could be beneficial as these help to improve and maintain soil structure, supply needed plant nutrients and quicken soil reclamation. Most organic amendments like straw, rice husk (rice hulls), groundnut and safflower hulls, farm yard manure (FYM), compost, poultry dropping, green manure, trees leaves, saw dust etc. on their decomposition produce high partial pressure of CO_2 and organic acids, which help in increasing the electrolyte concentration and lowering the soil pH. Such processes also help to increase the solubility of *kankar* to lower the ESP. Singh (1974) observed that when straw of barley and *Sesbania* was decomposed under aerobic conditions, their efficiency in terms of reduction in ESP and improvement in soil physical properties (Table 6.11) was less as compared to when those were decomposed under saturated (anaerobic) conditions. Thus, to get maximum benefits from organic amendments, it is advisable to maintain continuous ponding during the course of decomposition of the organic matter.

Table 6.11 Effect of organic materials on soil physical properties

Treatment	pH_s	*ESP*	*Modulus of rupture (bars)*	*Hydraulic conductivity, (cm hr^{-1})*	*Na in leachate (meq l^{-1})*
Barley straw aerated	9.1	81.5	12.9	0.03	16.6
Sesbania straw aerated	8.8	68.5	11.8	0.04	26.3
Barley straw saturated	8.4	56.1	11.3	1.72	30.2
Sesbania straw saturated	8.3	47.2	7.5	1.29	43.0
Original soil	9.5	95.0	-	-	-

Source: Singh (1974)

Organic materials together with inorganic amendments are more cost effective, hasten the reclamation process, increase the yield and therefore, their use should be encouraged (Dargan *et al.*, 1976). To be very effective alone, relatively large quantities (20 to 400 t ha^{-1} representing 1/5 to 1/3 of the soil volume) of organic amendments have to be used. If the C:N ratio of these materials is very high, as is the case with saw dust, rice husk and barley straw, then they decompose slowly and may be less effective as compared to Sesbania which has a low C:N ratio. Under these conditions deficiency of N may also occur and needs to be addressed. Under certain situation salinity effects, especially with cow dung slurry, may become limiting factors for their continuous use.

Industrial Wastes (spent wash, dairy waste)

In India, because of the high cost involved and operational difficulties, the use of H_2SO_4 has not become popular for the reclamation of alkali soils. However, acidic waste materials available from some industries are being increasingly used for the purpose at places where these are available. For example, spent wash, a distillery waste, has been found very useful in reclamation. The pH of the spent wash is about 5.0 and contains low Na (10.9 me l^{-1}) and high Ca + Mg (160 me l^{-1}). In addition it contains 1 percent K_2O and 3.7 mg l^{-1} of zinc. Singh *et al.* (1980) reported that the addition of spent wash was very effective in increasing the water intake rate of a highly alkali soil. ESP was reduced from 100 to 2 in the top 15cm of the soil used in the column. Field application of spent wash in Tamil Nadu has yielded encouraging results and is being popularized in the state. The application of spent wash followed by irrigation rather than the dilution of spent wash at the time of its application was very effective. Similarly, the dairy waste available after the testing of milk for its fat content is a very useful material for the reclamation of alkali soils. Shah (1975) used waste sulphuric acid (70 percent strength) in the field and achieved remarkable improvement in the alkali soils.

Comparative Evaluation

Sharma and Gupta (1986) observed that ESP decrease was similar in H_2SO_4 and gypsum treatments (Table 6.12). However, the saturated hydraulic conductivity of the soil was less and the water dispersible clay more in H_2SO_4 treatment. Similarly, the ESP drop and improvement in physical properties was more, when $(Al_2SO_4)_3$ was applied as amendment. This seems due to Ca of the gypsum and Al of $(Al_2SO_4)_3$ respectively, which are more effective flocculent as compared to H and H_2SO_4. Further $(Al_2SO_4)_3$ and $CaSO_4$ are slowly soluble and as a result of this, major part of these is not immobilised due to soluble $NaHCO_3$ and Na_2CO_3 but is effectively used to replace exchangeable sodium.

Electrical Method

Investigation have shown that the treatment with electrical current may stimulate the reclamation of alkali soils, although it cannot replace conventional procedures involving controlled leaching. A remarkable result was obtained by the U.S. Bureau of Reclamation on a field trail in Montana where saline, boggy land that produced no crop for 19 years had been improved to such an extent that a heavy growth of grasses and sweet clover covered the area 50 days later. In this work, after the current had been applied for a short time, the sodium content of the drainage water from the area increased from 1500 mg l^{-1} to 37,000 mg l^{-1}. The expenses for electrical current amounted to 6 dollars per hectare (Kovda *et al.*, 1973). The penetration of the chemical amendment at high densities of the electrical current (0.1 and 0.5 mA cm^{-2}) and complete reclamation of the alkali soil was achieved, the treatment proving to be the most efficacious. The results of these investigations have been used in field experiments also.

Table 6.12 Effect of amendments (applied @ 100% GR) on physico-chemical properties of a sodic Vertisol

Amend-ments	*pH (1:2)*	*EC* (dS m^{-1})	*ESP*	*Saturated hydraulic conductivity* ($mm\ hr^{-1}$)	*Water disper-sible clay (%)*	*Dispersion ratio*
Control	8.8	9.80	65	0.66	37.2	0.41
Gypsum	7.9	0.72	14	4.77	8.0	0.09
Pyrites	8.0	0.31	20	1.64	32.4	0.36
H_2SO_4	7.5	0.18	14	2.98	30.4	0.54
$Al_2(SO_4)_3$	7.6	0.27	8	4.49	8.6	0.09
$FeSO_4$	7.9	0.85	21	1.59	33.7	0.37

Source: Sharma and Gupta (1986)

Vadjunina and El-Sawaby El-Koumi (1972) conducted a laboratory experiment on alkali soil monoliths (15 x 15 x 50cm) to examine the effect of electrical reclamation as compared to gypsum and acid treatment. The following treatments were compared:

(i) Control

(ii) Gypsum @ 30 t ha^{-1}

(iii) H_2SO_4 @ 10 t ha^{-1}

(iv) H_2SO_4 @ 20 t ha^{-1}

(v) Electrical current for 3000 hr 0.01 mA cm^{-2} and 0.10 mA cm^{-2}

(vi) Electrical current for 1000 hr 0.50 mA cm^{-2}

The soils were leached after the above treatments. The changes in the soil pH, ESP and infiltration rate are shown in Table 6.13. The reclamation effect of electric current application at a density of 0.01 $mAcm^{-2}$ was found to be equal to the application of gypsum or H_2SO_4. The remarkable improvements in pH, ESP and the infiltration rate took place at the 0-30 cm soil depth.

Table 6.13 The effect of electrical and other treatments to the soil on pH, ESP and infiltration rate

Treatment	*0–10 cm*		*10-30 cm*		*Average infiltration rate (mm day^{-1})*
	pH	*ESP*	*pH*	*ESP*	
Original soil	10	72.8	10.09	89.9	–
Control	9.74	49.2	9.95	82.6	4.4
Gypsum	8.90	19.2	9.72	62.2	13.0
H_2SO_4 (10 t ha^{-1})	9.46	31.1	9.88	79.3	10.0
H_2SO_4 (20 t ha^{-1})	7.56	2.9	9.11	39.4	13.0
C (0.01 mA cm^{-2})	8.68	10.3	9.85	78.5	14.4
C (0.10 mA cm^{-2})	8.20	1.7	8.26	1.2	57.0
C (0.5 mA cm^{-2})	7.98	1.0	8.09	1.2	86.4

C = Electric current

Table 6.14 Effect of heating on properties of an alkali soil

Treatment	EC_e *(dS m⁻¹)*	*Soluble ions (m mol l⁻¹)*					*CEC*	*ESP*	*B*	*K (cm*
		Na	*Ca+Mg*	CO_3	HCO_3	*Cl*	*(me/100g)*		*(mg l⁻¹)*	*hr⁻¹)*
Control	13.4	108	1.5	54	25	49	8.3	92	9	0.2
75°C for 24 hr	12.0	102	1.5	44	25	45	8.3	91	–	–
100°C for 24 hr	11.5	97	1.5	35	19	45	8.3	92	–	–
200°C for 6 hr	10.4	88	1.5	16	9	45	8.3	91	–	–
400°C for 3 hr	5.8	52	1.5	2	4	35	7.6	68	–	–
500°C for 2 hr	4.8	30	1.5	0	3	35	6.8	37	1	1.0

Thermal Method

Investigation have shown that the heating an alkali soil to a high temperature results in significant reclamation. Gupta and Bandyopadhya (1975) achieved remarkable improvement in the alkali soil, which was heated to high temperature in the muffle furnace. On heating, an alkali soil containing illite, possibly vermiculite, at 500°C for 2 hr, the EC_e dropped from 13.4 to 4.8 dS m^{-1}, ESP reduced from 92 to 37, boron (saturation extract) decreased from 9 to 1 mg l^{-1} and hydraulic conductivity (K) increased from 0.2 to 1.0 cm hr^{-1} (Table 6.14).

The mechanism of the remarkable changes that take place due to heating is related with the clay mineral of the soil. Gupta and Bandyopadhya (1975) explained that on heating at high temperature (400-500°C), part of the sodium ions in the exchange complex of the soil penetrate into the vacant octahedral positions in the dioctahedral lattice of the illite, possibly vermiculite clay mineral. After entering the vacant octahedral positions, the sodium is rendered difficult to exchange or is fixed in a non-exchangeable form. However, the nature of the clay mineral did not undergo any change even after heating up to 500°C and illite possibly vermiculite dominated. The collapse of the interlayer space of the crystal lattice, follows the loss of swelling potential of the soil and increase in hydraulic conductivity from 0.2 to 1.0 cm hr^{-1} is therefore, quite obvious. Further, it seems that part of sodium carbonate is lost due to volatilization. Boron occurs in the organic form as well as inorganic form. Since the organic matter is destroyed beyond 200°C, some decrease in boron is quite probable. Boron may be reduced due to volatilization too.

Preliminary studies on germination and early seeding growth of wheat were further carried out in the saturation extract of original soil and that of one heated at 500°C for 2 hr. Ten seeds were selected for sowing. At the end of four days, the germination percentage was recorded and after 12

Fig. 6.3 Germination and seedling growth in the saturation extract of original alkali and heated alkali soil

Fig. 6.4 Seedling growth of wheat in a *in-situ* heated soil

days, the length of the seedlings was measured. The data presented in Table 6.15 show excellent growth of seedlings in the extract of the two soils (see Fig. 6.3 and 6.4).

Table 6.15 Germination percentage and seedling growth of wheat

Soil	*Germination percentage*	*Length of seedlings (cm)*
Original soil	0.0	–
Heated soil	100.0	14.3

It was further examined whether the type of clay minerals influences the reduction of ESP. It was observed that the illite mineral is more amenable to changes in ESP on heating to a high temperature followed by bentonite. The kaolinite mineral is not affected at all (Table 6.16).

Table 6.16 Effect of heating on ESP of different clay minerals

Clay mineral	*ESP*	
	Original	*After heating at 500°C for 2 hr*
Illite	63.0	24.5
Bentonite	80.1	63.8
Kaolinite	79.6	79.6

Although, experiments have been conducted on a laboratory scale but the results are very encouraging and promising. It is surmised that if a slow moving down draft furnace with its flame directed towards the ground on alkali lands is moved in the field, the soil could be reclaimed instantaneously. Such type of down draft furnace is manufactured in Australia. One such machine was gifted by Australia to the Central Scientific and Industrial Research, CSIR, New Delhi, for heating the black cotton soils around Bhopal and use the resulting hard substance, a kind of clinker, as a sub-base materials for making roads. The machine heats the soil to about 15 cm depth to a temperature of about 700°C. The results could be translated into field practice by the use of this type of machine. Alternatively, the soils could be heated in the field *in situ* by the use of electricity which may however, be prohibitive due to the high cost. Harnessing of solar energy in the near future seems to be more rational to implement this principle in practice.

REFERENCES

Bhumbla D.R.and Abrol I.P. 1975. Effect of application of different levels of gypsum on the yield of rice, wheat and barley grown in a saline soil. Proc. Int. Symp. New Development in the Field of Salt Affected Soils, Cairo, 1972, 537-44.

Dargan, K. S. 1979. Agronomic and cultural practices for crop production in salt-affected soils. Current Agric. 3:1-20.

Dargan, K. S., Gaul, B. L. and Abrol, I. P. 1976a. Effect of gypsum, farmyard manure and method of sowing on the yield of sugarcane in a sodic soil. Indian J. Agronomy. 21: 349-53.

Dargan, K. S., Gaul, B. L., Abrol, I. P. and Bhumbla, D. R. 1976b. Effect of gypsum, farmyard manure and zinc on the yield of berseem, paddy and maize in a highly sodic soil. Indian J. agric. Sci. 46: 335-41.

Gupta I.C. and Abichandani C.T. 1970. Seasonal variations in salt composition of some saline water irrigated soils of western Rajasthan I. Effect of rainfall. J. Indian Soc. Soil. Sci. 18: 428-35.

Gupta I.C. and Bandyopadhya A.K. 1975. Effect of heating in reclamation of a salt affected soil. Proc. Int. Symp. New Development in the Field of salt Affected soils, Cairo, 1972. 525-8.

Hira G.S. and Singh N.T. 1980. Irrigation water requirement for dissolution of gypsum in sodic soil. Soil Sci. Soc. Am. J. 44: 930-3.

Jaggi T.N. 1978. Use of Amjhore pyrites as alkali soil amendment. Proc. Sem. Use of Sedimentary Pyrites in Reclamation of Alkali soils, Lucknow. 37-43.

Khosla, B. K., Dargan, K. S., Abrol, I. P. and Bhumbla, D. R. 1979. Effect of depth of mixing gypsum on soil properties and yield of barley, rice and wheat on a saline sodic soil. Indian J. agric. Sci. 43:1024-31.

Kovda U.A., van den Berg C. and Hagan R.M. (Ed.) 1973. Irrigation, Drainage/Salinty FAO, Rome.

Leather J.W. 1897. Reclamation of reh and usar land. Agric. Ledger 4: 195-253.

Maharudrappa K., Baligar U.C., Prabhakar A.S. and Patil S.V. 1972. Effect of gypsum application with and without FYM to Karl on the yield of jayadhar cotton. Proc. Sem. Drought, Bangalore, 1968. 131-6.

Mehta K.K. and Yadav J.S.P. 1977. Phospho-gypsum for reclamation of alkali soils. Indian Fmg. 27: 6-7.

Oster J.D. and Halvorson A.D. 1978. Saline seep chemistry. In: Dryland Saline Seep Control. 11th Int. Cong Soil Sci. Edorontion, 2.7-2.29.

Overstreet R., Martin J.C. and King H.M. 1951. Gypsum, sulphur and sulphuric acid for reclaiming an alkali soil of the Fresno series. Hilgandia, 21 : 5.

Redly M., Darab K. and Csillag J. 1980. Solubility and ameliorative effect of gypsum in alkali soils. Int. Symp. Salt Affected Soils, Karnal. 313-21.

Richards L.A. (Ed.) 1954. Diagnosis and Improvement of Saline and Alkali Soils. USDA Hbk. 60, 160P.

Shah R.K. 1975. A note on quick and cheap reclamation method for saline-alkali soils using dairy waste sulphuric acid. ARCC Newsletter. 33 : 4-6.

Sharma, O. P. and Gupta, R. K. 1986. Comparative performance of gypsum and pyrites in sodic Vertisols. Indian J. agric. Sci. 56: 423-9.

Sharma, P. and Swarup, A. 1990. Microbial oxidation of pyrites in relation to its efficiency for reclamation of alkali soils. Ann. Rep. 1990-91. CSSRI, Karnal.

Singh, N. T. 1974. Physico-chemical changes in sodic soils incubated at saturation. Pl. Soil. 40:303-11.

Singh, N. T., Brar, G. S. and Singh, B. 1980. The composition of soluble salts in salt-affected soils of the Punjab state. Int. Symp. on Salt-Affected Soils, Karnal. 7-19.

Singh N.T., Hira G.S. and Singh R. 1978. Comparative effect of pyrites and gypsum on physic-chemical properties of a sodic soil. Proc. Sem. Use of Sedimentary Pyrites in Reclamation of Alkali soils, Lucknow. 69-80.

Vadjunina A.F. and El-Swaby El-kouni 1975. Chemical and electrical methods for reclaiming sodic-saline soils. Int. Symp. New Development in the Field of Salt Affected Soils. Cairo. 505-12.

Venkat Krishnan S. 1980. Mineralization of green manure (Sesbania aculeata) nitrogen in sodic and reclaimed soils under flooded conditions. Pl. Soil. 54: 149-52.

Yadav J.S.P. and Sharma B.M. 1981. An appraisal of alkali tolerance of gram (Cicer arietinum) in the field. Agrokeon. Talajt. 29: 456-62.

7

AGRONOMIC AND CULTURAL PRACTICES

Due to adverse soil physical environment, crops on alkali soils require certain special agronomic and cultural practices, which assist in the maintenance of soil health and help in sustaining the productivity of the crops. Adoption of best-suited practices helps to achieve optimum returns from the investment on land reclamation and other inputs. Cultural practices meant for normal lands and good quality water need to be suitably modified at least in first two-three years of land reclamation. Thereafter, normal crop growing practices could be adopted. The practices of immense value are: land preparation, irrigation, tillage, application of manure and fertilizers, seed rate, row to row and plant to plant spacing, date of planting, crop and cropping patterns. Some of these issues have been taken up in the relevant chapters. Few of the practices are included in this chapter.

Application of Manure

The organic manure as a source of humus and plant nutrients to increase the fertility levels of tropical soils has been well recognized. The organic matter content of the alkali soils, in general, is very low. Therefore, soil humus needs to be replenished through periodic additions of organic manure for maintaining soil productivity. A fraction of the plant nutrients removed by the crops can also be replenished through the application of organic manure. Organic manure supplies practically all the elements of plant nutrition, although the proportion of the elements may vary. The proportion of different elements in organic manure depends largely upon the nature, source and extent of the decomposition of the manure. Even when the nature of manure is similar, there could be considerable variations in the content of the micronutrients in the manure (Katyal *et al.* 1979).

Besides source of plant nutrients, organic manure has considerable influence on the physical and biological properties of the soils. The immediate physical effects are less marked, although improvements in aeration and infiltration of water in alkali soils are observed even in the short-term. Increased crop growth, resulting from application of manure, tends to promote aggregation and aids in retaining a good physical condition by protecting the soil against crust formation due to the beating action of rains.

Addition of organic manure counteracts the unfavorable effect of exchangeable sodium. The decomposition of manure liberates carbon dioxide and organic acids, which help to dissolve insoluble calcium salts in the solution and neutralize the exchangeable sodium.

In recent years, the concept of integrated nutrient management involving organic and inorganic fertilisers has become popular to meet the growing need of plant nutrient for high-yielding varieties under intensive agriculture. Therefore, regular application of organic manure is a sound practice for maintaining the soil fertility. Organic manures, which are frequently used in alkali soils, are farmyard manure and green manure. Besides these some organic materials such as molasses, press mud, rice straw and other crop residues are also used.

Farmyard Manure

It is the traditional and most commonly used organic manure by the farmers. It consists of a mixture of cattle dung, the bedding used in the animal house and of any remnants of straw and plant stalks fed to cattle. On an average, a well-rotten farm yard manure contains 0.5% N, 0.2% P_2O_5 and 0.5% K_2O. The quantities of different nutrients added through FYM, are not fully available to the crops in the year of application. Nitrogen is very slow acting and less than 30 percent of it is generally available to the crop grown following the application (Gaur *et al.*, 1984).

Farmyard manure has been successfully tried in alkali soils. At the Nissang experimental farm, application of 24 t ha^{-1} of farm yard manure to highly alkali soil doubled the yield of rice (Uppal, 1955). The experiment conducted at Karnal has shown that a combined application of gypsum and farm yard manure on a highly alkali soil resulted in much higher yield of rice grain and berseem green fodder than the application of gypsum or farm yard manure alone (Bhumbla, 1972; Dargan 1979) (Table 7.1).

The method of application of farm yard manure in our country is defective. Most of the farmers unload farm yard manure in small heaps in the field and leave it as such for a month or so before it is spread and subsequently ploughed in the field. Plant nutrients are lost considerably during the exposure of the manure to sun and rains. In summer, it results in rapid drying and considerable loss of nitrogen. To derive maximum benefit, the farmyard manure, immediately on being carted to the field, should be spread and mixed into the soil.

Green Manure

Green manuring is the practice of growing a suitable crop, generally a legume, and turned into the soil while green, at the appropriate time, for improving its productivity. The practice of green manuring was widely prevalent in India. However, the emphasis on it decreased after the sixties due to introduction of intensive farming system and with easy availability of chemical fertilisers. With the energy crisis of the mid seventies, green manuring has again become popular, mainly due to the limited supply of other organic matter sources and the high cost of chemical fertilisers. Green manure crop supplies readily decomposable organic matter as well as additional nitrogen. In alkali soil, green manuring is extremely important not only for supplying the nutrients to crop but also for buffering action of soil, and for improving the physical condition.

Table 7.1. Effect of farm yard manure (FYM) and gypsum on the yield of crops (t/ha)

Treatment	*Berseem fodder*	*Rice*	*Sugarcane stripped cane*
Control	0.15	2.45	–
FYM 25 t ha^{-1}	0.83	3.59	0.49
FYM 50 t ha^{-1}	1.74	3.74	0.47
Gypsum 25% GR	–	4.23	14.32
FYM 25 t ha^{-1} + Gypsum 25% GR	–	5.29	21.37
FYM 50 t ha^{-1} + Gypsum 25% GR	–	5.46	35.77
Gypsum 50% GR	9.49	5.70	28.65
FYM 25 t ha^{-1} + 50% GR	29.48	5.76	37.46
FYM 50 t ha^{-1} + 50% GR	31.89	6.89	39.11
CD at p = 0.05	4.77	0.89	9.29
Soil pH_2 at start	10.5	10.6	10.6

Source: Dargan (1979)

The crops most commonly used for manuring are: *dhaincha* (*Sesbania aculeata*), cluster-bean (*cyamopsis terragonoloba*), cowpea (*Vigna sinesis*), sunnhemp (*Crotalaria juncea*) and guar (*Cyamopsis psoraloides*). Among the above green manuring crops, dhaincha has been found to be the most beneficial. Uppal (1955) reported that out of three green manures tried, viz. *dhaincha*, sunnhemp and guar, dhaincha was found to be the most useful. Dhawan *et al.* (1958) found that dhaincha green manure crop, in addition contained the highest amount of calcium, having 34.2

percent of CaO on ash basis. The *dhaincha* when transplanted could withstand pH_2 above 9.5. Although, it contains lesser nitrogen than guar but because of its high yield potential, it is preferred on the basis of its overall total nitrogen content. In a barren alkali soil (pH_2 10.6), amended with gypsum @ 7.5 t ha^{-1}, dhaincha gave a fresh biomass of 16 t ha^{-1} (Rao, 1985). The plant has in general, a vigorous growth habit and in partially reclaimed alkali soil 20-24 t ha^{-1} fresh biomass is obtained in 45 days with the plant reaching 1.2 m in height. The plants nodulate vigorously in almost all types of soils including highly alkali soils. *Dhainxha* contains 0.7% N, 0.1% P_2O_5 and 0.6% K_2O on moist basis (Dargan *et al.*, 1982).

The sap of *dhaincha* leaves has a pH value of 4.0, and being strongly acidic, it exerts a marked influence in neutralising the high pH of the alkali soils. Because of actively fixing nitrogen in its root nodules, *dhaincha* also reduces the leaching losses of mineral nitrogen because of its vigorous root system. Through its deep roots, *dhaincha* mobilises phosphorus, potassium and other trace elements likely to be deficient in surface layers. The decomposition of organic matter liberates carbon dioxide leading to a lowering of soil pH and solubilisation of calcium, phosphorus, potassium and other trace elements. Apart from its alkali tolerance, this plant can withstand moderate salinity and waterlogged conditions.

There appears to be no need to allow extended periods for the decomposition of the green matter in case of *dhaincha*. Bhardwaj *et al.* (1977) have indicated that during green manuring of *dhaincha* for rice in alkali soils, rice could be transplanted immediately after the incorporation of green manure. Being succulent, having a low C:N ratio, it decomposes easily and quickly. The standing water in rice field hastens the decay without any harm to the rice crop. A growth period of about 45 days and no decomposition period between incorporation and transplanting resulted in better yield as well as saving in the time period of cultivation. Longer growth period renders the plant hardy and difficult to decompose, whereas allowing time for decomposition of a succulent 45-

days old *dhaincha* green matter results in greater losses of nitrogen through volatilisation and less nitrogen recovery by the rice crop (Table 7.2).

Green manuring with *dhaincha* contributes about 80 kg nitrogen to rice crop (Fig. 7.1). Depending upon the soil and rice variety, green manuring with *dhaincha* has been found to increase yields by 30 to 60% over control i.e. no N application (Rao, 1985). These results show green manuring with *dhaincha* is beneficial in alkali soils since it not only increases rice yield

Table 7.2. Effect of age and period of decomposition of *dhaincha* on rice yield

Age of dhaincha (days)	*Period of decomposition (days)*	*% N in the rice plant 25 days after transplanting*	*Rice grain yield ($t\ ha^{-1}$)*
45	0	2.73	5.93
45	10	2.09	5.69
45	20	1.99	4.39

Source: Dargan *et al.* (1982)

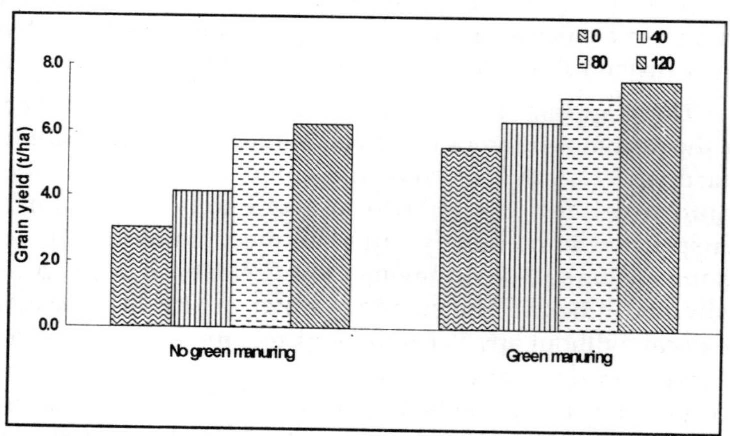

Fig. 7.1 Nitrogen contribution through green manuring ($kg\ ha^{-1}$) with *dhaincha* to rice crop

but also saves almost half the dose of nitrogen. The cost of growing the green manure crop (*dhaincha*), availability of irrigation water during summer months and other economic constraints generally influence the decision of a farmer for including a green manure crop in the crop rotation.

Nutrient Requirement

Alkali soils are generally considered poor in their nutrient supplying capacity. Low organic matter content, poor air-water relationships and high soil pH influence the transformation and availability of applied and native nutrients in alkali soils. Therefore, nutritional requirement for crop production in alkali soils is different from normal soils. Alkali soils have very low status of nitrogen and zinc but they have good reserve of phosphorus and potash. The analysis of barren alkali soils for N, P, K and Zn may not be very helpful in deciding the fertiliser requirements since following the application of amendments and leaching during reclamation the nutrient status of the soil might change. Therefore, soil should be analysed for available nutrients just after the application of amendments and leaching and prior to planting, so that the fertilisers may be applied judiciously. For the efficient use of fertilisers, points of primary concern are: (i) nutrient requirement of the crop, (ii) amount of nutrient available, (iii) chemical form of the applied nutrient, (iv) placement of nutrient in the soil and (v) time of nutrient application. For example, the fertilisers that supply P and K are generally applied at planting or sowing stage while N may be applied in three or more splits at different growth stages.

Nitrogen

Nitrogen is the most deficient and essentially needed plant nutrient in alkali soils. A number of field studies have shown that crops grown in alkali soils respond to higher level of applied nitrogen as compared to crops grown in normal soils. Moreover, the conditions for nitrogen losses through volatilisation and denitrification are ideal in alkali soils because of their high pH and poor physical condition. For this reason, the management of nitrogen in these soils for crop production is of prime importance.

Dose and source of nitrogen

The experiment conducted for two years on rice and wheat crops in alkali soils (Nitant and Dargan, 1974; Dargan, 1979) indicated that during the initial years of reclamation, ammonium sulphate was the best source of nitrogen for both rice and wheat crops. Next in the order of merit being, urea in rice and calcium ammonium nitrate in wheat crop. The optimum dose was found to be 150 kg N ha^{-1} for both the crops (Table 7.3). Therefore, it is obvious that crops grown in alkali soils, be fertilised with 20-25 percent more nitrogen than the recommended rates for normal soils i.e 120 kg N ha^{-1}.

The farmers prefer the application and use of urea because it is cheap as it costs less per unit nitrogen than ammonium sulphate. Moreover it is easily available. The results of studies conducted in a barren alkali soils on rice and wheat crops (Singh *et al.*, 1984 b; Singh and Sharma, 1984 a,b) showed that urea and ammonium sulphate were equally efficient as source of nitrogen for rice and wheat crops (Table 7.4). These studies revealed that urea and ammonium sulphate behave similarly when gypsum is applied as an amendment in required quantity. Ammonium sulphate would give better results in those situations where gypsum is not added in required amounts since in such a case sulphur present in the ammonium sulphate acts as a reclamative agent.

Table 7.3. Effect of doses of nitrogen on yield of rice and wheat crops (t ha^{-1})

Dose of nitrogen (kg ha^{-1})	*Rice*		*Wheat*	
	1971	*1972*	*1971-72*	*1972-73*
60	3.23	3.32	1.47	1.96
90	3.65	3.93	1.79	3.08
120	4.44	4.58	2.14	3.47
150	5.07	5.52	2.65	4.06
180	4.99	6.00	2.61	4.10
CD at p = 0.05	0.55	0.53	0.40	0.26

Table 7.4. Effect of source of nitrogen application on the grain yield of rice and wheat (t ha^{-1}) in a alkali soil

Source	*Rice*		*Wheat*	
	1981	*1982*	*1981-82*	*1982-83*
Urea	5.84	5.53	3.76	3.69
Ammonium Sulphate	5.69	5.53	3.69	3.99
CD at p = 0.05	ns	ns	ns	ns

Nitrogen fertilizer should be applied in split doses to reduce nitrogen losses through volatilization and denitrification. In earlier studies (Dargan, 1979) it was recommended that 50% nitrogen should be applied as a basal dose and remaining half in two equal splits after 3 and 6 weeks of transplantation in case of rice and wheat. Application of 50 percent nitrogen as a basal dose seemed to be on the higher side because higher dose promotes more losses of nitrogen. Nitrogen use efficiency of wheat and rice can be improved by slight modification in the time and method of application. For high nitrogen use efficiency in rice, one third nitrogen should be applied at transplanting, one-third at 3 weeks and remaining at 6 weeks after transplantation. In wheat, one-third nitrogen should be applied as a basal dose, one third at the time of first irrigation and remaining at second irrigation. Field studies (Singh *et al.*, 1984; Singh and Sharma, 1984) showed that application of nitrogen in four splits i.e. one-fourth basal and ¼ each at first, second and third irrigation to wheat-crop, proved superior to other methods of application (Table 7.5). Nitrogen application should not be missed at the time of sowing/transplanting and at panicle initiation stages.

Some saving in nitrogen can be effected if some of the nitrogen is applied as foliar spray rather than through soil application. Foliar application of urea @ 20 kg N ha^{-1}in two sprays, i.e. 10 kg N ha^{-1}at a time, was superior to even 60 kg N ha^{-1}through soil in case of rice crop, while in wheat crop, foliar application at 20 kg N $ha^{-1}$was better than 40 kg N ha^{-1}given through the soil (Dargan *et al.*, 1973, 1975). Under limited availability of nitrogen, i.e. 40 kg N ha^{-1}, whole of it should preferably be top-dressed at tillering stage.

Phosphorus and Potassium

Alkali soils contain very high amount of Olsen's extractable phosphorus (up to 67 mgl^{-1} P). A significant fraction of this is leached to lower depths following the application of amendments and ponding of water. Owing to high amount of extractable P, alkali soils do not respond to application of phosphatic fertilisers in the initial years of reclamation. Similarly, crops also do not respond to applied potassium because sufficient amount of K is released from the soil minerals. Dargan and Chhillar (1978) reported that rice and wheat grown in a sequence on a semi-reclaimed alkali soil did not respond to applied P and K over a period of three years. Chhabra (1983) further observed that in alkali soils, rice and wheat, grown in a sequence do not respond to application of phosphatic fertilisers for the initial 4 to 6 years and wheat for another 3 years.

However, in a 20 years field study (1974 to 1994) conducted on a gypsum amended alkali soil (pH_2 9.2 and ESP 32), Singh and Swarup (2000) reported that phosphorus applied at a rate of 22 kg P ha^{-1} to either or both rice and wheat in rotation significantly improved yields of rice and wheat from

Table 7.5. Effect of method of nitrogen application on grain yield of rice and wheat (t ha^{-1})

Method of application	Wheat	Rice		Wheat	
		1981	1982	1981-82	1982-83
$0B - \frac{1}{2} 5D - \frac{1}{4} 20D + \frac{1}{4} 40D$	$0B + \frac{1}{2} I_1 + \frac{1}{4} I_2 + \frac{1}{4} I_3$	5.45	5.46	3.95	3.74
$\frac{1}{4} B - \frac{1}{4} 20D + \frac{1}{4} 40D + \frac{1}{4} 60D$	$\frac{1}{4} B + \frac{1}{4} I_1 + \frac{1}{4} I_2 + \frac{1}{4} I_3$	6.62	6.22	4.09	4.76
$\frac{1}{3} B + \frac{1}{3} 20D + \frac{1}{3} 40D$	$\frac{1}{2} B + \frac{1}{4} I_1 + \frac{1}{4} I_2$	5.69	5.59	3.05	3.93
$\frac{1}{2} B + \frac{1}{4} 20D + \frac{1}{4} 40D$	$\frac{1}{2} B + \frac{1}{4} I_1 + \frac{1}{4} I_2$	5.91	5.36	3.72	3.93
CD at $p = 0.05$		0.22	0.31	ns	0.29

* B = Basal, D = Days after, I_1, I_2 and I_3 first, second and third irrigation etc.

1979 and 1985/86 onwards respectively (Table 7.6). Potassium applied at a rate of 42 kg ha^{-1} to either or both the crops had no effect on the yields.

Continuous cropping for 20 years reduced available N from initial level of 225 kg ha^{-1} to 103 kg ha^{-1} in unfertilized plots. However, continuous use of fertilizer N alone or in combination with P and K either maintained or slightly increased available N with final values ranging from 235 to 245 kg ha^{-1} (Table 7.7). With regular P application to crops in sequence, the available P increased from initial value of 33.6 kg ha^{-1} to 58 kg ha^{-1} in NP-NP and 57.6 kg ha^{-1} in NPK–NPK, in 0-15 cm soil depth. Where N alone was applied, available P declined progressively to 4.0 kg ha^{-1} from the initial value of 33.6 kg ha^{-1} . Continuous cropping for 20 years did not deplete available K in soil to a level where either rice or wheat or both could suffer k deficiency (Table 7.7).

Table 7.6. Effect of continuous cropping and fertilizers use on grain yield (t/ha) of rice (rough) and wheat in a sodic soil at Karnal

Treatment			*Rice*			*Wheat*	
Rice	*Wheat*	*1974*	*1985*	*1994*	*1974/75*	*1985/86*	*1994/95*
Control	Control	3.18	3.17	2.63	0.84	0.78	1.26
N	N	6.64	4.73	4.45	4.11	4.00	3.10
NP	NP	6.56	6.92	5.54	3.71	4.73	4.33
NP	N	6.63	6.97	5.62	4.14	4.62	3.98
N	NP	7.17	6.47	4.96	3.90	4.89	4.04
NPK	NPK	7.08	6.97	5.46	4.05	4.58	4.41
NPK	N	6.45	6.88	5.27	4.02	4.32	3.96
N	NPK	6.85	6.45	4.96	4.14	4.28	4.14
LSD (p=0.05)		0.96	0.55	0.65	0.82	0.36	0.45

Nitrogen (N). Phosphorus (P) and Potassium (K) applied at 120 kg N ha^{-1}, 22 kg P ha^{-1} and 42 kg K ha^{-1}

Source: Singh and Swarup (2000)

Table 7.7 Effect of continuous cropping and fertilizer use on available nutrients in the surface soil during 1994 at Karnal

Treatments		*Available nutrients (kg ha⁻¹)*		
Rice	*Wheat*	*N*	*P*	*K*
Control	Control	103	9.8	213
N	N	235	4.0	193
NP	NP	243	58.0	198
NP	N	240	15.6	193
N	NP	240	16.9	203
NPK	NPK	245	57.6	560
NPK	N	240	15.2	476
N	NPK	237	15.8	483
CD (P=0.05)		13	5.4	19
Initial values in 1974		275	33.6	358

N, P and K applied at 120 kg N, 22 kg P and 42 kg K ha^{-1}
Source: Singh and Swarup (2000)

Swarup (2000) further reported that response of applied P to rice was observed when Olsen's extractable P in the 0-15 cm soil depth had come down from the initial level of 33.6 kg ha^{-1} to 12 kg ha^{-1} which is very close to widely used critical soil test value of 11.2 kg ha^{-1}. Wheat responded to applied P when available P came down close to 8.7 kg ha^{-1} in 0-15 cm soil depth and nearly close to critical level (11.2 kg ha^{-1}) in the lower depth (15-30 cm). Chhabra (1985) also reported that in any individual year (1976-81), the yield of rice and wheat was not affected by the application of P and K. However, over a period of 6 years, the mean yield of rice in control plots was lower than the yield in the fertilised plots. Obviously, in recently reclaimed alkali soils, rice and wheat may be grown without P and K application for few years.

Zinc

Among the micro-nutrients, zinc is an important element for crop production in alkali soils, as these soils in their native state do not contain sufficient available zinc for optimum crop yield. High pH and presence of sodium carbonate decreases the solubility of zinc and cause medium to severe zinc deficiency in plants. Therefore, besides the addition of amendment and nitrogen, application of Zn is important for optimum crop yield in alkali soils (Kanwar and Randhawa, 1974). Response to zinc application differs widely among crops. The response also depends upon the degree of alkalinity. When alkali soils are amended with recommended gypsum doses (12 to 15 t ha^{-1}), application of zinc significantly increases the crop yield as compared to the application of gypsum alone (Swarup, 1991). An annual application of 20 kg $ZnSO_4$ ha^{-1} to both rice and wheat significantly increased the grain yield of rice by about 1.0 t ha^{-1} and that of wheat 0.5 to 0.8 t ha^{-1} over zinc control treatment (Table 7.8). Continuous application of 20 to 120 kg $ZnSO_4$ ha^{-1} did not increase the yield significantly over 10 kg $ZnSO_4$ ha^{-1}.

Among the various sources, zinc sulphate is the most common and widely used source for ameliorating zinc deficiency in the soils and plants. Besides, zinc phosphate, zinc oxide, zinc carbonate and zinc chelates have also been used. Soil application of zinc is better than other methods such as foliar spray, dipping of seedling roots in zinc oxide suspension, seed treatment etc. (Singh, 1985). Basal application of zinc at an early growth stage, mostly at the transplanting stage of rice and sowing of other crops, is more beneficial. In wheat, zinc may be applied up to 30 days of growth without substantial reduction in the yield but application of zinc after 50 days of sowing results in a significant reduction in the yield. When the basal application of zinc is missed or if zinc deficiency appears, top dressing of 25 to 30 kg ha^{-1} $ZnSO_4$ three to four times makes up the deficiency effectively.

Other Micro-nutrients

Next to zinc, iron and manganese are the other important micro-nutrients in alkali soils. It is not the total but available

Table 7.8. Effect of zinc level and application frequency on the grain yield of rice and wheat (t ha^{-1})

Zinc sulphate (kg/ha)	Rice First	Rice Second		Rice Third		Wheat First		Wheat Second		Wheat Third	
	S	S	C	S	C	S	C	S	C	S	C
0	5.06	4.95	5.06	6.49	6.56	1.09	1.15	1.36	1.40	1.99	2.02
10	6.01	5.67	6.14	6.87	7.54	1.34	1.64	1.73	2.22	2.14	2.84
20	6.04	5.91	5.82	7.08	7.70	1.75	1.69	1.87	2.42	2.43	2.93
40	6.00	5.89	5.93	7.53	7.54	1.66	1.56	2.19	2.25	2.46	3.12
80	6.07	5.89	5.72	7.54	7.58	1.55	1.66	2.32	2.29	2.94	3.10
120	6.97	6.11	5.87	7.62	7.52	1.59	1.63	2.22	2.42	3.08	3.03
CD (p = 0.05)											
Zinc	0.61		0.62		0.64		0.36		0.60		0.32
Frequency			ns		ns		ns		ns		0.23
Interaction			ns		ns		ns		ns		0.55

S = Single application of zinc to rice crop, C = Continuous application of zinc to each crop
Source: Singh and Abrol (1986)

iron, which is the limiting factor, because of high pH and $CaCO_3$ content. Iron deficiency has often been noticed in rice seedlings grown on raised seed beds in calcareous alkali soils (Takkar and Randhawa, 1978). Yadav and Kalra (1964) reported that highly calcareous, sandy and alkali soils under forest, contained smaller amounts of exchangeable Mn. Swarup (1979) reported that on submergence, the exchangeable Mn increased and under moist conditions it was converted into easily reducible Mn. Addition of iron or manganese salts to correct their deficiency may not be useful unless it is accompanied by prolonged submergence and addition of organic matter. Swarup (1984), reported that iron and manganese application did not affect the yield of rice and wheat crop but in combination with zinc the highest yield of rice was recorded (Table 7.9). Farmyard manure and zinc significantly enhances the rice and wheat yield.

Integrated Nutrient Management

Long-term fertility management experiments have revealed that disproportionate continuous application of chemical fertilizers has lowered the fertility status of the soils. As a result crop yields have stabilized or even declined over the years. Evidences also exist to show that application of farmyard manure and/or green manure helped to build-up nitrogen in the soil and over the years it has increased the yield of crops. Experiments in gypsum amended sodic soils have revealed that 110 kg nitrogen and 11 kg of phosphorus is made available if 50 days old *dhaincha* crop is turned into the soil. As a result, rice and wheat yield increased by 1.48 and 0.67 t ha^{-1} respectively (Swarup, 1991). Besides farmyard and green manure increased organic carbon and also increased the availability of plant nutrients. Integrated nutrient management consisting of a good blend of organic and chemical fertilizers can help to sustain crop production in reclaimed lands. It could also help to meet a part of the zinc requirement of the crops.

Table 7.9. Effect of micronutrients and farmyard manure on the grain yield of rice and wheat (t ha^{-1})

Treatment mg kg^{-1}	*FYM (t ha^{-1})*	*Rice*		*Wheat*	
		1983	*1984*	*1982-83*	*1983-84*
Control	0	3.92	5.28	2.10	2.01
	10	4.18	5.43	2.25	2.20
Fe 20	0	3.95	5.30	1.95	1.98
	10	4.25	5.50	2.15	2.25
Mn 20	0	3.99	5.35	2.10	2.10
	10	4.27	5.58	2.35	2.28
Zn 5	0	4.15	5.48	2.25	2.22
	10	4.46	5.68	2.40	2.39
Fe + Mn + Zn	0	4.35	5.57	2.18	2.28
	10	4.66	6.07	2.35	2.42
CD (p = 0.05)					
Micro-nutrient		0.21	0.20	0.14	0.15
FYM		0.26	0.23	0.15	0.17

Source: Swarup (1991)

An experiment to find out the beneficial effects of integrated nutrient management in terms of increased yield and/or fertility status of the soil has been conducted at the Institute research farm. The results revealed that yield level was higher when organic manure in the form of farmyard manure (FM) or green manure (GM) was mixed in the soil at half the rate of the chemical fertilizers (N60 P 13 and K 21 per ha). Maximum yield of the crop was obtained when organic manure was applied with N120 P 26 and K42 through chemical fertilizers (Table 7.10). The yield was equal to the yield obtained with N180 P39 and K36 applied solely through chemical fertilizers (Table 7.10). Similar statement can be made regarding organic carbon and available phosphorus in the soil.

Cultural Practices

Due to poor physical properties of alkali soils and their leaching requirement, crop production on alkali soils requires special cultural practices at least in the initial years of reclamation. The adverse effects can be minimised by avoiding puddling, adoption of special planting techniques, increasing the seed rate, resorting to close spacing, increasing the number of seedlings per hill, selection of seedlings of optimum age and time of transplanting and treatment of seeds/seedlings etc.

Table 7.10. Effect on yield and soil fertility status with integrated nutrient management in rice-wheat system

Treatment nutrients	*Yield (t ha^{-1})*		*Organic carbon (g kg^{-1})*	*Available (g kg^{-1})*		
	Rice	*Wheat*		*Phos-phorus*	*Potash*	*Zinc*
Control	3.25	1.36	3.0	9.8	205	0.75
N120	4.67	3.25	3.1	8.2	198	0.74
N120 P26	5.46	4.99	3.1	13.6	210	0.75
N120 P26 K42	5.54	5.07	3.2	14.0	240	0.76
N60 P13 K21	4.70	3.37	3.0	11.2	220	0.74
N60 P13 K21 + GM	5.56	3.62	3.2	15.8	250	0.85
N120 P26 K42 + GM	6.52	5.29	3.4	18.5	258	0.86
N60 P13 K21+ FM	5.09	3.63	3.5	16.0	246	0.87
N120 P26 K42 + FM	5.94	5.13	3.6	19.0	252	0.89
N180 P39 P63	6.01	4.96	3.2	19.8	250	0.74
CD	0.55	0.48	0.3	2.4	10	0.11

Source: Swarup (2000)

Puddling

Puddling is a common cultural practice on normal soils before rice transplanting. It acts as a mean to control deep percolation losses, minimises weed infestation and creates conditions conducive to proper transplanting of rice seedlings. In alkali soils, since the infiltration rate in the initial years is low and weed problem is also not very acute, the benefits of puddling needs investigation. Dargan (1979) reported that puddling in alkali soil reduced the rice yield by about 42 percent compared to no-puddling in the first year of reclamation. Since, leaching is beneficial in the reclamation process, puddling in the initial years might adversely affect the leaching of salts. Puddling should be adopted after 2-3 years of land reclamation when weed problem begins to appear (Singh *et al.*, 1982).

Hoeing

The alkali soils are highly dispersible and prone to spontaneous slaking and crust formation after irrigation or rain. In the initial years of reclamation, after each irrigation to wheat, a seal is formed on the soil surface. Upon drying, this surface seal becomes very hard and puts pressure on the young seedling by wrapping their delicate stems. This hard layer restricts the entry cf water and disrupts the normal exchange of gases between the soil atmosphere around the root zone and free atmosphere.

In a field study, hoeing after first and second irrigation significantly increased plant height, shoot and root dry weight, tillers, straw and grain yield of wheat (Table 7.11). one and two hoeings resulted in 17.4 and 28.3 per cent increase in grain yield of wheat, respectively (Sharma, 1988). Therefore, in the initial years of reclamation, the hard surface layer, formed after first and second irrigation should be broken by hoeing.

Table 7.11. Effect of hoeing on yield and yield components of wheat

Number of hoeing	*Plant height (cm)*	*Shoot dry weight (g m^{-1} row)*	*Root dry weight (mg $core^{-1}$)*	*Number of tillers m^{-1} row*	*Yield (t ha^{-1})*	
					Straw	*Grain*
0	83.3	125.0	385	88	4.44	3.10
1	90.3	150.2	500	102	5.17	3.64
2	93.0	165.5	675	111	5.85	3.98
CD (p=0.05)	2.5	13.7	–	5	0.56	0.42

Source: Sharma (1988)

Number of Seedling and Plant Population

Alkali soils need a higher seed rate to maintain higher density of plant population as a safeguard against some mortality and poor tillering in the initial years of reclamation. In order to have a higher plant population, rice should be transplanted at a closer spacing. Besides more number of plants be transplanted per hill. Therefore, higher seed rate for raising rice nursery is recommended. Similarly, for a good crop of wheat, higher seed rate is recommended to ensure adequate plant population in view of less tillering. A consensus is new emerging that seed rate in the initial years of reclamation be 25% higher than the seed rate recommended for the normal soils. Dargan (1979) reported that grain yield of rice increased with the increase in number of plants/hills (Fig. 7.2). In the initial years of reclamation at least 4 to 6 seedlings per hill should be transplanted. After taking 2-3 rice crops, the number of seedlings may be reduced to 2-3 per hill. Rice should be transplanted at a spacing of 15cm row to row and between plant to plant. The rice variety, CSR–1 transplanted at a spacing of 15 x 15 cm resulting in higher yield than other spacing (Singh, 1988) (Table 7.12).

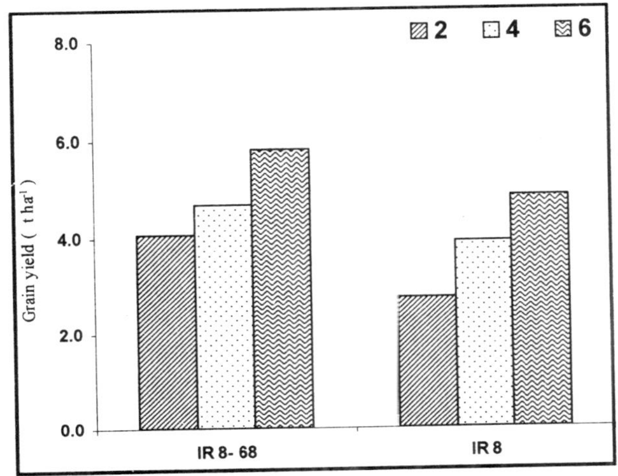

Fig. 7.2 Grain yield of two rice varieties as affected by number of seedlings

Table 7.12. Effect of spacing on the yield of rice (CSR 1) in a alkali soil

Spacing (cm)	*Grain yield (t ha^{-1})*	
	1983	*1984*
15 x 10	3.24	2.97
15 x 15	4.02	3.50
20 x 10	3.75	3.36
20 x 15	3.35	2.97
CD at 0 = 0.05	0.39	0.35

Initial pH_2 9.8, Source: Singh (1988)

Age of Seedling and Date of Transplanting

The young seedlings of rice are relatively more sensitive to alkali conditions. Somewhat older seedlings are, therefore, preferred for transplanting. In a field study, 35-40 days old seedlings gave significantly higher yield compared to young seedling (Dargan and Gaul, 1974) (Table 7.13). For better yields, more than 40 days old seedlings should be used under conditions of delayed planting (Singh, 1985).

Date of transplanting of rice is very important for a region because it must help in better rainwater management but at the same time, any delay in this respect must not cause reduction in crop yield. Singh (1987), observed that transplanting on 30th June gave significantly higher yield than on 18th July (Table 7.13). Based on the rainfall analysis, the optimum time for transplanting of high yielding medium duration varieties like IR 8 is from 25th June to 10th July. This would help in reducing the irrigation requirement. Medium duration varieties like Basmati 370 and short duration high yielding varieties like P_2-21 and PR 106 should be transplanted from middle to end of July. Transplanting beyond this period results in reduced yield.

Table 7.13. Effect of date of transplanting and age of seedling on grain yield of rice, var. IR-8-68 (Mean of two years).

Date of transplanting	*Yield ($t\ ha^{-1}$)*	*Age of seedlings (days)*	*Yield ($t\ ha^{-1}$)*
24 June	6.3	24	5.40
30 June	7.1	28	5.70
6 July	6.2	32	5.72
12 July	5.7	36	6.20
18 July	4.5	40	6.10
C.D. p = 0.05	0.71		0.44

Soil pH_2 (0-15 cm)=9.3 to 9.5, Source: Singh (1988)

Planting Technique

Poor germination in alkali soils is a serious limiting factor in crop production. Therefore, special planting technique used to be designed or be modified to overcome unfavourable soil conditions for germination and crop establishment. Sugar beet is a highly salt tolerant crop but it cannot be grown successfully in alkali soils because of poor germination. In a trail on sugar beet cultivation, Dargan and Chhillar (1973) found that sowing the seed on one side of the ridge half way between top and bottom, opposite to the sun direction gave significantly higher yield than other methods (Table 7.14). However, Garg (1987) reported that in an alkali soil (ESP 45), flat sowing gave higher yield than sowing on ridges.

Table 7.14. Effect of method of sowing on the yield of sugar beet

Treatment	*Survival percentage*	*Root yield (t ha^{-1})*	*Foliage yield (t ha^{-1})*
Flat sowing	37.5	12.8	12.1
Ridge sowing	71.6	19.5	17.0
Sowing on both sides of alternate ridge	67.8	15.9	12.4
Transplanting on flat surface	58.2	13.4	17.0
Transplanting on ridges	84.3	13.7	14.7
CD at p = 0.05	–	3.24	

Source: Singh (1988)

Dargan *et al.* (1973) found that trench method of sowing gave significantly higher yield of sugarcane than flat sowing in a highly alkali soil having pH_2 10.6 before gypsum application. In trench sowing, ridges were made 65cm apart and trenches were dug in furrows where setts were sown after applying gypsum, FYM and fertilizers. Higher yield in trenches was due to less concentration of salts, which moved up to the top of adjoining ridges.

In Vertisols, major emphasis has been laid on improved surface drainage to save the crops from water stagnation, which could be a regular feature of these soils. Precise land grading and growing crops on beds and furrow system are the major features of this model. While rice is grown in the furrows, other crops such as maize and cotton are cultivated on the beds. With this system, while submergence of maize and cotton is avoided, the drainage water from the beds supplements the rainwater for the rice crop grown in furrows.

As already mentioned, the model has been applied to alkali Vertisols in the states of M.P., Gujarat and Maharashtra where irrigation water is available in limited quantities.

Treatment of Seed/Seedlings

One of the main cause for the poor germination or stand of the crop in alkali soil is the disruption in the permeability of roots due to which it fails in balanced ion absorption. The sodium ions which are in predominance get free access inside the cell and become toxic which are in predominance get free access inside the cell and become toxic to plants. The calcium ions have been reported to maintain the cell membrane permeability and antagonise the toxic effect of sodium in plant tissue and growing media (Clarkson and Hanson, 1980). The plants which are able to maintain their chemo-osmotic potential in their cells under salt stress agrophysical treatment of seeds and seedlings is known to induce salt tolerance. Since the germination and survival of seedlings/plants are the initial basic problems under alkali conditions, the treatment are being given to seed and seedlings. The rice seedlings (var. Jaya) treated with calcium nitrate and calcium chloride solutions for 15 hr before transplanting increased the grain yield (Table 7.15).

Table 7.15. Effect of treatment of seedlings on grain yield of rice (t ha^{-1}) at different pH_2 levels

Treatments	*pH₂*				*Mean*
	8.5	*9.5*	*9.8*	*10.0*	
Control	6.91	6.77	4.00	1.69	4.84
Ca $(NO_3)_2$ 1%	7.26	7.09	5.77	2.58	5.67
Ca $(NO_3)_2$ 2%	7.10	6.81	4.76	3.14	5.45
$CaCl_2$ 1%	7.24	7.29	5.93	3.44	5.98
$CaCl_2$ 0.5%	9.82	7.03	5.36	3.36	5.64
Mean	7.06	7.00	5.16	2.84	

CD at $p = 0.05$; pH = 0.28; Treatment = 0.32; Interaction = 0.64
Source: Qadar *et al.* (1979)

Cropping Pattern

Selection of suitable crops and their sequence are very important considerations in reclamation and management of alkali soils. There are intra and inter-genic differences in the tolerance of crops. Some crops are sensitive, whereas others are either semi-tolerant or tolerant, at a given level of alkali. Therefore, the selection of the first crop will depend upon the degree of alkali after the basic reclamation measures have been implemented. The crops, which are relatively more tolerant and can bear well with the alkali conditions are preferred in the early phase of reclamation. Cropping pattern for alkali soils should not solely be decided on the basis of economic returns, but emphasis should also be placed on the improvement in the soil properties due to cropping and also to the quality or produce, particularly those of oilseeds and forages. The other important criterion in the selection of a crop rotation is the nitrogen fixation in the soil to save on nitrogen application besides avoiding nitrogen leaching that may cause environmental degradation. The nitrogen fixed in the soil can be utilised by non-legume crop during the following season.

Basu and Tagare (1943) tried several crops on moderately alkali soils of Deccan Canal area for two years. From the increase in Ca/Na ratio, the order of effectiveness in ameliorating alkali soil was found in order: Berseem > rice >dhaincha > cotton > tobacco > wheat. Talati (1947) concluded from a series of crop rotation experiments that dhaincha-sugarcane-cotton rotation was the best suited for alkali soil of southern states. Satyanarayna (1953) observed that temporary substitution of a second crop of rice in place of pulses, normally following rice reduced alkalinity in soils of Krishna East Bank Canal. This enabled the cultivation of pulse crop in the second year. Thus, the rotation suggested were as, rice-rice in the first year and rice-pulse in the second year.

In alkali soils, rice has been commonly recommended as the first crop in Punjab. After first initial leaching, rice was transplanted during monsoon. It was followed by berseem or senji in the winter season. Kanwar and Bhumbla (1961) reported that *dhaincha*-rice-berseem was the best cropping pattern for alkali soils of Punjab. Uppal *et al.* (1961) observed that *dhaincha*, rice and sugarcane in summer season and oats, barley, berseem, senji and methi in winter season, were the most suited crops for alkali soils of Punjab. In Uttar Pradesh, rice alone or *dhaincha*-rice in summer are the usual crops taken during the first stage of reclamation, which is often followed by berseem, wheat or barley in winter (Agarwal and Gupta 1968). Kanwar and Singh (1968) observed, that in field experiments at Ludhiana (Punjab) on alkali soils (pH_2 9 to 10), the rotation, *dhaincha* (green manure)-rice-sugarbeet gave the best results. From practical considerations, it is difficult to grow *dhaincha* as the first crop on farmer's field.

On the basis of several field studies conducted at Karnal, Dargan (1979) concluded that two cropping patterns viz. rice-wheat-*dhaincha* (green manure) and rice-berseem were more suitable and remunerative in the early phase of reclamation. When the crops are cultivated successfully for about 3 years, it is possible to grow even semi-tolerant crops like raya (*Brassica juncea*), pearl millet, sorghum, sugarcane etc. However, Singh (1988) showed that oil seed crops could also be raised successfully even as first crop on highly alkali soils, if reclamation has to be commenced from the winter season (Table 7.16). After the harvest of oilseed crops, pearl millet and sorghum crops can be grown during summer (April to June) as forage crop (Table 7.17).

Rice-wheat/berseem-*dhaincha* (green manure) is a better crop rotation, but reclamation process is slow under rice-wheat rotation. The yield of berseem during the first year of reclamation is very low, therefore farmers generally follow the rice-wheat or rice-wheat-*dhaincha* rotation. Sharma *et al.* (1983) studied the effect of four cropping patterns in an alkali soil (pH_2 10.0). It was revealed that the grain yield of subsequent rice crop was higher after rice-persian clover

Table 7.16. Effect of levels of gypsum on the yield of oilseed crops (t ha^{-1})

Gypsum (t ha^{-1})	*pH$_2$ at sowing (0-15 cm)*	*Toria*	*Rapeseed*	*Raya*	*Taramira*	*Mean*
Control	10.2	-	-	-	-	-
6.25	9.7	0.51	0.82	1.02	0.47	0.71
12.50	9.4	0.86	0.91	1.14	0.58	0.82
18.75	9..2	0.86	0.91	1.24	0.59	0.90
25.0	8.8	0.87	0.98	1.27	0.62	0.93
Mean	-	0.78	0.91	1.17	0.57	
CD (p = 0.05)	Gypsum =0.07 and Crop=0.08					

Initial pH$_2$ (0-15 cm) = 10.4, Source: Singh (1988)

Table 7.17 Effect of levels of gypsum on dry forage yield (t ha^{-1}) of sorghum and pearl millet

Gypsum (t ha^{-1})	*pH$_2$ at sowing (0-15 cm)*	*Sorghum*					*Pearl millet*				
		S109	*S136*	*S120*	*JS20*	*Mean*	*LC2*	*LC5*	*LC6*	*LC7*	*Mean*
Control	10.1	-	-	-	-	-	-	-	-	-	-
6.25	9.7	10.2	9.2	8.6	10.7	9.7	7.9	7.4	8.2	6.6	7.5
12.5	9.4	12.8	9.6	11.3	12.7	11.3	9.0	9.8	8.0	9.9	9.0
18.75	9.2	9.8	10.9	12.6	13.3	11.6	7.4	9.1	9.4	10.5	9.1
25.0	8.8	11.5	11.9	13.8	12.7	12.5	10.1	12.9	12.3	10.8	11.5
Mean		10.8	10.4	11.5	12.3		8.4	9.8	9.5	9.4	
CD (p = 0.05)	Gypsum=1.30; Crop=1.5						Gypsum=1.20; Crop=1.0				

Source: Singh (1988)

(shaftal) and rice-berseem rotations than after rice-wheat-*dhaincha* (green manuring) rotations (Table 7.18). It was more profitable to raise persian clover or berseem for fodder in winter than wheat on farmer's fields.

Table 7.18. Average yield (t ha^{-1}) of different crops under different crop rotations on farmer's fields

Rotation	*Rabi yield* 1979-80	*Rabi yield* 1980-81	*Kharif yield* 1980	*Kharif yield* 1981	*Profit (Rs. ha^{-1})*
Rice-wheat	1.7	1.9	5.7	6.0	7,528
Rice-wheat-dhaincha	1.7	2.1	6.1	6.7	8,403
Rice-berseem	18.0	52.8	6.8	7.2	8,810
Rice-Persian clover (shaftal)	24.0	55.8	7.0	7.1	9,930
CD at p = 0.05	–	–	0.7	0.6	–

Source: Sharma *et al.* (1983)

Under resource constraints where amendments and fertilisers are not available, Karnal grass (*Diplachne fusca*) and paragrass (*Brachiria mutica*) can be grown successfully on alkali soils (Kumar *et al.* 1980; Rana and Prakash, 1980). After growing these grasses for 2-3 years, it is possible to follow the recommended cropping patterns.

Based on extensive trials and field experiences, the short and long-term cropping sequences for alkali lands under reclamation have been worked out (Table 7.19 and Table 7.20)

Table 7.19. Cropping patterns recommended for alkali soils (During reclamation phase)

Season	*Year of reclamation* Ist	2nd	3rd
Summer (April–May)	Leaching/ Sesbania for green manuring	Sesbania green manuring	Sesbania green manuring/Fallow/ Cow pea (fodder)/ Maize (fodder)
Kharif	Rice/ Sesbania	Rice	Rice

Rabi	Barley/ Wheat	Wheat/ Barley/ Raya/Shaftal Senji/ Sugar beet	Wheat/Barley/Raya/ Berseem/Senji/ Sugar beet

Table 7.20. Cropping sequences recommended for alkali soils (Post reclamation phase)

Soil pH₂ of 0-15 cm layer	*Years after reclamation*	*Crops*	
		Kharif	*Rabi*
9.2 to 9.3	3 to 4	Cotton, sorghum, pearl millet, rape seed	Mustard
8.9 to 9.0	5 to 8	Sugarcane, groundnut, *arhar*, soybean	Berseem, sunflower, safflower, gram, pea, lentil
8.5 to 8.8	*After 8 to 10 years*		Any kind of crops including vegetables, flowers etc.

Biological Reclamation Model for Resource Poor Farmers

The biological reclamation approach aims at the reclamation of alkali soils by growing salt tolerant crops and their varieties. It is not a substitute for chemical amendment model, but as an alternate approach for adoption by resource poor farmers who are unable to invest on recommended doses of the chemical amendments. In this approach, alkali tolerant varieties of rice, wheat and mustard are grown either without or with a small dose of the amendment. A brief outline of this model is given in the following paragraphs.

Highly Alkali Soils (pH > 10.0)

It is recommended to grow CSR 10 variety of rice during *kharif* and sugar beet during the *rabi* season (rice-sugar beet cropping sequence) for three years. Within this period, the soil pH_2 will come down from 10.0 to 9.3. In the fourth year and later any other high yielding variety of rice in *kharif* and wheat (KRL 1-4) or raya CS_52 can be grown successfully.

Moderately Alkali Soils (pH 9.2 to 9.8)

Grow rice CSR 10 in the *kharif* season as the first crop without application of soil amendment. As a result, the soil pH_2 will come down to a level so that wheat KRL 1–4 or Indian mustard varieties such as Pusa bold, Kranti, Varuna or CS_52 can be grown during the *rabi* season.

Agronomic Practices for Important Crops

General principles and practices for crop production in alkali lands have been discussed in this and other chapters of this book. Since, rice–wheat cropping sequence is recommended during the first few years of reclamation, improved agronomic and cultural practices for these crops are discussed in the following sections. Besides, the practices for growing the green manuring crop (sesbania) are also included.

Rice (*Oryza sativa L.*)

Rice is grown in almost all the states of India. This crop occupies an area of 44361 thousand ha producing 8487.1 thousands tons of grain with an average yield of 1.911 t ha^{-1} (2000-01).

Soils

Rice is adapted to all types of soils, but is particularly suited to the clay and clay loam soils. Rice plant is able to tolerate a wide range of soil reaction, but it does have a preference for acidic soils. Rice is an ideal crop for growing in alkali soils having pH_2 up to 9.6. Semi-aquatic nature of the plant requires submerged moisture regime for optimum growth. These conditions are normally easy to achieve in alkali soils due to their poor water transmission characteristics. Transplanted rice is known to be highly tolerant to alkali conditions but in soils having high pH, alkali tolerant varieties should be grown or some amendments should be applied to reduce the pH_2 up to 9.6. The plant has reclamative effect on the soil and with its cultivation pH is likely to go down.

Varieties

High yielding varieties like IR 8, Jaya and PR 106 have been grown successfully during initial stages of reclamation. Short duration varieties like P 2-21 are suitable for late transplanting. *Basmati* rice can also be grown under late transplanting conditions, especially from the second year onwards. Recently developed varieties by the CSSRI, Karnal such as CSR 10, CSR 13 and CSR 30 could also be grown during initial years of reclamation.

Seed rate and seed treatment

To safeguard against high mortality and poor tillering in the initial years of reclamation, a seed rate of 55-60 kg ha^{-1} is required to raise the seedling for transplanting one hectare of alkali land as compared to 30-35 t ha^{-1} for normal soil. Heavy and good seeds of a suitable variety should be selected by soaking the seeds in 10 percent common salt solution. After removing the floating seeds, the selected seeds should be washed 2 to 3 times with normal water. Then selected seeds should be soaked in solution of Ceresan (0.1%) or in 60 litres of water containing 6 g streptocycline and 60 g of Ceresan wet for 8 to 10 hr before sowing, as prophylactic measure against any seed-borne infection.

Nursery raising

The rice seedlings should be raised in a normal soil since rice seedlings are sensitive to alkali at 1-2 leaf stage. Select a fertile, well-drained upland piece in the field near the source of irrigation. For raising medium-duration and high yielding varieties, the seeds should be sown in the nursery from 10 to 30 May for timely transplanting from the last week of June to the first week of July. For late transplanting from second week of July to end of July, seeds of short duration varieties should be sown in the nursery from the first week of June to the third week of June. For transplanting one-hectare area, about 1000 m^2 area is required for nursery raising. Before preparing the field, 2.5 tons compost or farmyard manure should be applied. For raising a wet nursery, the field should be puddled in standing water with a puddler or a *desi* plough. In case of dry nursery, about 1 or 1.25 m wide raised beds should be left in between the beds. Before sowing, fertilizers at the rate of 1 kg N and 1 kg P_2O_5 per 100 m^2 should be broadcast and thoroughly mixed in the nursery beds. In case of wet nursery, the seed should be broadcast on the bed saturated with water. Keep the seed bed saturated for the first five days and then as the seedling grow, gradually increase the level of water up to 5-6 cm. In dry nursery, the treated seeds should be sown in lines and covered with mixture of farmyard manure and soil. Another dose of nitrogen @ 1 kg/100 m^2 should be applied 15 days after sowing. The nursery should be kept free from weeds and should be regularly irrigated.

Field preparation

Reclamation of alkali soils starts from the top and rarely proceeds to deeper depth because gypsum application has been limited to the gypsum requirement of top 15 cm of the soil layer. Therefore, shallow ploughing of the land without inverting the soil is recommended. The land should not be tilled in too wet or too dry condition. At proper soil moisture content, 3 to 4 shallow cross ploughing should be done to pulverize the soil.. After last ploughing, the field should be levelled with a *sohaga* (leveller). Puddling i.e. ploughing in standing water, an important operation in normal soil for transplanting of rice, is not recommended during the initial years of reclamation (2 to 3 years after gypsum application). The seedlings should be transplanted in the well prepared fields immediately after irrigation. Some time, due to some unavoidable reasons, the surface of field becomes hard before transplanting. Under such conditions, field should be ploughed in standing water to shallow depth with a harrow. This will loosen the soil to facilitate easy transplanting.

Age and number of seedlings

The transplanting should be done when the seedlings are 35 to 40 days old as compared to 25-30 days in case of normal soils. For better yield, more than 40 days old seedling should be used under delayed transplanting. About 4-5 seedlings per hill should be transplanted, at 15 cm row to row and plant to plant. After 2-3 years, the spacing can be increased to that in normal soils and number of seedlings may also be reduced to 3-4 per hill.

Application of fertilizers

During the initial years of reclamation, the alkali soils need higher dose of nitrogen, i.e. 150 kg N ha^{-1} for medium duration high yielding varieties and 120 kg N ha^{-1} for short duration high yielding varieties. Ammonium sulphate, during the early stage of reclamation, is better source of nitrogen but due to its non-availability and also higher cost, urea may be used profitably in alkali soils (Singh *et al.*, 1984).

To reduce nitrogen losses through volatilisation and denitrification, nitrogenous fertilisers should be applied in split doses. In rice, nitrogen should be applied in 3 equal splits viz. one-third at transplanting, one-third at 3 weeks and remaining at 6 weeks after transplanting. Nitrogen efficiency can be further increased, if it is applied in 4 equal splits, i.e. one fourth at transplanting, and remaining in three equal splits at 3, 6 and 8 weeks after transplanting (Singh and Sharma, 1984a).

Application of 10 kg N ha^{-1} as a foliar spray (3.0% urea solution) and remaining as soil application has been found beneficial over the application of total dose of nitrogen as soil application. If rice crop is taken after *dhaincha* green manuring, the total dose of nitrogen can be reduced to about 70-75 kg N ha^{-1} as *dhaincha* green manuring enables as much rice yield as obtained with an application of 80 kg N ha^{-1}. There is no need to apply phosphorus and potassium in initial 4-5 years of reclamation. Whenever soil test shows phosphorus and potassium deficiency, the fertilizers should be applied at the time of transplanting.

Application of Zinc

Application of 25 kg zinc sulphate ha^{-1} at transplanting has been found beneficial for rice production (Fig. 7.3 and 7.4). If zinc sulphate is applied to both rice and wheat crops then 10 kg $ZnSO_4$ ha^{-1} is sufficient. After about 3-4 years when the soil is improved, it should be applied on soil test basis.

Water management

High yielding dwarf rice varieties require only shallow submergence (5 ± 2 cm) as deeper submergence reduces the yield. The crop generally requires about 15 to 20 irrigation after transplanting. Water should be kept standing except for one or two days after about 8-10 days of transplanting. At this stage if water is present in the field, it should be drained out and irrigation should be withheld for about 2-3 days for better development of root system. Water should also be drained out prior to fertilizer application. Thereafter, about 5 to 7 cm submergence should be maintained. It has also been observed that during period of reduced water availability, ponding of irrigation water one day after disappearance of ponded water result in as much grain yield as in the continuous submergence. There are certain stages when water requirement is high and, therefore crop should not suffer due to lack of water at seedling establishment stage, vegetative or tillering stage, panicle initiation stage and milking and grain development stage. The water should be completely drained from the field about 10-12 days before the harvest of crop.

The areas where alkali soils occur extensively, usually receive a rainfall of about 700-800 mm annually. Most of this rainfall occurs in rainy season (July to September). All the rainfall can be stored in the rice fields and the farmers may not worry much about the drainage except when the storms are quite heavy such as rainfall exceeding 15 cm received in one day. In such events excess water should be drained into a surface drainage system provided for this purpose. The storing of rainwater in the fields helps in reducing the irrigation water requirement of the crop.

Fig. 7.3 Poor growth of rice in alkali soils with no application of zinc

Fig. 7.4. Excellent growth of rice in alkali soils with application of zinc

Interculture and weed control

Weed problem is generally not serious in alkali soils for the first 2-3 years of reclamation. If algal growth is noticed, rice weeder can be used to minimize it or the standing water be replaced with fresh water. The weed problem after 2-3 years of cropping can be controlled by hand weeding. Grassy weeds can be controlled by applying Machette @ 30 kg granules ha^{-1} in 4-5 cm standing water, 3-4 days after transplanting or spray with 2 kg liquid active ingredient in 400 to 600 liter of water per hectare. The water from the field should be drained out before the application of herbicide.

Plant protection measures

The incidence of pest and diseases in rice grown in alkali soils is no different than normal soils. The methods to control insects, pests and disease are therefore the same. BHC 10% @ 20-25 kg ha^{-1} should be dusted against grass hopper, leaf-hoper, rice hispa, rice bug, rice thrips etc. Against stem borer, 0.1% Methylparathion (Metacid 50 EC) @ 750 t ha^{-1}should be sprayed 20-30 days after the first spray. Sometimes brown hopper causes great damage to the crop when the crop is near maturity. It could be prevented by broadcasting Furadone @ 8 to 10 kg/ha in standing water.

To control diseases like blast, bacterial blight, leaf spot, sheath blight etc. use disease free seed, treated with Agrosan G.N. or Cersean @ 2.5 g. For leaf spot, crop should be sprayed with any copper fungicide containing copper oxychloride using a concentration of 2 to 3 g l^{-1} of water. The spray may be repeated after every 7 to 10 days if the rainy and humid weather persists.

Yield

The rice yields are normally quite good in alkali soils. In the very first year of reclamation with improved agronomic and cultural practices, an average grain yield of 4.5-5.0 t ha^{-1} can be obtained in case of medium duration, high yielding varieties and 4.0-4.5 t ha^{-1} in case of short duration, high yielding varieties. The yields increase appreciably in the subsequent years. From second year onwards yields up to 6.0 t ha^{-1} and 5.0 t ha^{-1} can be obtained from medium and short duration varieties, respectively.

Wheat (*Triticum aestivum* Linn. Fiori and Paol)

Wheat is the world's most widely cultivated crop. In India, it is the main cereal crop. In respect of area and production, it occupies the second position being exceeded only by rice. Wheat crop occupies an area of 25068 thousand hectares producing 68763 thousand tonnes grain (2000-01) with an average yield of 2.74 t ha^{-1}.

Soils

Wheat can be grown in a variety of soils except highly alkali, highly saline and waterlogged soils. Soils with sandy loam to clay loam texture and moderate water holding capacity are ideal for wheat cultivation. In alkali soils, wheat can be grown fairly if ESP is less than 30 or pH_2 is below 9.3. If the ESP is high, it is desirable to apply gypsum and grow rice as the first crop. Subsequently wheat can be grown without any additional application of gypsum. Although, several crops can be grown following rice in the reclaimed land, farmers prefer to grow wheat after the harvest of rice crop.

Field preparation

Wheat crop requires a well-pulverised seedbed having optimum soil moisture for good and uniform germination. After the harvest of rice crop, plough the field and irrigate. Once the field is in workable condition plough the field 2-3 times. After every ploughing carry out the planking operation. If rice is harvested late, and there is sufficient moisture in the field, then make use of the residual moisture and sow the wheat by ploughing and planking 2 to 3 times. In this case there is no need to apply pre-sowing irrigation as it would delay the sowing of wheat. If the rice is harvested in the month of November and moisture is also insufficient to sow wheat, pre-sowing irrigation should be applied without ploughing the field so that field comes in ploughable conditions at an early date. Remember, working in too wet or too dry condition will deteriorate the physical properties of the soils and affect productivity.

Varieties

Some of the high-yielding short stature varieties recommended for cultivation are:

For Timely sown crop: HD 2009, WH 157, HD 1982, HD 2329, KRL 1-4, KRL 19

For Late sown crop: HD 1553, HD 1981, WL 343

Seed rate and seed treatment

The seed rate varies with variety as well as with time of sowing. High seed rate between 100 and 125 kg ha^{-1} should be used to have optimum plant population. In case of late sowing, it should be increased by 20-25 percent.

To safeguard against the soil and seed borne diseases, the seed should be treated with Thiram or Agrosan GN or Captain @ 2.5 gm kg^{-1} seed. Areas where loose smut is a problem, seed should be treated with vitavax @ 2 gm kg^{-1} of wheat seed before sowing.

Time and method of sowing

The time of sowing is one of the important aspects in obtaining good yield of wheat. It depends upon the variety as well as the local conditions. The optimum time for wheat sowing is the first fortnight of November. The average temperature at the time of sowing should be around 20-25°C. There is gradual decline in yield if sowing is delayed beyond 15th November. Under late sowing condition, HD 1553, HD 1981 and WL 343 varieties should be preferred. Wheat sowing after middle of December results in very poor yield.

Sowing should be done in optimum moisture condition. Even slightly less moisture would affect the germination. The seed should be sown in lines 20 cm apart, at a depth of 5 cm with bullock or tractor driven seed drill. Seed-cum fertilizer drill should be preferred to ensure uniform placement of seed and fertilizers at the optimum depth. If seed drill is not available, the seed should be sown by 'Kera' or 'Pora' method.

Fertilizer application

Nutritional requirement of wheat for alkali soils is different than the normal soils. It is recommended to apply 25 percent more nitrogen (150 kg ha^{-1}) as compared to the dose usually recommended for normal soils (120 kg ha^{-1}). Urea and ammonium sulphate are equally efficient as source of nitrogen (Singh and Sharma, 1984a). During the first year 150 kg N ha^{-1} should be applied in 3-4 splits for better nitrogen use efficiency. If applied in three splits, one third as basal, at the time of sowing, one-third at first irrigation and remaining should be applied at second irrigation. Nitrogen use efficiency of wheat can be further improved by slight modification by applying 150 kg N in four equal splits that is ¼ basal + ¼ at first irrigation + ¼ at second irrigation and ¼ at the third irrigation. Nitrogen application should not be missed at the time of sowing and at panicle initiation stage.

Apply 10 kg $ZnSO_4$ ha^{-1} to wheat crop at sowing time. Basal dose of nitrogen and full dose of zinc sulphate should be drilled after final preparatory tillage. Phosphorus and potassium do not respond for first 4-5 years and these should be applied if the soil test shows their deficiencies.

Irrigation

Alkali soils, being structurally unstable, are prone to spontaneous slaking and crust formation upon irrigation, which impedes water intake and therefore, the storage capacity of the soils. Effective water storage is further reduced owing to the restriction of roots only in the upper few centimeters of soils, depending upon the extent of soil improvement. Because of low hydraulic conductivity, the movement of stored water to plant roots is very slow and drying of surface soil layer is rapid. For these reasons, wheat in alkali soils requires irrigation more frequently with small depths at each irrigation than for crops grown in normal soil conditions. Due to very low water intake, heavy irrigation is quite harmful to the crop, particularly at the early stage of crop growth (Sharma and Swarup, 1988 a,b; 1989a). Therefore, to ensure optimum wheat yield excess irrigation water must be drained out within one day of irrigation (Fig. 7.5 and 7.6).

Fig. 7.5 Poor growth of wheat in undrained plots

Light irrigations are preferred in these soils. To obtain good yield of wheat, 5-6 shallow irrigations would be sufficient. If excess water stands on the land surface, it should

Fig. 7.6 Excellent growth of wheat in drained plots

be removed within a day to minimize adverse effect on crop yield (Table 7.21).

Table 7.21 Response of various *rabi* crops to short-term water stagnation in semi-reclaimed alkali lands

Duration of water stagnation (Days)	*Yield (t ha^{-1})*		
	Mustard	*Wheat*	*Barley*
Drained	1.43 (100)*	4.01 (100)	3.65 (100)
1	1.31 (92)	3.70 (92)	3.52 (96)
2	1.20 (84)	3.32 (83)	3.39 (93)
4	1.12 (78)	2.93 (73)	3.18 (87)
6	1.02 (71)	2.43 (61)	2.75 (75)
CD (p=0.05)	0.22	0.28	0.28

* Values in parenthesis are the relative yield

The time of first irrigation to wheat grown in alkali soil is also different than normal soil. If first irrigation is given 21 days after sowing as in the case of normal soils, the yellowing of seedling starts because of higher salt concentration near the root zone. Therefore, the first irrigation to wheat sown in the first fortnight of November should be applied after 28 days of sowing. In case of late sowing the first irrigation should be delayed by one week. Second irrigation should be applied after 20-25 days of the first irrigation. Frequency of irrigation can be increased in the months of February and March. In all 5-6 irrigation are sufficient to get good yield. It is better to give irrigation in borders, each border being approximately 6 m x 40 m, wherever possible.

Interculture operations

Since following irrigation, a hard surface layer (crust) is formed in these soils, it affects the young seedling adversely and also restricts the water entry and normal exchange of gases from the root to free atmosphere. Therefore, two hoeing should be given one each after first and second irrigation. The hoeing improves the soil aeration and help in the root development.

Weed control

In alkali soils, for the first two years of reclamation, weed problems is not anticipated much. But from third year onwards, the weed problem becomes as severe as in normal soils (Singh *et al.*, 1982). Dominant weeds which infest wheat crop are : *Phalaris minor (Mandusi), Chenopodium album (Batua), Melilotus alba* (Wild Senji) and *Polypogon monspliensis* (Rabbit foot grass). These weeds could be controlled by applying the weedicides such as: Dosanex, Arelon, Tolean, Graminon and Delron. Any one of these weedicides can be applied @ 1.0 kg a.i/ha after 4 to 5 days of first irrigation for effective and economic weed control (Singh *et al.*, 1984 a).

Plant protection measures

Termites damage the crop soon after sowing and some time near maturity. For the control of termites, use Aldrin 5 percent dust or BHC 10 percent dust at the rate of 20-25 kg ha^{-1} and mix it well in the soil at the time of last ploughing before sowing. Against surface grass hopper and army worms, BHC 10 percent dust should be applied @ 25 kg ha^{-1}. Against wheat aphids and jassids, apply 0.5 litre Folithion or Thiodan or one litre Ekalux 25 EC in 800 litres of water per hectare. For the control of brown rust, black rust or yellow rust spray 0.2 percent Zineb or Dithane M-45.

Yield

Good grain yield of wheat can be obtained from alkali soils under reclamation if soil pH_2 is between 9.3 to 9.0. About 1.8 to 3.0 t ha^{-1} yield can be obtained in case of timely sown wheat. If pH_2 ranges between 9.0 and 8.5 or below, 3 to 4 t ha^{-1} yields could be obtained.

Dhaincha (Sesbania aculeata)

Dhaincha is mainly grown in alkali soils for green manuring. It is quick growing leguminous plant and can withstand adverse conditions of water logging, salinity and alkalinity. It is sensitive to salts at germination stage but is an ideal green manure crop for rice growing soils. It can be cultivated with minimum time and inputs while providing maximum benefits of a green manure crop.

General growth habits

Dhaincha can be grown in almost all-climatic conditions, dry or moist and in soils either drained or waterlogged. In waterlogged soils, it can attain a height of 1.5-1.8 m in a very short time. In standing water, it gives out lateral roots from the stem to have a firm grip in the soil so as to withstand strong winds. Once a good germination is achieved, it can also withstand drought. *Dhaincha* is tolerant to alkali conditions and can withstand pH_2 of 9.5. The plant has vigorous growth habit and nodulates in almost all types of soils including saline and alkali soils (Fig. 7.7).

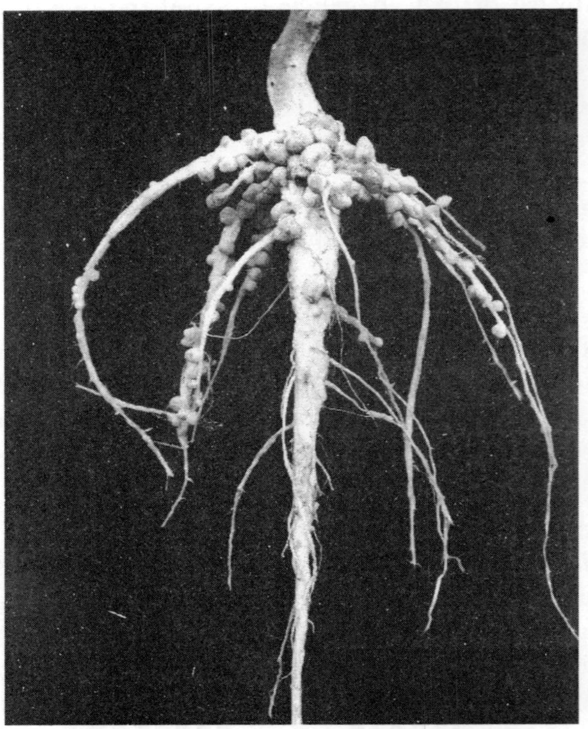

Fig. 7.7Nodules of *dhaincha* plant in an alkali environment

Land preparation and time of sowing

Land for the cultivation of *dhaincha* is prepared by giving 1-2 ploughings and plankings. Special care be taken to level the fields. If the pH_2 is more than 10.0, gypsum need to be added @ 7.5 t ha^{-1}. The soils in that case are leached with good quality water for about 10 days. On soils where rice-wheat crops have already been taken, there is no need to apply gypsum.

Dhaincha is grown during the summer and the rainy season. Although, it is difficult to take *dhaincha* as the first crop but with appropriate addition of gypsum, it can even be taken as the first crop. It is generally recommended to follow rice-wheat-*dhaincha* rotation. The sowing time for the crop extends throughout the month of May although the recommended time is the first week of May. The appropriate time, however, need to be decided depending upon the time at which rice is to be transplanted.

Seed rate and sowing method

Before the crop is sown, a light irrigation need to be applied. Seeds of *dhaincha* need to be soaked in water overnight. The seeds @ 60 kg ha^{-1} should be broadcasted in a thin standing water. If the seeds are properly handled and stored, these remain viable for 3-4 years.

Nutrient requirement and irrigation scheduling

In normal soils, the efficiency of green manuring increases with the application of phosphatic fertilizer @ 40 kg P_2O_5 ha^{-1}. However in alkali soils application of phosphatic fertilizers is not necessary. Application of 15-20 kg N ha^{-1} as basal dose would be beneficial. Light and frequent irrigation are beneficial. First irrigation may be applied after a week of sowing. Other irrigation may be applied as and when required. A total of 5-6 irrigation are required for raising a 45 days old crop in the summer season.

Incorporation of crop

The crop is turned into the soil using a disc plough or a disc harrow. A 45 days old crop adds 20-24 t ha^{-1} green matter containing about 95-115 kg of nitrogen (Rao, 1985). There is no need to allow any time for the decomposition of the green matter. After the incorporation of the crop, irrigate the field and transplant rice in the standing water. Being succulent, it decomposes easily upon incorporation into the soil. The standing water in the rice fields hastens the decomposition of the green matter without causing any harm to the rice crop. About 50 percent of the added nitrogen is converted into readily available ammonical form in 4-6 days and the rest in 10-20 days of application under the normal temperature conditions that prevail during the main rice crop.

It has been found that the incorporation of 45 days old *dhaincha* plants with no decomposition period resulted in better yields of the rice crop. Besides, it also saved time. If the plants are older than 45 days, the plants are rendered hardy and are difficult to decompose. Similarly, if the plants are allowed time for decomposition, the losses of nitrogen through volatilisation is more resulting in lesser recovery by the rice crop.

Advantages of *Dhaincha* Green manuring

Dhaincha, a salt tolerant crop, has been observed to offer many benefits to the reclamation programme. One of the major benefits of cropping of *dhaincha* in the first few years of reclamation is that it provides shading effect. As a result, the salt accumulation in the root zone is much less in comparison to a situation where fields are left fallow. The carbon-dioxide liberated by the roots as well as that produced during decomposition of the green matter solubilizes calcium carbonate from the natural calcium carbonate present in alkali soils, thereby promoting reclamation. The lowering of the pH as a result of liberation of carbon-dioxide helps in the mobilization of calcium, phosphorus, potassium and other trace elements and make these available to the rice crop.

In a partially reclaimed alkali soil, it supplies about 40-80 kg N ha^{-1} depending upon the stage of growth at which it is incorporated in the soil.

The increased permeability and relatively more amounts of salts leached from the soil root zone are also attributed to its extensive and sturdy root system. The green manure crop improves the water holding capacity of the soil, improves its tilth, improves soil aeration and facilitates natural drainage.

REFERENCES

Agarwal, R.R. and Gupta R.N. 1968. Saline Alkali Soils in India. Tech. Bull. (Agric. Series), ICAR, New Delhi. 221 p.

Basu, J.K. and Tagre, V.D. 1943. Soils of the Deccan canals. IV. The alkali soils, their nature and management. Indian J. Agric. Sci. 13: 157-81.

Bhardwaj, K.K.R., Venkat Krishna S. and Batra, L. 1977. Studies on manurial value of dhaincha as a green manure crop. Ann. Rep. CSSRI, Karnal, 36.

Bhumba, D.R. 1972. Reclamation and utilization of salt-affected soils. Indian Fmg. 22: 151-4.

Chhabra, R. 1983. Phosphorus requirement of rice and wheat at different stages of reclamation of sodic soils. Ann. Rep. CSSRI, Karnal 36-43.

Chhabra, R. 1985. Crop response to phosphorus and potassium fertilization of a sodic soil. Agron. J. 77: 699-702.

Clarkson, D.T. and Hanson, J.B. 1980. The mineral nutrition of higher plants. Ann. Rev. Pl. Physiol., 31: 239-98.

Dargan, K.S. 1979. Agronomic and cultural practices of crop production in salt-affected soils. Curr. Agric. 3: 1-20.

Dargan, K.S., Chandra, H. and Bhumbla, D.R. 1973. In saline alkali soil-urea spraying for more paddy. Indian Fmg. 22: 9-10.

Dargan, K.S. and Chhillar, R.K. 1973. Technique for sugar beet and vegetables cultivation in saline-alkali soils. Indian Fmg. 22: 13-6.

Dargan, K.S. and Chhillar, R.K. 1978. Studies on the effect of nitrogen and missing application of P and K in the rice wheat sequence in alkali soils. Indian. J. Agron. 23: 14-8.

Dargan, K.S. and Gaul, B.L. 1974. For paddy in alkali soil-seedling age and planting date vital. Indian Fmg. 24: 11-2.

Dargan, K.S., Gaul, B.L. and Abrol, I.P. 1973. Growing sugarcane in saline–alkali soils. Indian Fmg. 23: 9-10, 19.

Dargan, K.S., Nitant, H.C. and Bhumbla, D.R. 1975. In alkali soils urea spraying for saving nitrogen and more wheat. Indian. Fmg. 27: 11.

Dargan, K.S., Singh, O.P. and Gupta, I.C. 1982. Crop Production in Salt-Affected Soils. Oxford and IBH Publishing Co. New Delhi, 276 pp.

Dhawan, D.L., Bhatnagar, B.B.L. and Ghai, P.D. 1958. Role of green manuring in reclamation. Proc. Natn. Acad. Sci. India, 27(A): 168-75.

Garg, V.G. 1987. Grow sugar beet on sodic soils. Indian Fmg. 36(10): 19-21.

Gaur, C., Neelakanthan, S. and Dargan K.S. 1984. Organic Manures (Revised Ed). ICAR, New Delhi.

Kanwar, J.S. and Bhumbla, D.R. 1961. Ann. Rep. Scheme on Reclamation of Saline Alkali Soils in Punjab (1960-61), PAU, Ludhiana.

Kanwar, J.S. and Singh, N.T. 1968. Suitability of sugar beet for saline and saline-alkali soils of northern India. I. Adaptability. Indian J. Agric. Sci. 38: 115-21.

Kanwar, J. S. and Randhawa, N. S. 1974. Micronutrient Research in Soils and Plants in India. Tech. Bull. (Agric.) 50. ICAR, New Delhi.

Katyal, J.C., Randhawa, N.S. and Roy, R.N. 1979. Micro-nutrients problem in agriculture. Joint Proc. India/FAO/Norway Seminar on Micro-nutrients in Agriculture, New Delhi, 1979.

Kumar, Ashok., Abrol, I.P. and Dargan, K.S. 1980. Effect of exchangeable sodium on growth and yield of five forage grasses. Forage Res. 6: 123-7.

Nitant, H.C. and Dargan, K.S. 1974. Influence of nitrogen fertilisers on yield and nitrogen uptake of wheat in saline sodic soils. J. Indian. Soc. Soil Sci. 22: 121-4.

Qadar, A., Joshi, Y.C., Bal., A.R. and Dwivedi, R.S. 1979. Induction of salt resistance in crop plants. I. Chemical treatment. Ann. Rep. CSSRI, Karnal, 95-6.

Rana, R.S. and Prakash, Ved. 1980. Karnal grass grows well in alkali soils. Indian Fmg. 30: 17-9.

Rao, D.L.N. 1985. Sesbania for green manuring. Better Fmg. Salt-Affected Soils, CSSRI Ext. Series No. 6, 7 pp.

Satyanarayana, M. 1953. Crop and land improvement under the Krishna East Bank Canal (T.N.) Madras Agric. J. 40: 293-4.

Sharma, D.P. 1988. Effect of surface crust breaking on growth and yield of bread wheat in alkali soils. Indian J. agric. Sci. 58: 699-701.

Sharma, D. P. and Swarup, A. 1988a. Effect of short-term flooding on growth, yield and mineral composition of wheat in alkali soils under field conditions. Plant Soil. 107:137-143.

Sharma, D. P. and Swarup, A. 1988b. Remove excess water for higher wheat productivity in alkali soils. Indian Fmg. 38(6):18-19.

Sharma, D. P. and Swarup, A. 1989. Effect of short-term water logging on growth, yield and nutrient composition of wheat in alkaline soils. J. agric. Sci. (Cambridge). 112:191-197.

Sharma, D.P., Mehta, K.K., Yadav, J.S.P. and Singh, G. 1983. Effect of crop rotation on growth and soil properties in sodic soils on farmers' fields. Indian J. Agric. Sci. 681-5.

Singh, G., Mehta, K.K. and Sharma, D. P. 1982. Note on weed problem in wheat grown in alkali soils. Curr. Agric. 6: 181-2.

Singh, G. and Sharma, D.P. 1984 a. Rice in sodic soils. Intensive Agric. 22: 15-9.

Singh, G. and Sharma, D.P. 1984 b. Nitrogen management for wheat in sodic soils. Indian Fmg.34: 37-9.

Singh, G., Sharma, D.P. and Mehta, K.K. 1984 a. Chemical weed control in wheat in alkali soils under reclamation on farmer's fields. Curr. Agric. 8:26-32.

Singh, G., Sharma, D.P. and Mehta, K.K. 1984b. Effect of sources, levels and methods of N application on rice in sodic soils. Natn. Symp. Nitrogen, Plant, Soil and Fertiliser, Hisar, 190-6.

Singh, K.N. 1985. Cultural practices for growing rice in alkali soils. Better Fmg. Salt-Affected Soils, CSSRI, Ext Series no. 9, 10 pp.

Singh, K.N. 1987. Technology for rice cultivation in alkali soils. Indian Fmg. 37: 3-7.

Singh, K. N. 1988. Cultural practices for crop production in alkali soils. Indian Fmg. 38:21-23, 43.

Singh, K. N. and Sharma, D.K. 1984. Effect of cultural practices and nitrogen levels on rice grown in a highly sodic soils. Ann. Rep. CSSRI, Karnal, 75.

Singh, K. N. and Swarup, A. 2000. Effect of long-term rice-wheat cropping sequence on yield and soil properties in a reclaimed sodic soil. In Long-term Soil Fertility Experiments in Rice-wheat cropping Systems. (Abrol, I. P., Bronson, K. E., Duxbury, J. M. and Gupta, R. K. Eds.). Rice-wheat Consortium Paper Series 6, New Delhi. 40-49.

Singh, M.V. 1985. Zinc nutrition of crops in alkali soils. Better Fmg. Salt-Affected Soils, CSSRI, Ext. Series No. 4, 8 pp.

Singh, M. V. and Abrol, I. P. 1986. Split application of zinc better than in a single dose. Indian Fmg. 36:35-37.

Swarup, A. 1984. Effect of micronutrients and farmyard manure on yield and micro-nutrient content of rice and wheat grown on sodic soil. J. India Soc. Soil. Sci. 32: 397-9.

Swarup, A. 1979. Availability of manganese under moist and submerged conditions in sodic soil. J. Indian Soc. Soil. Sci. 27:485-5.

Swarup, A. 1991. Effect of gypsum, green manure, farmyard manure and zinc fertilization on the zinc, iron and manganese nutrition of wetland rice on a sodic soil. J. Indian Soc. Soil. Sci. 39: 530-6.

Swarup, A. 2000. Nutrient management for crop production in alkali lands. In Salinity Management in Agriculture (Gupta et al. Eds.). 99-108.

Swarup, A. and Singh, K. N. 1989. Effect of 12 yeas rice/wheat cropping sequence and fertilizer use on soil properties and crop yield in a sodic soil. Field Crops Research. 21: 277-287.

Takkar, P.N. and Randhawa, N.S. 1978. Micro-nutrients in Indian agriculture. Fertil. News. 23(8): 3-26.

Talati, R.P. 1947. Field experiments on the reclamation of salt lands in Baramati of Bombay Deccan. Indian J. Agric. Sci. 11: 959-77.

Uppal, H.L. 1955. Green manuring with special reference to Sesbania aculeata for treatment of alkali soils. Indian J. Agric. Sci. 25: 211-35.

Uppal, H.L. Agarwal, R.R. and Kibe, M.M. 1961. Reclamation of Saline and Alkaline Land. Farm Bull. 66, Ministry of Food and Agriculture, New Delhi.

Yadav, J.S.P. and Kalra, K.K. 1964. Exchangeable manganese in certain forest soils of India. J. Indian Soc. Soil. Sci. 12: 225-53.

8

IRRIGATION PRACTICES

Irrigation is an old art and is believed to be as old as the history of agriculture. The main purpose of irrigation is to provide water to crops in adequate quantity at the right time and at the right place without causing adverse effects on crops or the soil resource. The aim is to get high crop yields and a product of good quality. With the rapid increase in area under irrigation, expansion of area under high yielding varieties, the competitive demands from domestic, industrial and other sectors, shrinking base of land and water resources for agriculture is quite evident. It appears that use of marginal and poor land and water resources is the only answer to feed the ever-increasing population. Utilization of these resources on long-term basis calls for scientific knowledge on soil-water-plant relationship and its modifying influence on the irrigation methods and technologies. Management of irrigation water through improved irrigation practices can possibly increase agricultural production of soils with poor physical state than any other single agricultural practices.

Modification of Irrigation Practices

The problem of soil or water salinity/alkalinity is not realized till the crop production is entirely eliminated or at least drastically reduced. Unfortunately, use of poor land and water is considered at par with normal land and excellent quality irrigation water. As a result of this belief, not only one ends up with poor crop yields but also with immediate or gradual reduction in fertility of the land resource. Irrigation practices, therefore, should be modified such that basic objectives for which irrigation is applied are attained satisfactorily.

Moisture Movement and Irrigation Cycles in Alkali Soils

In saline soils, osmotic potential of the soil solution is the primary variable to which crops respond. Total moisture stress is the sum of matric potential and the osmotic potential. Salinity generally produces symptoms, which closely resemble those of drought. Contrary to this concept, water shortage in alkali soils appears to be mainly due to the poor physical conditions coupled with poor water transmission characteristic, which impede the moisture and air movement in the root zone. This fact is clearly explained in Fig. 8.1. The surface layer of a high ESP soil dries quicker than a similar soil of low ESP. Cumulative loss of water in a gypsum treated soil is 25 cm in 10 days compared to 31.6 cm in the same period from the upper 8 cm of the soil profile of an alkali soil. The loss is 9.85 cm and 3.35 cm from 8-16 cm layer in 10 days under similar conditions. This is due to low upward flux in high ESP soils. The differences in unsaturated hydraulic conductivity of the soils explain this behaviour. Clearly, alkalinity significantly affects the magnitude and pattern of water content changes in the soil profile following evaporation. In a period of 120 days, losses from normal soil amounted to 19.29 cm compared to 8.77 cm in an alkali soil. Moreover, there was practically no depletion from layer below 60 cm in an alkali soil. Contrary to it, a considerable fraction of the total water was lost from lower soil layers in the case of normal soils. In a similar study, Acharya *et al.* (1979) revealed that water extraction rate *in Brassica juncea* reduced from 0.23 cm day^{-1} to 0.14 cm day^{-1} as the ESP of the soil increased from 4 to 38. While, only 76% of the water was extracted from 0-30 layere in the soil with ESP of 4, 100% of water was extracted from this layer with an ESP of 38 (Table 8.1).

Table 8.1 Water extraction by *Brassica juncea* as affected by the ESP of the soil

Water extraction	*ESP of the surface (0–15 cm) soil*				
	4	*11*	*16*	*23*	*38*
Extraction rate cm day^{-1}	0.23	0.24	0.20	0.18	0.14
Soil layer(cm)			*Percentage of total extraction*		
0–15	46.4	40.0	67.5	75.0	78.0
15–30	30.0	31.7	28.0	25.0	22.4
30–45	16.3	18.7	4.5	0	0
45–60	7.3	6.2	0	0	0

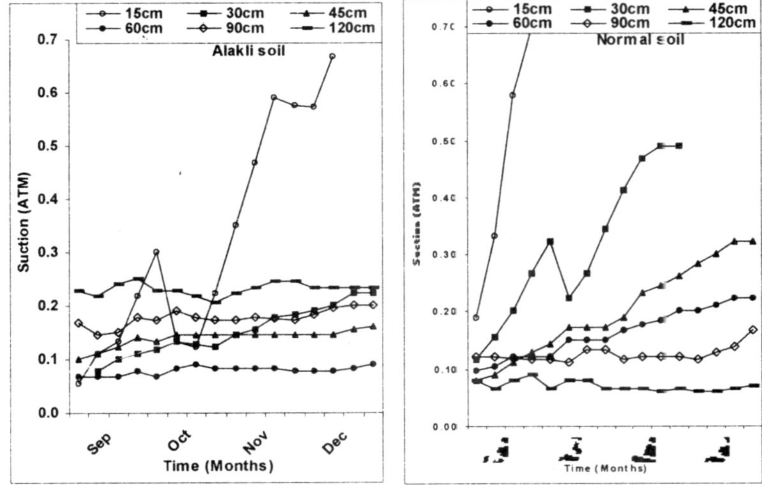

Fig. 8.1 Moisture content changes in the top 120 cm soil profile following wetting in an alkali soil and a normal soil

From this brief discussion and the information included in other chapters, following conclusions relevant to irrigation of alkali lands can be drawn.

- The capacity of alkali soils to absorb water or their infiltration rate continues to be low even after reclamation. For this reason, if a heavy irrigation is applied, water is likely to stand on the land surface for considerable period and affect the crop yield. Therefore, light irrigation should be preferred for alkali land reclamation.
- The sub-soil layers in these soils continue to have high ESP which confines the crop roots to only upper soil layers. A consequence of this root distribution is that the soil depth from which plants extract moisture is restricted. Therefore, the soil moisture needs to be replenished at shorter intervals.
- The contribution of lower layers to crop water requirement is much less because of poor water transmission characteristics of the lower layers. It also highlights the need for light and frequent irrigation.

Obviously, in land reclamation of alkali lands, traditional irrigation cycle for the normal soils consisting of a brief period of infiltration followed by an extended period of water extraction has to be changed in favour of infiltration-dominated process. It would be appropriate to change the frequency of water application without changing the total depth of water applied since evapotranspiration requirement of the crops does not change much. Thus, in alkali soils one has to follow a 'low depth-high frequency' irrigation system. A field experiment on frequency of irrigation in alkali lands indicated that 9-11 irrigation resulted in maximum production of wheat (Table 8.2) (Gaul *et al.*, 1973). Abrol *et al.* (1975) studied the effect of number of irrigation on wheat yield in an alkali soil at two stages of improvement. The results reveal that there was a linear increase in yield up to 11 irrigations in soil with pH of 9.5 whereas in a soil with pH of 9.0, there was no significant increase in the yield beyond 9 irrigations (Table 8.2). Later studies also established that for optimum yield of summer *dhaincha* (*Sesbania aculeata*) for green manuring, 9 irrigations with shallow depth seemed appropriate.

Table 8.2. Effect of number of irrigation on the yield of wheat

Treatment E (mm)	*1970–71*		*Treatment E (mm)*	*1971-72*	
	No. of irrigations	*Grain yield (t ha^{-1})*		*No. of irrigations*	*Grain yield (t ha^{-1})*
40	11	1.99	30	14	2.63
60	8	1.46	50	9	2.57
80	6	0.96	70	7	2.32
100	5	0.78	90	6	2.04
120	4	0.68	110	5	1.45
CD at 5%		0.45	0.46		

E= Cumulative pan evaporation in mm; Irrigation depth 0.8* E (mm) in first year and 0.6* E (mm) in second year.

Alkali Soils and Quality of Irrigation Water

Saline water has been used world over to reclaim alkali lands. Recommendations have also emerged to that effect. However, a combination of alkali soils-saline water should be used after careful analysis of both the soil and water samples. The data should be examined for individual anions and cations. For example, water rich in CO_3 or Na should altogether be avoided on alkali soils. These waters even when applied to a normal soil will produce alkali hazards and therefore, should be applied only when needed with appropriate management. A complete monitoring of the system is needed annually. Instances are not lacking when the traditional one time application of gypsum failed to sustain the reclamation when sodic (high RSC) waters were used to irrigate the reclaimed land. It is apparent that in such cases, annual application of gypsum to neutralize the RSC of the high RSC water needs to be applied to sustain cop production.

Methods of Irrigation

Broadly, the irrigation methods can be classified in four categories, viz. (i) surface, (ii) subsurface, (iii) sprinkler and (iv) drip. Several indigenous alternatives to drip irrigation have been developed to suit local conditions and to reduce cost (Gupta and Gupta, 1987). Surface methods of irrigation have been divided and subdivided into several classes as illustrated below:

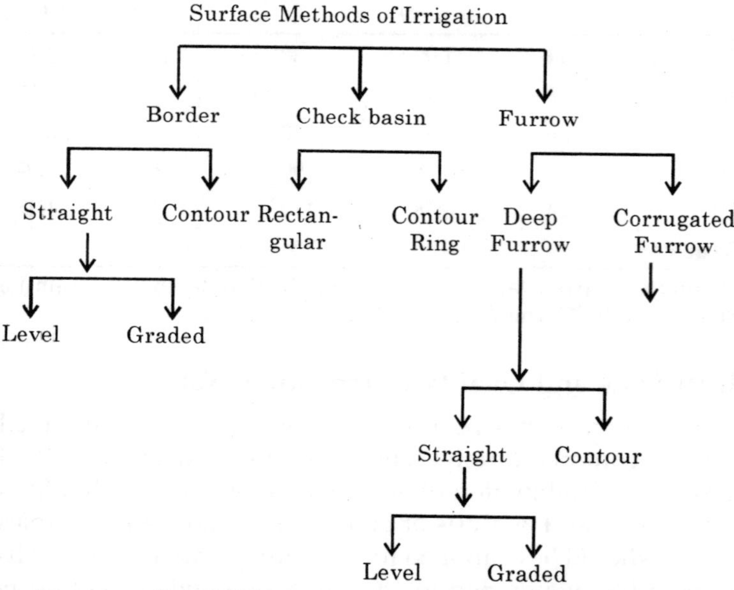

In case of sprinkler irrigation we have the perfo-system and the rotating head system. To apply a particular method of irrigation, the two main considerations are: its technical feasibility to meet the physical requirements and the cost. It is difficult to formulate any thumb rule in this regard. At some places one method of irrigation might be feasible, while at other locations more than one method could be suitable. Cost wise, surface methods of irrigation are the best. With little investments and design skills, surface methods of irrigation can be successfully employed to achieve result similar to the improved irrigation techniques.

Technically speaking, in choosing an irrigation method, several factors need to be considered. Among them, land levelling requirement and its cost, soil type and its variation, quality and amount of irrigation water available, climate, crop rotation, initial and operational cost of the system and ease in operation and maintenance are important. As land levelling is an essential pre-requisite of a reclamation programme, limitations on this account are only few. However, to achieve better results, precision of levelling has to be much higher.

High Frequency–Low Depth Irrigation

Irrigation frequency refers to the number of days between water application or irrigation. It depends upon the consumptive use and moisture extraction depth. As the moisture extraction depth in alkali soils is limited, amount of water available to crop will be much less compared to a crop in normal soil (or gypsum treated soil) where moisture is extracted from lower depths as well. Thus, these soils require high frequency irrigation, which must be provided to achieve optimum crop yields.

Irrigation methods most suited to meet this requirement of high frequency-low depth are the sprinkler and the drip irrigation systems. However, in alkali soils, the scope of these methods is limited due to the following reasons:

1. For the recommended crop rotation (lowland rice-wheat) drip irrigation cannot be utilized, whereas sprinkler irrigation has application only for wheat cultivation. Thus, investment cannot be properly utilized.
2. Initial investments are very high. Coupled with investments on reclamation, the cost of reclamation could be prohibitive.
3. The crops for which drip irrigation is suitable can be grown only after the lands are reclaimed fully. Only at that stage, investments on drip irrigation can be thought of.

4. Initially, more deep percolation losses in surface irrigation methods will be useful as such losses would help leaching the salts and aid in the reclamation process to continue over time.

5. Ground water quality in these regions is generally good and therefore, any advantage of sprinkler or drip irrigation on account of increased tolerance to saline water irrigation is not met with.

In a comparative study on border, perfo-and sprinkler irrigation methods, water use efficiency in all the methods was at par (Pandey and Singh, 1977). It is apparent that surface methods of irrigation will be most useful in alkali lands.

Precision Land Levelling viz.-a-viz. Depth of Application

It is generally believed that as much as 50 percent of the water applied in a surface irrigation method contributes to deep percolation loss. However, the precision with which land levelling is performed greatly determines the minimum amount of water that can be applied per irrigation. Greater the precision, lesser is the depth per irrigation. It has been estimated that if deviations in land levels are up to ± 3 cm around the mean value, nearly 40 percent extra water has to be applied to irrigate the land. Tyagi (1984) reported that to apply 4.2 cm of water per irrigation, it is necessary to achieve a land levelling index of 1.5 (Table 8.3). It is apparent that to apply about the same quantity of water, frequency of irrigation would increase with decreasing (improved) levelling index. At an index of 3.0 cm, one can apply the desired number of 7 irrigations. With increasing levelling index amount of water applied per irrigation is increased. It causes water stagnation, which is likely to affect the yield. It is now known that yield decrease with increasing duration of submergence. Goel and Gupta (1986) revealed that the decline is relatively early in case of alkali soils (Fig. 8.2). Thus, yield will be much less at spots with low elevations as water will stagnate for longer duration at these points. Tyagi (1984) attributed this as a major cause of yield loss in poorly levelled lands. Agarwal and Goel (1981) in a similar study reported that to irrigate the plots completely, cumulative amount of water applied tc wheat increased to 47.0 cm at an index of 3.7 compared to 38.3 cm at an index of 2.0. The water use efficiency consistently increased with decreasing levelling index. Therefore, 'High frequency-low depth' irrigation criterion for alkali lands can be easily met with surface methods of irrigation. Only some additional investments are needed to improve the precision of land levelling. This would avoid the investment on sprinkler irrigation for the wheat crop.

Table 8.3 Levelling index and depth of water applied in one irrigation

*Range of levelling index**	*Depth of water applied (cm)*	*No. of irrigation at IW/CPE = 0.9*
0-1.5	4.2	8
1.5-3.0	5.0	7
3.0-4.5	6.2	5
4.5-6.0	8.2	4
6.0-7.5	9.9	4

$$\text{Levelling index} = \frac{|\Sigma\ (\text{Desired level–actual level})|}{\text{Number of observations}}$$

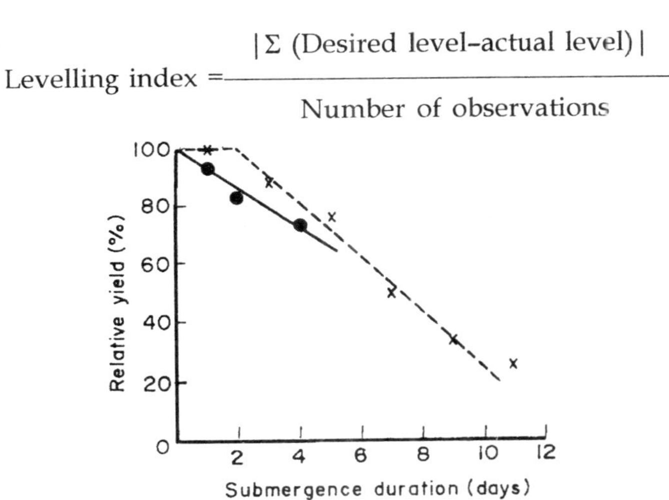

Fig. 8.2 Effect of land submergence on the yield of wheat in normal and an alkali soil

Surface Methods of Irrigation

Flooding, border and ridge and furrow methods are the most common in alkali lands. Basin irrigation (contour ring) is used wherever forest trees are planted.

Flooding

Flooding is the most simple but least desirable method of irrigation because it is quite inefficient. For initial leaching of salts, flooding method is commonly used because of its simple and less technical nature. This method is also used by the farmers in checking precision of the land levelling of their fields. Once the fields are flooded, higher spots become visible. Thus, the earth from those points is cut and dumped at low spots. Later on, the fields are laid out such that improved surface irrigation methods are used.

Border irrigation

Border method of irrigation is controlled flooding, in which land is divided into number of long strips called borders that are separated by low ridges. The border strip has a uniform slope in the direction of flow, which usually varies from 0.05 to 0.2 percent. Cross-slope can be to a maximum of 0.2 percent. The width varies from 3 to 15 m and length from 20 m for a sandy soil to 400 m for a heavy textured soil. This method of irrigation is suitable for all crops and for all soils except with extreme (very high or very low) rates of infiltration.

Levels versus graded borders

Alkali lands are situated in flat terrain and have a general slope of up to 0.1 percent. It was earlier considered that these lands should be perfectly levelled. It is now known that gentle slopes can be advantageously incorporated in the graded borders and perfectly levelled fields are not needed. Comparative performance of the level and graded borders (0.09 percent slope) revealed that graded borders are superior to level borders in respect of water application and distribution efficiencies as well as in the water use efficiency (Table 8.4). In this experiment, stream size was 10 l s^{-1} and the irrigation was applied when depth of irrigation to pan evaporation ratio was 0.7. The cut off ratio was 70 percent except for the first irrigation where it was 85 percent. The cut off ratio needs to be higher during the first irrigation to allow the water to spread all over the border. With these cut off ratios, fields are neither over irrigated nor under irrigated and chances of flooding at the tail end of the borders is minimized.

Table 8.4 Comparative performance of level and graded borders in alkali lands

Items	*Graded border with cut off ratio*				*Level border with cut off ratio*			
	0.55	*0.75*	*0.85*	*1.00*	*0.55*	*0.70*	*0.85*	*1.00*
Irrigation depth (cm)	23.08	27.9	29.1	29.8	30.9	34.5	35.5	32.5
Excess application in level border (cm)	–	–	–	–	7.1	6.6	6.4	2.7
Percentage area covered	84	100	100	100	65	81	93	100
Number of Irrigation	8	7	6	5	7	6	5	4
Application efficiency (%)	83.0	78.0	64.0	57.5	69.8	56.0	52.6	42.7
Distribution efficiency (%)	59.2	82.0	64.6	58.0	39.3	51.0	61.7	70.9
Crop yield t ha^{-1}	3.3	4.2	4.1	3.8	3.1	3.4	3.5	3.4
Water use efficiency (kg $ha^{-1}cm^{-1}$)	131	150	141	131	106	98	108	105

Source: Tyagi (1978)

Size of borders

Discharge of shallow cavity wells in Karnal and Kurukshetra districts on an average is 10 ls^{-1}. To work out the best dimensions of the graded borders for such a stream size (usually it is not possible to reduce the discharge) a replicated trial was conducted with various widths and lengths of the border (Dhruva Naryana *et al.*, 1980).

The borders with lengths of 50-70 m and widths of 4-6 m gave the best performance (Table 8.5). This means that a unit stream size of 1.66-2.5 l s^{-1} is most useful for these soils. The earlier recommendations of 70 percent cut off ratio, with 85 percent cut off ratio for the first irrigation need to be practiced with these sizes of the borders as well.

Table 8.5 Comparative performance of borders of different dimensions

Length (m)	*Width (m)* **4**	**6**	**8**	**10**
		Distribution of efficiency (%)		
50	58	87	70	50
70	45	72	64	44
90	41	69	73	70
		Application efficiency (%)		
50	69	79	79	65
70	42	74	63	64
90	61	58	63	67
		Yield of wheat (t ha^{-1})		
50	4.1	5.2	5.4	4.9
70	4.6	5.4	5.4	5.0
90	4.6	4.7	4.9	4.5

Technology for modifying borders for rice cultivation

Long sloping borders are desirable for good water management in alkali lands particularly for wheat cultivation. Such a situation, however, is not conducive for rice cultivation because it causes differential depths of ponding along the length. Even at the tail end, yield of rice is likely to be reduced because of relatively large depth of submergence. To achieve uniformity at the tail end, Pandey *et al.* (1977) designed a monoclinal border based on a mathematical formulation and translated it to field situations (Fig. 8.3). The techniques when adopted improved uniformity coefficient and crop yield (Table 8.6). The system consists of sub-diving a single border for wheat into 2-3 compartments by raising temporary bunds with suitable outlets at pre-decided heights (Fig. 8.3). The yield in 93 m long border with 0.1 percent slope can be increased with compartmentalisation. The yield in three compartments is significantly greater than one compartment. The yield in two compartments is not significantly different than the three compartments. The trend, however, suggest that there is increase in yield with the increasing uniformity of ponding. To achieve best results therefore, the uniformity coefficient should be in the range of 70-80 percent.

Table 8.6 Rice yield under different treatments of compartmentalisation

Compartment	*Uniformity coefficient (%)*	*Yield ($t\ ha^{-1}$)*	
		*1975**	*1976***
One	42	6.18	6.32
Two	71	6.48	6.54
Three	81	7.10	6.77
CD at 5%		0.61	0.43

* Pusa 2-21, ** Jaya , Source: Pandey *et al.* (1977)

The mathematical analysis was used to show that if head-end depths are kept constant in the three treatments to avoid differential drying up of head end, compartmentalization saves irrigation water that is needed to be applied in the first irrigation (Table 8.7). This confirms the utility of this technique as a management practice.

Fig. 8.3 Use of long borders for rice cultivation through compartmentalization

Based on mathematical equations, which relate the length of the border, slope and height of outlets for different number of compartments; calculations were made to suggest the number of compartments and height of the outlets. This table should be helpful to field workers as the use of mathematical equations could be dispensed with (Table 8.8).

Table 8.7 Effect of compartmentalization on irrigation water depth to be applied during the first irrigation

Compartment	*Average depth of water to be applied (cm)*	*Percent saving over the single compartment*
One	9.65	–
Two	7.33	24.0
Three	6.55	32.1

*Neglecting the amount of water infiltrated common to the three treatments

Table 8.8 Selection of number of compartments and outlet height

Length of border (m)	*Number of compartments and outlets height (cm) in border of slope (%)*			
	0.05	*0.1*	*1.5*	*0.2*
60	1(10.0)	1(10.5), 2 (9.5)	2 (10.0)	3(10.0)
80	1(10.0)	2(10.0)	3 (10.0)	4(10.0)
100	1(10.0)	2(10.5), 3 (9.5)	4 (10.0)	5(10.0)
120	1(10.5)*, 2 (9.5)	3 (10,0)	4(10.5), 5 (9.5)	6(10.0)
200	2(10.5), 3 (9.5)	5 (10,0)	7(10.5), 8 (9,5)	10(10.0)

*Outlet height in parenthesis for given number of compartments

Ridge and furrow method

Alkali soils have low infiltration rate and therefore, are liable to be affected by water stagnation particularly in soils of heavy texture. Therefore, in many cases ridge and furrow method of irrigation has been found superior to flat method of irrigation. In a saline soil at Kanpur (EC_e 4.8 dS m^{-1} and ESP 55), flat method of sowing was not found useful for both maize and wheat. Sowing on the side of ridges was superior to other treatments in the case of maize, whereas for wheat sowing on sides of ridges as well as in furrows were at par, closely followed by sowing in two meter wide beds (Table 8.9). The

Table 8.9 Yield of maize and wheat in different methods of irrigation in saline alkali soil (Kanpur)

Sowing method	*Grain yield (t ha^{-1})*	
	Maize (Ganga-5)	*Wheat (Sarbati Sonora)*
Flat	0.93	2.19
Side of ridges	1.85	2.51
Side of ridges as well as in furrows	1.19	2.52
2 m wide beds	0.95	2.35

Source: Sharma and Verma (2000)

ridge planting was superior to flat bed planting for sorghum and cotton at Indore in black soils. The best results were obtained when (Sharma and Verma, 2000) furrows between ridges were laid out at 0.65% slope (Table 8.10).

Table 8.10 Yield (t ha^{-1}) of sorghum and cotton as influenced by gradient of furrows and method of planting

Slope (%)	*Sorghum*			*Cotton*		
	Ridge	*Flat*	*Mean*	*Ridge*	*Flat*	*Mean*
			1983			
0.30	2.00	1.39	1.69	0.99	0.96	0.97
0.65	3.00	2.33	2.67	1.13	0.97	1.05
1.00	2.34	1.92	2.13	0.89	0.80	0.84
Mean	2.40	1.91	-	1.00	0.91	-
			1984			
0.30	2.41	2.04	2.23	0.96	0.69	0.83
0.60	2.94	2.58	2.76	1.08	0.86	0.97
1.00	1.88	1.73	1.81	0.60	0.70	0.65
Mean	2.41	2.12		0.88	0.75	-

Irrigation Water Management–Field Applications

Irrigation water management broadly covers many aspects that help to make the best use of water supply available at the farm. It includes improvement in the irrigation system as a whole, which in essence consists of the following three components:

1. Source of water
2. Conveyance system
3. Field application system

In alkali soils, entirely irrigated by tube wells with recommended rice-wheat rotation, the overall system efficiency was observed to be 54 percent for the wheat crop and 39 percent for the rice crop. The average water requirement was found to be 46 cm for wheat and 150 cm for rice with water use efficiency of 70 kg ha^{-1} cm^{-1} and 46 kg $ha^{-1}cm^{-1}$ for wheat and rice, respectively. Still there was scope of improvement in irrigation application efficiencies as well as in the cultural management, which consists of improving field layout and levelling index. Studies in operational research revealed that border width, stream size and time of application worked out under the field experiments can be recommended for adoption by the farmers. It would help to improve irrigation water management on their lands. Briefly, ideal land and water management practices for rice-wheat rotation in alkali soils can be listed as under.

1. Level the land to an extent that no water stagnation occurs in the wheat season. Ideally the levelling index should be less than 3.0 cm. This criterion will naturally meet the criterion for rice cultivation.
2. Long and narrow strips, popularly known, as borders should be used. In heavy textured soils where surface stagnation of water is feared, ridge and furrow method can be applied. For rice cultivation these borders can be modified in temporary compartments.
3. Light and more frequent irrigation should be applied in wheat. This should result as a consequence of step 1.
4. In rice, conjunctive use of rainfall and irrigation water should be made. As much as 75 percent of the rainwater can be stored in rice fields. This should naturally reduce the irrigation requirement.
5. Any stagnation of water in wheat should be removed within 24 hr (Sharma and Swarup, 1989).

A part of the discrepancy in yield between the experimental farm and demonstration farm on the one hand and farmers' field on the other can be attributed to non-ideal irrigation water management (see chapter 12). The border strip method of irrigation can be one of the most efficient methods of irrigation in alkali lands. Most modifications involve simple changes in management practices though some may involve capital investment such as precision land levelling. If water application efficiency can be improved to 75 percent from 50 percent, it will permit one and a half time as much land to be irrigated with the same amount of water. Probably it will be necessary to make an economic evaluation of the improved application efficiency viz.-a-viz. cost of land levelling.

Quality of Irrigation Water

The characteristics of the irrigation water that have been conventionally associated in determining its quality are the EC, SAR and RSC besides some toxic elements. Briefly the four properties are:

1. Salinity (Total concentration of soluble salts measured as EC and expressed as dS m^{-1}).
2. Alkali (Relative proportion of sodium to other cations calculated as SAR ($Na/\sqrt{[(Ca + Mg)/2]}$) and expressed as $(mmol\ 1^{-1})^{1/2}$. However, in case of Sodium to Calcium Activity ratio, SCAR ($Na/\sqrt{Ca}$).
3. Sodicity (Relative concentration of bicarbonate as related to calcium + magnesium determined as RSC = $(CO_3 + HCO_3)-(Ca + Mg)$ and expressed as meq l^{-1}. However, in case of waters of pH < 8.5 due to absence of carbonates, it is determined as Residual Sodium Bi-Carbonate, RSBC = (HCO_3-Ca).
4. Toxicity (Concentration of boron, fluorine and lithium etc. expressed as mgl^{-1}).

Salinity

The salinity of water per se is not harmful to the crop. It is the salinity of the soil solution that builds-up over time, which affects the crop adversely. Thus, classification of irrigation water with respect to salinity hazard on the basis of EC is based primarily on the development of salinity in the soil to the extent that yields are affected adversely. On the basis of electrical conductivity, the irrigation water may be classified into six salinity classes (Gupta 1986, Gupta 1989, Gupta and Gupta, 2001).

C-O, Non-saline water (EC < 0.2 dS m^{-1}) may create severe permeability problem in the soil because infiltration rate into the soil is adversely affected due to lack of salts in the water to such an extent that the crop is not adequately supplied with water and yield is reduced.

C-1, Non-saline water (EC < 0.2–1.5 dS m^{-1}) can be used for irrigation with most crops on most soils with little likelihood that soil salinity will develop. Large areas of citrus trees (very sensitive plant) have been irrigated for many years with waters having EC < 1.5 dS m^{-1}. These waters do not require any substantial leaching and are relatively high in Ca and low in chlorides. There is seldom any problem of high SAR/SCAR, RSC/RSBC or toxic elements in the waters falling under this group.

C-2, Low salinity waters (EC–1.5-3.0 dS m^{-1}) can be used if a moderate amount of leaching occurs under the current irrigation practices. Most of the crops except sensitive ones comprising some horticultural and leguminous plants can be grown on all soils except heavy textured, with impeded drainage. These waters do not have any significant problem of SAR/SCAR and toxic elements but may have some problem due to RSC/RSBC.

C-3, Medium salinity waters (EC 3.0-3.5 dS m^{-1}) can be used on soils provided with good drainage such that leaching fraction is not less than 0.3. Most of semi-tolerant and tolerant crops can be grown under good management. The water may have moderate problem of high SAR/SCAR and RSC/RSBC but seldom-significant problems of toxic elements. It is interesting to add here that there is evidence to show that optimum yields of many tolerant crops are obtained under irrigation with waters belonging to this EC group.

C-4, High salinity waters (EC 5.0-10.0 dS m^{-1}) are suitable for irrigation on soils provided with very good drainage and leaching fraction always greater than 0.3, such that EC_e does not exceed EC_{iw}. Only salt tolerant crops can be grown under good management. Higher the total and seasonal rainfall during the crop growth period, better the usability of such waters. These waters generally have significant problem of medium to high SAR/SCAR but rarely due to RSC/RSBC. However, high SAR (>30) values disqualify these waters for satisfactory use for prolonged periods. Summer fallowing is some times necessary for affecting desalinisation, and amendments may also be used to take care of hazards due to sodium and or toxic elements.

C-5, Very high salinity waters (EC > 10 dS m^{-1}) are directly not suitable for irrigation but may be used in conjunction with low salinity waters for field crops. However, some salt tolerant trees and grasses can be grown.

Alkali

Among the soluble salts of irrigation water, sodium is considered to be most hazardous. The water, which might be considered suitable according to salinity, may not be suitable if sodium predominates. The classification of irrigation waters with respect to alkali hazard on the basis of SAR/SCAR is based primarily on the increase of exchangeable sodium and its effect on the physical condition of the soil. ESP of the soil is known to be equal to SAR of the soil in equilibrium in tune with SAR of the water when EC_{iw} and EC_e are less than 5 dS m^{-1} and Mg to Ca ratio is less than one. Thus, SAR of the irrigation water directly reveals whether it is excessive for crop and if it will deteriorate the physical properties of the soil. When EC_{iw} is high (5.0-10.0 dS m^{-1}) and Mg/Ca ratio is also higher than one then SCAR will give better idea than SAR if ESP is to be depended upon for the soil appraisal and/ or crop performance (Gupta 1984, Gupta 1986, Gupta 1990).

On the basis of SAR/SCAR, the irrigation waters may be classified in six classes:

S-0, Non-alkali water (SAR/SCAR <5) can be used for irrigation on almost all soils for all crops even those sensitive to sodium such as stone-fruit trees or woody trees.

S-1, Normal water (SAR/SCAR 5-10) can be used for irrigation on almost all soils with little danger of the development of harmful levels of exchangeable sodium for growing all crops except some stone-fruit or woody trees which are specially sensitive to sodium. These waters do not require leaching and/or amendments.

S-2, Low alkali waters (SAR/SCAR 10-20) can be used for crops, which are semi-tolerant or tolerant to sodium on almost all soils such that LF is around 0.3. If soils contain gypsum or calcium carbonate, these waters can be used more successfully. EC should not be less than 1-2 dS m^{-1} lest permeability problem should develop.

S-3, Medium alkali waters (SAR/SCAR 20-30) can be used only for crops which are tolerant to sodium on soils provided with good drainage such that LF is always greater than 0.3. If soils contain gypsum or calcium carbonate and if rainfall is appreciable and effective, these waters can be used very successfully. EC should not be less than 2-3 dS m^{-1} lest permeability problem should develop.

S-4, High alkali waters (SAR/SCAR 30-40) are not suitable directly for irrigation but may be used in cycle or conjunction with low sodicity waters or with the use of amendments such as gypsum.

S-5, Very high alkali waters (SAR/SCAR > 40) are directly not suitable for irrigation without drastic treatment.

Sodic (RSC/RSBC)

The classification of irrigation waters with respect to carbonate or bicarbonate hazard on the basis of RSC or RSBC is based primarily on the precipitation of Ca and Mg in the soil resulting in increased SAR/ESP characterizing it as alkali soil. Since appreciable amount of carbonates occur in such waters pH (>8.5), RSC should be calculated for high pH waters and RSBC for low (<8.5) waters. These waters also cause permeability problem in the soils (Gupta 1980a, Gupta 1983).

On the basis of RSC/RSBC, the irrigation water may be classified in six classes:

A-0, Non-sodic water (RSC/RSBC–ve) can be used for irrigation on almost all soils for all crops for indefinitely long periods without any problem.

A-1, Normal waters (RSC/RSBC 0 meq l^{-1}) can be used for irrigation on almost all soils for all crops even those very sensitive to carbonates or bicarbonates. These waters may not create any permeability problem.

A-2, Low sodic waters (RSC/RSBC trace-2.5 meq l^{-1}) can be used for irrigation on almost all crops. These waters may not create any permeability problem unless drainage is impeded, rainfall is unduly low and evaporation is very high.

A-3, Medium sodic waters (RSC/RSBC 2.5-5.0 meq l^{-1}) can be used for irrigation on almost all soils with little danger of the development of harmful levels of alkali for growing all crops except those which are specifically sensitive to carbonates or bicarbonates. Optimum yields of several alkali tolerant crops are obtained when RSBC is in this range.

A-4, High sodic waters (RSC/RSBC 5.0-10.0 meql^{-1}) can be used for irrigation on soils provided with good drainage such that LF is not less than 0.3, for growing semi-tolerant and tolerant crops to sodium. EC should be <3.0 dS m^{-1} and SAR < 10. Rainfall should be appreciable and effective (> 500 mm). If SAR is 10 or more, use of gypsum may be required.

A-5, Very high sodic waters (RSC/RSBC 10.0 meq l^{-1}) are not suitable directly for irrigation but may be used in cycle or conjunction with the good quality water or with amendment such as gypsum. High alkalinity with preponderance of carbonates associated with high EC and SAR/SCAR, prohibits the use of these water for irrigation.

REFERENCES

Abrol, I. P., Gaul, B. L. and Acharya, C. L. 1975. Efficient water management-key to success in alkali soils. Indian Fmg. 25(4):15-17.

Acharya, C.L. and Abrol, I. P. 1975. Comparative study of soil water behaviour in a sodic and in an adjacent normal soil. J. Indian Soc. Soil Sci. 23: 391-400.

Acharya, C. L., Sandhu, S. S. and Abrol, I. P. 1979. Effect of exchangeable sodium on the rate and pattern of water uptake by raya (Brassica juncea L.) in the field. Agron. J. 71:936-941.

Agarwal, M.C. and Goel, A.C. 1981. Effect of field levelling quality on irrigation efficiency and crop yield. Agric. Water Mgmt. 4: 457-64.

Dhruva Narayana, V.V., Kalra, V.D. and Singh, O.P. 1980. Design of a farm layout for saline-sodic soils. Indian Fmg. 23(4): 14-5.

Gaul, B. L., Abrol, I. P. and Dargan, K. S. 1973. Frequent and light irrigation best for saline-sodic soils. Indian Fmg. 23:14-15.

Goel, A.C. and Gupta, S.K. 1986. Drainage requirement of wheat in relation to its cultivation in Haryana. Haryana Agric. Univ. J. 26(1): 30-36.

Gupta, I.C. 1980a. The effect of irrigation with high sodium waters on soil properties and wheat growth. Intern. Symp. Salt-Affected Soils, Karnal, 382-8.

Gupta, I.C. 1980b. The effect of irrigation with boron waters on the growth of wheat. Curr. Agric. 4: 51-5.

Gupta, I.C. 1982. The effect of irrigation with high lithium waters on the growth of wheat. Curr. Agric. 6: 84-5.

Gupta, I.C. 1983. Quality of irrigation water and the concept of residual sodium carbonate. Curr. Agric. 7: 150-5.

Gupta, I.C. 1984. Reassessment of irrigation water quality criteria and standards. Curr. Agric. 8:113-26.

Gupta, I.C. 1986. Quality of irrigation water: recent criteria and classification. Curr. Agric. 10: 1-142.

Gupta, I.C. 1990. Use of Saline Water in Agriculture. Revised Edition. Oxford & IBH Publishing Co. 308 pp.

Gupta, I.C. and Chandra, H. 1972. Effect of gypsum in reducing boron hazard of saline waters and soils. Ann. Arid Zone. 11: 228-30.

Gupta, S.K. and Gupta, I.C. 1987. Management of Saline Soils and Waters. Oxford & IBH Publishing Co. New Delhi. 339 p.

Gupta, I. C. and Gupta, S. K. 2001. Use of Saline Water in Agriculture. Third Revised Edition. Scientific Publishers, Jodhpur.

Pandey, R.N., Dhurva Narayana, V.V., Tyagi, N.K. and Gupta, S.K. 1977. Management of sloping borders for rice cultivation in alkali soils. Indian. J. agric. Res. 47: 613-6.

Pandey, R.N. and Singh, O.P. 1977. Evaluation of irrigation methods under salt-affected soils. Ann. Rep. CSSRI, Karnal. 95.

Sharma, D. P. and Swarup, A. 1989. Effect of short-term water logging on growth, yield and mineral composition of wheat in alkali soils. J. Agric. Sci. (Cambridge). 112:191-197.

Sharma, O.P. and Verma, S.K. 2000. Surface drainage requirement of black soils. In Salinity Management in Agriculture (Gupta, S.K., Sharma, S.K. and Tyagi, N.K. Eds.) CSSRI, Karnal. 87-98.

Tyagi, N.K. 1978. Some design aspects of ponded borders with cut-back stream in alkali soils. Curr. Agric. 2: 13-18.

Tyagi, N.K. 1984. Effect of land surface uniformity on irrigation quality and economic parameters in sodic soils under reclamation. Irrig. Sci. 5: 151-60.

9

ALKALI TOLERANCE OF PLANTS

The plants differ widely in salt tolerance from sensitive ones whose normal growth is inhibited by low concentration of salts to the most resistant halophytes, which grow profusely on saline habitats. Glycophytes, in general, grow well in non-saline conditions. Though most crop plants are glycophytes, but there is rather wide range of salt tolerance among them. Beetroot probably tolerates maximum while carrots tolerate the minimum (Strogonov, 1964). Crop plants even exhibit differences in their resistance to salinity, alkalinity and salinity of the irrigation water. Similar to salinity, though alkalinity is not incompatible with plant life, yet crop and crop varieties respond differently to alkali conditions. Therefore, the selection of a crop to be cultivated on alkali soil is a subject of practical and great economic importance. This should allow exploiting saline-alkali lands and putting them to use at little cost.

Criteria for Crop Tolerance

Four criteria are generally followed to evaluate comparative tolerance of crops:

1. Germination of crops
2. Plant survival

3. Absolute plant growth or yield
4. Relative growth or yield

Large numbers of investigations on differential response of crops or varieties have been reported at germination stage and attempts made to extrapolate the tolerance limit for final performance. More than often-such attempts are likely to be frustrating because tolerance characteristics differ from one stage of growth to another.

Plant survival has been used as a criterion by ecologists but without yield, plant survival alone has little value to the farmer. On the other hand, it can be useful criterion for plant breeders. Absolute plant growth or yield is of greatest interest to the farmers. However, this criterion does not permit comparison between crops because yields for different crops are not expressed in comparable terms. The relative growth or yield is defined as the yield on an alkali soil as a fraction of the yield on a non-alkali soil under similar environment and nutritional conditions. This criterion is reliable provided the level of other essential factors such as nutritional factor or water does not affect yield reductions. The main difficulty with this method, however, is to decide at what level of yield reduction, different plants should be compared. A researcher comparing the salt tolerance at 10 percent yield reduction may essentially end up differently than the other who is comparing the salt tolerance at 50 percent yield reduction. Nevertheless, this criterion is favoured world over and is widely used for relative comparison.

In addition to these four criteria, attempts have also been made to evolve a criterion based on metabolic parameters. The sodium and potassium contents in plant tissues and particularly their ratio have been found to be suitable parameters to adjudge the relative alkali tolerance. Studies on few varieties known for their differential affinity to alkali conditions, revealed that at tillering stage, high K/Na ratio would characterize a tolerant variety compared to a variety which has low K/Na ratio (Joshi *et al.*, 1980). Free proline status of leaves at seedling stage has also been found a good indicator of alkali tolerance (Bal, 1976). But in later tests, it was observed that it is not very much reliable. The change in pH of the cell sap as a result of alkali stress also has been found to be useful for comparing relative tolerance of crops and varieties (Dwivedi, 1979). The alkali halophytes showed only a nominal rise in pH of their cell sap at ESP 40 as compared to ESP 10. The tolerant *Kharchia* variety of wheat similarly exhibited a rise of only 1 percent in its sap pH at ESP 40 at 35 days growth stage. In spite of the concerted efforts that have been made in this direction, more information needs to be generated on such tests so as to arrive at a sound criterion.

Adverse Effects of Exchangeable Sodium

The adverse effects of exchangeable sodium on crop growth may be due to the following factors:

1. Direct toxic effects
2. Structural deterioration of the soil (adverse physical condition) restricting moisture transmission and aeration. It may physically impede root elongation and seedling emergence.
3. Nutritional imbalance

In general, the adverse effect appear as a result of the combination of the above three factors. For example an excess of specific ion may be toxic to various physiological processes. At the same time or in some other cases it may also cause nutritional disorders. In alkali soils, specific ions, which may be accumulated by plants are Na^+ or HCO^-_3. When ion imbalance affects the plants, the situation can often be diagnosed and ameliorated.

In alkali soils, emergence of plumule is rendered difficult because of poor physical properties particularly in the absence of proper moisture conditions. If these soils are irrigated prior to emergence, a hard crust is formed, which restrict the emergence of germinating seeds. Poor physical conditions also adversely affect the moisture availability and aeration, which influence the overall plant growth. Some of the attributes of vegetative growth that get reduced are plant height, leaf number, leaf area, tiller number and root and shoot dry weight.

Iron chlorosis, zinc deficiency and boron toxicity are some of the problems that are experienced while cropping on alkali soils. Nutritional problem can often be corrected by ameliorating soil to fit the crop. In alkali soils of India where iron chlorosis and zinc deficiency have been observed, boron toxicity has not been of much consequence. Gupta (1979) observed that even if toxic amounts of boron are present in the original alkali soil, gypsum application would reduce boron to non-toxic levels partly by converting the soluble sodium metaborate to insoluble calcium metaborate and partly through leaching.

Modelling Salt Tolerance of Crops

Salt tolerance of crops could be studied by appropriately modelling crop response to saline/alkali environment. Maas and Hoffman (1977) extensively evaluated the experimental data on crop production of many crops in saline environment and proposed a piecewise linear model which states that yield of a crop essentially remain unaltered with increasing salts unless a threshold value is reached. Beyond this level, decrease in crop yield is linear till it becomes zero. Mathematically, such a crop production function could be described with a piecewise linear model such that:

$$Y = \begin{cases} 100 & 0 \le EC_t \le EC_e \\ 100\text{-}S\,(EC_e\text{-}EC_t) & EC_t \le EC_e \le EC_o \\ 0 & EC > EC_o \end{cases} \qquad (9.1)$$

Here, Y is the relative yield as a fraction of yield in non-saline conditions, EC_t is electrical conductivity of the soil up to which there is no reduction in yield and is described as threshold EC, EC_e is EC of the soil measured in saturation extract, EC_o is the salinity of the soil at or beyond which there is no yield and S is the slope of relative yield versus salinity curve between EC_t and EC_o. It represents yield reduction per unit increase in the soil salinity beyond the threshold. Model proposed by Maas and Hoffman (1977) has been extensively tested for different saline environment such as for boron toxicity (Francois, 1982), exchangeable sodium percentage (Gupta and Sharma, 1990) and electrical conductivity of the irrigation water (Mishra *et al.*, 1990). In all cases piecewise linear model has been found very effective in describing crop response. In these conditions EC_e in Eq. 8.1 is replaced with level of boron (mg l^{-1}), ESP or electrical conductivity of irrigation water, respectively.

In a study, van Genuchten and Hoffman (1984), observed that in many cases, piecewise linear model fails to describe the complete response curve particularly at the tail portion. Therefore, they proposed a new equation for evaluating crop tolerance, which could be written as:

$$Y = \left[\frac{1}{1 + (EC_e / EC_{50})}\right]^P \tag{9.2}$$

Here, P is the parameter, which controls the shape of the response curve, and EC_{50} is the electrical conductivity of the soil at which yield is 50 percent of the control value.

Simultaneously, with the development of Eq. (9.2) and to take into account situation where yield increases initially with increasing EC and then declines, a third model was also proposed (van Genuchten, 1983). This model is written as:

$$Y = \exp\,(a\, EC_e - b\, EC_e^{\,2}) \tag{9.3}$$

Here, a and b are constants which control the shape of the response function. The EC at which yield will be maximum can be given by the relation $EC_e = a/2\,b$. It may be noted that such situation do occur in practice. Yield of various vegetable crops was observed to be initially increasing with increasing EC of the irrigation water before starting declining in several experiments carried out with pitcher irrigation technique. These models could also be used for estimating crop tolerance to alkali conditions provided EC_e is replaced with ESP (Gupta and Sharma, 1990) or any other relevant parameter such as SAR.

Another model to assess crop response has been the SegReg model released by ILRI (Oosterbaan, 1998). It is designed for segmented linear regression with one dependent variable (crop yield) and one or two independent variables (crop growth factors). Introducing a breakpoint makes the segments. Thus, one can obtain a broken line. The selection of the best breakpoint and function is based on maximizing the statistical coefficient of explanation and performing tests of significance.

It is believed that with the four models available, any kind of crop response could be simulated by appropriately selecting a model.

Relative Salt Tolerance Rating

Salt tolerance rating in respect of some important crops listed on the basis of germination (Mehrotra and Gangwar, 1964) revealed that during summer, maize and *mahua* perform well in alkali soil both under high and low alkalinity (Table 9.1). For winter season, wheat appears to be best performer. Rice, which is reported to be highly tolerant, appears to follow maize and *mahua* under low salinity and is least tolerant among the crops tried at high salinity. This observation should not create confusion, as data from some other places have put rice as the most tolerant crop for alkali conditions. The variation in the conclusion drawn could be traced to the difference in the testing technique. While in the studies reported, direct sown rice has been taken for comparison, in case of studies elsewhere, rice has been grown with 30-40 days old seedlings. Dargan (1979) reported that age of seedlings significantly affects the tolerance of rice. The seedlings aged 5-6 weeks were found more tolerant than younger seedlings. According to Mehrotra and Gangwar (1964) also, rice after germination (25 days later) is more tolerant to alkali conditions and surpasses even the maize and *mahua* crop. The American literature also lists rice as a semi-tolerant crop as far as alkali conditions are concerned and this listing should be viewed in the context that there also rice is grown by direct seeding. A relative crop tolerance list of crops at 50% yield reduction has been prepared (Table 9.2).

Table 9.1 Relative tolerance of crops to alkaline conditions at germination stage

High	*Low*
Kharif crops	
Maize	Maize
Mahua	Mahua
Cotton	Rice
Arhar	Urd
Urd	Cotton
Rice	Pearl millet
	Arhar
	Dhaincha
	Moong bean
	Sanai
	Kodon
	Sorghum
Rabi Crops	
Wheat	Barley
	Pea
	Berseem

Table 9.2 Tolerance of crops to various levels of soil sodicity

Range of ESP	*Crops*
10–15	Safflower, mash, peas, lentil, pigeon pea, *urd* bean
15–20	Bengal gram, soybean, maize
20–25	Groundnut, cow pea, onion, pearl millet
25–30	Linseed, garlic, guar, lemon grass, pamarosa, sugarcane, cotton
30–50	Wheat, raya, sunflower, berseem, shaftal, senji, blue panic, gutton panic
50–60	Barley, sesbania, para grass, Rhodes grass, matricaria
60-70	Rice, Karnal grass

Relative crop yield is only 50 percent of the maximum in the alkalinity range indicated

The salt tolerance indices in terms of threshold ESP, slope and ESP_{50} as related to eq. (9.1) for various crops are listed in Table 9.3. It is an updated version of the crop tolerance table proposed by Gupta and Gupta (1987) where in critical limits of ESP for various crops for yield reduction of 10, 25 and 50 percent were reported (Table 9.4) which also lists critical limits of ESP for various grasses. The yield of all crops decline with increasing ESP beyond a threshold (Table 9.3). Piecewise linear model describes the data sets well in all crops except transplanted rice where it failed to describe the yield beyond 50 percent yield reduction. This situation could also arise in other tolerant crops with initially flat slopes but sharper decline in yield beyond a particular ESP (Generally ESP_{50}-the ESP at which the yield is 50 percent of the control value). Response curves for tolerant (Either ESP_t is high or slope is less so that $ESP_{50} > 50$), moderately tolerant and sensitive crops (ESP > 25) are represented in Fig. 9.1 which show that crop plants cover a fairly wide spectrum from sensitive to fairly tolerant. The relative tolerance of various grasses to soil pH or ESP has also been worked out (Kumar and Abrol, 1986, See Chapter 11).

The most important crop rotation for alkali soils is rice-wheat. The observed and predicated response curve of rice and wheat indicated that rice is much more tolerant to alkali conditions than wheat (Fig. 9.2). The standard deviations from the mean values used in fitting the piecewise linear model for each point are also shown. It may be noted that deviations from the mean are much larger in case of wheat compared to rice. Deviation is more at middle point than at extremes. This could be due to relatively large spatial variability of ESP in reclaimed alkali soils.

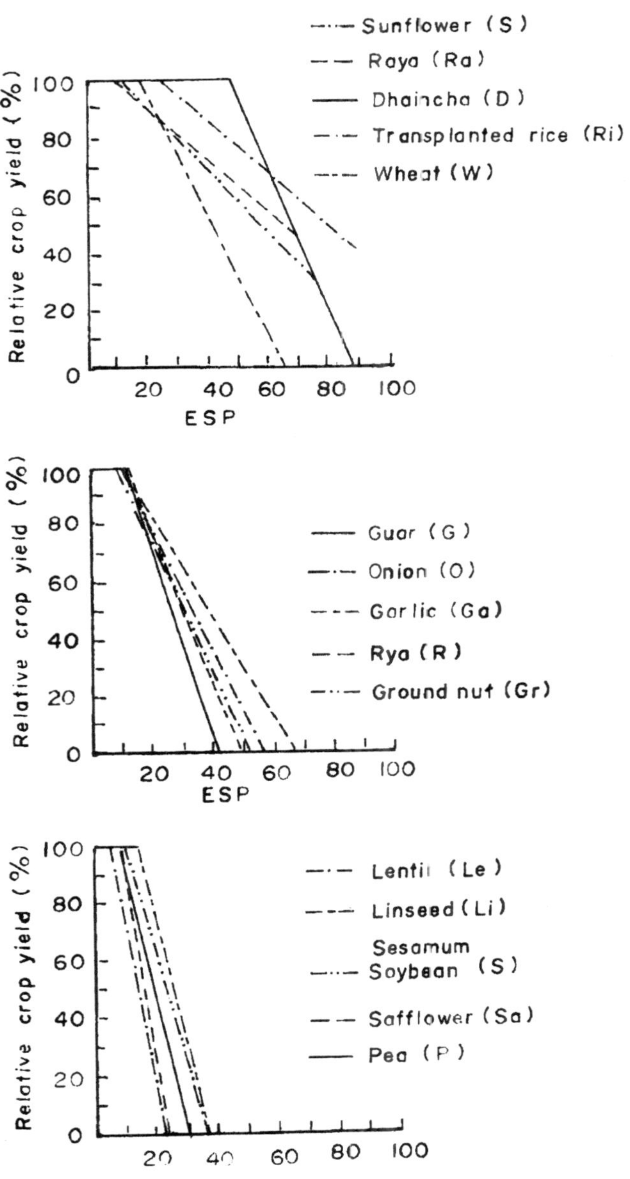

Fig. 9.1 Relative tolerance of crops to alkali environment

Table 9.3. Threshold, slope and ESP_{50} of crops for medium textured soils (sandy loam)

Crop		*Piecewise linear model*		
		ESP_t	(%) *Slope*	ESP_{50}
Barley	*Hordeum vulgare (P)*	8.5	3.5	22.3
Cowpea	*Vigna unguiculata*	13.5	9.1	19.0
Sesbania	*Sesbania aculeata*	46.9	2.4	67.7
Gram	*Cicer arietinum*	7.7	5.0	17.7
Groundnut (Peanut)	*Arachis hypogaea*	8.0	2.2	29.7
Guar (Cluster bean)	*Cyamopsis psoraloides D.C.*	11.9	3.2	27.5
Lentill	*Lens esculentum*	4.9	5.5	14.0
Linseed	*Linum unitatissinum L.*	13.3	2.3	25.0
Pear millet	*Pennisetum typhoideum*	13.6	2.6	32.8
Raya (Indian mustard)	*Brassica juncea L.*	7.6	0.8	70.1
Rice	*Oryza sativa*	24.4	0.9	80
		32.7	1.3	71.2
Rye	*Secale cereale*	11.0	2.6	30.2
Sesamum	*Sesamum indicum*	9.0	3.6	22.8
Soybean	*Glycine max*	8.0	3.5	22.3
Sunflower	*Helianthis annus L.*	11.3	1.1	56.8
Saffflower	*Carthamus tinctorius*	7.6	5.2	17.2
Wheat	*Triticum aestivum (P)*	16.4	2.1	40.2
		20.4	2.6	39.6
Pea	*Pisum sativum*	7.7	4.1	19.9
Onion	*Allium cepa*	9.8	2.2	32.5
Garlic	*Allium sativum*	9.5	1.8	37.3

ESP values indicate average soil ESP of 0-15 cm layer
ESP_t are the lower ESP values at which trails were conducted
P = The studies have been conducted in pots

Intra-crop variability, besides its role in crop selection, reflects on the future success of any breeding program for stressed environments. Based on the work at CSSRI, Karnal, the range of intra-crop variability is reported in Table 9.5 (Mishra *et al.* 2000). It is apparent that rice has the maximum range of genetic variability for sodicity tolerance while barley has the maximum for salinity tolerance.

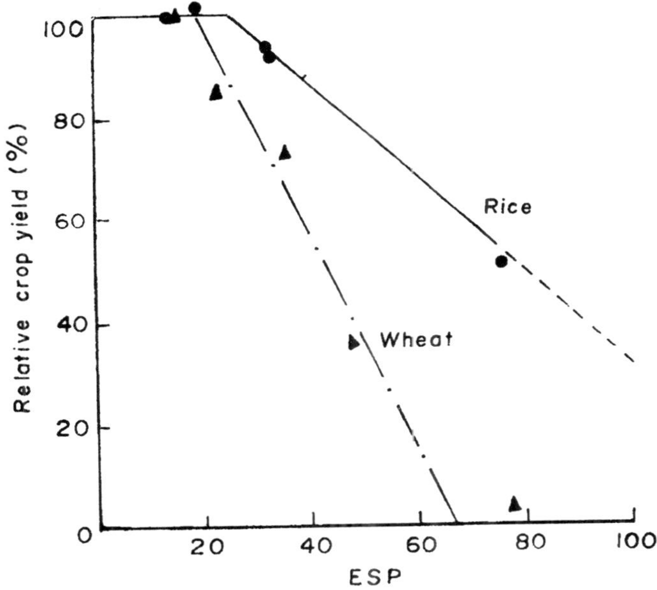

Fig. 9.2 Observed and predicted response curves for rice and wheat

Genotypic Differences

There are large genotypic differences and as such crop varieties differ in their tolerance widely. Therefore, not only selection of crops is important, but also selection of crop varieties is equally important. Comparison of salt tolerance indices for 5 genotypes of rice indicated that CSR 3 (a natural selection from indica types) is the most tolerant to alkali with an ESP threshold of 26.16 while M 1-48 is the least tolerant with an ESP threshold of only 8.02 (Table 9.6). Similar test with 6 genotypes of wheat indicated that Kharchia 65 was the

Table 9.4 Critical limits of soil ESP at different yield levels

Crop	*Critical limits for yield reduction of*		
	10%	*25%*	*50%*
Rice	38.0	54.0	72.5
Wheat	22.5	33.3	46.0
Barley	29.5	42.0	52.2
Castor	14.5	22.5	37.0
Sunflower	22.5	36.8	52.5
Pear millet	13.5	19.0	24.5
Linseed	14.2	22.0	34.5
Pea	9.8	12.5	18.5
Raya	19.5	37.5	68.0
Rye	14.0	18.5	28.0
Dhaincha	15.5	38.5	80.5
Bermuda grass	60.0	85.0	–
Karnal grass	12.5	–	–
Hybrid Napier	21.0	33.0	52.5
Para grass	30.0	52.0	89.5
Setaria grass	24.5	37.5	60.0
Marvel grass	23.0	49.0	92.0
Rhodes grass	14.5	76.5	87.0

most tolerant both in respect of ESP threshold and ESP_{50} (Table 9.7). The order of alkali tolerance is Kharchia 65>KRL 4-13 > KRL 3-23 > KRL 1-4 = HD 2009 > HD 4502. It may be noted that there are not much significant differences among the last four genotypes. Similar differences in the genotypes of barley are shown in Fig. 9.3. A view of the salt tolerant genotypes CSR 10 (rice) and KRL 19 (wheat) is shown in Fig. 9.5 and 9.6 respectively.

Table 9.5 Intra-crop variability of salt tolerance in some important crops

Crop	*Sodicity (pH)*	*Salinity (EC dS m^{-1})*
Rice	9.2-10.2	4.0-10.0
Wheat	8.8-9.3	6.5-11.0
Barley	9.0-9.3	4.0-6.5
Indian mustard	8.9-9.2	4.0-5.5
Toria	8.8-9.0	4.0-6.0
Taramira	8.7-8.9	4.0-6.0
Linseed	8.7-8.9	4.0-6.0
Safflower	8.7-8.8	4.0-6.0
Sunflower	8.6-8.8	4.0-6.0
Sugarcane	8.8-9.0	-
Cowpea	8.6-8.8	4.0-5.0
Green gram	8.6-8.8	-
Pigeon pea	8.3-8.6	-
Pea	8.6-8.8	4.0-5.0
Gram	8.6-8.8	4.0-5.0
Bakla	8.6-8.8	4.0-7.0
Sugar beet	9.2-9.8	4.2-10.0
Pearl millet	8.7-8.9	4.0-8.0

Table 9.6 Alkali tolerance of rice genotypes

	CSR^{-1} Mutant	*M1-48*	*Basmati 370*	*CSR^{-1}*	*CSR-3*
Threshold ESP_t	20.36	8.02	15.92	20.63	26.16
Slope	2.03	2.22	1.84	0.82	0.73
ESP_{50}	45.00	30.60	43.10	81.60	94.65
Mean yield (t ha^{-1})	1.49	1.62	1.32	1.49	1.64

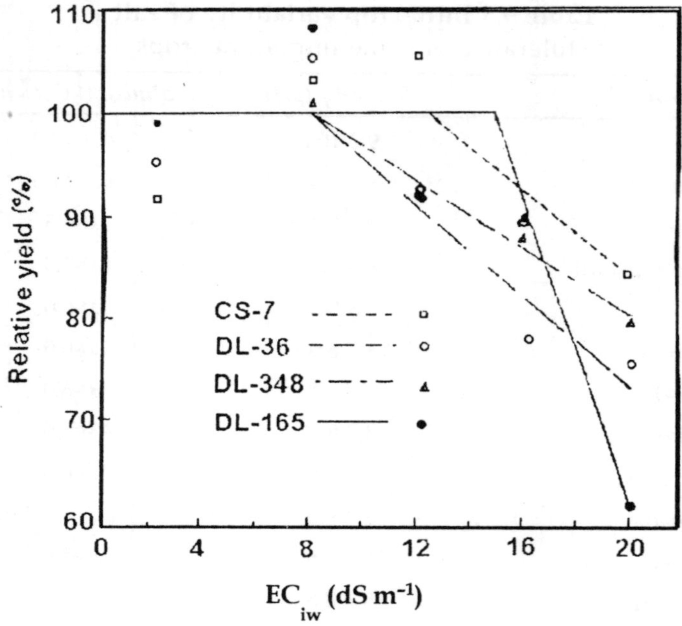

Fig. 9.3 Relative tolerance of barley genotypes to irrigation water salinity

Fig. 9.4 A view of the alkali tolerant rice variety CSR10

Fig. 9.5 A view of the alkali tolerant rice variety KRL 19

Ionic imbalance and leaf water potential

As discussed previously, alkali condition of the soil affects most crops because of the deterioration in soil physical properties, ionic imbalance, nutrition related problems and toxicity. Increasing levels of alkali lead to accumulation of Na and depletion of K in all genotypes of wheat but to a greater degree for sensitive ones, HD 4502 and HD 2009. Better performance of the tolerant genotypes, kharchia 65 and KRL 4-13 appears to be due to regulation of ionic uptake and distribution within the plant (Sharma, 1987). Higher concentration of Na is accompanied by reduced concentration of K in case of the sensitive genotypes. It is made worse by less favourable water relations as indicated by sharper decline in leaf water potential. Relatively, more favourable water relations in the case of tolerant genotypes enable them to perform better under adverse conditions of alkali (Table 9.8).

Table 9.7 Alkali tolerance of wheat genotypes

Genotypes	*Grain yield*			*Plant dry weight*[1]		
	Threshold ESP_t	*Slope*	ESP_{50}	*Threshold*	*Slope*	ESP_{50} ESP_t
HD 4502	14.00*	2.83	31.7	14.05	2.22	36.6
HD 2009	14.00*	2.76	32.1	14.00*	2.43	34.6
KRL 3-23	14.00*	2.45	34.4	14.00*	1.32	51.9
KRL 1-4	14.00*	2.77	32.1	15.56	2.19	38.4
KRL 4-13	14.00*	2.10	37.8	14.00*	1.67	43.9
Kharchia 65	14.00*	1.85	44.9	14.00*	1.25	54.0

[1]Shoot dry weight excluding grain

* The threshold is taken as 14.0, the lowest ESP at which experiment was conducted

Table 9.8 Effect of increasing levels of alkali on water potential of flag leaf, sodium and potassium concentrations of leaves of wheat genotypes at grain filling stage

ESP	*HD 4502*	*HD 2009*	*Kharchia 65*	*KRL 4-13*
		Leaf water potetnial (MPa)		
14	-1.57 ± 0.37	-1.59 ± 0.32	-1.30 ± 0.15	-1.42 ± 0.31
28	-1.90 ± 0.18	-1.86 ± 0.34	-1.51 ± 0.28	-1.60 ± 0.16
39	-2.30 ± 0.25	-1.94 ± 0.11	-1.70 ± 0.16	-1.68 ± 0.19
50	-3.24 ± 0.35	-2.70 ± 0.21	-1.72 ± 0.12	-1.80 ± 0.08
61	–	–	-1.78 ± 0.09	-1.88 ± 0.09
		Leaf Na (% dry weight)		
14	0.29 ± 0.05	0.28 ± 0.80	0.33 ± 0.70	0.20 ± 0.05
28	1.41 ± 0.12	1.37 ± 0.15	1.15 ± 0.20	1.18 ± 0.31
38	2.16 ± 0.16	2.06 ± 0.24	1.20 ± 0.20	1.16 ± 0.12
50	3.74 ± 0.22	3.65 ± 0.30	1.36 ± 0.18	1.38 ± 0.14
61	–	–	1.28 ± 0.21	1.35 ± 0.18
		Leaf K (% dry weight)		
14	2.58 ± 0.34	2.29 ± 0.21	2.87 ± 0.34	3.56 ± 0.41
28	1.50 ± 0.20	1.95 ± 0.16	2.31 ± 0.19	2.41 ± 0.31
38	1.15 ± 0.14	1.49 ± 0.16	1.72 ± 0.21	2.41 ± 0.31
50	0.53 ± 0.17	0.68 ± 0.14	1.27 ± 0.17	1.38 ± 0.19
61	–	–	1.25 ± 0.18	1.32 ± 0.24

Central Soil Salinity Research Institute, Karnal has developed few salt tolerant varieties that can be well adopted in alkali soils. These varieties and others available are reported in Table 9.9.

Table 9.9 Promising varieties of important crops released and in pipe line for cultivation in alkali soils

Crop	*pH/ESP*	*Salinity, EC ($dS\ m^{-1}$)*	*Varieties*
Rice	9.8-10.2	10.0	CSR10, CSR11
	9.4-9.8		CSR10, CSR11 CSR12, CSR13 CSR19,CSR20 CSR21,CSR24 CSR26
Wheat	9.2-9.3	6.5	KRL 1-4, WH157 Raj 3077
	8.7-9.0	5.5	HD 2009, HD2285, HD2329, WH542, C306
Indian mustard	8.8-9.2	6.5	Pusa bold, Varuna, Kranti
	ESP 12.0-38.3		CS52
Barley	up to pH 9.3	11.0	CSB1, CSB2 CSB3,DL200 Ratna, BH97 DL348
Sugarbeet	9.5-10.0	10.0	Ramonskay 06 Poly rava-E, Tribal Meribo-resistapoly
Sugarcane	<9.0		CO453, CO1341, CO6801, CO62329 and CO1111

Source: Mishra (1996)

Alkali Tolerance of Forest Species

Much like crops, forest species also differ among themselves in their tolerance to alkali conditions (Yadav and

Pathak, 1967; Khan and Yadav, 1969). Yadav and Singh (1970) in an investigation in Vrijbhumi Forest Division of Uttar Pradesh found that all the planted species failed to grow on soils having pH more than 10 and soluble salt content above 3.42 percent in the top layer and above 1.14 percent in the subsurface with kankar nodules. Safe limit for *Prosopis juliflora* was found to be up to a pH of 9.5 and soluble salt content of 0.54%. *Acacia nilotica* on the other hand could grow satisfactory on the soils having pH value above 10.0 and soluble salt content below 0.3 percent. Singh *et al.* (1993) and Singh *et al.* (1997) worked extensively on the afforestation of alkali lands. More details on this aspect and a list of forest plants that can grow under different pH ranges are listed in Table 11.4 of Chapter 11 of this book.

Tolerance of Crops to Soil Salinity

In many cases salinity problem occurs along with the problem of alkali. It is particularly true in the case of saline-alkali soils. Therefore, crop selection in such cases may have to be made on the basis of tolerance to soil salinity than alkali. The yield reductions due to excessive salts could be ascribed to the following three factors, which may influence plants singly or in combination.

1. A general osmotic effect in which growth and yield are determined by the osmotic pressure of the medium.
2. Imbalance in the uptake of ions
3. Toxic effects on specific plants due to accumulation of the causative ions in the plant.

Maas and Hoffman (1977) prepared a comprehensive table listing EC_t, slope and EC_o of many crops utilizing the piecewise linear model. Such comprehensive data for Indian conditions is lacking. Gupta (1992) collated the existing information on this subject and utilizing eq. (9.1) determined EC_t, slope and EC_o for several crops and soil/climatic conditions (Table 9.10). More comprehensive data are available for the Indian conditions in respect of crop tolerance to irrigation with saline water. Gupta and Yadav (1986) based on a review of the experimental evidence reported the critical limits of salinity of the irrigation water at which yield would decline by 10, 25 and 50 percent of optimum yield that is expected with fresh water. Mishra *et al.* (1990) utilized the same data and with the help of eq. (9.1) listed EC_t, slope and EC_{50} in terms of EC of the irrigation water (Table 9.11). Such data could be used to work out tolerance of a crop to soil salinity provided leaching fractions could be properly estimated.

Table 9.10 Crop tolerance to soil salinity for working out leaching requirement

Slits	*Soil type*	*Crop*	*Threshold ES* ($dS\ m^{-1}$)	*Slope* (%)	EC_{50} ($dS\ m^{-1}$)
Sample	Sandy loam	Wheat	4.0	29.0	5.7
		Mustard	6.0	15.0	9.3
		Barley	7.0	19.0	9.6
Karnal	Sandy loam	Mung bean	1.8	20.7	3.3
		Mustard	3.8	6.9	11.0
		Sorghum	2.2	10.6	6.9
Agra	Sandy loam	Wheat	8.2	19.8	10.7
		Mustard	6.1	20.7	8.5
		Berseem	3.5	12.5	7.5
		Tomato	1.3	6.5	9.0
Dharwad	Black clay	Wheat	2.3	20.5	4.7
		Safflower	2.8	20.7	5.2
		Sorghum (w)	2.1	3.9	14.9
		Itallian millet	6.1	50.0	7.1
Indore	Black clay	Berseem	2.3	20.5	4.7
		Safflower	2.8	20.7	5.2
		Sorghum (w)	2.1	3.9	14.9
		Italian millet	6.1	50.0	7.1
		Sataria	1.1	2.2	23.9
Indore	Black clay	Berseem	2.0	11.2	6.5
		Safflower	2.8	5.0	12.8
		Maize	0.5	7.9	6.8

The tolerance of plant species to soil salinity has also been worked out (Table 9.12). In areas where salinity is not associated with shallow water table conditions, *Acacia auriculifarmis, Acacia auriculifarmis, Lencaena lenocephala* can be grown. Where high salinity and shallow water table are encountered, species like *casuarina glauce, Tamarix articulata* and *Prosopis juliflora* have been found to do well (Tomar and Gupta, 1986; Tomar *et al.* 1998).

Table 9.11 Threshold irrigation water quality, slope and EC_{50} of selected crops

Crop	*Soil texture*	*Location*	*Piecewise linear model*		
			EC_t	*Slope (%)*	EC_{50}
Wheat	Sandy loam	Agra	7.0	4.50	10.1
	Loamy sand	Jodhpur	3.5	8.90	9.1
	Sandy loam	Karnal	7.9	8.70	13.6
	Dune sand	Karnal	11.1	2.90	28.3
	Sandy loam	Hisar	3.4	4.50	12.5
	Sandy loam	Sampla	1.7	1.75	30.3
	Sandy loam	Kanpur	1.0	4.60	11.9
	Black clay	Dharwad	1.0	4.60	11.9
	Black clay	Indore	4.4	4.70	15.0
Barley	Sandy loam	Agra	8.3	2.2	31
	Sandy loam	Jobner	10.8	3.95	23.5
Rice	Sandy loam	Karnal	1.3	7.57	7.9
	Clay (S)	Bapatla	1.0	7.79	7.4
	(W)		1.0	12.52	5.0
Maize	Black clay	Indore	1.0	7.17	8.0
	Black clay	Dharwad	1.0	2.84	18.6
Sorghum	Sandy loam (F)	Agra	3.2	2.96	20.1
	(G)	Agra	6.2	3.82	19.3
	Black clay	Dharwad	1.0	5.80	9.6
Pearl millet	Sandy loam	Agra	4.6	2.03	29.3
	(576.0)				
	(408.0)		2.2	3.92	14.9
	(358.5)		4.1	5.80	9.6
Mustard	Sandy loam	Agra	6.6	7.35	13.4
	Sandy loam	Jobner	2.0	1.96	27.5

Sunflower	Sandy loam	Agra	4.9	7.82	11.3
	Sand (W)	Bapatla	1.0	3.76	14.3
Safflower	Sandy loam	Agra	3.8	3.31	18.9
	Black clay	Dharwad	1.0	2.41	21.8
Groundnut	Sand	Baptla	1.0	11.54	5.3
Pigeon pea	Sandy loam	Agra	0.6	4.50	13
Cluster bean	Sandy loam	Jobner	2.0	7.77	8.4
Onion	Sandy loam	Agra	0.6	12.75	4.6
	Sand	Bapatla	4.6	11.87	8.8
Lady's finger	Sandy loam	Agra	0.6	4.23	12.4
Fenugreek	Sandy loam	Jobner	2.0	5.59	10.9
Berseem	Sandy (F)	Agra	2.2	13.9	5.8
Italian millet	Black clay	Dharwad	8.8	11.30	13.3
Finger millet	Black clay	Bapatla	1.0	5.25	10.6
Potato	Sandy loam	Agra	1.7	6.26	9.7
Brinjal	Sandy loam (P)	Karnal	9.8	10.6	14.5
	Sand	Baptla	1.0	7.1	8.0

S = Summer; W = winter, F = Fodder, G = grain; P = Pithcer irrigation
Numbers in parenthesis indicate average rainfall

Table 9.12 Salinity tolerance of trees

Tolerant (EC_e 25-35 dS/m)	*Tamarix troupii* (Pharans), *T. articulata* (Pharanas), *Prosopis julifora* (Pahari Kikar), *Pithecellobium dulce* (Junglee jalebi), *Parkinsonia aculeata* (Parkinsonia), *Acacia farnesiana* (Pissi Babul)
Moderately tolerant (EC_e 15-25 dS/m)	*Callistemon lancheolatus* (Bottle brush), *Acacia nilotica* (Kikar), *A. pennatula* (Babul), *A. tortilis* (Israeli kikar), *Casuarina glauca 13155* (Casuarina), *C. glauca 13987* (Casuarina), *C. obesa 27, C. glauca* (FRI), *C. equisetifolia* (FRI) (Casuarina), *Eucalyptus camaldulensis* (Safeda), *Leucaena leucocephala* (Subabool), *Erescentia alata* (Erescentia)

Moderately sensitive (EC_e 10-15 dS/m)	*Casuarina cunninghamiana* (FRI) (Casuarina), *C. cunninghamina* (Aust) (Casuarina), *Eucalyptus tereticornis* (Safeda), *Acacia auriculkiformis* (Australian kikar), *Terminalia arjuna* (Arjan), *Pongamia pinnata* (Papri), *Gauzuma ulmifolia, Leucaena shannoni* (Subabool), *Samanea saman* (Rain tree), *Albizia cartibea* (Siris), *Senna atomaria* (Senna)
Sensitive (EC_e 7-10 dS/m)	*Syzgium cuminii* (Jamun), *S. fruitcosum* (Jamoa), *Tamarindus indica* (Imli), *Salix spp.* (Willow), *Acacia deami* (Acacia), *Albizia guachepela* (Siris), *Alelia herbertismithi* (Alelia), *Caesalpinia eriostachyyas* (Caesalpinia), *C. velutina* (Caesalpinia), *Haemotoxylon brasiletto* (Haemataxylon)

REFERENCES

Bal, A.R. 1976. Salinity tolerance through seed germination and proline. Bio. Pl. 18: 227-229.

Dargan. K.S. 1979. Agronomic and cultural practices for crop production in salt-affected soils. Curr. Agric. 3: 1-20.

Dwivedi, R.S. 1979. Plant physiology. In: A Decade of Research, CSSRI, Karnal. 99-116.

Francois, L.E. 1982. Effect of excess boron on tomato yield, fruit size and vegetative growth. J. Am. Soc. Hort.Sci. 109: 322-7.

Gupta, I.C. 1979. Note on the effect of leaching and gypsum on the detoxification of boron in a saline-sodic soil. Curr. Agric. 3: 231-4.

Gupta, I.C. and Yadav, J.S.P. 1986. Crop tolerance to saline irrigation waters. J. Indian Soc. Soil. Sci. 34: 279-86.

Gupta, S.K. 1992. Leaching of saline soils. Bull. 17, Central Soil Salinity Research Institute, Karnal.

Gupta, S. K. and Gupta, I.C. 1987. Management of Saline Soils and Waters. Oxford and IBH Pub. Co. New Delhi. 339 p.

Gupta, S.K. and Sharma, S.K. 1990. Response of crops to high exchangeable sodium percentage. Irrig. Sci. 11: 173-9.

Joshi, Y.C., Qadar, Ali., Bal, A. R. and Rana, R. S. 1980. Sodium/ potassium index of wheat seedling in relation to sodicity tolerance. Intern. Symp. Salt-Affected Soils, Karnal, 1980. 457-60.

Khan, M.A.W. and Yadav, J.S.P. 1969. Characteristics and afforestation problems of saline-alkali soils. Indian Forester 88: 259-71.

Kumar, A. and Abrol, I. P. 1986. Grasses in alkali soils. Bull. 11. Central Soil Salinity Research Institute, Karnal. 95p.

Maas, E. V. and Hoffman, G.J. 1977. Crop salt tolerant: Current assessment. J. Irrig. Drain Div. ASCE, 103 (IR): 115-34.

Mehrotra, K.L. and Gangwar, B. R. 1964. Studies on salt and alkali tolerance of some imprortant crops in Uttar Pradesh. J. Indian Soc. Soil. Sci. 12: 75-84.

Mishra, B. 1996. Highlights of Research on Crops and Varieties for Salt-affected Soils. Research Bull, CSSRI, Karnal. 28p.

Mishra, B., Singh, R. K. and Senedira, D. 2000. Enhancing genetic resources and breeding for problem soils. In Using Diversity: Enhancing and maintaining Genetic Resources On-Farm (Sperling, L. and Loevinsohn, M. Eds.) IDRS Resource Book (On-Line)

Mishra, K.L., Porwal, A. K. and Gupta, S. K. 1990. Assessment of crop tolerance to saline irrigation waters. Bhujal News. 5: 35-40.

Oosterbaan, R. J. 1998. SEGREG. Lecture Note 4 and Manual. ILRI, Wageningen, The Netherlands.

Rana, R.S., Ahuja, P.S. and Singh, K.N. 1979. Growth in salt-affected areas. Indian Fmg. 29(5): 5-6,11.

Sharma, S.K. 1987. Effect of exchangeable sodium on growth, yield and ionic relations in sodicity sensitive and resistant genotypes. Pl. Physiol. Biochem. 14: 87-91.

Singh, G. B., Singh, N. T., Singh, H., Dagar, J. C. and Sharma, V. P. 1997. Evaluation of agriculture, forestry and agro-forestry practices in a moderately alkali soil in north-western India. Agroforestry Systems. 37: 279-295.

Singh, G. B., Singh, N. T. and Tomar, O. S. 1993. Agroforestry in salt-affected soils. Bull. 17. CSSRI, Karnal. 65 p.

Singh, G.B., Gupta, S.K., Sharma, D.P. and Tyagi, N.K. 2000. Reclamation and Management of Waterlogged Salt-Affected Soils. Deptt. of Land Resources and Central Soil Salinity Research Institute, Karnal.

Strogonov, B.P. 1964. Physiological Basis of Salt Tolerance in Plants. IPST, Jerusalem.

Tomar, O. S. and Gupta, Raj K. 1986. Performance of tree species in saline soils. Ann. Rep. CSSRI, Karnal. 20-30.

Tomar, O. S., Gupta, Raj K. and Dagar, J. C. 1998. Afforestation techniques and evaluation of different tree species for waterlogged saline soils in semi-arid tropics. Arid Soil Res. And Rehabilitation. 12: 301-316.

Van Genuchten M. Th.1983. Analyzing Crop Salt Tolerance Data: Model Description and User's Manual. Res. Rep. 120. USDA, U.S. Salinity Lab., Riverside, USA.

Van Genuchten M. Th. and Hoffman, G.J. 1984. Analysis of crop salt tolerance data. In: Shainberg, J., Shalhevet J. (Eds.). Soil Salinity Under Irrigation. Springer Berlin. 258. Pp.

Yadav, J.S.P., Bhumbla, D.R. and Sharma, O.P. 1975. Performance of certain forest species on a saline sodic soil. Proc. Symp. New Dev. in the Field of Salt-Affected Soils. Cairo (1972), 683-90.

Yadav, J.S.P. and Pathak, T.C. 1967. Study on alkaline soils and their possible improvement by afforestation. J. Soil. Water Cons. India 5: 24-9.

Yadav, J.S.P. and Singh, K. 1970. Tolerance of certain forest species to varying degrees of salinity and alkalinity. Indian Forester 96: 587-99.

10

POST RECLAMATION BEHAVIOUR

To monitor and evaluate the soil health and productivity is an essential pre-requisite to maintain sustainability of a land reclamation programme. In the process of reclamation, alkali soils pass through a number of stages, which can be utilized to test or judge the nature of the reclamation methods under operation as well as the degree of their effectiveness. Moreover, some changes would also reveal whether additional measures are needed to make reclamation more effective or to prevent resodication or secondary salinization. The effect of reclamation is apparent on the stand of the crops being grown as well as on the physical, chemical and biological changes introduced in the soil properties (Table 10.1). Although crop growth is usually regarded as a good index to judge the progress of reclamation, soil tests provide a more reliable and precise basis for such an appraisal. The extent of variation depends largely on inherent soil properties, amount of amendment applied, cropping pattern adopted, amount of water applied, applied cultural practices and prevailing climatic conditions of the area. Although, degree of changes in soil properties following gypsum application is known to a greater extent, information on effect of gypsum application over a reasonably long period is limited. Since, the knowledge of the long-term changes in soil properties is of importance for the management of alkali soils, some of the physico-chemical properties and crop yields after gypsum application over a period of time under different cropping patterns are discussed in this chapter. It is not necessary to monitor all the parameters listed in the Table 10.1 regularly, since all the parameters would not be affected by reclamation as effectively as the others. Therefore, it is advisable to select those soil parameters that are influenced the most by reclamation. Also, some of the parameters could be measured regularly while others once in a while or when the effect is directly or indirectly observed.

Table 10.1 Chemical, physical and biological parameters for monitoring soil health

Chemical	*Physical*	*Biological*
Organic carbon	Bulk density	Biological worm population
Soil nutrients	Organic matter	Bio-diversity
pH	Soil water holding capacity	Crop yield
EC	Soil porosity	
ESP	Hydraulic conductivity	
	Soil crusting	
	Infiltration rate	
	Soil cracking	
	Depth to ground water	
	Surface stagnation	

Chemical Properties

The changes in soil chemical properties during the reclamation of a alkali soil are discussed below :

pH, EC and ESP

The effect of gypsum applied @ 12.5 t ha^{-1}, on an alkali wasteland was evaluated on soil properties after 1 to 5 year of gypsum application. After one year of gypsum application, soil pH_2 decreased from 10.5 to 9.2 in 0-15 cm layer and it further decreased to 8.5 after 5 years (Fig. 10.1). The pH values beyond 30 cm depth were more than 9.0 indicating the slower rate of improvement in the deeper layers. High alkalinity of deeper layer tends to restrict the root growth, therefore, crops having shallow root system should be grown in alkali soils till such time that the deeper layers are improved. A bulk of the soluble salts in the profile got leached down during five years of cultivation and residual salinity of the soil was within the safe limits for plant implying the beneficial effect of standing water during rice cultivation (Table 10.2).

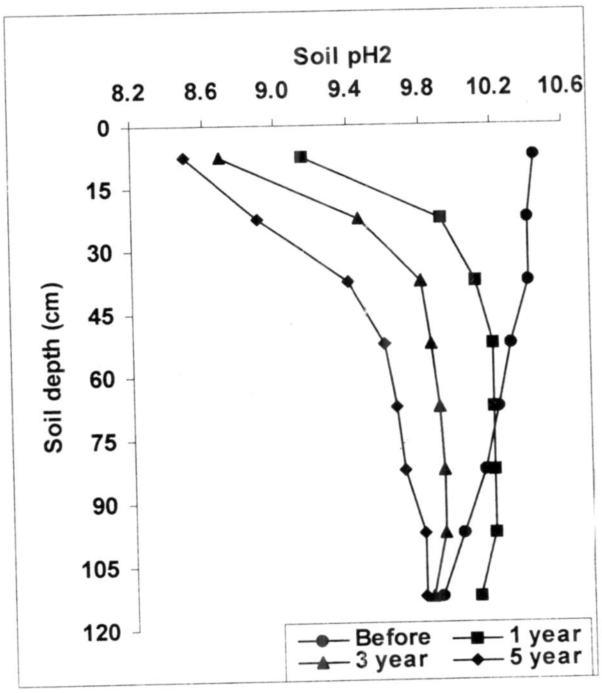

Fig. 10.1 Changes in soil pH_2 at different soil depths before and after 1, 3 and 5 years of gypsum application on farmer's fields

In a long-term field experiment initiated in 1974, continuous cropping with rice and wheat grown in rotation from 1974/75 to 1994/95 (except for 1986-1993, when rice was replaced with pearl millet), Singh and Swarup (2000) observed that continuous cropping for 21 years decreased soil pH_2 from 9.2 to 8.2 and exchangeable sodium percentage from 32 to 8.0

in 0-15 cm soil depth (Fig. 10.2 and 10.3). The drop in soil pH_2 was sharp in first 3 years, gradual for next 5 years and afterwards (1982/83 onwards) remained almost static at 8.2. However, at lower depths soil pH_2 and ESP, though decreased progressively, were still higher than the initial values of surface soil (0-15 cm). The inclusion of either berseem or shaftal in cropping patterns, during the reclamation of alkali soils hastens the reclamation process (Table 10.3). Cultivation of Karnal grass with mesquite for a period of about 74 months reduced soil pH and EC significantly as compared to without grass (Table 10.4).

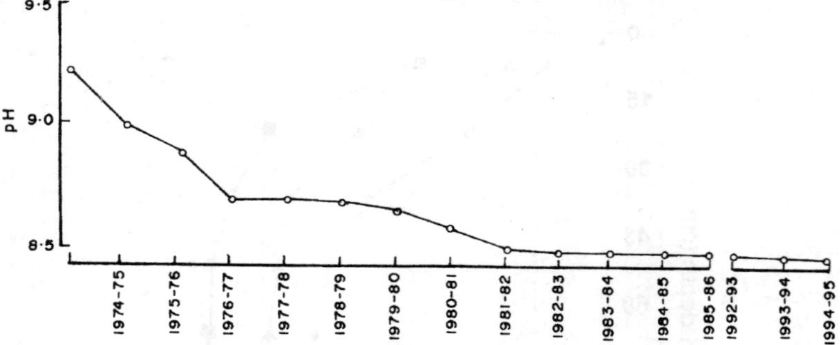

Fig. 10.2 Long-term effect of rice-wheat cultivation on soil pH during 1974-95 at Karnal

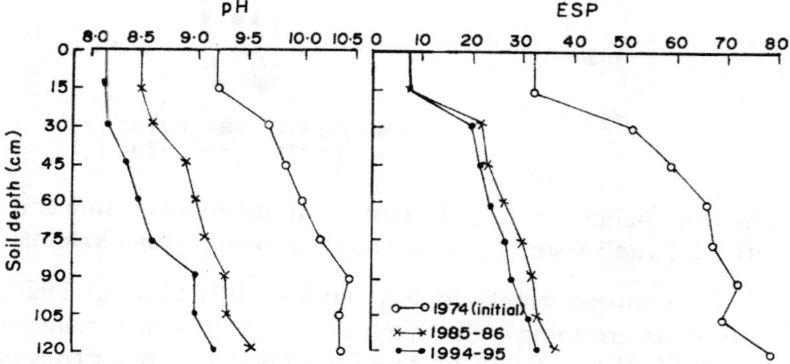

Fig. 10.3 Long-term effect of rice-wheat cropping on pH and ESP of a sodic soil at Karnal (India)

Calcium carbonate and organic matter

Alkali soils of the Indo-Gangetic plains invariably contain free $CaCO_3$ concretions at some depth in the soil profile. These concretions of $CaCO_3$ play a significant role in reclamation of alkali soil. Due to liberation of CO_2 and other biological activities of the rice roots, more $CaCO_3$ is dissolved and in turn calcium replaces exchangeable sodium. Solubilisation of $CaCO_3$ increases due to improved surface soil conditions including marked decrease in pH values. $CaCO_3$ (< 2mm) decreased from 1.85 to 0.48 percent in 0-15 cm layer after 5 years of gypsum application but in deeper layer change was very less (Table 10.2).

Table 10.2 Effect of gypsum application on soil properties under rice/wheat cropping

Year after gypsum application	*Depth (cm)*	*EC_2 (dS m^{-1})*	*$CaCO_3$ (%)*	*Organic carbon (%)*
1	0-15	0.96	1.60	0.15
	15-30	1.00	2.00	0.11
	30-60	1.23	2.60	0.09
3	0-15	0.38	1.00	0.19
	15-30	0.61	1.90	0.15
	30-60	1.00	2.52	0.12
5	0-15	0.22	0.48	0.23
	15-30	0.25	1.82	0.18
	30-60	0.40	2.50	0.13
Before gypsum application	0-15	3.25	1.85	0.10
	15-30	3.00	2.10	0.09
	30-60	2.46	2.62	0.08

Source : Sharma (1986)

Alkali soils are quite poor in organic carbon content. Continuous cropping increases organic carbon content with time and the increase is more in 0-15 cm layer mainly because of the decay of roots and stubble of crops. A slightly higher build-up of organic carbon was observed under rice–wheat–*dhaincha*, rice-berseem rotations than rice-wheat rotation (Sharma *et al.*, 1983, 1984). An appreciable increase in organic carbon content was observed (Singh 1994) where inter-space between mesquite was planted with Karnal grass. (Table 10.4). Even without grass, organic carbon content in soil increased as compared to its initial value. The mean organic carbon in 0-15 cm soil increased from 0.18 to 0.43 and 0.58 percent in no-grass and grassed soil, respectively in 74 months.

Table 10.3 Effect of different cropping sequences on the chemical properties of soil under reclamation

Crop rotation	*Depth (cm)*	*May, 1981*		*May, 1983*	
		pH_2	*EC_2 ($dS\ m^{-1}$)*	*pH_2*	*EC_2 ($dS\ m^{-1}$)*
Rice-wheat	0-15	8.9	0.60	8.8	0.32
	15-30	9.9	0.73	9.6	0.50
Rice–wheat–dhaincha	0-15	8.7	0.51	8.7	0.30
	15-30	9.8	0.67	9.5	0.45
Rice-Shaftal	0-15	8.6	0.36	8.6	0.23
	15-30	9.7	0.59	9.5	0.42
Rice-berseem	0-15	8.5	0.49	8.6	0.24
	15-30	9.5	0.63	9.4	0.48
Before the start of experiment (May, 1979)	0-15	10.0	1.13	-	-
	15-30	10.2	1.37	-	-

Source : Sharma *et al.*, (1983, 1984)

Physical Properties

The poor physical properties of alkali soils due to high ESP acts as a severe constraint to optimum crop production. The changes in soil physical properties and their interaction with plants contribute to efficient soil water management and evaluation of reclamation practices of alkali soils.

Table 10.4 Effect of *Prosopis juliflora-Laptochloa fusca* after 74 months of planting on some properties of an alkali soil

Soil properties	*Depth (cm)*	*Initial*	*After 74 months of planting*	
			Prosopis	*Prosopis + grass*
PH_2	0-15	10.3	9.3	8.9
	15-30	10.3	9.7	9.4
EC_2 (dS m^{-1})	0-15	2.2	0.46	0.36
	15-30	1.5	0.68	0.60
Organic C (%)	0-15	0.18	0.43	0.58
	15-30	0.13	0.29	0.36
Available N (kg ha^{-1})	0-15	79	133	165
	15-30	73	98	134
Available P (kg ha^{-1})	0-15	35	36	30
	15-30	31	34	26

Source : Singh (1994)

Dispersion and Hydraulic Conductivity

The amount of dispersible clay regulates various physical and mechanical properties of the soil such as swelling, porosity, water retention capacity, hydraulic conductivity and modulus of rupture. In alkali soils due to high ESP nearly 90 percent silt + clay is found in water dispersible form in the entire profile. The dispersion decreased to 72, 66 and 58 percent in 0-15 cm layer after 1, 3 and 5 years of gypsum application (Table 10.5). This reduction continued in the lower depths also but at a slower rate. The more reduction in 0-15 cm layer was due to the replacement of exchangeable sodium with calcium and also due to slight increase in organic carbon content which acts as the binding agent of soil particles (Sharma *et al.*, 1981). Similarly, saturated hydraulic conductivity of 0-15 cm layer increased from 2 mm day^{-1} to 12, 21 and 38 mm day^{-1} after 1, 3 and 5 years of gypsum application. The physical properties of alkali soil improve more when either berseem or shaftal is included in the rotation than wheat (Table 10.6). Chawla and Chhabra (1991) reported that continuous cultivation of rice-wheat in rotation for 11 years and application of fertilizers significantly improved the soil physical properties.

Table 10.5 Changes in soil dispersion and hydraulic conductivity after 1-5 year of gypsum application

Year after gypsum application (12.5 t ha^{-1})	*Depth (cm)*	*Dispersion* (%)*	*Hydraulic conductivity (mm day^{-1})*
1	0-15	72	12
	15-30	90	4
	30-60	95	2
3	0-15	66	21
	15-30	82	8
	30-60	84	5
5	0-15	58	38
	15-30	75	15
	30-60	78	9
Before gypsum application	0-15	88	2
	15-30	92	1
	30-60	94	0

Source: Sharma (1986)

$$* \text{ Dispersion } (\%) \frac{\text{Water dispersible (slit + day)}}{\text{Total (silt + clay)}} \times 100$$

Water Infiltration and Storage

Infiltration characteristics largely determine the total water storage in the profile. During the process of alkali land reclamation, addition of gypsum considerably improves the infiltration characteristics. The amount of water infiltrated in 24 hr in unreclaimed alkali soil and after 1, 2, 3, 4 and 5 years of reclamation was 3.3, 5.1, 6.0, 7.1, 7.8 and 9.1 cm, respectively (Fig. 10.4) (Sharma, 1986). Cumulative infiltration followed the relationship, 1 = at^n + b, where I indicates cumulative infiltration (cm), t is the elapsed time (hr) and a, n and b are constants. The values of these constants for original alkali soil and after 1 to 5 year of reclamation are reported in Table 10.7. The increase in all the constants indicated continual improvement in the physical conditions as reflected on the cumulative infiltration of these soils in different years of reclamation.

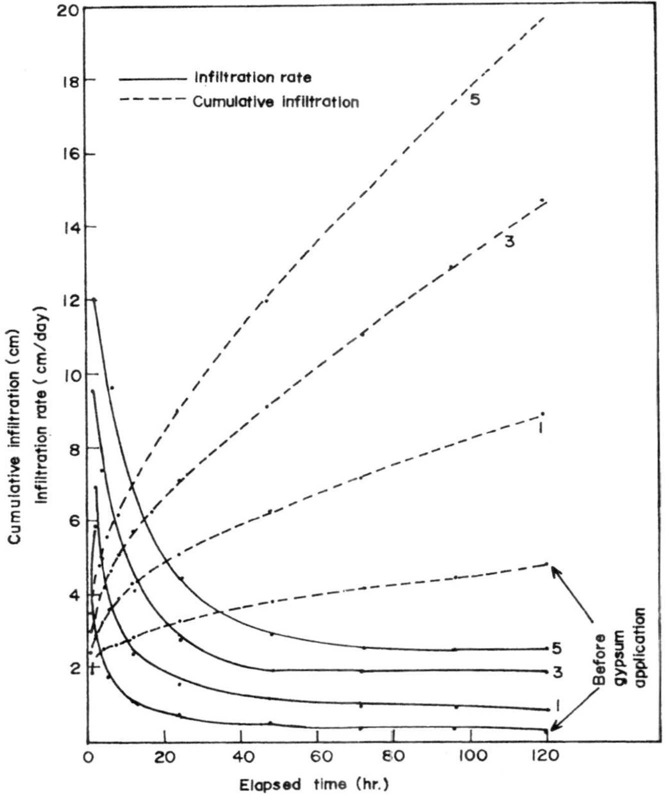

Fig. 10.4 Infiltration rate (Ir, cm/day) and Cumulative infiltration (CI, cm) before and after 1, 3, 5 years of gypsum application on farmer's field

Table 10.6 Effect of different crop rotations on dispersion and hydraulic conductivity of a alkali soil*

Rotations	*Soil dispersion (%)*		*Hydraulic conductivity (mm day^{-1})*	
	1981	*1983*	*1981*	*1983*
Rice-wheat	66	65	22	24
Rice-wheat-dhaincha	64	61	43	48
Rice-berseem	53	51	53	60
Rice-shaftal	55	54	48	53
Before the start of the experiment (1979)	87		2	

* Gypsum was applied @ 12.5 t ha^{-1} in all the rotations.
Source : Sharma *et al.*, (1983b)

Table 10.7 Improvement in the values of infiltration constants

Year after reclamation	*Constants*		
	a	*n*	*b*
0	0.96	0.28	1.02
1	0.99	0.41	1.50
2	1.04	0.46	1.80
3	1.13	0.49	1.93
4	1.14	0.52	1.95
5	1.26	0.54	2.21

Source : Sharma (1985)

Application of gypsum and continuos cropping increased the infiltration rates of these soils from 3 mm day^{-1} to 9, 14, 18, 23 and 25 mm day^{-1} after 1, 2, 3, 4, and 5 years of reclamation, respectively. Although the infiltration rate increased nearly 8 times as the pH_2 of 0-15 cm layer decreased from 10.5 to 8.5, but high pH_2 of lower layers continued to influence the infiltration rates. Slope of the curve in equation log Y = 6.256-0.571X, obtained by plotting log infiltration rates against soil pH_2 of surface 0-15 cm layer is indicative of amount of improvement in infiltration rate with fall in pH_2 during the reclamation (Fig. 10.5). A relationship of the type, $I = at^n$ was obtained between infiltration rate and year of reclamation, where I is infiltration rate (mm day^{-1}), t the period of reclamation in year and n is the slope of the curve. The values calculated from the equation, $i = 8.79\ t^{0.67}$ were comparable with the observed values (Fig. 10.6).

Soil moisture distribution to a depth of 120 cm indicated increased moisture storage after different years of reclamation (Fig. 10.7). After 5 years of reclamation deeper layers stored 5 to 7 percent more moisture as compared to unreclaimed alkali soil. The higher moisture content in the deeper layers is attributable to continual improvement of soil properties during reclamation.

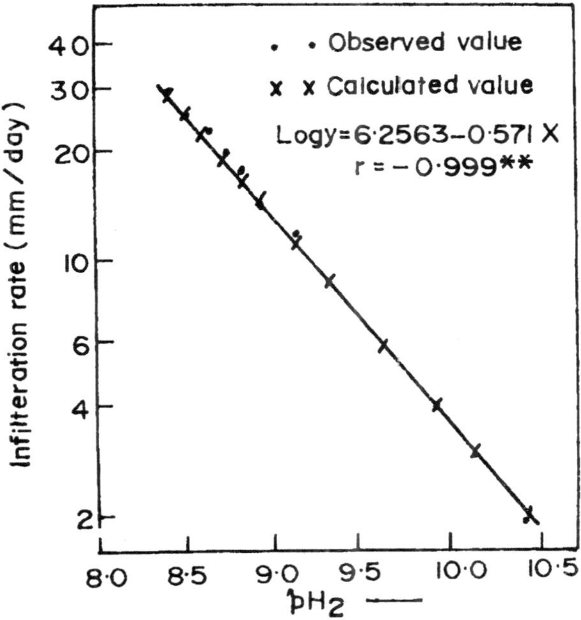

Fig. 10.5 Relationship between infiltration rate and pH_2

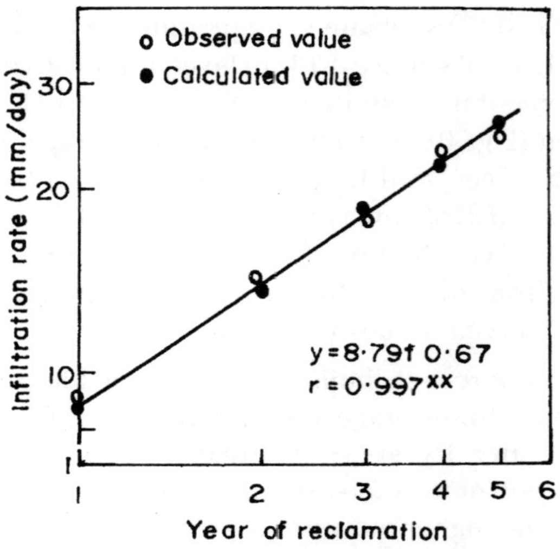

Fig. 10.6 Relationship between infiltration rate and year of reclamation

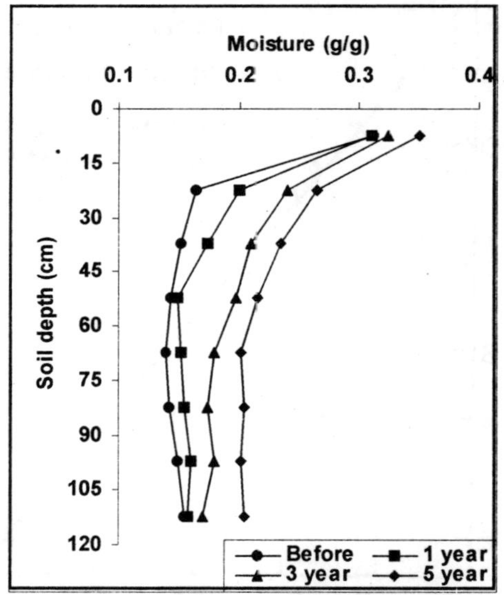

Fig. 10.7 Post infiltration moisture distribution before and after 1, 3, 5 years of reclamation on farmer's field

Available Nutrients

Continuous cropping for 20 years in a alkali soil reduced available N from initial level of 225 kg ha^{-1} to 103 kg ha^{-1} in unfertilized plots (Singh and Swarup, 2000). However continuous use of fertilizer N alone or in combination with P and K either maintained or slightly increased available N with final values ranging from 235 kg ha^{-1} to 248 kg ha^{-1} . With regular P application to crops in sequence, the available P increased from initial value of 33.6 kg ha^{-1} to 58 kg ha^{-1} in NP-NP and to 57.6 kg ha^{-1} in NPK-NPK in the 0-15 cm soil depth (Table 10.8). Where N alone was applied, available P declined progressively to 4.0 kg ha^{-1} from initial value of 33.6 kg ha^{-1} . Potassium applied to either or both the crops in rotation increased available K. Continuous cropping for 20 years in no way depleted available K in soil to a level where either rice or wheat or both could suffer K deficiency.

Table 10.8 Effect of continuous cropping and fertilizer use on available nutrients in the surface soil (0-15 cm) during 1994 [1]

Treatment [2]		*Available nutrients* [3]*(kg ha^{-1})*		
Rice	*Wheat*	*N*	*P*	*K*
Control	Control	103	9.8	213
N	N	235	4.0	193
NP	NP	243	58.0	198
NP	N	240	15.6	193
N	NP	240	16.9	203
NPK	NPK	245	57.6	560
NPK	N	240	15.2	476
N	NPK	237	15.8	483
CD (p=0.05)		13	5.4	19

[1] Estimated after the harvest of wheat 1993/94

[2] Nitrogen (N), Phosphorus (P) and Potassium (K) were applied at 120 kg ha^{-1}, 22 kg ha^{-1} , and 42 kg ha^{-1}.

[3] Initial values in 1974 were 225 kg N ha^{-1}, 33.6 kg P ha^{-1} and 358 kg K ha^{-1}.

Source: Singh and Swarup (2000)

Crop Yields

The rice-wheat-*dhaincha* green manuring and rice-berseem/shaftal cropping sequences are more remunerative in the initial stages of reclamation than rice-wheat rotation, which is generally followed by the farmers due to many constraints. In research experiments where best agronomic and cultural practices are followed, the crop yield obtained and the improvement brought about in soil properties are generally of higher order than under farmers' management practices.

Rice

Rice is an ideal and the most popular rainy season crop grown during the initial years due to its high alkali tolerance and reclaiming effect. Rice yields are good (4-5 t ha^{-1}) even in the first year of reclamation and yields tend to reach normal value with time. The rice yield continues to increase up to 4th

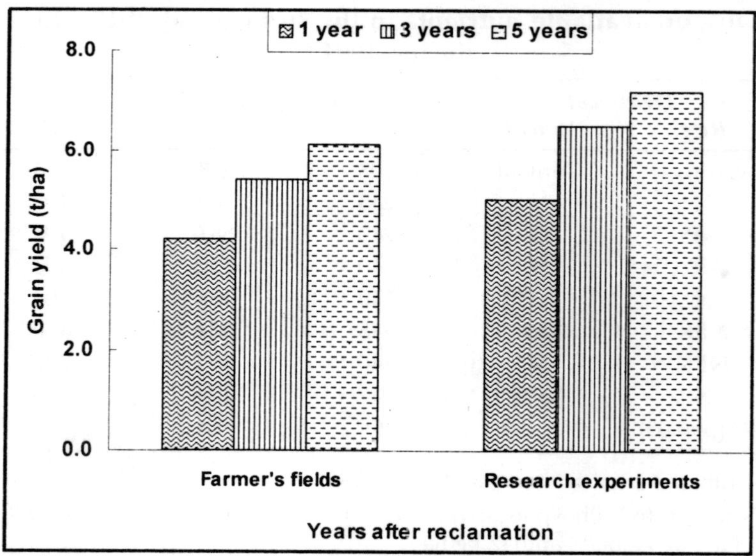

Fig. 10.8 Progressive improvement in rice yield of wheat on farmer's fields and experimental farm (*Source: Sharma, 1986*)

year as compared with the first year of reclamation. The average yield on farmer's fields in 5 successive years was compared with those obtained in research experiments (Fig. 10.8). In the first year of reclamation, on farmer's fields, the average rice yield was 4.2 t ha^{-1} and this increased to 6.1 t ha^{-1} in the 5th year. The trend of increase was similar to that observed in research experiments, but yields were higher in the later case (Sharma, 1986). The fluctuations in the grain yield of rice in a gypsum amended alkali soil over a period of 20 years is shown in Fig. 10.9 (Chhabra and Thakur, 2000).

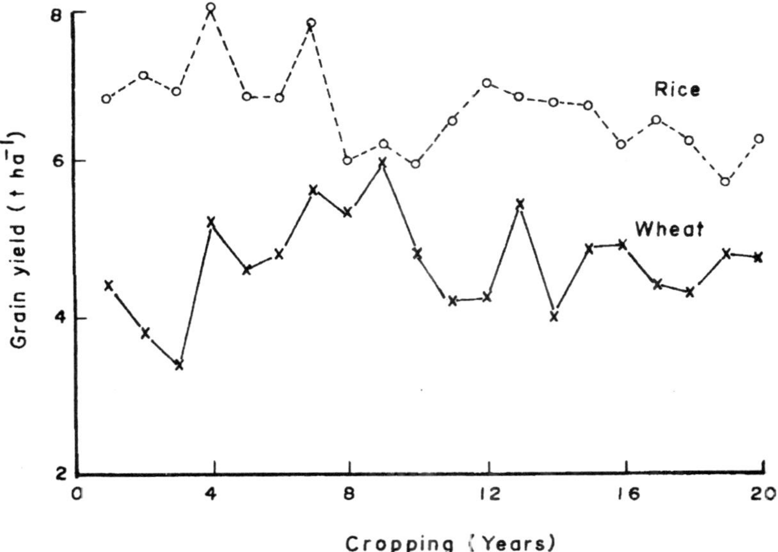

Fig. 10.9 Variation in grain yield of rice and wheat in fertilized plots (N_{120} P_{22} K_{50} Zn_5) in a gypsum amended sodic soil over a period of 20 years (1976-1995)

Pearl millet

In alkali soils, pearl millet could be grown after 2-3 years of reclamation. Pearl millet performs well if the pH_2 of the reclaimed lands is less than or equal to 9.0. In soils having pH_2 in the range of 9.1 to 9.3, transplanted crop performs better than direct seeded crop. The performance of pearl millet crop over a period of 8 years (1986-1993) is shown in Table 10.9. In general pearl millet yield increased with fertilizer application.

Table 10.9 Effect of continuous cropping and fertilizer use on grain yield of pearl millet on an alkali soil at Karnal [1]

Treatment [2]		*Grain yield (t ha^{-1})*					
Pearl millet	*Wheat*	*1986*	*1987*	*1989*	*1991*	*1992*	*1993*
Control	Control	0.54	0.70	0.65	0.54	0.91	1.16
N	N	1.47	1.39	1.45	1.89	1.92	2.18
NP	NP	1.80	1.65	1.72	2.17	2.34	2.04
NP	N	1.80	1.58	1.68	2.00	2.34	2.18
N	NP	1.73	1.54	1.65	1.99	2.43	2.33
NPK	NPK	2.02	1.68	1.85	2.77	2.55	2.33
NPK	N	1.95	1.67	1.80	2.04	2.52	2.45
N	NPK	1.91	1.60	1.78	1.97	2.40	2.42
CD (p=0.05)		0.35	0.30	0.34	0.30	0.52	0.43

[1] In rice wheat cropping system, rice was replaced by pearl millet during 1986-1993.

[2] Nitrogen (N), Phosphorus (P) and Potassium (K) were applied at 120 kg ha^{-1}, 22 kg ha^{-1}, and 42 kg ha^{-1}.

Source: Singh and Swarup (2000)

Wheat

Wheat yield depends upon time of sowing and soil pH. If soil pH_2 is between 9.3 to 9.0, yields between 1.5 to 3.0 t ha^{-1} can be obtained in the first year of reclamation. Average grain yield of wheat on farmer's field in the first year of reclamation was 1.8 t ha^{-1}, whereas the yield obtained in research experiments was 3.2 t ha^{-1} (Fig. 10.10). Wheat yields increased slowly in the subsequent years, but remained low compared to normal yields of wheat under optimum management and relatively non-alkali condition in the region. In a long-term experiment Chhabra and Thakur (2000) estimated that in treatment receiving full fertilizer doses (N_{120} P_{22} K_{50} Zn_5), the yield of wheat fluctuated every year (Fig.

10.10). However, in general the overall yield of wheat did not show a declining trend over a period of 20 years.

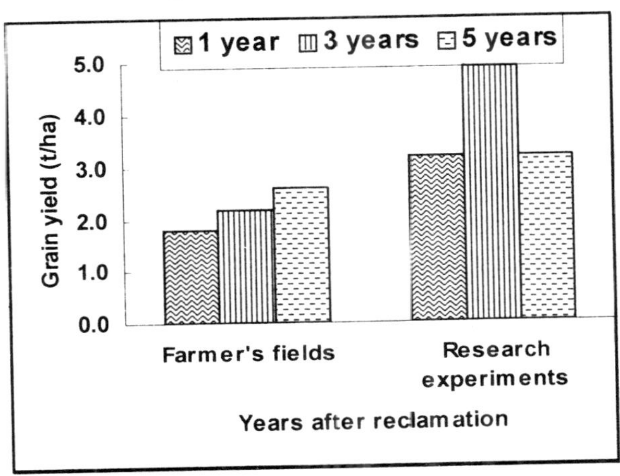

Fig. 10.10 Progressive improvement in grain yield of wheat on farmer's fields and experimental farm (*Source: Sharma, 1986*)

Hydrological Effects of Reclamation

Land use changes as a consequence of alkali land reclamation affect the following hydrological components :

1. Infiltration rate
2. Catchment retention storage
3. Runoff and peak rate of run-off
4. Ground water recharge

Infiltration Rate

The changes in infiltration rate have been discussed earlier. It has been reported that as reclamation progresses, basic infiltration rate as well as constant and exponent of the power function describing infiltration rate characteristics of the soil increase. Similar results have been reported by Tiwari *et al.,* (1981). On the other hand Singh (1980) utilized an equation proposed by Horton (1940) for studying changes in infiltration characteristics of the soils under reclamation. It was observed that three parameters of the Horton equations are functions of the ESP as follows :

$$fc = \text{Exp.}\ (1.90-0.07\ \text{ESP}) \qquad (10.1)$$

$$fo = \text{Exp}\ (3.46-0.04\ \text{ESP}) \qquad (10.2)$$

$$K = 0.15\ \ln\ (\text{ESP}) + 0.24 \qquad (10.3)$$

Here, fc is the constant rate at which the capacity rate of infiltration approaches asymptotically with time; fo is the initial capacity infiltration rate where the soil moisture status of the watershed is equal to zero and K is a positive constant depending upon the soil characteristics. Thus, it is apparent that as ESP decreases, both fc and fo increase while K decreases indicating increased infiltration rate with decrease in ESP.

Catchment Retention Storage

The watershed retention storage increases owing to the increased infiltration rate and bunding of fields to store water to grow rice. Based on an equation proposed by Linsley *et al.*, (1949) for watershed storage and observed changes in basic infiltration rate, Singh *et al.*, (1979) proposed that rain water retention in the catchment with rice crop could be given by the following relation. :

$$RW = a + b\ (1-e^{-ct}) + Sd\ [1-e^{-k(P-f(I)-E)}] \qquad (10.4)$$

Here, RW is the rain water retention due to increased infiltration and bunding, a is the basic infiltration rate of the unreclaimed catchment, b and c are constants indicating increase in infiltration rate after complete reclamation and the rate of increase in basic infiltration rate during the time span of reclamation respectively, t is the time in year from the start of reclamation, Sd is the maximum storage capacity, k is a constant, P is the gross rainfall, E is the evaporation rate and f (I) is the basic infiltration rate in the ith year of reclamation. Thus the term (P-1(I)-E) could be described as the excess rainfall. While evaluating catchment retention storage for a 1200 ha alkali watershed which was being progressively reclaimed, for the low magnitude of storms there was not much difference in the water retention values corresponding to percentage of the area reclaimed (Singh *et al.*, 1979). However, for high magnitude storms, there was considerable difference in the amount of water stored within the watershed. In general, the water retention capacity of the watershed was found to increase with increase in the area reclaimed.

Runoff and peak rate of runoff

The reclamation of alkali watersheds considerably alters the time distribution characteristics and the total amount of run-off. In a study on identical plots of 1.26 ha each, the run-off volume was reduced by 75 percent while peak rate of run-off was reduced by 50 percent from a reclaimed plot compared to an unreclaimed one (Singh *et al.*, 1979) (Fig. 10.11). Based on Instantaneous Unit Hydrograph Technique, Singh (1980) showed that due to reclamation, the flow duration characteristics are changed resulting in reduced run-off and delayed peak discharges. For this purpose a multiple regression analysis was undertaken considering depth of rainfall, intensity of rainfall, antecedent precipitation index, slope, area and

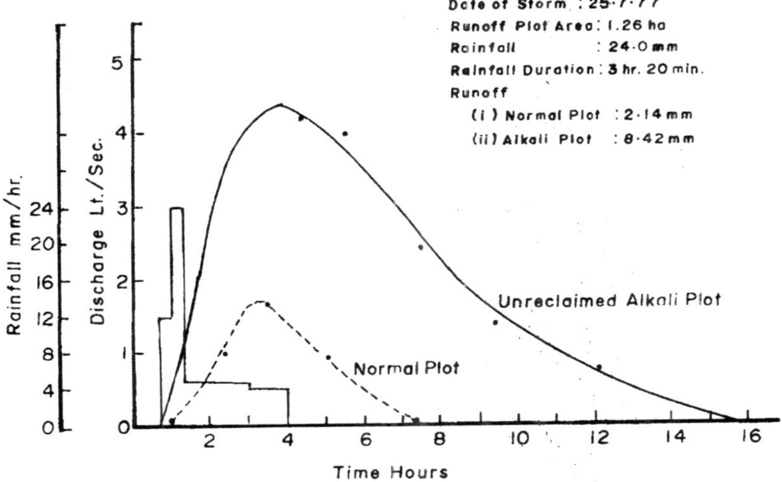

Fig. 10.11 Effect of reclamation on total and peak run-off

shape of the watershed and reclamation factor as the variables. It was found that shape of the watershed and reclamation factor are the two most influencing parameters for run-off estimation. Reclamation factor was defined as (1 + reclaimed area/ total area). Thus, it varied from 1 for a completely unreclaimed watershed to 2 for a completely reclaimed watershed. It was shown that with complete reclamation, runoff volume could reduce to 45 percent of the total volume expected from the unreclaimed watershed (Singh, 1980).

Table 10.10 Water balance analysis of the CSSRI,Karnal farm

Supply	*1972*	*1973*	*1974*	*1975*	*1976*	*1977*
Precipitation	69.5	58.9	38.4	60.4	86.7	58.9
Canal seepage	4.0	4.0	4.0	4.0	4.0	4.0
Total measured supply	73.5	62.9	42.4	64.4	90.7	62.9
Demand						
Run-off	12.1	9.4	0.5	1.2	10.0	5.5
Evapotranspiration	34.2	37.9	37.9	35.8	43.6	26.3
Addition to soil moisture storage	9.0*	8.0	6.8	8.8	10.9	7.5
Addition to ground water	29.1	18.7	17.1	23.9	25.5	22.8
Total demand	84.4	73.3	62.3	69.7	90.0	62.1
Probable groundwater recharge from other areas						
Total demand–total supply	10.9	10.4	19.9	5.3	(-) 0.7	(0.7) 0.8
Amount of water stored on the farm	57.4	49.5	37.9	67.2	76.7	53.4
Percentage of rainfall	82	84	99	89	89	91

Ground Water Recharge

As reclamation progresses, there is more opportunity for infiltration and ground water recharge. Satisfactory assessment of increased ground water recharge as a consequence of reclamation is difficult because of the problems associated with direct measurements in the field. Therefore, water balance technique is commonly adopted in assessing this component. Water balance components for 6 years were measured at C.S.S.R.I., Karnal where reclamation has been undertaken and improved rain water management practices have been adopted (Table 10.10). The analysis for the June-September period, indicated that the total net seasonal run-off decreased, the ground water recharge from local rainfall is increased even while the net ground water inflow from outside the area is decreasing. The percentage of rainfall conserved showed an increasing trend although the percentage varied from year to year with the total amount of rainfall.

REFERENCES

Chawla, K. L. and Chhabra, R. 1991. Physical properties of a gypsum amended sodic soil as affected by long-term use of fertilizers. J. Indian Soc. Soil Sci. 39: 40-45.

Chhabra, R. and Thakur, N. P. 2000. Long-term study on phosphorus fertilization for rice-wheat cropping system in an alkali soil in the Indo-Gangetic plains. (In) Long-term Soil Fertility Experiments in Rice-wheat Cropping Systems. Rice-Wheat Consortium Paper Series 6 (Eds. Abrol et al.). New Delhi. India. Rice-Wheat Consortium for the Indo-Gangetic Plains. 31-39.

Horton, R.E., 1940. An approach to the physical interpretation of infiltration capacity. Proc. Soil. Sci. Soc. Am. 5 : 399-417.

Linsley, R.K., Jr., Kohler, M.A. and Pauthus, J.L.H. 1949. Applied Hydrology. Mc-Grew-Hill Book Co., New York, 689 pp.

Sharma, D.P. 1985. Evaluation of water infiltration characteristics during the reclamation of sodic soils. J. Indian Soc. Soil Sci. 33 : 893-5.

Sharma, D.P. 1986. Effect of gypsum application on long-term changes in soil properties and crop growth in sodic soils under field conditions. J. Agron. Crop. Sci. 156 : 166–172.

Sharma, D.P., Mehta, K.K. and Yadav, J.S.P. 1981. Effect of reclamation practices on soil properties and crop growth on farmer's fields–a case study. J Indian Soc. Soil Sci. 29 : 356-60.

Sharma, D.P., Mehta, K.K., Yadav, J.S.P. and Singh, G. 1983 a. Effect of crop rotation on crop growth and soil properties in sodic soils on farmer's fields. Indian J. Agric. Sci. 53 : 681-5.

Sharma, D.P., Mehta, K.K., Yadav, J.S.P., Singh, G. 1983b. Usar bhumi mein shaftal aur berseem upyogi. Kheti 35 (12) : 23-5, 30.

Sharma, D.P., Singh, G. and Mehta, K.K. 1984. Influence of different cropping patterns on available nitrogen and organic carbon status of sodic soils on farmer's fields. Curr. Agric. 8 : 164-8.

Singh, G. 1994. Afforestation and agro-forestry for salt-affected soils. (In) Salinity Management for Sustainable Agriculture (Rao, D.L.N. et al., Eds.), CSSRI, Karnal. 260-261.

Singh. K. N. and Swarup, A. 2000. Effect of long-term rice-wheat cropping sequence on yield and soil properties in a reclaimed sodic soil. (In) Long-term Soil Fertility Experiments in Rice-wheat Cropping Systems. Rice-Wheat Consortium Paper Series 6 (Eds. Abrol et al.). New Delhi. India. Rice-Wheat Consortium for the Indo-Gangetic Plains. 40-49.

Singh, O.P. 1980. Analysis of the hydrological changes taking place in alkali soil watersheds during reclamation. Ph.D. Thesis, JNTU, Hyderabad.

Singh, O.P., Narayana, V.V.D. and Tiwari, A.K. 1979. Analysis of the hydrologic changes taking place in alkali soil watersheds during reclamation. Canadian. Agric. Engg. 21 : 147-150.

Tiwari, A.K., Pandey, R.N. and Gupta, S.K. 1981. Transient behaviour of infiltration rate in alkali lands under reclamation. J. Agric. Engg. 18 : 21-8.

11

ALTERNATE LAND USE

Reclamation of alkali soils for arable purposes is technically feasible, economically viable and an eco-friendly proposition. It can tremendously augment the food grain production in the country. It is estimated that if 2.5 m ha of alkali soils are reclaimed for crop production, it would add at least 15 million tonnes of food grain annually to the national production. However, there are situations where this technology can not be adopted. Lands in the possession of village *Panchayats* or owned by the Government are some examples where reclamation technology for crop production has failed to make a dent. It is because under the community ownership no one owns the responsibility. Resource poor farmers may also fail to take advantage of the technology for arable cropping. This chapter examines the constraints and describes alternate land management techniques, which could be adopted not only to put this resource in some use but also to start the reclamation process so that these lands do not offer a desolate look. Indeed, successful efforts have been made to manage and even reclaim these soils by such means that require less cash inputs.

Constraints in Reclamation

Cost of Gypsum

Over the years, the cost of gypsum has gone very high due to the transportation and handling charges. State Land Reclamation Corporations have withdrawn a portion of subsidy on gypsum cost. Presently, it costs a farmer more than Rs. 600 per tonne. The increased cost discourages many farmers to undertake land reclamation.

Panchayat Lands

A large area of alkali lands belongs to village *Panchayats* which neither have the funds nor the will to carry out the reclamation of these lands. In addition to the financial constraints, the fact that the land is required for various common needs of the community, it is not being reclaimed for cultivation of the crops. As per the provision of land utilization act, the land cannot be leased out on long-term contract basis. Therefore, when a short-term lease is given, the farmer, who has got the land on lease, works half heartedly and does not take any long-term investment and management decisions.

Lack of Education

The reclamation is a knowledge based technology and a user need to know about the salient features of the technology. It is the first pre-requisite for action. In developing countries, because of many difficulties, farmers fail to obtain or get the desired feed back. Sometimes they use traditional practices and do not wish to learn new skills that is required for reclamation.

Land Ceiling

In alkali affected areas some farmers have large land holding. As per the land-ceiling act, they cannot keep more land than a certain prescribed limit of good quality. These farmers do not invest in land reclamation as upon reclamation they have to part with the land if it comes under the land ceiling. Since, they do not attach much importance to these lands, these soils remain unreclaimed for a longer period.

Institutional Support

Institutional support plays a very catalytic role in land reclamation. The role played by land reclamation corporations in Punjab and Haryana has proved this beyond doubt. These corporations acted as a single window for providing technical know-how as well as inputs necessary to take up land reclamation. This is being replicated at few places but at other places such support is lacking.

Due to the above constraints, a large fraction of alkali lands is still lying barren. In such circumstances these lands can be profitably be put to other uses which require less inputs, skill and after care. In fact, emphasis is now being laid on exploiting these lands with endemic plant species where reclamation technology can not be adopted for one reason or the other.

Grasses for Alkali Lands

Ecological studies on undisturbed sites in Karnal and Kurukshetra districts of Haryana where such soils are found in abundance indicate that certain distinct alkali land grasses can be identified based on the frequency, density and abundance of native flora by its characteristic predominant species. The grass species identified are: *Diplachne fusca, Sporobolus diander, Sporobolus marginatus, Chloris barbata, Kochia indica, Desmostachya bipinata* and *Cynodon dactylon*. The occurrence of different grasses in alkali soils in nature is a pointer to their potential for growing in these soils possibly without use of amendments and/or fertilizer and manure.

Grasses without Amendment and Fertilizer

The native grass, *Displachne fusca* (Australian Grass) or now well known in India as Karnal grass with two cultivated grass species *Panicum antidotale* (Blue panic) and *Brachiaria mutica* (Para grass) were tried in a alkali soil. These were planted alone as well as in a mixture on a soil with average pH_2 of 9.8 and ESP of 71 in the 0-15 cm layer. The para grass yielded the maximum green fodder followed by para grass + Karnal grass mixture (Table 11.1). Though it was expected that the later will give more yield because of the creeping nature of the para grass and erect nature of Karnal grass but this was not observed probably because of limited nutritional and soil factors. The other grasses which have been found tolerant are: *Sporobolus diander (ren ki ghas)* and *Cynodon dactylon (doob)* among the native grasses and *Chloris gayana* (*Rhodes grass)* among the cultivated grasses.

Table 11.1 Forage yield of three grasses in monoculture and mixed planting under alkali conditions (pH_2 = 9.8, ESP 71).

Grass species	*Green fodder yield (t ha^{-1})*			
	1st	*2nd*	*3rd*	*Total*
	Cutting			
Para	16.3	18.6	13.1	48.0
Blue panic	11.6	14.8	5.4	31.8
Karnal	9.4	11.9	4.0	25.3
Para + Blue panic	10.6	13.8	8.2	32.3
Para grass + Karnal	15.4	18.9	13.0	47.3
Blue panic + Karnal	11.3	15.8	5.1	32.2

Source: Chandra (1979)

Grasses with Fertilizer and Amendment

The original barren alkali soils have pH_2 as high as 10.6. Such soils are most dispersed. Grasses even under these conditions can be grown, however, with little more efforts and inputs. For this, levelling and bunding of lands is essential as it helps to manage rain water. Application of amendments and water for leaching are required to remove excess exchangeable sodium to some extent. A comparative evaluation of 5 grass species in a pot house trial revealed that Rhodes grass performed the best at all ESP levels (Table 11.2)

Table 11.2. Green yield (g plot^{-1}) of 5 grasses at different alkali levels

Grass			*ESP*			*Mean*
	5	*25*	*64*	*78*	*85*	
Marval	307	281	198	178	173	228
Rhodes	488	415	409	380	268	392
Bermuda	283	271	248	241	202	249
Pangola	176	142	113	76	49	111
Karnal	270	210	214	208	206	222
Mean	305	264	236	216	180	80

CD at 5%, grasses or ESP = 23.5, Interaction = 5.14
Source: Kumar *et al.*, (1980)

Response to Gypsum Application

The amount of amendment required depends upon the initial alkali status of the soil and the nature of crops to be grown. The grasses, in general, are more tolerant to alkali conditions than the cereal crops. Different grass species differ in their tolerance to alkali conditions and obviously also in quantity of gypsum required for their optimum yield. The effect of gypsum application on the performance of 5 perennial forage grasses on a highly alkali soil (pH_2 10.6) is summarized in Table 11.3. Due to the nature of the grasses and differences in their tolerance to alkali conditions, in 1979, 3 cuts from Karnal grass, 2 cuts each from Rhodes grass and blue panic and *Paniucm leavifolium* and only one cut from Coastal Bermuda, could be obtained.

Table 11.3. Green forage yield (t ha^{-1}) of 5 grasses as affected by gypsum application

Grass	*Year*	*Gypsum level (t ha^{-1})*			*Mean*
		0	*5.2*	*10.4*	
Karnal	1979	18.8	19.9	22.2	20.3
	1980	51.6	48.9	47.9	49.4
Panicum-laevifolium	1979	2.5	9.1	11.8	7.8
	1980	13.9	57.8	67.2	46.3
Blue panic	1979	3.68	9.0	11.0	7.9
	1980	1.5	50.2	60.3	37.3
Rhodes	1979	12.5	27.1	24.2	21.3
	1980	70.7	82.5	86.0	79.7
Coastal Bermuda	1979	4.0	6.9	8.0	6.3
	1980	28.3	33.4	34.0	32.0
CD (p = 0.05)	1979	2.6			
Grasses	1980	10.5			
Gypsum levels	1979	2.2			
	1980	2.6			

Source: Kumar and Abrol (1983)

Blue panic and *Panicum leavifolium* had significantly lower forage yield than the Rhodes and Karnal grasses. Rhodes and Karnal grass did not differ significantly in their mean yields. In 1980, 5 cuts from all the 5 grasses were taken. Rhodes grass gave the highest green forage yield, which was significantly higher than all other grasses. The green forage yield of *Panicum laevifolium* and Blue panic improved with each increment of the gypsum level. In general, there was an appreciable improvement in the forage yield of all the grasses during 1980 as compared to 1979 in plots where gypsum was applied. In the following years the yield of Karnal grass declined progressively. The yield of the Rhodes grass also decreased with time after second year but at a much lesser rate than the Karnal grass. Coastal Bermuda did not show much variability in its yield, after second year. *Panicum laevifolium* and Blue panic had almost similar growth pattern throughout with maximum production in the third year. The Karnal grass,

Rhoades grass, Bermuda grass and para grass are therefore, the four promising grasses for large scale utilization of alkali lands.

Characteristics of Some Alkali Tolerant Grasses

Karnal Grass (*Diplachne fusca* Linn. P. Beauv.)

This grass is most tolerant to alkali conditions and it can come on its own at relatively lower elevations in alkali fields where monsoon rain water stands for comparatively longer duration (Fig. 11.1). In Uttar Pradesh, this grass is locally known as *Chhoti dandar* or *Narri*. It is perennial, erect type and

Fig. 11.1 Grasses in a barren alkali land without application of gypsum

grows as high as 75 to 100cm. This grass can be propagated both by root slips and stem cuttings. The stem should be below the soil. Though it is difficult to collect its seeds but the grass can also be propagated by seeds. Once the grass is established at a place, replanting is not required as the fallen seed germinate in due course of time. The grass yields 40-50 t ha^{-1} green matter at ESP level as high as 60. Even at the higher ESP level, the yield reduction is minimal. Irrigation to this grass is necessary after planting and subsequently except during monsoon (semi-arid climate). Drainage requirement are minimal and rain water can be stored in bunded fields for as much as 8 days without loosing the yield.

Rhodes Grass *(Chloris gayana Kunth.)*

This grass is also an erect type and grows as high as 1 to 1.5 m. Initially, it is more affected by alkali but once established, it grows well under such conditions. It requires less number of irrigation since the grass is able to tolerate aridity and high temperature. Rhodes grass can be propagated by root slips or by seeds. In alkali soil, propagation by root slips is preferred because surface crust formed at the soil surface hinders the germination. It is planted in the month of July without any amendment but immediately after planting irrigation is necessary. In first year it can yield 15-20 t ha^{-1} green matter which increases to 65-75 t ha^{-1} in the second year. One of the disadvantages of this grass is that it cannot tolerate water stagnation, which are of common occurrence in the Indo-Gangetic plains during monsoon season, particularly in the alkali lands. Therefore, it is necessary to provide surface drainage for best results.

Bermuda Grass (*Cynodon dactylon Linn. Pers*)

This grass is commonly known as *doob* and is commonly grown in pastures and soil conservation programmes. Bermuda grass is less tolerant to alkalinity. It can tolerate ESP up to 50, but at 80 ESP its yield decrease to about 60 percent compared to yield at ESP 50 or less. It is a perennial grass, with creeping habit and rooting from many nodes. The grass is propagated by seeds as well as by root slips. In alkali soils, root slip method is preferred for propagation. During summer months, irrigation at an interval of 10 to 15 days is required. At ESP 50, the yield of this grass is around 50 t ha^{-1}. Similar to Rhodes grass, Bermuda grass also requires a well laid out surface drainage system since it cannot tolerate standing water. Yield reduction to the extent of 50 % occurs if water stands in the grassed land for 8 days. The grass is not only good for land reclamation but also helps to reduce soil erosion, which is quite common in alkali soils since these are dispersed soils.

Para Grass (*Brachiaria mutica* (Forsk) Stapf.)

This grass is grown in medium alkali conditions. It grows well in standing water. The grass is propagated by root-slip or stem cuttings. This grass requires irrigation more frequently than others, but drainage requirements in the monsoon season are minimal. At 50 ESP, the grass can yield up to 50 t ha^{-1} annually.

The relative tolerance of some grasses to sodicity is depicted in Fig. 11.2 which illustrates the differences in salt tolerance of these grasses.

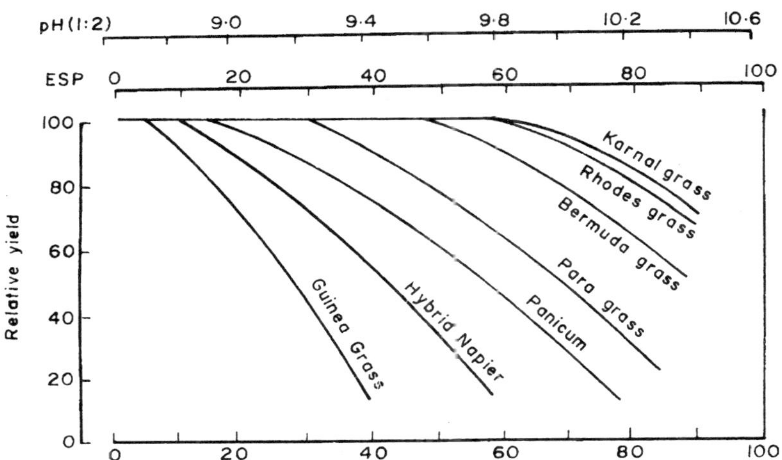

Fig. 11.2 Relative tolerance of grasses to soil ESP and pH$_2$

Tree Plantation in Alkali Soils

The National Commission on Agriculture has reported that there is a big gap between the demand and supply of both the fuel-wood and the industrial wood. With burgeoning population, this mismatch is anticipated to widen further. Considering the gravity of the situation, the Commission stressed the need for afforestation of about 40 million ha of land presently lying barren due to such problem soils as alkali, saline, waterlogged, ravine lands, lateritic soils, coastal areas, stony and gravelly lands, high altitude and steep sloping lands.

As such, the utilization of alkali soils for growing trees appears to be a promising land use. Besides meeting the wood requirement such an approach offers an opportunity to increase the forest cover of the country, which presently is far below the minimum requirement of one third of the total land surface. Afforestation in these barren lands would also contribute to the maintenance of healthy agro-ecological system and averting the environment hazards. As a caution, it may be added that as a result of ever increasing demand for food, it would not be desirable to divert all alkali lands to forestry but, specific areas should be identified where trees can be grown without affecting crop production. Village community (*Panchayat*) lands and alkali lands with undulating topography offer enormous scope for afforestation. Besides, tree plantation could also be encouraged in alkali areas where industries, schools, offices and other installations are located.

Suitable Tree Species for Alkali Soils

Certain forest species have been identified which are tolerant to the alkali conditions. Some species like *Capparis aphylla, Caparis horrida, Salvadora oleoides* and *Zizyphus* sp. occur naturally under moderate alkali conditions (Yadav, 1978, Sharma and Bhargava, 1978). Species like *Acacia nilotica* (Babul), *Prosopis juliflora* (mesquite), *Butea monosperma (Dhak*), *Tamarix articulata* and *Albizzia lebbek* (Siris) can grow within certain limits in alkali soils (Khan and Yadav, 1962). Among fast growing exotic species, *Leucaena leucocephala,* (Varieties K8 and Fiji) has shown good growth in moderate to heavy alkali soils (Lohani, 1979). *Acacia nilotica* and *Prosopis spicegera* were found to promising in Punjab. On the basis of available data, some species have been arranged tentatively in descending order of their tolerance to soil alkali as: *Prosopis juliflora, Acacia nilotica, Eucalyptus* hybrid, *Zizyphus* species, *Capparis decidua, Capparis horrida, Pongamia pinnata, Butea monosperma, Casuarina equisetifolia, Acacia aurtiduliformis, Phyllanthus emblica, Terminalia arjuna, Azadirachta indica, Dalbergia sissoo, Tamarindus indica, Albizzia procera, Albizzia lebbek, Syzygium cumini, Leucaena leucocephala, Populus deltiodes, Ailanthus excelsa* (Yadav, 1989).

The most promising forest species identified for planting in highly alkali soils are Pahari Kiker (*Prosopis juliflora),* kikar (*Acacia nilotica)*, Pharans (*Tamarix articulata)*. The relative tolerance of different species to soil alkalinity is given in Table 11.4. Besides the tolerance of the plant, the utility and total bio-mass production are the other of considerations for selecting the species.

The technology for tree plantation is much less complex and requires less inputs. But for successful plantation adoption of appropriate practices is important. A successful plantation should take into account the following:

1. Good survival and rapid early growth of saplings.
2. Choice of a right species matching the planting sites.
3. Adequate site preparation.
4. Application of fertilizer, if necessary.
5. Irrigation during initial stages.
6. Weed control and protection against insects/pests, disease, etc.
7. Protection from animals.

Table 11.4 Relative tolerance of forest tree species to soil pH/sodicity/alkalinity

Highly tolerant $pH_2 > 10.0$	*Tolerant* pH_2 *9.5-10.0*	*Moderately* pH_2 *9.0-9.5*	*Sensitive* $pH_2 < 9.0$
Pahari Kiker (*Prosopis juliflora*) Kikar (*Acacia nilotica*), Pharans (*Tamarix articulata*) Jor-tor (*Casuarina* equietifolia*)	Jangal jalebi (Pithecellobiumdulce), Safeda (*Eucalyptus tereticornis*), Arjan tree (*Terminalia arjuna*), Imly (*Tamarindus indica*), Papri (*Pongamia pinnata*), Khair (*Acacia catechu*), Dhak (*Butea monosperma*), Lasura (*Cordia rothii*), Siris *Albizia lebbeck Parkinsonia aculeata*	Kigelia (Kigelia pinnata), Shisham (*Dalbergia sissoo*), Siamea (*Cassia siamea*), Neem (*Azadirachta indica*), Silver oak (*Grevilla robusta*), Dhaincha (*Sesbania sesban* Bakain (*Melia azedarach*), Subabul (*Leucaena leucocephala*), Saunjana (*Moringa olifera*), Bamboo (*Bambusa spp.*), Sehtoot (*Morus alba*), Siris (*Albizia procera*), *Acacia auriculiformis, Acacia senegal*	Poplar (*Populus deltoides*), Teak (*Tectona grandis*), *Ficus virens, Bombax ceiba, Hardwickia Binnata, Thespesia populnea Bauhinia variegata, Lagerstro-emia speciosa, Cadrella toona*

* Not suitable for deep ground water areas
Source : Singh et. al., 1977

For successful tree plantation in alkali environment, proper method of site preparation is of utmost importance. Some principals' of good site preparation are as follows.

1. Production of a loose soil amenable to rapid proliferation of the root system.
2. Modification of root environment to retain and supply moisture to plants.
3. The addition of chemical amendments only around the plant than in the entire area.

4. Application of nutrients, like nitrogen, zinc, etc.
5. Perforation of hard pan in the sub-soil if any, as it hampers the root growth.

Site preparation should aim at achieving high survival and rapid growth of tree plants. The investments on site preparation depends on the properties of site, species to be planted and the purpose of plantation.

Tree Plantation Techniques in Alkali Soils

Depending upon the alkali conditions, topography and resources, one of the following technique can be successfully used for tree plantation.

1. Pit method
2. Auger hole method
3. Ridge plantation
4. Trench plantation

Pit method

Depending upon the type of soil, and the depth of the *kankar* layer, pits of different sizes are used for planting trees. The soil of the pits is either replaced by a good soil from nearby place or amended suitably by gypsum or other amendments. FYM and basal dose of nutrients is also added at this stage. In alkali soils, the pits are dug to a depth of about 1m, so that the *kankar* layer if any, is broken. The deep pits having good soil or soil amended with addition of gypsum and FYM are found to give better results (Yadav, 1980).

Species like *Eucalyptus terticornis, Prosopis juliflora* and *Acacia nilotica* were planted in pits 60cm x 60cm x 60cm filled with good soil. Not much success was, however, achieved in Haryana (Yadav, 1980). *Eucalyptus hybrid, Acacia nilotica* and *Albizzia lebbek* were planted at a spacing of 4m x 4m in an alkali soil after treating each pit with 5 kg gypsum + 20 kg FYM. The survival percentage in the case of *Eucalyptus* hybrid and *Acacia nilotica* was 60 percent, while it was only 16 % in the case of *Albizzia lebbek.* Replacement of the original soil with good soil as well as the original soil treated with gypsum yielded almost similar results. *Prosopis juliflora* performed better compared to *Acacia nilotica.*

In another field experiment, pits of 90cm depth (90cm x 90cm) were dug in alkali lands (pH_2 10.0) before the onset of rainy season. The pits wre refilled after giving the following treatments: (1) original soil, (2) addition of FYM @ 25 kg pit^{-1}, (3) addition of gypsum @ 50 percent GR (3.5 kg pit^{-1}), (4) addition of gypsum @ 50 percent GR plus FYM and, (5) replacement of original soil by normal soil. Two types of seedlings of each species viz. small and tall were used for transplanting in the fields. The small seedlings represented those raised in the polyethylene bags and the tall seedlings represented those, which were first raised in polyethylene bags and subsequently allowed to grow in a temporary nursery bed. The age of seedlings was the same in both the cases. An additional treatment of fertilizer application (N and P) was also superimposed. The survival percentage of the planted seedlings was the lowest in the control (Yadav *et al.,,* 1972). Though the treatment of FYM gave the higher survival percentage than the control, application of gypsum resulted in more than 90 percent survival in case of *Albizzia lebbek, Eucalyptus* hybrid, and *Prosopis juliflora.* Gypsum + FYM was as good as the soil replacement and were at par. *Eucalyptus* hybrid and *Prosopis juliflora* attained maximum height as compared to remaining species. In the untreated soil, performance of *Prosopis juliflora* and *Acacia nilotica* was better than other three species. The height increment was greater in case of plants raised from the tall seedlings as compared to those from the small seedlings. The fertilizer application increased the height, the magnitude being maximum in case of *Eucalyptus* hybrid (Table 11.5). It was concluded that the species like *Eucalyptus* hybrid, *Prosopis juliflora* and *Acacia nilotica* can be grown successfully by treating the soil of the planting pit with gypsum + FYM.

Table 11.5. Height increment (cm) of different forest species on an alkali soil (1 year).

Treatment	*Acacia nilotica*	*Prosopis-juliflora*	*Eucalyptus hybrid*	*Albizzia lebbek*	*Terminalia arjuna*
Soils :					
Normal	107	100	119	87	98
FYM + Gypsum	76	102	120	71	95
Gypsum	88	92	91	62	85
FYM	76	81	62	46	68
Original	40	46	33	15	25
Type of seedlings :					
Tall	90	88	93	58	77
Small	77	82	83	55	72
Fertiliser :					
Fertilised	91	94	103	57	80
Unfertilised	95	76	74	56	69

Auger hole technique

This technique of tree plantation in alkali soils has been devised keeping in view that a hard *kankar* layer is always encountered at about 1 to 1.5 m depth. Thus to pierce this layer, a auger hole is made from 1.2 m to 1.8 m depth. The diameter of the auger hole is about 15 cm. A manually or mechanically operated auger could be used (Fig. 11.3). Auger holes are refilled by either the normal soil from adjoining areas or properly amending the original alkali soil before planting the saplings. The technique is cheaper than the pit method as it involves reclamation of a very small percentage of the soil and aims at training the roots to grow deeper into the soil where relatively better soil environment is present (Fig. 11.4). This technique was first described by Agarwal and Gupta (1968) but has recently been adopted on large scale in tree plantation at the Central Soil Salinity Research Institute and Forest Department of Haryana. Initially deep auger hole 150cm has a distinct advantage over the pit method or a shallow auger hole (90 cm) in which *kankar* layer is not pierced through.

Mixing of 2-3 kg gypsum and 8 kg FYM with the original alkali soil from the planting site per post hole of 15cm diameter and 150cm depth yielded good survival and growth of selected species as with 12 kg gypsum and 24 kg FYM in conventional pit method of planting (Table 11.6). *Acacia nilotica* (Babul), *Prosopis juliflora* (Mesquite), *Casuarina equisetifolia* (Jor-tor) and *Sesbania* (Dhaincha) have shown promising results when planted in a highly alkali soils using auger hole technique. The moderately good species are *Albizzia labbek (Siris), Azadirachta indica (Neem)* and *Eucalyptus tereticornis*. However, it was observed that later on the growth of eucalyptus plants was restricted. Visual symptoms like yellowing or chlorisis indicated possibility of nutritional disorders.

Fig. 11.3 A tractor operated auger for making auger holes for tree plantations

The main advantages of auger hole technique are:

1. The cost of plantation is less, as small amount of amendment is required.
2. The process of planting can be mechanized such that planting can be speeded up.
3. The *kankar* layer can be pierced to facilitate root penetration to greater depths.

Fig. 11.4 Plant roots move deeper when planted in auger holes

While auger hole technique has several plus points, it has some limitations as well. This technique is useful only when carried out mechanically. Making auger holes manually is a tedious task and needs large labour force. It is also observed that the initial advantage gained with this method in the first 2-3 years is evened out in later years. This was particularly observed in the case of *Eucalyptus* plantations. It seems that roots proliferation in this case is vertical and the lower soil layers which are deficient in the nutrients. In the surrounding area around the auger hole, the pH value remains higher than the auger hole and therefore, root proliferation in the horizontal direction is restricted.

Table 11.6. Per cent survival and growth parameters of *Eucalyptus tereticornis* and *Acacia nilotica* after 7 years of planting in an alkali soil

Post hole filling mixture O.S. + + G+F (kg)	*Size of the post hole (cm × cm)*	*Eucalyptus*			*Acacia*		
		Survival (%)	*Height (cm)*	*DSH (mm)*	*Survival (%)*	*Height (cm)*	*DSH (mm)*
3+4	10x120	100	822	138	100	659	140
3+6	10x180	100	884	158	100	666	155
3+8	15x120	88	838	144	100	680	153
3+8	15x180	100	902	163	100	733	164
12+24	90x90	100	921	167	100	741	177
Mean		98	873	154	100	696	158

O. S. = Original soil (pH 10.3-10.5); DSH = Diameter at stump height
Source: Gill and Abrol (1986)

Table 11.7. Mean biomass production after one year of planting in shallow and deep auger holes on oven dry basis (g)

Tree species	*Flat surface plantation*				*Ridge plantation*			
	With grass		*Without grass*		*With grass*		*Without grass*	
	Shallow	*Deep*	*Shallow*	*Deep*	*Shallow*	*Deep*	*Shallow*	*Deep*
Eucalyptus	160	860	125	667	342	897	314	816
Acacia	80	697	90	540	212	925	186	857
Parkinsonia	124	714	120	585	265	878	226	757

Source: Grewal and Abrol (1983)

Ridge plantation technique

Alkali lands have high potential of run-off. The run-off from these barren lands causes flooding in low-lying areas. Thus, a technique to conserve rainwater within the planted area, has been devised. In this technique ridges of different sizes, shape and spacing were made at different planting sites. Plant saplings were planted on the ridges while trenches were used to store the rainwater. The biomass of the plants was much higher in the ridge than the flat method of planting (Table 11.7). The biomass was higher in deep than shallow auger holes in the case of both the methods. The ridge method, besides giving higher biomass, helped in rainwater management and soil conservation. The cost of ridge making and the overall economics would determine the application of this technology by the forest department.

Trench plantation technique

In this technique, trenches of different sizes and shapes are opened either manually or mechanically. Trenches are

Table 11.8. Effect of treatments and planting techniques on survival, height, DSH and DBH of mesquite 2 years after plantation

Treatment	*Survival (%)*	*Height (cm)*	*DSH (mm)*	*DBH (mm)*
With grass	92	294	38.6	13.1
Without grass	92	370	48.0	18.3
C. D. (p=0.05)	Ns	62	6.9	4.9
Filling mixture :				
Original soil	63	153	18.0	5.8
Gypsum	88	323	38.8	13.9
Gypsum + Rice husk	100	394	55.0	21.1
Gypsum + FYM	100	412	54.0	18.9
C. D. (p=0.05)	24	67	16.8	7.9
Planting technique :				
Pit	100	323	47.5	17.2
Auger	100	358	46.5	17.3
Trench	88	349	38.8	13.9
C. D. (p=0.05)	ns	ns	7.0	ns

Original soil pH_2 =10.4-10.6 , DBH = Diameter at breast height, DSH = diameter at stump height; Source: Singh and Abrol (1988)

refilled by adding suitable amendment in the soil. The plants are then planted in these trenches. It was observed that mesquite could be successfully established with this technique. (Singh and Abrol, 1986; Singh *et al.* 1988). Mesquite performed better in the case of no grass compared to with grass when Karnal grass was grown in association with mesquite (Table 11.8 and Fig. 11.5). The technique is inferior to the pit or the auger hole method but is cheaper and easier to apply for large scale plantations.

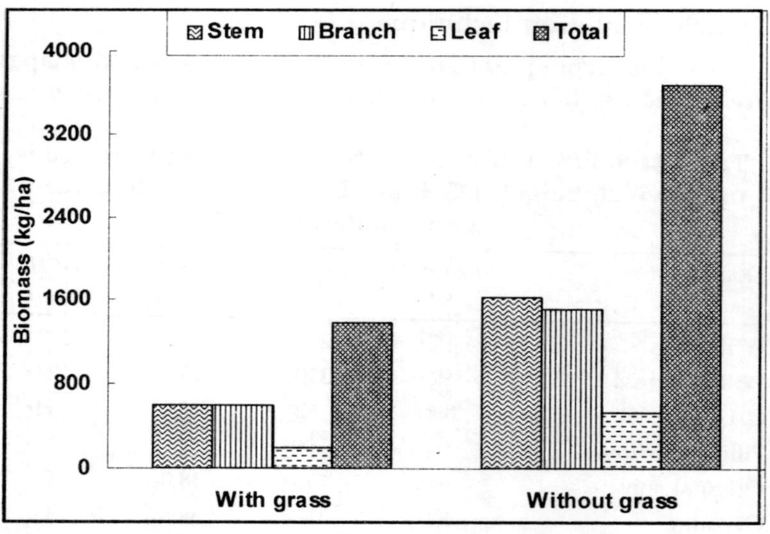

Fig. 11.5 Oven dried biomass of mesquite 720 days after planting

Cultural Practices for Growing Trees in Alkali Lands

The success of tree plantation depends to a great extent on the kind of planting technique, soil preparation, selection of suitable species and use of amendments. Besides, cultural practices can help to improve the performance of tree species under the adverse environment. Some practices are as follows.

Planting time

Generally there are two planting seasons for woody species-February to March and July to September. The latter is preferred under rainfed or scarce irrigation situations. However, if assured irrigation facilities are available and the trees are sensitive to cold during the establishment stage, the February-March season should be preferred. Deciduous trees like *shisham* and poplar should always be planted in this season.

Irrigation

Irrigation specially during the establishment stage of the woody species is a critical input. Application of irrigation, fortnightly for the first three months, and monthly during the later growth period up to two years, results in significant increase in survival, growth and bio-mass production of some forest tree species (Fig. 11.6). After two years, irrigation may be withdrawn, if the monsoon is normal.

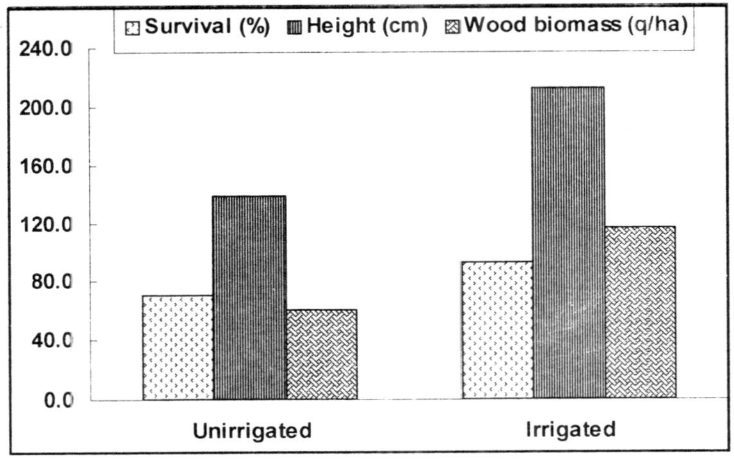

Fig. 11.6 Effect of irrigation on mesquite plants

Tree spacing

If the primary purpose of plantation is firewood production or energy plantation then 2m x 1m or 2m x 2m spacing should be adopted. In alkali soils, closer planting covers the risk of high mortality. In agro-forestry, the minimum spacing between rows and plant should be kept at 4m and 2m, respectively (Fig. 11.7). If the tree is spreading type like *Prosopis, Acacia, Dalbergia* etc. the spacing should not be less then 5m x 3m. Further, if the purpose is both firewood and timber production, high density plantation may be preferred. After about 3 or 4 years, 50 per cent of the plants may be harvested to meet periodic firewood needs and the remaining 50 per cent may be kept for timber production.

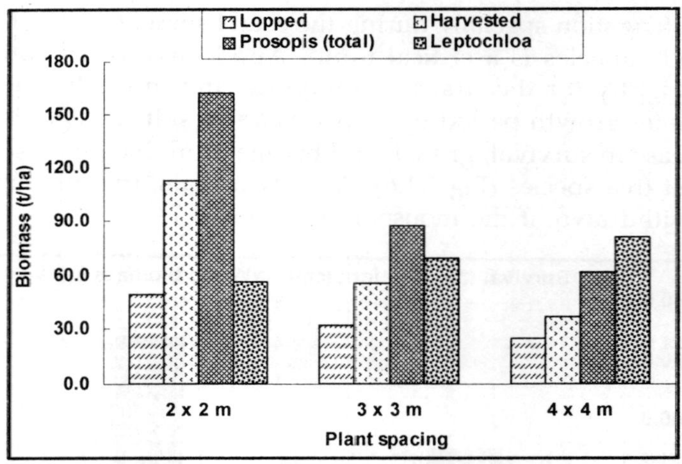

Fig. 11.7 Effect of spacing on *Prosopis* and *Leptochloa* grass

Fertilization

Alkali soils are generally deficient in N, Ca and Zn. Application of N to the non-nitrogen fixing trees improve the growth significantly. On the other hand, N application is not required for N-fixing species. For non-N-fixing trees, a basal dose of N (50 g urea plant^{-1}) should be mixed in the soil mixture used to fill the auger-holes. Zinc sulphate at the rate of 10 g auger-hole^{-1} may also be applied at the time of planting. Later, 50 gram urea should be applied in two equal splits every year, one during the monsoon season and the second in February-

March. Application of Phosphorus and Potash are not needed as these are present in sufficient quantities. Application of farm-yard manure does help in meeting the iron needs of the woody species.

Pruning/Lopping

Pruning refers to the removal of unwanted side branches of trees which are photo synthetically less active. It is practiced to give proper shape to the trees and to enhance the growth of vegetation underneath and inter crops. The biomass received during lopping could be used as firewood. Lopping of *Prosopis juliflora* at 16 and 40 months after planting (at 2m x 2m spacing) yielded about 13 t of woody bio-mass per ha and increased the green forage yield of inter-planted Karnal grass (Fig. 11.8). At the first looping, all the side branches should be removed up to one meter height, and at the second lopping 2 m stem should be kept free of unwanted side branches. Most of the trees of the tropical regions should be lopped between November and January when they are in dormant growth phase.

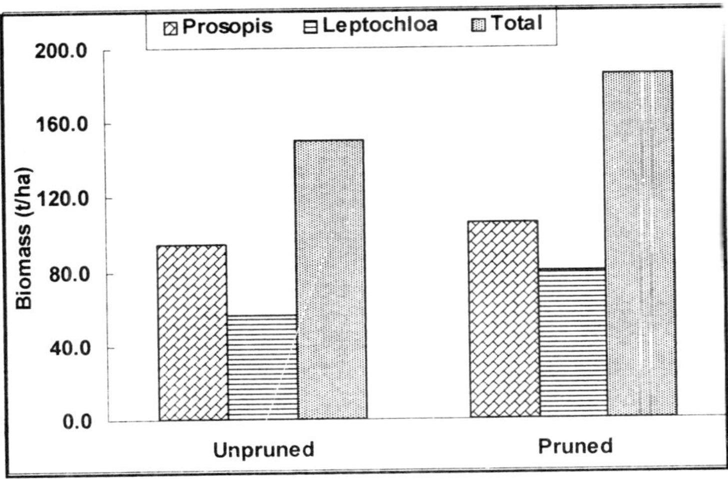

Fig. 11.8 Biomass of *Prosopis* and *Leptochloa* grass in unpruned and pruned situations

Soil Amelioration by Trees

In addition to bio-mass production, growing of trees on alkali soils results in their amelioration by improving physical, chemical and biological properties of the soil. The incorporation of organic matter through leaf litter and other foliage results in favourable changes in the physico-chemical properties of the soil (Table 11.9). Growing leguminous trees like *Prosopis, Acacia* and *Casuarina* ameliorates these soils at a much faster rate than non-leguminous trees, because of the build-up of organic matter and the recycling of important nutrients. It has also been proved that highly sodic soils reclaimed through tree plantations can be successfully used for growing all kinds of agricultural crops after removing the trees.

Table 11.9 Amelioration effect of tree plantation on an alkali soil

Species	*Original soil*		*After 20 years*		*Yield (g pot^{-1})*	
	pH_2	*O.C. (%)*	*pH_2*	*O.C. (%)*	*Wheat*	*Oat*
Eucalyptus tereticornis	10.3	0.12	9.18	0.33	32	43
Acacia nilotica	10.3	0.12	9.03	0.55	56	62
Albizia lebbek	10.3	0.12	8.67	0.47	45	53
Terminalia arjuna	10.3	0.12	8.15	0.58	44	46
Prosopis juliflora	10.3	0.12	8.03	0.58	62	88
Cropped land					13	24

Source: Singh and Dagar (1998)

Agro-forestry for Moderately alkali or Reclaimed Lands

Most promising trees for agroforestry on reclaimed alkali lands identified are: *Populus deltoides* (Poplar), *Eucalyptus tereticornis* (Safeda), *Acacia nilotica* (Kikar) and *Tectona grandis* (Teak). The suitable intercrops during establishment stage are rice-berseem and rice-wheat. From third year onwards, as tree canopies develop, shade loving species such as berseem, guinea grass, turmeric and colcasia perform well. Poplar based agroforestry is more remunerative because of its faster growth and high wood price in the market compared to *safeda* and *kikar* based systems. The intercrops have been found to aid the growth of the trees.

Six years results of a study on comparative evaluation of agriculture, forestry and agroforestry practices in terms of productivity, sustainability and economics in a moderately alkali soil are summarized as follows:

- Poplar and eucalyptus growth was better when grown with intercrops, whereas acacia grew better without crops.
- Yields of almost all the intercrops were maximum with eucalyptus while minimum with acacia.
- Effect of trees on the fertility build-up in the soil was in the order acacia > poplar >eucalyptus > sole crops.
- The benefit cost ratio was highest in the case of poplar based and minimum in the case of acacia based system.

Agro-forestry Systems for Commercial Farms

Viewing agro-forestry as a viable proposition, many progressive farmers like to grow trees and inter-crops simultaneously in the very first year of land reclamation. In this set-up, the trees are planted with standardized auger-hole technique and the inter-space between the trees is reclaimed with amendments like gypsum or pyrites. For good returns and speedy reclamation, rice crop is recommended as in the case of normal land reclamation. Singh *et al.* (1997) evaluated this agro-forestry system on a moderately alkali soil (pH < 9.2) for 6 years. Three commercial trees viz. Poplar (*Populus deltoides*), Eucalyptus (*E. tereticornis*) and babul (*Acacia nilotica*) were planted either sole or in association with rice-wheat, rice-berseem, pigeon pea/sorghum-mustard rotations. Results at 5 years showed that inter-crops of berseem, rice, wheat and mustard can be successfully grown along with these trees during initial 3 years (Table 11.10). Later on these crops could be replaced with shade-loving crops such as turmeric. These inter-crops help Poplar and Eucalyptus to grow faster but adversely affect the growth of low water demanding trees like Acacia.

Table 11.10 Total grain (G), fodder (F) and rhizome (R) yields from various crop rotations in 5 years

Crop rotation	*Yield (t ha^{-1})*			
	Eucalyptus	*Acacia*	*Poplar*	*Open*
Rice-wheat/cowpea-berseem				
Rice (G)	14.4	12.5	11.8	21.6
Berseem (F)	239.7	212.7	234.6	389.1
Cowpea (F)	18.0	4.6	2.5	45.0
Rice-wheat/ Guinea grass-oat				
Rice (G)	13.4	11.8	10.3	21.0
Wheat (G)	9.0	8.1	8.4	16.0
Guinea grass (F)	18.1	12.3	2.5	30.0
Oats (F)	23.8	24.0	25.6	42.0
Pigeon pea-mustard/turmeric				
Pigeon pea (G)	0.7	0.8	0.2	0.7
Mustard (G)	2.3	1.8	2.0	4.0
Sorghum (G)	18.3	8.6	22.8	50.0
Turmeric (R)	22.3	5.9	8.3	22.1

Source: Singh *et al.* (1997)

Horticulture in Alkali Soils

Earlier, it was considered highly difficult to raise fruit trees in highly alkali soils of $pH_2 > 10.0$. But recent experiments at ND University of Agriculture and Technology, Faizabad and CSSRI, Karnal with some salt tolerant species of fruits have shown that there are about half a dozen fruit plants which can be grown in highly alkali soils by adopting proper site preparation techniques and by using higher dose of organic and inorganic amendments. The fruit species which can be established successfully in alkali soils identified are: ber (*Zizyphus mauritiana*) guava (*Psydium guajava*), pomegranate (*Punica granatum*), amla (*Emblica officinalis*), Karaunda (*Carrisa carandus*), Imly (*Tamarindus indica*) and Jamun (*Syzygium cuminii*). The fruit species, which have shown high degree of salt tolerance and were found promising at the ND University of Technology at Faizabad in alkali soils, are reported in Table 11.11.

Table 11.11 Some suitable fruit species and their relative tolerance

Fruit species	*Tolerance*		*Suitable varieties*
	pH	*ESP*	
Aonla-*Emblica officinalis*	9.5	40	Chakaiya, NA-7, NA-6
Guava-*Psidium guajava*	9.2	30	Sardar (L-49)
Ber-*Ziziphus mauritiana*	9.5	45	Banarasi, Karaka, Ponda
Bael-*Aegle marmelos*	9.0	30	Narendra-5, Narendra-9
Mahua-*Madhuca latifolia*	9.2	-	Narendra selection
Grape-*Vitis vinifera* Perlette	9.0	30	Beauty seedless,
Karaunda-*Carrisa carandus*	9.2	35	Narendra selection

Source: Singh *et al.* (1994)

The planting techniques consisted of making pits of 60 cm x 60 cm x 60 cm dimensions manually. In the center of each pit an auger hole of 20-25 cm diameter and 140-160 cm deep (to pierce through the *Kankar* pan) is made using tractor mounted augers. These pits cum auger holes are filled back with a mixture of original soil + 8 to 10 kg gypsum + 10 kg FYM + 20 kg river sand. To improve upon survival and quality, rootstock should be planted, followed by in-situ grafting for desired characters. Some of the fruit species are sensitive to water logging and frost such as pomegranate and sapota. So, proper drainage in the rainy season and protection of the young tender saplings during winter is a pre-requisite for the over all success of the horticulture plants. Apply regular irrigation to keep the orchard soil moist to off-set frost damage. For better growth of the plants, apply 25 percent higher dose of nitrogen and FYM every year than recommended for normal soils. Grow *Sesbania* during rainy season as a green manure crop to improve soil fertility.

Multi-story mixed plantations in which multiple combination of fruit species are used for plantation was tested at Faizabad. In this model, *aonla*, guava and *ber* were planted at a spacing of 8x8 m and *karaunda* and *phalsa* in between the rows at 4x4 m spacing. Initially the soil had high pH (9.5-10.6) and ESP (76-80). The pits used to plant the trees (1x1x1 m for *aonla*, guava and *ber*) and (0.6x0.6x0.6 m for *karaunda* and *phalsa*) were filled with a mixture of normal soil + BHC (100g) + FYM (25 kg). The recommended practices were followed to raise the plantations. The species, varieties and combination used in plantations are reported in Table 11.12.

Table 11.12 Species combination, variety and plant density of the experimental set-up

Species combination	*Variety*	*Type of plant*	*Plant density ha^{-1}*
Aonla+	Chakaiya+NA-7	Budded	144
Guava+	L-49 (sardar)	Budded	100
Karaunda	Local selection	Seedling	100
Aonla+	Chakaiya+NA-7	Budded	144
Ber+	*Umran*	*Budded*	*100*
Guava+	L-49 (sardar)	Budded	144
Ber+	Gola+kaithli	Budded	100
Phalsa	*Local selection*	*Seedling*	*100*

Data on growth in terms of trunk girth of plants of 1-10 years age indicate fast growth (Table 11.13). *Ber* appears to have excellent growth after 6th year and onwards under both *aonla*+ *Ber* and guava + *ber* + *phalsa* models. *Aonla* recorded higher girth than the guava under *aonla* + guava + *karaunda* model.

Table 11.13 Growth performance of fruit species under mixed plantation

Combination	*Average trunk girth * (cm) in successive years*									
	1	*2*	*3*	*4*	*5*	*6*	*7*	*8*	*9*	*10*
Aonla+	15.3	24.8	29.7	38.8	45.2	48.5	52.0	57.8	60.1	62.0
Guava+	8.4	12.8	19.5	24.5	33.0	40.2	46.0	50.2	54.1	56.2
Karaunda	*2.2*	*4.5*	*8.8*	*10.2*	*11.6*	*12.2*	-	-	-	-
Aonla+	14.6	22.5	28.4	38.2	42.1	45.8	50.2	54.3	56.0	57.1
Ber	*13.0*	*22.5*	*26.8*	*36.6*	*39.3*	*49.8*	*58.5*	*62.8*	*71.2*	*75.2*
Guava+	8.8	13.7	20.2	23.6	28.5	39.5	48.4	56.5	61.2	64.0
Ber+	10.5	20.7	25.7	29.8	42.1	56.3	59.2	61.0	62.4	63.4
Phalsa	-	-	-	-	-	-	-	-	-	-

* Average of 20 plants, Source: Singh (1996)

Budded plants of guava and *ber* and seedlings of *karaunda* and *phalsa* started bearing from the 3rd year. This suggests that these plants are more precocious in bearing than *aonla* plants. *Karaunda* and *phalsa* lost productivity after 5th year. It was probably as a result of the shading effect of the other trees. Total productivity of guava + *ber* +*phalsa* was the highest till 6th year followed by *aonla*+guava+ *karaunda* and *aonla* + *ber* (Table 11.14). Higher productivity of *ber*+guava + *phalsa* was again observed in 9th and 10th years as compared to other combinations. Changes in some soil properties after 5th and 10th year of plantation were monitored (Table 11.15). Guava + *ber* + *phalsa* model was found to be the most effective in improving the soil properties. Apparently, mixed plantation helps to reclaim alkali wastelands.

Table 11.14 Productivity of multi-story mixed plantation

Combination	*Average yield * (t ha^{-1}) in successive years*							
	3	*4*	*5*	*6*	*7*	*8*	*9*	*10*
Aonla+	-	-	2.5	4.5	5.0	5.8	6.3	7.5
Guava+	1.3	2.2	3.2	4.0	5.2	5.5	6.0	6.6
Karaunda	*0.4*	*0.8*	*1.2*	*0.2*	-	-	-	-
Total	1.7	3.0	6.9	8.7	10.2	11.3	12.3	14.1
Aonla+	-	-	2.3	4.2	4.8	5.1	5.5	6.0
Ber	*0.7*	*2.0*	*2.8*	*4.0*	*4.5*	*4.8*	*5.0*	*5.5*
Total	0.7	2.0	5.1	8.2	9.3	9.9	10.5	11.5
Guava+	1.2	2.6	3.9	5.2	5.5	6.0	7.2	8.0
Ber+	0.6	2.0	3.0	4.5	4.7	5.2	6.0	6.5
Phalsa	*0.3*	*0.6*	*0.8*	*0.3*	-	-	-	-
Total	2.1	5.2	*7.7*	10.0	10.2	11.2	13.2	14.5

*Average of 20 plants, Source: Singh (1996)

Table 11.15 Physico-chemical properties of soil (0-45 cm) as affected by mixed plantation

Combination	*Years after plantation*	*pH_2*	*EC_e (dS m^{-1})*	*ESP*	*Hydraulic conductivity (cm hr^{-1})*	*Organic carbon (%)*
Aonla+						
Guava+ *Karaunda*	5	9.8	15.7	67	0.12	0.17
	10	9.2	13.4	60	0.17	0.21
Aonla+						
Ber	*5*	*9.8*	*13.3*	*65*	*0.18*	*0.16*
	10	9.4	12.0	57	0.23	0.22
Guava+	*5*	*9.2*	*10.9*	*59*	*0.24*	*0.25*
Ber+	10	9.0	8.3	47	0.38	0.30
Phalsa						
Control (barren land)	5	10.5	21.2	80	0.08	0.13
	10	10.6	18.3	76	0.09	0.15

Source: Singh (1996)

A number of models have been tried to make horticultural plantations economically viable alternative and to get returns during initial years of plantation. Following are few of the models that have been found appropriate for adoption.

Agri-horti System

In this system agricultural crops are grown in association with fruit species. Rows between the fruit trees are used for crop cultivation. In a study conducted at Faizabad, mustard and sunflower were grown in association with guava and *aonla*. Mustard yield in both the years is more than sunflower (Table 11.16). Total productivity of mustard and sunflower is relatively higher with guava than with *aonla*. However, it seems that cultivation of these oil seed crops could be one of the options to utilize inter-space between guava and *aonla* orchards during the first few years. It would provide additional income to the farmers during a period when the fruit plants do not yield any income.

Table 11.16 Productivity of oil seeds as inter-crop

System	*Variety*	*Productivity (t ha^{-1})*	
		2nd year	*3rd year*
Guava+	Sardar	-	-
Mustard+	Baruna	0.14	0.18
Sunflower	Modern	0.10	0.13
Aonla+	Chakaiya	-	-
Mustard+	Baruna	0.11	0.16
Sunflower	Modern	0.08	0.11

Silvi-horti System

In this system, forest species are planted in association with fruit species. Some horticultural based agro-forestry models have been introduced by ND University of Agriculture and Technology, Faizabad (Singh, 1996). In the silvi-horti-pasture model, the growth rate of guava + eucalyptus + subabul was faster and production was higher in terms of fruits, fodder and fuel wood (Table 11.17). Reduction in fruit yield particularly in guava and *aonla* was noticed in the 7th year. It could be due to the suppression in growth and fruiting by the forest species. Hence the forest species were removed from the model at this time.

Table 11.17 Productivity of silvi-horti system

System	*Product*	*Average productivity (t ha⁻¹) in successive years*						
		4	5	6	7	8	9	10
Guava+	Fruit	1.8	2.7	3.0	2.5	3.3	3.5	4.0
Eucalyptus+	Wood	-	-	-	10.5	-	-	-
Subabul	Fodder+ wood	0.7	1.2	1.4	1.0 (2.0)	-	-	-
Aonla+	Fruit	-	2.2	4.1	3.6	4.0	4.3	4.8
Eucalyptus+	Wood	-	-	-	9.0	-	-	-
Subabul	Fodder+ wood	0.6	1.0	1.2	1.0 (2.1)	-	-	-
Bael+	Fruit	-	0.9	1.8	2.2	3.0	3.1	3.5
Eucalyptus+	Wood	-	-	-	7.8	-	-	-
Phalsa	Fodder+ wood	0.1 (0.2)	0.21 (0.3)	0.2 (0.4)	0.1 (0.4)	-	-	-

Wood-dry, Fodder-green, Values in parenthesis are for wood

Data recorded on physico-chemical properties of soil in relation to silvi-horti systems reveal a clear-cut improvement in hydraulic conductivity and increase in organic carbon content of the soil (Table 11.18). Corresponding reduction in pH, electrical conductivity and exchangeable sodium are also noticed in all the treatments compared to the control. Guava + eucalyptus + subabul was found to be the most effective system in improving the soil properties (Table 11.18).

Table 11.18 Changes in properties of salt-affected soil under silvi-horti systems after 7 years (0-45 cm soil depth)

Systems	*Hydraulic conductivity (cm hr⁻¹)*	*Organic carbon (%)*	pH_2	EC_e *(dS m⁻¹)*	*ESP*
Guava+*Eucalyptus*+subabul	0.28	0.26	9.2	10.0	49
Aonla+*Eucalyptus*+subabul	0.26	0.20	9.8	13.3	53
Bael+ *Eucalyptus*+phalsa	0.26	0.21	9.7	12.8	55
Control (barren land)	0.09	0.16	10.4	18.3	76

Oleri-horti System

In this system vegetable crops are grown in association with horticultural plants. Two kinds of cropping systems were

Table 11.19 Productivity of guava based vegetable cropping system

System	*Varieties*	*Spacing*	*Productivity (t ha⁻¹)*		*Net returns in 4th year (Rs.)*
			2nd year	*4th year*	
Guava	Sardar	8x8 m	-	2.4	18,632
Cauliflower	Pusa Synthetic	60x40 cm	5.3	5.6	
Onion	Pusa Red	15x10 cm	8.5	9.0	
Guava	Sardar	8x8 m	-	2.6	16,800
Cabbage	Golden Acre	60x45 cm	4.8	5.2	
Okra	Parbhani Kranti	30x15 cm	5.6	5.8	
Guava	Sardar	8x8 m	-	2.5	10,450
Tomato	Pusa Ruby	60x45 cm	4.7	5.6	
Bottle gourd	P. S. Prolofic long	2x1.5 m	4.0	4.6	
Guava	Sardar	8x8 m	-	2.2	5,837
Chillies	Pusa Sadabahar	45x30 cm	2.0	2.5	
Bitter gourd	Faizabadi	2x0.6 m	1.0	1.2	

tried. One had guava plantation alone while the other had a mixed plantation of *aonla* + guava. In the first instance the total productivity of the system was highest when cauliflower + onion were grown in association with guava plants (Table 11.19). It was followed by cabbage + okra, tomato + bottle gourd and chillies + bitter gourd. The net returns were also highest with cauliflower + onion followed by cabbage + okra in the 4th year.

In the second case of mixed planatation, productivity of bottle gourd + cabbage was higher than the tomato + Spinach when grown in association with aonla + guava (Table 11.20).

Table 11.20 Productivity of vegetables as inter-crops with aonla + guava plantation

System	*Variety*	*Spacing*	*Average yield (t ha⁻¹)* 1st year	2nd year
Bottle gourd+	P.S. Prolific long	2x1.5 m	2.6	3.8
Cabbage	Golden acre	60x45 cm	3.0	4.0
Tomato +	Pusa Ruby	60x45 cm	2.3	2.8
Spinach	All green	Broad cast	2.0	2.6

Note: In both the systems aonla + guava were grown at a spacing of 8x8 m

Silvi-oleri System

In this system vegetable crops are grown in association with forest plantations. Studies at N D University of Agricultural and Technology at Faizabad, revealed that the productivity of brinjal + bottle gourd is maximum when grown in association with teak plantation (Table 11.21). It is followed by tomato + onion, cauliflower + okra and bitter gourd + okra. The net returns per unit area were, however, found to be highest in the case of cauliflower + okra in the 5th year of cultivation.

Table 11.21 Productivity of vegetables as inter-crops under teak plantation

System	*Variety*	*Spacing*	*Average yield ($t\ ha^{-1}$)* 1st	2nd	5th	*Net returns in 5th year (Rs. ha^{-1})*
Brinjal	Pant Samrat	60x45 cm	7.8	9.5	9.8	9,750
Bottle gourd	P. S. Prolofic long	2x1.5 m	4.0	4.2	4.5	
Cauliflower	Pusa Synthetic	60x40 cm	5.2	5.4	5.8	21,508
Okra	Parbhani Kranti	30x15 cm	4.3	5.0	5.2	
Tomato	Pusa Ruby	60x45 cm	4.0	4.6	5.0	16,580
Onion	Pusa Red	15x10 cm	7.6	8.0	8.3	
Bitter gourd	Faizabadi	2x0.6 m	0.8	1.2	1.5	16,232
Okra	Parbhani Kranti	30x15 cm	4.0	4.5	5.0	

Note: In each system teak wood was grown at a spacing of 4x4 m

Medicinal and Aromatic Crops

Medicinal and aromatic plants are in great demand to meet the national requirement and for export. Since these crops are minor in nature, it is not always possible to produce these crops on fertile lands, which can be used to produce food grains. Wastelands especially the lands affected by alkalinity and salinity problems where profitable returns are not possible from agricultural crops, could be utilized for the cultivation of these high-valve crops with marginal inputs. The threshold limits of pH and ESP for some of the medicinal and aromatic plants (Table 11.22) indicate that most of the aromatic grasses (except citronella) can withstand alkalinity levels given by a soil pH_2 of 9.5 or an ESP of 55. Among the medicinal crops, rye for ergot can be grown successfully in soils having pH_2 up to 10.0. Further studies on ameliorative potential of these crops for different kinds of alkali soils and their efficacy to withstand different stresses are required for their cultivation under specific situations. These crops can also be grown in inter-spaces between fruit plants and rows. In case pH_2 is less than 9.5, crops of Babuna (*Matricaria camomila*) and Isabgol (*Plåntigo ovata*) can be grown in between fruit trees.

Table 11.22. Safe limits (threshold) of alkalinity for some important aromatic and medicinal crops

Crop	*pH_2*	*ESP*
Aromatic :		
Palmarosa	9.5	55
Lemongrass	9.0	50
Vetiver	9.5	55
Citronella	8.5	25
Jamrosa	10.0	55
Medicinal :		
Periwinkle	9.5	-
German Chamomile	9.5	-
Rye for ergot	10.0	-

Source : Patra and Singh (1998).

Fish Ponds in Alkali Soils

The infiltration rate of alkali lands is poor and as a result rainwater keeps on standing for a longer period especially in the low-lying depressions. Thus, these depressions provide opportunities to convert and use these as fishponds (Fig. 11.9). These fishponds can be located in the lowest portion of the farm while the remaining upland portion could be put under agricultural cropping. These ponds could also serve as drainage ponds for the cropped area. The field studies have shown that except during the first rain storm of the monsoon season, the surface drainage water quality is good enough and has no deleterious effect on the growth of the fishes. Alternative arrangement for filling the pond in the post monsoon season has to be made to ensure the fish farming.

Fig. 11.9 A semi-reclaimed alkali lands converted to a fish pond

In a study conducted at N.D. University of Agriculture and Technology, Faizabad, a pond of 0.4 ha was constructed for evaluation of fishes. The boundaries of fishpond are planted with *Casuarina equisettifolia*. The results presented in Table 11.23 reveal that in general the survival of fishes was less than 50%. Grass carps recorded highest survival (59%) followed by common carps (56%). A total productivity of 0.637 t was obtained meaning thereby that the productivity could be around 1.6 t ha^{-1}.

Table 11.23 Fish productivity after 12 months in a 0.4 ha pond

Fishes	*Fish seed Fry-5-6 cm (Number)*	*Survival (Number)*	*Average weight/fish (kg)*	*Yield (t)*
Rohu	300	98	0.8	0.078
Catlu	250	92	1.0	0.092
Grass carps	300	178	1.1	0.195
Silver carps	200	102	1.3	0.132
Common Carps	500	280	0.5	0.140
Total	1550	750	-	0.637

Source : Singh (1996).

REFERENCES

Agarwal, R. R. and Gupta, R. N. 1968. Saline Alkali Soils in India. Tech. Bull. Indian Council of Agricultural Research, New Delhi. 221 pp.

Chandra, S. 1979. Genetics and Plant Breeding. In A Decade of Research. CSSRI, Karnal. 80-98.

Gill, H. S. and Abrol, I. P. 1985. Tree plantation in alkali soils. Better Farming Series Salt-affected Soils. CSSRI, Karnal. 8: 11pp.

Gill, H. S. and Abrol, I. P. 1986. Effect of site preparation and composition of filling mixture on the performance of Eucalyptus and Acacia in a highly sodic soil. Ann. Rep. CSSRI, Karnal. 25-27.

Grewal, S. S. and Abrol, I. P. 1983. Studies on rain water conservation for the establishment of an agro-forestry system in a highly sodic soil. Ann. Rep. CSSRI, Karnal. 31-33.

Khan, W. A. M. and Yadav, J. S. P. 1962. Characteristics and afforestation problems of saline alkali soils. Indian Fmg. 83:259-261.

Kumar, A. Abrol, I. P. and Dargan, K. S. 1980. Effect of exchangeable sodium on the growth and yield of five forage grasses. Forage Res. 6:123-127.

Kumar, A. and Abrol, I. P. 1983. Effect of gypsum on five tropical grasses grown in normal and extremely sodic soils. Exptl. Agric. 19:169-177.

Kumar, A. and Abrol, I. P. 1986. Grasses in Alkali Soils. CSSRI Bull. 11. 96 pp.

Lohani, D. N. 1979. Preliminary trials with high yielding varieties of Luecaena leucocephola. Indian For. 105:199-202.

Patra, D. D. and Singh, D. V. 1998. Medicinal and aromatic crops. In Salinity Management in India (Eds. Tyagi, N. K. and Minhas, P. S.). Central Soil Salinity Research Institute, Karnal. 499-506.

Sharma, R. C. and Bhargava, G. P. 1978. Soil survey of the operational research project area for the reclamation of alkali soils. CSSRI Rep 8. 72pp.

Singh, G. B. 1987. Agronomic investigations on production of mesquite in highly alkali soils. Ann. Rep. CSSRI, Karnal. 120-128.

Singh, G. B. and Abrol, I. P. 1986. Agronomic investigations on production of mesquite in highly alkali soil condition. Ann. Rep. CSSRI, Karnal. 98-107.

Singh, G. B., Abrol, I. P. and Cheema, S. S. 1988. Agroforestry in alkali soils: Effect of planting methods and amendments on initial growth, biomass accumulation and chemical composition of mesquite with inter-space planted with and without Karnal grass. Agro-forestry Systems. 7: 135-160.

Singh, G. B. and Dagar, J. C. 1998. Agroforestry in salt-affected soils. (In) Agricultural Salinity Management in India (Tyagi, N. K. and Minhas, P. S. Eds.) 473-487.

Singh, G. B., Singh, N. T. and Tomar, O. S. 1993. Agro-forestry in salt-affected soils. Bull. 17. CSSRI, Karnal. 65 p.

Singh, G. B., Singh, N. T. and Abrol, I. P. 1994. Agro-forestry techniques for the rehabilitation of salt land. Land Degradation and Rehabilitation. 5: 223-242.

Singh, G. B., Singh, N. T., Singh, H., Dagar, J. C. and Sharma, V. P. 1997. Evaluation of agriculture, forestry and agro-forestry practices in a moderately alkali soil in north-western India. Agro-forestry Systems. 37: 279-295.

Singh, I. S. 1996. Agro-forestry for Salt Affected Lands. Bulletin, N. D. University of Agriculture and Technology, Faizabad, UP. 23p.

Singh, I. S., Singh, R. K. and Khanna, S. S. 1994. Management of Sodic Soils Through Planation. Bulletin, N. D. University of Agriculture and Technology, Faizabad, UP. 51p.

Yadav, J. S. P. 1978. Studies on reclamation and utilization of salt-affected soils at Central Soil Salinity Research Institute. Fert. News. 23: 14-21.

Yadav, J. S. P. 1980. Salt-affected soils and their afforestation. Indian Forester. 106: 259-272.

Yadav, J.S.P., Bhumbla, D.R. and Sharma, O.P. 1972. Performance of certain forest species on a saline sodic soil. Proc. Symp. New Dev. in the Field of Salt-Affected Soils. Cairo (1972), 683-90.

12

SOCIO-ECONOMIC CRITERIA

India is confronted with a challenging task of increasing agricultural production to feed the ever-increasing population. A target to double the food production by 2020 has been placed before the nation by The Prime Minister of India. With shrinking land under plough and keen competition between various demands on water, it appears that agriculture has to exploit marginal and poor quality soil and water resources. In the present scenario, horizontal expansion of the agriculture on good soil resources is likely to be negligible. On the other hand large agriculturally productive lands would be taken out of agriculture for domestic and industrial sectors. Therefore, the only possibility to increase agricultural production is through the vertical expansion i.e., by increasing food production per hectare of land under plough including increase in the cropping intensity. A redeeming feature, however, is that nearly 8.6 million ha, of land is now out of cultivation of which 4 million ha is alkali land. Thus, horizontal expansion to that extent is possible by reclaiming this land for agriculture. If barren alkali land are reclaimed, it would enable the nation to have an additional food grain production of 24 0 m tonne assuming a modest production of 6 t ha^{-1} per annum. Such a strategy would require large investments in the private and public sectors. Primary investments in this case will be mainly done by the private sector (farmer), whereas large-scale secondary investments have to be made by the private and public sector (industrial houses and the government).

Economic Criteria

A project is successful and worthy of investment, only if it is economically viable. The judgment of economic viability is made on the basis of one of the following three criteria:

1. Net benefits or financial feasibility
2. Benefit-cost ratio
3. Rate of internal return

Though there are no hard and fast rules for selecting a particular criterion, it is expected that benefits should exceed cost or benefit-cost ratio should be more than one. Since the poor farmer makes the investments for reclamation of alkali lands, the proposition must be financially feasible. The social benefits become secondary in this case.

Constraints in Land Reclamation

Technical feasibility of reclamation of alkali lands has been proved beyond doubt. It will be shown later, that the proposition is also economically lucrative. In spite of this, it is observed that the pace of reclamation is not as fast as one would expect it to be. It is due to several constraints, which can be grouped into following three categories:

1. Financial
2. Social
3. Administrative and political

Financial Constraints

Any reclamation programme at the farmers level can be initiated only if he has substantial funds for initial investment. The items of investment include the cost of gypsum, land preparation, tube well installation, rice production and other subsidiary works. The farmers who own only alkali lands or those with small holdings besides such barren lands, do not have that much amount to invest on reclamation work. In spite of the loan facilities in the three states of Punjab, Haryana and Uttar Pradesh, farmers because of the illiteracy or other inhibitions, do not wish to take loans, which they describe as a vicious circle. Tedious and time-consuming nature of the processing of loan applications is also one major reason for the lack of interest in taking loans. To overcome this hurdel, it would be useful to associate agriculture development officers of the lead banks in the training programmes. Moreover, this technology is effective and viable only if it is implemented as a package. Manytimes, small farmers are unable to implement this package resulting in partial reclamation.

Social Constraints

The reclamation technology has wide acceptance among the farmers as few social constraints inhibit the implementation of this package. It is due to the fact that there were no traditional technologies for land reclamation, which might hinder the spread of new technology. As a result of illiteracy particularly amongst the marginal and small farmers, the knowledge level regarding reclamation of alkali soils is low (Parsad and Singh 1980). The movement of these farmers is also restricted to their communities and villages and therefore, they are unable to learn from others experiences. They also do not respond to the extension workers because of their inhibitions. Probably an extensive mobile training network with some agricultural institute as the focal point may help in spreading the message quickly and effectively.

Administrative and Political Constraints

Governments of Punjab, Haryana and Uttar Pardesh have encouraged reclamation of alkali lands. Land Reclamation Corporations have been set up which undertake the reclamation work on behalf of the farmers. They also have their own pilot projects to demonstrate the feasibility of the technology and to identify technological gaps. Subsidy on gypsum is provided and priority is given for electrical connection.

Some of the constraints, which remain to be addressed, are with regard to Panchayat lands. These lands are given on lease to an individual farmer who does not take interest in the reclamation of these lands. As these lands are auctioned, he fears that in the next auction some other person will take this land or he will have to pay much higher price next time.

Another constraint is that of surplus lands declared by landlords. They take no interest in these lands and continue to drag the cases pending in the courts. Some farmers are hesitant to reclaim their lands because once it is reclaimed a part of their holding would become surplus. A suitable strategy to deal with such problems should be evolved so as to encourage land reclamation. For example, in the case of Panchayat lands, lease for at least 10 years should be granted to recover the cost and to enjoy the benefits of labour that has been put in for land reclamation.

In spite of these constraints and the active support provided by many state governments, the alkali land reclamation programme has gone well with the farmer. Positive features that have helped this technology to gain the support of the farmers are listed in Table 12.1. It is believed that if some of the constraints as listed above are also addressed, the technology would gain further support and even the lands under Panchayats would turn from white deserts to green.

Table 12.1. Adoption potential of alkali land reclamation technology

Technologies likely to be adopted easily	*Alkali land reclamation programme*
Direct effects visible	✓
Technically flawless	✓
Individual farmer oriented	✓
Economically viable under farmers practices and inputs	✓
Low initial investments	✓
Simple technology	✓
Policy incentives are available	✓
Institutional support	✓
In line with the existing social norms	✓

Economics of Land Reclamation

The economics of land reclamation can be calculated by working out the cost and benefit arising out of the investments. The cost component can be divided into two groups ie. The capital cost and the annual cost (Table 12.2). The capital cost, which is of non-recurrent nature, is made once in the first year. In subsequent years only interest on this investment can be included towards expenditure. Though investment on tube well is of non-recurrent nature, this is not included as an investment on reclamation. Instead irrigation charges are worked out and are included suitably in the reclamation and crop production programme. In some cases, it is included as investment and the operational and maintenance cost is included in the crop production programmes.

The annual cost in case of reclamation is due to cultivation cost of rice and wheat. In some cases, green manuring crop is raised to improve the physical condition of the soil. The cost-benefit on this account is also included. Based on this principle, cost benefit of reclamation has been worked out at different places and under different sets of conditions. It is difficult to cover all these conditions in this chapter. However, typical examples from the three states of Punjab, Haryana and Uttar Pardesh are included.

The relative cost on various components of land reclamation reveal that maximum investments are needed for application of amendment (Table 12.3).

Table 12.2. Work components as envisaged in reclamation of alkali soil

Sr. No.	*Kind of work*	*Quantity/length/Number*
	Recurrent cost	
1	*Bunding* (m/ha)	470
2	Irrigation channels (m/ha)	100
3	Drainage channels (m/ha)	100
4	Outlet (small)	1
5	Land levelling (Tractor/hrs)	10
6	Tube well	1 per 4 ha
7	Pump set (no. per tube well)	1
8	Soil amendment and application(t/ha)	8-12
	Annual Costs	
9	Crop production (Rice)	Per ha
10	Crop production (Wheat)	Per ha
11	Crop production (green manuring)	Per ha

Table 12.3 Initial reclamation and operational cost of alkali land reclamation

Particulars	*Percentage of total cost*
On-farm land development	3.64
Tube well	15.76
Gypsum application	32.93
Rice cultivation	24.72
Wheat cultivation	22.95

Punjab

Chhiba and Singh (1978) worked out the economics of alkali land reclamation in the Operational Research Project, Kaputhala. The initial pH_2 of the soil was 10.5 indicating that land under reclamation was highly deteriorated. Gypsum @ 10 t ha^{-1} was added. A statement of expenditure and returns show that cost of reclamation is recovered within 2 years (Table 12.4). Although, a marginal loss of Rs. 170/-is indicated in the first year if the land reclamation cost is also included in the total cost, but in the second year, not only the total cost is recovered but a net gain of Rs. 3530/-is also made. Apparently, land reclamation in Punjab is a viable proposition.

Table 12.4. Expenditure and returns (Rs. ha^{-1}) statement for ORP Kapurthala

Particulars	*Period*	
	1975-76	*1976-77*
Cost of operations		
Bunding and levelling	540	–
Gypsum application and leaching	1230	–
Green manuring (Growing and burying)	1070	560
Production cost of rice	1990	1340
Production cost of wheat	1970	1260
Gross cost	6700	3160
Sale of rice and its by-products	3730	3950
Sale of wheat and its by-products	2800	2910
Total	6530	6860
Net returns	(-) 170	3700
Net gain in 2 years	3530	

Figures are nearest to ten rupees

Haryana

Economics of reclamation in Haryana calculated on the basis of data collected from 60 farmers fields shows that if the increase in land value is taken into account, the total cost of reclamation is more than offset by this increase alone (Table 12.5). The net profit from cultivation alone, however, is much less in this case as compared to Punjab. The net profit estimated at Rs. 2420/-is not sufficient, to recover the cost of reclamation which is estimated at Rs. 3260/-. However, profits could have been more and the cost of reclamation would have been recovered in 2 years provided:

1. The subsidy on gypsum is taken into account. If the subsidy component at the rate of 50 % of the cost of gypsum is included, the cost of reclamation would reduce to that extent.
2. In calculating the cost of crop production, rental charges of the land @ Rs. 500/-per annum have been included. If the farmer owns the land, a sum of Rs. 1000/-would be deducted from the total cost making the net profits for 2 years as Rs. 3420/-.

Clearly, land reclamation is a viable proposition. Most recent information reveal that the cost of reclamation could be recovered within three years with minor benefit over the total investments (Table 12.6). Thus, one could say that the cost of reclamation can be recovered in two to three years depending upon the subsidy component and whether the land is taken on lease or is owned by the farmer. A pertinent policy issue that emerges from this analysis calls for approparite changes in the Panchayat act allowing lease of alkali lands for a period of at least 10 years. It would provide the farmer with an incentive to invest more on land reclamation. He would be able to receive his investments back in about three years and for the remaining period, he can reap the harvest of his efforts and investments made. Apparently, the lease of the land for 5 years under the prevalent system is not at all sufficient to encourage the farmers to invest on land reclamation.

Table 12.5 Cost and returns per ha on alkali soils under reclamation in the first two years of crop production

Cost	*Amount (Rs.)*	*Returns*	*Amount (Rs.)*
1975-76			
Cost of land preparation and amendment application	3260	Increase in land value after one year of reclamation	4620
Cost of rice cultivation	1690	Returns from rice crop	2410
Cost of wheat cultivation	1640	Returns from wheat crop	1720
Total cost of cultivation	3330	Total returns	4130
Net Returns			800
1976-77			
Cost of rice cultivation	1950	Returns from rice crop	3310
Cost of wheat cultivation	1650	Returns from wheat crop	1890
Total cost of cultivation	3600	Total returns	5220
Net returns			1620

Table 12.6. Initial establishment and operational costs for reclamation of alkali lands

Particulars	*Cost (Rs ha^{-1})*	*Percentage of total*	*Returns (Rs ha^{-1})*
Ist year			31,600
Bunding and levelling	2,050	1.85	
Tube well installation	8,925	8.07	
Gypsum application	18,650	16.85	
Rice cultivation	14,000	12.66	
Wheat cultivation	13,000	11.75	
2nd year			39,500
Rice cultivation	14,000	12.66	
Wheat cultivation	13,000	11.75	
3rd year			42,850
Rice cultivation	14,000	12.66	
Wheat cultivation	13,000	11.75	
Total (3 years)	**110,626**	**100.00**	**113,750**

The cost-benefit of land reclamation on lands adopted by the Central Soil Salinity Research Institute, Karnal and the land reclaimed by the farmers was also worked out. The analysis suggests that the benefit-cost ratio even at the farmer's level of adoption is 3 or more than 3 depending upon the component of the subsidy. With a subsidy of 70 per cent, the B-C ratio is 4.6 (Table 12.7). The B-C ratio is still higher if the complete package is implemented compared to when it is partially implemented as happens under real field situations. The cost of reclamation is generally recovered within 3 years. Economics studies carried out by Haryana Land Reclamation and Development Corporation brings out that a fair return on investments including repayment is possible even in the very first year.

Table 12.7. Benefit-cost ratio, net present worth (NPW), net benefit investment ratio and payback period of alkali soil reclamation technology

Indicators	*Subsidy level*		
	Without subsidy	*50% subsidy*	*70% subsidy*
As per CSSRI recommendation			
Benefit-cost ratio	4.6	6.0	7.0
Net present worth (10^3 Rs ha^{-1})	66.0	70.4	72.5
Net benefit investment ratio	7.0	11.4	16.7
Payback period (years)	2.0	1.8	1.6
As per farmer's level of adoption			
Benefit-cost ratio	3.0	3.9	4.6
Net present worth (10^3 Rs ha^{-1})	36.7	41.0	43.0
Net benefit investment ratio	3.0	4.6	5.6
Payback period (years)	3.4	2.0	2.6

Reclamation Cost-Pyrites versus Gypsum : Uttar Pradesh

Pyrites is commonly used as an amendment in the state of Uttar Pradesh. Singh (1978) worked out the land reclamation cost at Kanpur on the basis of pyrites and gypsum applied at the rate of 40 % gypsum requirement (Table 12.8). It was further observed that increasing the rate of gypsum application from 40 % GR to 60 % GR, involved an additional expenditure of Rs. 1432. Differences in the rice yield as a result of higher dose of the amendment were insignificant but the yield of wheat increased by 0.3-0.4 t/ha in gypsum treated plots. Pyrites was observed to be economically viable proposition.

Table 12.8. Reclamation cost of alkali lands

Item	*Total cost (Rs. ha^{-1})*	
	Pyrites (22% Sulfur)	*Gypsum*
Land preparation and layout	403	403
Amendment	2254	3150
Amendment application and leaching	198	265
Total	2855	3818

Indirect Benefits

Feasibility of a project is often judged by the returns on investments or the benefit-cost ratio. Often, a project is sanctioned, only if its benefit-cost ratio exceeds one. Recent guidelines from various funding organizations indicate that even those projects which have a benefit-cost ratio less than one can be sanctioned provided the project helps to generate employment or helps in poverty alleviation or meets one or more of social objectives of the state. It is a part acceptance of the importance of indirect benefits. It should, therefore, be prudent to examine the indirect benefits of an alkali land reclamation programme. It is beneficial to account for these benefits to justify such projects or to assess the utility of a programme of this nature. Some of the indirect benefits are:

1. Generation of employment opportunities.
2. Effective utilization of rain water and reduced flood hazards.
3. Better environment with improved quality of life.
4. Enhanced social status of the resource poor farmer in a rural setting.

Employment generation

The employment opportunities in a reclamation project can be classified into two groups:

1. On-farm employment generation such as for land preparation, amendment application and crop production.
2. Indirect employment opportunities such as at mining sites, tube wells installation, in new industries that may come up in the region to meet additional requirements of the project and for handling additional produce in the market.

Screening of complete records of 24 demonstration plots on land reclamation revealed that direct employment for 202 man days is generated in response to reclamation of one ha of land (Table 12.9). It is apparent that employment generation in terms of human labour, bullock days, farm machinery hours were higher in case of plots under the Institute's demonstration than in the case of areas reclaimed by the farmers. It is because of the fact that farmers while adopting the technologies miss or leave many finer points of the technology. As a result the work generated is less and so are the yield of crops, which are also less compared to the demonstration plots (Fig. 12.1). If the one time employment generation opportunities are deducted from the total, 148 and 110 man days of employment per annum are generated in the demonstration plots and the plots reclaimed by the farmers respectively. It may be understood that with time the employment generation in the plots reclaimed by the farmers would also approach that of the demonstration plots.

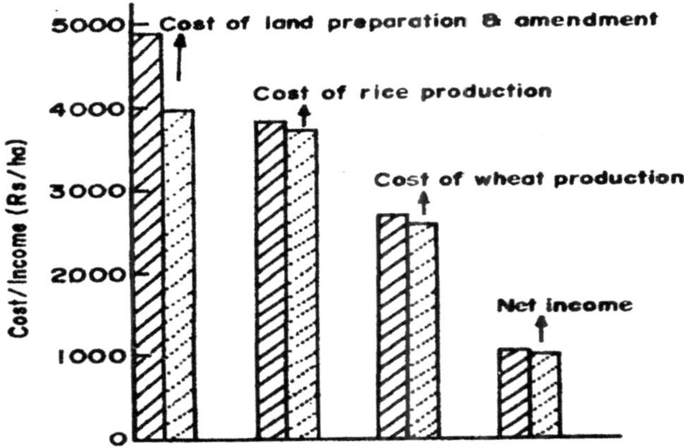

Fig. 12.1. Relative cost of reclamation, crop production and net income

Table 12.9. Employment generation potential of alkali lands

Particulars	*Human labour (days)*	*Bullocks (days)*	*Farm machinery (hr)*		
			Tractor	*Tube well*	*Thresher*
	Institute demonstration plots				
Land reclamation	54.3	11.7	8.0	23.0	–
Rice production	94.2	1.8	0.4	138.7	–
Wheat production	53.9	12.2	3.7	78.2	10.0
Total	202.4	25.7	12.1	239.9	10.0
	Area reclaimed by the farmer				
Land reclamation	34.0	4.3	11.3	20.3	–
Rice production	74.2	1.0	0.1	124.4	–
Wheat production	35.5	7.5	5.6	61.3	8.7
Total	143.7	12.8	17.0	206.0	8.7

If the employment generated under the indirect employment opportunities is also added, it should add enormously to the figures quoted for the direct employment at the farm. A simple calculation could be made to show that enormous work would be generated as a result of reclamation programme on 2.0 million ha land which is just half of the total land affected by this problem. For example, 400,000 tube wells, tube well rooms and pumping sets, 30,000 tractors and matching implements, 4.5 million tons of additional nitrogen, fertilizers and 20 million tons of amendments will be needed. As the reclamation may take around 15 years or so, it is understood that employment generation will be spread over a sufficiently long period of time.

Fig. 12.2 A scene resembling flooding in an alkali catchment following rainfall

Effective utilization of rainfall and reduced floods

Most of the rainfall occurring over barren alkali lands is converted into run-off causing long-term water stagnation and imposes heavy load on under designed drainage systems of the area (Fig. 12.2). In some cases, even if water were removed from the area, congestion would occur at the tail end of the watershed. Experimental evidence now available reveals that with reclamation, a major part of this run-off is conserved in the catchment itself. Not only the total run-off is reduced, peak is also reduced and has a delaying effect on its appearance at the outlet. The water retention capacity of the watershed is also increased, thereby reducing flood hazard. Land reclamation results in increased ground water recharge which is badly needed in areas where water table is depleting. A study at the Central Soil Salinity Research Institute, Karnal has indicated that with good management more than 90 per cent of the rainfall can be conserved within the catchment. Naturally it contributes to reduction in drainage requirement and thereby reduced investments on drainage. Flood hazard is reduced substantially as a result of rainwater conservation.

Better environment with improved quality of life

Barren alkali lands where water stagnation occurs for few weeks to months serve as breeding places for mosquitoes. With reclamation, barren fields are not only converted into lush green fields, the breeding places for the mosquitoes are also destroyed. Although there has not been any direct evidence on the reduction of malaria hazard in the surroundings where land has been largely reclaimed, people certainly are happier and agree that they have a much healthier life than before. If Panchayat lands can also be put under trees, it should go a long way in improving the environment in the village as a whole.

Enhanced status of the poor in rural setting

In rural India, poor men are treated badly. Particularly hurt are those, who have land but can not put them under plough because of excessive salts. Sometime they loose their investment in a bid to get something out of the lifeless barren land, which is the only property they possess. Recent studies have revealed a substantial increase in land value upon land reclamation in Uttar Pradesh (Table 12.10). Such a change in the land value would raise the status of the poor farmers in their villages. Migration of the people from rural areas to urban areas gets initiated. If man folk migrate, the women are treated badly resulting in gender related discrimination. With reclamation, poor farmers become proud owners of lush green fields and are able to give employment to some of the landless labourers or at least engage their family members in some useful tasks. They leave working on somebody else's field where they are ill treated. Thus, with reclamation, they can play an independent role in socio-politico-economic functions of the village.

Table 12.10. Land value before and after reclamation in Uttar Pradesh

Category of land	*Land value (Rs. ha^{-1})*	
	Before reclamation	*After reclamation*
B+	115,000	170,000
B	55,000	155,000
C	30,000	125,000

Long-term Effect on Farm Income

Land reclaimed during 1974-75 continued to display a dynamic behavior in cropping pattern, farm income and employment (Agnihotri, 1985). Substantial changes in profit, cost of production and yield variation were observed over the years. Relative data for the two years provide enough evidence of these changes (Table 12.11). It may be seen that after reclamation, barley was the unique crop, which yielded more returns while cost of production reduced over the years. The yield of basmati rice and berseem crops stabilized during this period.

Subsidy on Land Reclamation

There is ample justification for granting subsidy to the farmers on land reclamation. Reclamation of lands leads to an overall community and regional development the fruits of which will be shared by all whether he is a owner of the land or not. As others will be sharing the benefits and not the cost, compensation in the form of subsidy is justified. Besides this, reclamation of alkali lands will enhance the prospects of achieving national goals and thus, it is a priority area for investments. Appropriate amount of subsidy should encourage the farmers to become partner in this task of national importance. Many times it is argued that subsidy is misused by the farming community. This alone can not be a sufficient ground to deny the subsidy to the farmers. To avoid misuse, subsidy could be in the form of adjustment in land revenue or in terms of cash against purchases made.

Table 12.11. Effect of land reclamation on farm-income, cost and yield variability

Particulars	*IR8*		*Basmati*		*Wheat*		*Barley*		*Berseem*	
	N	*A*	*N*	*A*	*N*	*A*	*N*	*A*	*N*	*A*
Returns (Rs. ha^{-1})										
1975-76	1581	796	1714	633	1398	387	479	380	1665	739
1980-81	2154	1228	2330	1682	1869	1523	565	541	2431	2178
Cost (Rs. ha^{-1})										
1975-76	925	836	687	937	1030	792	625	528	816	293
1980-81	2614	2746	2219	1914	2091	2075	364	393	2987	2516
Instability (CV)										
1975-76	0.28	0.28	0.27	0.62	0.17	0.36	0.14	0.32	0.20	0.31
1980-81	0.28	0.28	0.27	0.42	0.17	0.36	0.14	0.32	0.20	0.29
Change in returns (%)	36	54	36	166	34	293	18	42	46	195
Change in cost (%)	183	228	223	104	103	162	(-)42	(-)26	266	270

N= Normal, A= Alkali . The change in returns and costs is from 1975-76 to 1980-81, CV = coefficient of variation

Progress of Reclamation

With the advent of green revolution and a technology of land reclamation made available at about the same time by CSSRI, many state governments realized the potential of land reclamation for increasing food grains production and established Land Reclamation Corporations in their states. A notable mention of Punjab, Haryana and Uttar Pradesh can be made in this regard. Environmentalists also played a key role in raising the adverse environmental impacts particularly in regard to water logging and soil salinization in the irrigation commands. Migration of the rural poor also helped to plan this activity so as to halt this menace. As a result, Government of India came out with many schemes providing incentives and subsidies on several components of land reclamation programmes. These attempts lead to reclamation of large areas. On the basis of Gypsum distributed by Land Reclamation Corporations, an assessment of the area reclaimed has been made (Parsad, 1989). Although, this approach is still used to assess the area, Gupta (2001) assessed the reclaimed areas in these states by deducting the area reported as salt-affected in 1971 and during the last five years (Table 12.12). It is assessed that more than 1 million ha of alkali lands in these three states have been reclaimed. A redeeming feature of this assessment is that the value obtained in this assessment matches well with the assessment made with the other technique. Attempts are now being made in Bihar to reclaim alkali lands. It is believed that with site specific technologies being made available and the experiences so far, land reclamation and management programme in the country would get the desired fillip. By providing institutional support and policy backstopping, Government can provide the necessary incentive to this activity. It is believed that the time is not far when India would be free from the problem of alkali wastelands.

Table 12.12. Extent of the salt-affected area (million ha) and area reclaimed (million ha) in different states

State	*Area affected (1971)*	*Area affected (1995-2001)*	*Area reclaimed*
Punjab	0.530	0.164	0.366
Haryana	0.700	0.153	0.547
Uttar Pradesh	1.200	1.060	0.140
Total			1.053

Source: Gupta (2001)

REFERENCES

Agnihotri, A. K. 1985. Effect of sodic soil reclamation on income, employment and cropping pattern. Ann. Rep. CSSRI, Karnal. 110-111.

Chhiba, I. M., Singh, N. T. 1978. An ex-armyman reclaims his alkali land. Indian Fmg. 28(2): 15-17.

Gupta, S. K. 2001. Extent and distribution of salt-affected soils in India. Lecture delivered at the National Course on Agricultural Water Management. CSSRI, Karnal.

Parsad, R. and Singh, P. 1980. Some socio-economic constraints in the adoption of alkali soil reclamation technology by the farmers. Ann. Arid Zone. 19:351-358.

Parsad R. 1989. Technology for the reclamation of sodic soils. Indian Fmg. 39(5) : 26-7

Singh, P. 1980. An appraisal of the economics of reclamation of alkali soils. Proc. Int. Symp. Salt-Affectd Soils, Karnal. 555-561.

Singh, P. and Gupta, J. N. 1979. Income and employment generation in reclamation of alkali soils on marginal farms. Curr. Agric. 3: 109-114.

Singh, P. and Gupta, J. N. 1979. Economics of crop production on sodic soils under reclamation. Ann. Rep. CSSRI, Karnal. 141-142.